THE ECONOMICS OF AGING

Seventh Edition

James H. Schulz

AUBURN HOUSE
Westport, Connecticut • London

Library of Congress Cataloging-in-Publication Data

Schulz, James H.
    The economics of aging / James H. Schulz.—7th ed.
      p. cm.
    Includes bibliographical references and index.
    ISBN 0–86569–294–7 (alk. paper)—ISBN 0–86569–295–5 (pbk. : alk. paper)
    1. Old age pensions—United States.   2. Retirement income—United States.
    3. Age—United States—Economic conditions. I. Title.
    HD7105.35.U6S38 2001
    330.973'0929'0846—dc21   00–034873

British Library Cataloguing in Publication Data is available.

Library of Congress Catalog Card Number: 00–034873
ISBN: 0–86569–294–7 (hc)
     0–86569–295–5 (pbk.)

First published in 2001

Auburn House, 88 Post Road West, Westport, CT 06881
An imprint of Greenwood Publishing Group, Inc.
www.greenwood.com

Printed in the United States of America

∞™

The paper used in this book complies with the
Permanent Paper Standard issued by the National
Information Standards Organization (Z39.48–1984).

P

Copyright Acknowledgments

The author and publisher gratefully acknowledge permission to reprint material from the following copyrighted sources:

Figure 1–5, from J. R. Gist and J. Mulvey, "Marginal Tax Rates and Older Taxpayers," *Tax Notes* (November 5, 1990): 679–694. Reprinted with the permission of the American Association of Retired Persons.

Excerpt from Alan Downs, "Tale of a Reformed Corporate Executioner," *The Christian Science Monitor* (March 15, 1994): 8. Reprinted with permission.

Figure 2–6, from Alan Downs, "Tale of a Reformed Corporate Executioner," *The Christian Science Monitor* (March 15, 1994): 8. Reprinted with permission.

Figure 2–7, from James H. Schulz, "The Economics of Mandatory Retirement," *Industrial Gerontology* 1(1), New Series (Winter 1974): 1–10. Reprinted by permission of The National Council on the Aging, Inc.

Table 3–3, from National Center on Women & Aging, *Financial Challenges for Mature Women* (Waltham, Mass.: Heller Graduate School, Brandeis University, 1998). Reprinted with permission.

Figure 8–3, from James H. Schulz, Allan Borowski, and William H. Crown, *Economics of Population Aging: The "Graying" of Australia, Japan, and the United States* (Westport, Conn.: Auburn House, 1991), p. 78; and James H. Schulz, *The Economics of Aging*, 6th ed. (Westport, Conn.: Auburn House, 1995), p. 271. Reprinted by permission of Auburn House, an imprint of Greenwood Publishing Group, Inc., Westport, Conn.

Contents

PREFACE   xi

1. **The Economic Status of the Aged**   1

   Diversity among the Elderly   3
   Aged Income   4
   The Aged Are Not a Homogeneous Group   10
   The Impact of Taxation, Assets, and In-Kind Income   19
   The Adequacy of Income in Old Age   31
   The Impact of Inflation   47
   Chapter 1 Highlights   55
   Suggested Readings   56

2. **To Work or Not to Work**   59

   The Right to Retire   59
   The Work-Leisure Trade-off   60
   Economic Problems of Older Workers   73
   Training Older Workers   81
   The Retirement Decision   85
   Mandatory versus Flexible Retirement Options   89

Do the Aged Want to Work?   94
Chapter 2 Highlights   97
Suggested Readings   98

3. **Retirement Planning**   **99**

Retirement Provision by Individuals   100
The Role of Pensions   105
Public or Private?   110
What Mix of Public and Private Pensions?   115
Arguments against and for Social Security   116
Arguments in Support of Private Pensions   121
The Pension Mix in Various Countries   124
Planning for Retirement   124
Finding Someone You Can Trust   125
Chapter 3 Highlights   128
Suggested Readings   129

4. **Social Security: Old Age and Survivors' Benefits**   **131**

The Changing Social Security System   132
The Principles of Social Security   134
Retirement Benefit Provisions   136
Social Security Pension Reforms   147
Chapter 4 Highlights   168
Suggested Readings   169

5. **Social Security Financing: Who Pays? Who Should Pay?** **171**

Rising Pension Expenditures and Growing Controversy   172
Financing Social Security   173
Social Security and the Federal Budget   183
Financing Equity   187
Social Security Financial Reform Proposals   197
Chapter 5 Highlights   203
Suggested Readings   204

6. **Health, Disability, and SSI Benefits**   **205**

Health Insurance for the Elderly   206
Long-Term Care   213

Financing Health Care 219

Other Social Security Programs: Disability and SSI 225

The Supplemental Security Income Program 232

Chapter 6 Highlights 240

Suggested Readings 240

7. **What Role for Employer-Sponsored Pensions?** 243

Who Is Covered? 245

Private Plan Characteristics 254

Private Pension Regulation 264

ERISA Helps but . . . 266

Financing Private Pensions 268

Women and Private Pensions 273

Government Employee Pension Plans 274

Chapter 7 Highlights 280

Suggested Readings 281

8. **Population Aging: Generational Conflict?** 283

Generational Conflict? 284

Aging Populations 284

Dependency Ratios 286

Financing an Aging Population 292

The Generational Equity Debate 295

"Put the Old Folks Back to Work!" 300

Age Is Not the Key Variable 304

Chapter 8 Highlights 305

Suggested Readings 306

NOTES 309

GLOSSARY 315

REFERENCES 325

INDEX 353

Preface

With the arrival of the new century, reflections on events over the *last* century have increased. One dramatic happening was the spectacular economic growth that occurred in the West as a result of technological innovation and mass production. The industrial revolution that began in the 18th century quickened in the 19th century, but seemed to surge and then slow down briefly in the 20th century, only to be replaced by an electronic and information revolution that promises even greater prosperity.

Accompanying the economic growth was another equally important development. Instead of only a small elite in the population enjoying a decent living, the larger output was shared with a rising "middle class." Of course, not everyone shared. In the early part of the century, for example, most retired workers and their families did not share in the rising standard of living. Poverty in old age was the dominating reality. That situation, unacceptable in the face of long-term economic growth, set the stage for a radical change in the way people prepared for retirement.

Preparing for the years in retirement has never been an easy task. Planning for many years into the future in the face of numerous uncertainties that will impact on the outcome is daunting to most people. Historically, the tendency had been to "hope for the best"—which often meant reliance on family and charity—but in the 20th century it came to mean reliance on social security.

Over the years, social security has improved dramatically. For many, employer-sponsored pensions supplement those benefits; and financial institutions are now offering an ever-growing variety of ways for the saver to invest his or her money to meet future retirement needs.

As we start a new century, however, many questions continue to confront the typical worker and his family:

- How does social security work, and will it be there when I need it?
- How much should I personally save for retirement, who can I trust to advise me, and how do I choose among the seemingly endless number of financial investment options?
- What role, if any, will be played in my retirement planning by my employer-sponsored benefit plan? And suppose I don't have one?
- What does it take to retire with the confidence that my income in old age will be "adequate"? And how do I deal with unpredictable expenditure needs—such as rising health care costs and long-term care?
- When is the best time to retire, and will there be meaningful options if I decide to continue working?
- What if I want to continue to work? How can I keep my skills up to date?

This is a book about these questions—and many others—that all of us will have to deal with in one way or another.

There are other questions, however, that are of special significance for women. Despite all the progress to date, very large numbers of older women, both today and tomorrow, will live in poverty; poverty in old age has become a "women's problem"! Being assured of adequate income in retirement is especially difficult for women because of the traditional sex biases in the workplace, the complexity of women's roles, their longer life expectancy, lower private pension coverage, inadequate survivors' benefits, and a long tradition in many families that "managing the finances" is not women's work. How are women to cope with these issues? And what roles should employers and government play in the solutions?

All people not yet old (especially women) must think explicitly about their future. It is my hope that this book will be of some help in those efforts. However, *The Economics of Aging* has never been a "self-help" book designed solely to help individuals with *their* retirement planning. Many of the answers to each individual's questions about the economics of aging depend on evolving trends, policies, and practices of business and government (in large part outside the individual's control).

Therefore, this book also examines in depth the nation's evolving private and public policies on retirement, pension, and health. There is no doubt that policies in these areas are changing rapidly. For example, as we discuss at length in the text, the area of employer-sponsored pensions is undergoing dramatic change as employers shift much more of the responsibility for pension planning, adequacy, and management to their employees.

Evolving private pensions is just one of many important changes occurring. This new edition gives attention to all the major developments that have occurred (or are occurring) with regard to "the economics of aging." Perhaps the issue that has received the most attention in recent years is the rising cost of so-called "entitlements" and the future impact they may have on the economy, taxes, and workers' incomes. What does the future hold for the American "welfare state" and for those growing old in it?

In this regard, major attention is being given to the retirement of the "Baby Boomers" and the various "financing of old-age" issues raised by the demographic transition we must pass through during the early part of the 21st century. Unfortunately, much of the discussion has been based more on assertions than facts and analysis. A recent report of the National Academy on an Aging Society reminds us that *Demography Is Not Destiny* (Friedland and Summer, 1999). But one would never know that from most of the dire warnings we hear almost every day of rising "dependency ratios" and unsustainable pension and health costs. Thus, with each passing year the aged become more and more a target of criticism, mainly because of issues related to the rising costs of retirement benefits.

This book tries to provide a balanced view of the facts, arguments, and options related to the debate over the economic implications of "demographic aging." This edition expands the prior edition's extensive discussion of the topic.

Other additions to the new edition include:

- A discussion of the National Academy of Science's proposed new way to measure poverty.
- An update on the U.S. experience with "reverse annuity mortgages."
- An analysis of what is happening to the labor force participation rates of older men.
- An examination of the issues surrounding "life-long learning" and training options for older workers, including the Workforce Investment Act of 1998.
- An introduction of the new concept of "productive aging."
- Descriptions of the "hybrid" pension plans now being offered by many employers.
- A detailed discussion of "pension privatization" issues.
- An expanded discussion of issues related to older women, especially with regard to financial planning.
- A review of the latest information on the question: Who will get their "money's worth" from social security?

- Increased attention to the emerging issues related to disability insurance programs.

As in the prior editions, I have tried to open up to nonspecialists the now-burgeoning storehouse of relevant social science knowledge and research bearing on the economic aspects of aging, and in doing this I have tried to minimize economic jargon and the more technical aspects of this highly specialized literature—attempting at the same time to bring the reader close to the cutting edge of our knowledge to date.

The success of past editions (and hopefully this new edition) owes much to those who have taken the time to review, critique, and suggest improvements. The list of such contributors over the years now numbers over 100 people. My heartfelt thanks to all of them, and a special thanks to my staff assistant, Margaret Stubbs, who has shared with me the joys and frustrations of preparing all seven editions.

The first edition of *The Economics of Aging* came out in 1976. At that time providing for adequate income in retirement was still a major social problem in the United States. More than two decades have passed, and many things have changed—most for the better. My biggest concern continues to be that just as we have come so close to "solving" that big social problem (i.e., providing everyone with adequate income in retirement), a new problem has arisen. The push for "privatization" of pensions takes us down a path that, in my opinion, is likely to lead to social *insecurity*, not social *security*. Many of the additions to this edition speak to that possibility.

Chapter 1

The Economic Status
of the Aged

The treatment of old people in America, many of whom have a hard life behind them, is remarkable. . . . [This is illustrated by] the terrifying extent to which old people are left in poverty and destitution. . . . It cannot possibly be the considered opinion of the majority of Americans that so many of those who in America are often called "senior citizens" should be left in misery, squalor and often forbidding loneliness, unattended though they are in need of care. The situation is overripe for a radical reform of the old age security system.

So wrote the well-known social commentator Gunnar Myrdal in his book *Challenge to Affluence* (1963). Myrdal was writing in the early 1960s. In those days it was relatively easy to write about the economic situation of the elderly population. All one needed to do was cite statistics that confirmed what most people knew from either personal experience or observation: *most of the elderly suffered from serious economic deprivation*—that their incomes were inadequate, that **inflation**[1] worsened the situation by reducing real incomes and eroding savings, and that the aged were one of the largest poverty groups in the country.

Today the situation is much better, due in large part to collective action taken over the past few decades. In fact, major breakthroughs have occurred in the development of private and public programs to deal with the economic problems of old age. Here are some of the major changes that have occurred in the United States:

1. Since 1950, social security old age benefit levels have increased by almost 300 percent, significantly faster than inflation over the same period.
2. During the three decades following World War II, employer-sponsored pensions spread throughout large corporations and grew rapidly—with dramatic increases in benefit levels (available at increasingly earlier ages).
3. Major government health benefits (Medicare and Medicaid) were legislated.
4. Property tax relief laws for the elderly have been legislated in all our states.
5. Mandatory retirement because of age was made illegal.
6. Old Age Assistance programs in the states were abolished, and a new national Supplemental Security Income program (SSI) was put in their place.
7. Social security, military and federal employee pensions, SSI, and the Food Stamp program were automatically indexed for inflation.

Despite the economic problems that remain (which will be discussed later in this book), we must not lose sight of the important gains that have been made. Dramatic changes have occurred in the levels of income provided older persons, especially from public and private pensions. Consequently, there has been a significant improvement in the general economic status of this group—traditionally viewed as poverty stricken.

Contrast Myrdal's comment with a recent statement by a well-known pension think tank in Washington, D.C. (EBRI, 1989):

The economic well-being of the elderly as a group is now equal to or greater than that of the nonelderly as a result of a large and sustained decrease in poverty among people over age 65 during the past 20 years. . . . Although to be old is no longer to be poor, substantial pockets of economic insecurity and near poverty still exist among the elderly.

Is it true that today's elderly are economically "better off" than the nonelderly? We think not. Recent research studies (discussed later)˙do indicate big changes, but we would characterize them in a different way. *From a statistical point of view, the elderly in this country are beginning to look a lot like the rest of the population: some very rich, lots with adequate income, lots more with very modest incomes (often near poverty), and a significant minority still destitute.* This is very different from the past, when a great many were destitute.[2]

Given public concern about the social security system meeting its projected obligations (see Chapter 5), news of a greatly improved economic situation for the aged is to be welcomed. And it is certainly heartening to hear that older people today are *economically much better off* than they were a little more than two decades ago. The decline in the seriousness of *some* economic problems for *some* elderly people means that the task of helping the aged may not need to be as high on the social agenda as in prior years. In fact, given the rising costs of providing for the aged, some people have begun to argue that we have already gone too far. This chapter (and much of the book) provides information relevant to assessing that issue.

We begin by explaining why the typical money income statistics usually reported do not give a full and accurate picture of the aged's economic status, and discuss a variety of factors—including assets, in-kind income, and taxes—that should be taken into account. We then discuss measures of adequacy and the poverty problem. Finally, we look at the impact of inflation on the elderly.

DIVERSITY AMONG THE ELDERLY

Once we recognize that the economic similarities between the old and younger populations are increasing, we must also recognize the important differences. While clearly most of those disadvantaged before old age remain disadvantaged, they are joined in old age by many for whom certain economic problems are unique:

- The elderly widow who finds her income but a small fraction of the income enjoyed when her retired husband was alive.
- The appliance salesman living only on social security—who was never covered by a private pension and neglected ("could not afford") to contribute money into an Individual Retirement Account or some other personal investment program.
- The retired couple whose supplemental income cushion was wiped out when the electric power consortium in the state of Washington defaulted on bonds sold to build nuclear power plants that were no longer economically viable.
- The engineer who, despite years of private pension coverage, never gained a large **vested** pension because of repeated job changes.
- The retired executive who must sell most of his financial assets to pay for the institutional care needed for his wife with Alzheimer's disease.
- The retired junior high school teacher without social security whose pension has fallen far behind needed purchasing power as a result of inflation, especially the double-digit inflation experienced in the late 1970s and early 1980s.
- The gas station mechanic who becomes unexpectedly disabled at the age of 50 and has nothing to supplement his meager social security disability pension.

The list could go on and on. But the point of the list is not so much to elicit sympathy for the aged or to prove the need to do more. Rather, we seek to emphasize and make more concrete the heterogeneity of the aged and warn against those glib generalities: "the aged" are poor; or now, with greater frequency, "the aged" are well-off.

Prior to the 1960s there were relatively few data available to analyze the economic situation of the aged population in the United States. This situation changed dramatically in the early 1960s as a result of the Social Security Administration's very comprehensive survey of the aged in 1962 (Epstein and Murray, 1967). Since then, a wide range of statistics has been published by the Social Security Administration, the Census Bureau, the Department of Labor, and various private organizations. These data provide a variety of information on various aspects of the elderly's financial status.

Two important notes of caution are immediately in order, however. First, because it takes time to collect, check, analyze, and publish statistics, there is often a considerable lag in the availability of information. Throughout the chapter we present illustrative statistics—the latest that were available at the time of writing. Many readers, however, will want to seek the newer data available. Second, all statistical information is subject to great abuse; unless users are very careful, they may misinterpret or misuse the available data. Therefore, in addition to giving information on various subgroups of the elderly, the discussion below also attempts to deal with two important questions: What are the most useful kinds of data for evaluating the economic status of the aged, and what are the major problems in interpreting the data available?

AGED INCOME

We begin our discussion of the elderly's economic status by looking at the **income** they receive. Income is not the only resource contributing to the economic welfare of the aged; later sections of this chapter will look at a number of other important factors (for example, assets). But as Mollie Orshansky (who developed the American poverty index) has observed, "while money might not be everything, it is way ahead of whatever is in second place" (Irelan and Bond, 1976).

Income Distribution

Table 1–1 shows the distribution of **money income** for both aged couples and nonmarried individuals. In 1996, only 4 percent of aged couples had money income of less than $10,000; one-quarter had money income of less than $15,000. However, the income situation of nonmarried individuals age 65 or older—most of whom live alone—was much different. About one-third had income below $10,000, and 51 percent had income below $15,000.

Figure 1–1 compares the distribution of money income for *aged* families with the distribution of *middle-aged* families. We see that in 1998, the median incomes varied greatly.

In Table 1–1, all of the aged (except those in institutions) are included.

Table 1–1
Distribution of Total Money Income of Aged Families[a] in 1996

Total Money Income	All Aged Families	Married Couples	Nonmarried Persons
Less than $5,000	3%	1%	5%
$5,000–9,999	17	3	26
$10,000–14,999	16	9	20
$15,000–19,999	13	13	13
$20,000–34,999	23	32	18
$35,000–49,999	11	17	8
$50,000–64,999	6	9	4
$65,000–74,999	3	4	2
$75,000 or more	9	12	6
Median Income	$20,535	$30,040	$14,834
Total Percent	100[b]	100	100[b]

[a]Tabulation is for units where at least one person is age 65 or older. It includes aged persons living with a younger relative who is considered the "householder"; such units are classified in Bureau of the Census tabs as members of nonaged families (see text).
[b]Does not add to 100 percent due to rounding.
Source: Based on data in Social Security Administration (SSA), *Income of the Population 55 or Older, 1996* (Washington, D.C.: SSA Office of Policy, 1998), Table II.1.

This is not always the case. In Bureau of the Census publications using Current Population Survey data, persons living with a younger relative who is considered the **householder** are classified in "families under age 65."

If an aged person lives with his children or if the children live with their aged parent(s), should the two units be reported separately, or should the income be lumped together into one big family? It often makes a significant difference in the final results that are reported. There is a tendency to combine all the incomes of related people living together. The result has been that a lot of aged poverty in the past has been hidden because the poorest aged—those who are unable to live by themselves—were statistically aggregated into the bigger and usually more prosperous family unit.

One might argue that if the aged are living with a member of a younger family unit and the family unit is not itself poor, then the aged's standard of living is not likely to be poor. Using this perspective, one can argue further that there is no problem in such cases and that if you statistically separate the aged out (perhaps to try to justify higher pension benefits), you are basing the analysis on an artificial situation.

Figure 1–1
Median Family Income by Age of Householder,* 1998

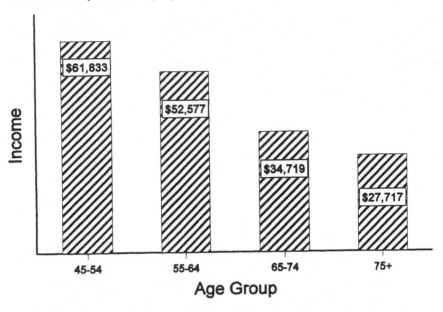

*For definition of householders see Table 1–1, footnote a.
Source: U.S. Bureau of the Census, *Money Income in the United States, 1998*, Current
    Population Reports: Consumer Income (Washington, D.C.: U.S. Government Printing
    Office, 1999), Table 4.

The opposing view, however, is that some of these people are not
necessarily treated as members of the family. They may be there by necessity, and sometimes families do not permit them to share fully in the
higher standard of living of the rest of the family. Or, even if the younger
members of the family want them to share fully, many aged people are
too independent to be willing to draw heavily upon the resources of the
rest of the family. They would rather—even though they live within the
family—live at a lower, perhaps subsistence, level.

Changes over Time

Historically, we know that as social security benefit levels have increased, many aged persons have stopped living with relatives and set up
independent households. Statistically, as a result of these family units
breaking up, new units headed by an aged person show up in Bureau of
Census data. Since these new aged units almost always have very low
income, the process tends to increase the reported incidence of poverty
among the aged. We find, for example, that during certain periods the

Table 1–2
Changes in Median Money Incomes of Aged Persons, 1986 versus 1996ᵃ

	Median Income		
Marital Status	1986	1996	Percentage Change
All Units (Age 65+)	$10,950	$16,644	52%
Married Couples	18,890	28,178	49
Nonmarried Men	8,510	14,108	66
Nonmarried Women	6,870	10,938	59

ᵃAmounts are in current dollars, unadjusted for inflation.
Source: Based on data in Social Security Administration (SSA), *Income of the Population 55 or Older* (Washington, D.C.: SSA Office of Policy, various years).

number of persons in poverty has declined among nonaged groups but has risen among the aged (partly as a result of the movement of the aged out of other families).

Thus, when the statistics show aged poverty increasing, it is not necessarily true that the situation is actually getting worse. In fact, the statistics may be a reflection of things getting better. As pension benefits go up, some of the poor aged who prefer independent living are able to break out of other family units and thus become identifiable statistical units. But, again, it can be argued that they were always poor, and all that has changed is their living arrangements.

Statistics from surveys show the significant increase in elderly income that has occurred over the 1986 to 1996 period. Table 1–2 shows for a 10-year period the percentage increases in income for couples and nonmarried women and men. Over this period, nonmarried men experienced the largest increase in **median** income.

Sources of Income

Figure 1–2 shows the sources of income for the elderly. While social security is the major source (40 percent), asset income (18 percent), pensions (19 percent), and earnings (20 percent) make large contributions. We must remember, however, that various income sources are distributed unevenly among the subgroups of the aged population. Earnings go mostly to the non-retired; asset income goes mostly to a few high-income elderly. In a subsequent section we examine more closely these differences.[3]

Figure 1–3 shows the trend in income sources for the elderly between 1962 and 1996. While the share from social security has been relatively stable, employer-sponsored pensions clearly increased.

Earnings still remain an important source of income for some elderly.

Figure 1–2
Sources of Money Income, 1996*

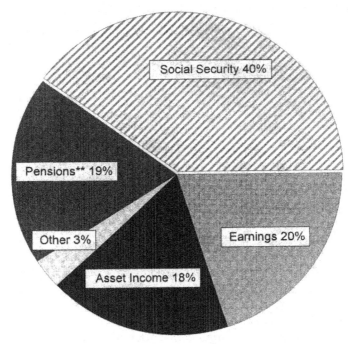

*Aged persons 65+.
**Employer-sponsored pension (and annuity), IRA, Keogh, and 401(K) payments.
Source: Social Security Administration (SSA), *Income of the Aged Chartbook, 1996* (Washington, D.C.: SSA Office of Research, Evaluation, and Statistics, 1998).

In 1996, as Figure 1–3 shows, more than one in five elderly units received employment income. The proportion with earnings drops rapidly with age, however; about 40 percent of those 65 to 69, but only four percent of those over age 84, work.

An Important Statistical Warning

Almost all the statistics that have been presented in the prior sections were based on the government's Current Population Survey (CPS). The CPS is a household survey conducted by the Bureau of the Census. The survey is designed to gather monthly information on labor force participation and unemployment. At least once a year, however, detailed information is obtained in the CPS on the kinds and amounts of income individuals and families receive.

Income information from surveys like the CPS is subject to substantial

Figure 1–3
Shares of Aged* Income from Various Sources, 1962–1996

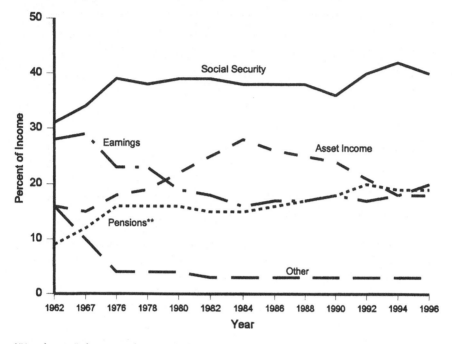

*"Aged units" that are either married couples living together with at least one age 65+ or
   65+ nonmarried persons.
**Employer-sponsored pension (and annuity), IRA, Keogh, and 401(K) payments.
Source: Social Security Administration (SSA), *Income of the Aged Chartbook, 1996* (Washington, D.C.: SSA Office of Research, Evaluation and Statistics, 1998).

reporting errors by those interviewed. Respondents sometimes do not
know, remember incorrectly, refuse to answer, or give false information
out of anger or fear of government retribution. Such errors can produce
substantial underestimates of income and can distort our view of the
relative income positions of various socioeconomic groups. Thus, while
the CPS data are relatively reliable for the great bulk of aged whose income is low, they are not for the small group of aged with extensive
property, farm, or other self-employment income.

The Social Security Administration's Office of Research and Statistics
has been researching this reporting problem for many years. It has published startling findings with regard to the seriousness of the problem
(Radner, 1982). Errors were found to be very large, especially for the
elderly.

The Social Security Administration study found that in 1972 the CPS
underestimated the mean income of families and single units of all ages

Table 1–3
Adjusted Mean Income of Family Units, 1979

	Mean Income	
Age of Head	CPS	CPS Adjusted
14–24	$10,511	$10,300
25–34	17,953	18,530
35–44	23,220	25,670
45–54	24,664	28,460
55–64	20,809	25,280
65 or older	10,837	15,860

Source: Daniel B. Radner, "Distribution of Family Income: Improved Estimates," *Social Security Bulletin* 45 (July 1982): 13–21.

by 11 percent. However, the incomes of family units headed by persons age 65 or older showed an increase, when adjusted for underreporting, of 41 percent! The extent of CPS underestimating was much larger for those with higher incomes and relatively small for those at the low-income levels. The major cause of error in the income estimates was underreporting of property income (interest, dividends, rent, royalties, and trust income) and to a lesser extent self-employment income (especially farm income). The study also made less precise estimates for the year 1979. The adjusted mean income numbers for this later year are equally surprising, as shown in Table 1–3.

The Social Security Administration's findings dramatically emphasize the need to be cautious in using and interpreting income statistics. Later in this chapter, when we look at asset statistics, the same caution applies—probably more so.

If only the above problems were the only ones involved in measuring the economic status of the elderly. Unfortunately, once we understand the underreporting limitations of the CPS data, our problems are only beginning.

THE AGED ARE NOT A HOMOGENEOUS GROUP

It is common for writers and analysts to give only the mean or median income for all or large groups of the aged. But as we saw from the income distribution statistics in Table 1–1, for example, there is a wide divergence in income if the elderly are grouped by marital status. Similar distortions result from grouping all the aged together and generalizing about their social problems. Most people who study old age and the process of aging (gerontology) are familiar with this aggregation problem in the social and psychological areas. There is no such thing as the collective aged; the aged are as diverse as the population itself, and this is as true for economic status as it is for other areas.

If one views the aged as one homogeneous group, there is a tendency to try to develop for them one appropriate economic policy—just as in other areas, we have tried at times to develop one appropriate housing policy and one appropriate health policy. We have learned over the years that such attempts almost always fail when dealing with diverse groups. The most useful types of data for analysis and evaluation are those that break down the aged population into smaller subgroups.

The Retired versus the Nonretired

The first step toward disaggregation of the data is very simple: separate the aged into at least two broad categories—the retired and the nonretired. Unfortunately, most of the data sources do not or cannot provide such a breakdown. They do not because often it simply does not occur to those presenting the data that this is an important distinction. They cannot because in determining when a person is retired one must deal with difficult conceptual problems, and the questions asked in the survey providing the data do not always include the information necessary for judging whether a person is retired. Hence one typically sees data that group aged wage earners together with people without earnings. The earners, of course, tend to have much higher and more adequate incomes. When they are averaged together with the non-wage earners, both the mean and median income for "the aged" are increased. This makes the situation look better than it actually is for retired people and much worse than it actually is for the employed.

If one wants to segregate the retired from the nonretired, one immediately runs into the problem of how to define retirement for statistical purposes. Many aged persons work to supplement their pension and other retirement income. Is a person who is working twenty hours a week to be counted as a retired person, or is he or she partially retired? If the latter, what does that mean? Thus, even if we divide the aged population on the basis of retirement, it is not clear whether there should be two categories or more than two. A three-category tabulation, for example, might be full-time workers, part-time and unemployed workers, and the "fully retired." In general, most discussions of the economic status of the aged do not even attempt to deal with this problem when presenting data. This omission is unfortunate because (as we will show) this is such an important issue in evaluating the economic well-being of elderly people. Table 1–4 shows the differences in total income tabulated by whether aged units had any earnings from work in 1992. Note the dramatic dif-

Table 1–4
Money Income of Older Persons with and without Earnings, 1992

Aged Units	Median Income
Age 65 or older	
Earnings, Yes	$26,717
Earnings, No	$11,915
Married Couples	
Earnings, Yes	$32,850
Earnings, No	$20,530
Nonmarried Persons	
Earnings, Yes	$17,569
Earnings, No	$8,838

Source: Susan Grad, *Income of the Population 55 or Older, 1992* (Washington, D.C.: U.S. Department of Health and Human Services, 1994), Table 111.6.

ferences between those who had worked some part of the year and those totally retired.

Different Elderly Age Groups

Another major problem in analyzing data on the aged is that it often is not appropriate to group people together who differ in age by as much as fifteen or twenty years. Often statistics on the economic status of aged people group all persons age 65 and over. Again, certain conclusions drawn from such data may be misleading. To begin with, it is important to realize that the needs of people at the two extremes of the retirement period are often quite different.

Consumption Patterns

A study by McConnel and Deljavan (1983) of *retired* persons' expenditures in comparison with those of older people *still working* found that the retired spend a significantly larger proportion of their budgets than those still working on shelter, food for home meals, and health care. However, as income increases, retired families commit a smaller proportion of additional income to necessities and a much larger proportion to gifts and charitable contributions.

Similar expenditure differences exist if one looks at those elderly age 65 to 74 in comparison with those age 75 or older. Table 1–5 shows for

Table 1–5
Expenditure Patterns of the Aged, 1989

| | Age Group | | |
Item	Under 65	65-74	75 and over
Total expenditures	$30,191	$21,152	$15,919
Food at home	8.3%	9.7%	10.8%
Food away from home	6.5	5.5	5.0
Housing	24.5	23.4	23.8
Transportation	19.0	17.5	14.1
Health care	4.0	9.4	14.8
Entertainment and reading	5.3	4.0	3.4
Personal insurance and pensions	9.7	5.0	1.9
Apparel	5.8	5.4	3.6
Utilities, fuels, and public service	6.2	8.6	9.6
Cash contributions	2.8	4.8	7.5
Other[a]	7.7	6.8	5.6
Total	100.0%	100.0%	100.0%

[a]Tobacco products, alcoholic beverages, personal care, reading, education, and miscellaneous expenditures.
Source: *Aging America: Trends and Projections*, 1991 edition (Washington, D.C.: U.S. Department of Health and Human Services, 1991).

each age group the proportion of total expenditures accounted for by different types of purchases. Not surprisingly, the 75-plus group spends, on average, much more on out-of-pocket medical care. In fact, the difference between the two subgroups of the elderly is as great as that between the elderly age 65 to 74 and the population under age 65. The older aged subgroup also spends a greater proportion of its budget on housing and a lower proportion on transportation, apparel, insurance, and entertainment. Also, expenditures have been shown to vary as a result of differences in work status and income levels (see, for example, Moehrle, 1990).

Another reason for separating the aged into various age groups is that the accustomed standard of living for the *very* old is usually quite different from that of the *newly* old. Each group grew up and worked over different periods of history. Each group's final earnings, and the resulting levels of living prior to retirement, are different. Given the lengths of time involved, these differences can be quite substantial. Thus, in evaluating the adequacy of income for aged people, one might want to allow for the fact that the *very* old themselves may have lower expectations about their standard of living than aged persons who retire a decade or two later.

There is, however, another factor that works in the opposite direction. Among the very old the incidence of exceptionally high expenditures for chronic illness and institutionalization rises dramatically. As Table 1–5 shows, the proportion of personal expenditures that goes for health care is nearly four times bigger for the group of aged who are age 75 and over than it is for those under 65. And for those elderly persons who experience very serious medical problems, economic need can rise catastrophically.

A study by Cook and Settersten (1995) focused on these age and income distinctions. Using data from the government's Consumer Expenditure Survey, they divided people age 45 and older into four age groups. Then they divided households in these groups by five income thresholds above and below the poverty level. Among the many interesting things they found are that:

- Income group differences are dramatic for virtually all types of expenditures, especially when age is held constant. But statistics on differences in expenditures by age alone can be misleading and should be interpreted very carefully.

- With regard to political contributions, higher income groups of the elderly tend to be more charitable. They "give more," but on average the elderly in all income groups "give virtually nothing" (0% to 0.1% of total expenditures).

- The elderly who have very low incomes do not spend a much greater proportion of total expenditures on health care than do higher elderly income groups.

With health costs rising dramatically (see Chapter 6), the question arises as to the impact of these costs on personal health expenditures. Rubin and Nieswiadomy (1997) and Acs and Sabelhaus (1995) report that out-of-pocket payments have risen dramatically for the elderly, faster than for other age groups. They show that these increases were mainly the result of buying more and higher-priced health insurance, rather than for medical goods and services. This seems to indicate that as their income rises, the elderly are trying to better shield themselves from the unpredictability and risks of the American health care system.

Differences in Income Histories

The incomes of those who have recently retired are often much better than those who have been retired a long time, mainly because the former group's earnings were typically higher, and pensions based upon them are consequently better. Also, the newer retirees are more likely to reap

Table 1–6
Age, Marital Status, and Poverty

	All	Married Couples	Nonmarried Persons
Age	Poverty Level		
62–64	11%	4	19
65–74	10	3	16
75+	15	4	20

Source: Social Security Administration (SSA), *Income of the Population 55 or Older, 1996* (Washington, D.C.: SSA Office of Policy, 1998).

gains from the relatively recent establishment of private pensions or improvements in old plans. Table 1–6 shows the percentage of aged in various age and marital categories who had money incomes below the poverty level in 1996. The data indicate that whereas one in five nonmarried persons over age 74 has money income below the poverty level (20 percent), the incidence of poverty for all those age 62 to 64 is only 11 percent.

Different Retirement Patterns

There is a final reason that one should be sensitive to age differences in assessing the economic status of the elderly. In recent years it has become increasingly unsatisfactory to talk of only those people 65 and older as being aged, given the rise of early retirement in the United States. We know that to designate arbitrarily as old those who have reached a specific chronological age is a most inadequate way of approaching the problem of defining the aged. It takes no account of people's varying capacities for physical and mental activities and social involvement, among other things. We know that people age differently in terms of various characteristics.

The more serious economic problems of aging commonly arise from, or are aggravated by, the cessation of earnings following retirement. Thus it is important to study that part of the older population having the most economic problems—those families where there are no regular workers. Increasingly, this group includes people who are less than 65 years of age. If we look at persons younger than age 65, we can logically divide them into two groups: those younger than age 62 and those age 62 to 64. Age 62 seems to be an appropriate dividing point because this is the earliest age at which eligible persons can first receive social security old age benefits (except for widows, who can qualify at age 60).

Persons who retire before age 62 must rely on employer-sponsored pensions and/or their own assets and income from these assets. Data

Table 1–7
1992 Money Income of Older Age Units[a] **(Married and Nonmarried), Ages 55 and Older**

Age	Median Income	Less than $10,000	$10,000-40,000	$40,000 or more	Total Percent[b]
55-61	15,177	35	47	18	100
62-64	14,905	35	53	12	100
65-69	12,727	39	51	11	100
70-74	11,787	41	52	7	100
75-79	12,361	40	55	5	100
80-84	11,435	40	57	4	100
85+	10,126	50	47	4	100

[a]Tabulations are for units where at least one person is in the age category specified. Units include persons living with a younger relative who is considered the "householder"; such units are classified in Bureau of Census tables as members of nonaged families.
[b]May not add to 100 percent due to rounding.
Source: Based on Susan Grad, *Income of the Population 55 or Older, 1992* (Washington, D.C.: U.S. Department of Health and Human Services, 1994), Table iii.1.

indicate that this group tends to be composed of both very high-income people and very low-income people (Kingson, 1979; Packard and Reno, 1988). That is, we find among this very early retirement group those people who *have* to retire early even though they do not have enough money and those people who *can* retire very early because they have sufficient economic resources to live satisfactorily.

Those who retire reluctantly tend to be workers with health problems, difficulties obtaining and maintaining a job, and lacking a pension to supplement social security. Those who retire voluntarily tend to be those with good employer-sponsored pensions—especially where the spouse also has a pension and the home is mortgage-free (Morgan, 1980).

Shifting from those who retire before age 62 to those ages 62–64, we focus on a group that is eligible for social security retirement benefits but at a reduced level. Ever since the early retirement provisions under social security were first introduced (in 1956 for women and 1961 for men), more than half of the men and women starting to receive social security old-age retirement benefits have opted for reduced benefits before age 65.

Published economic data on the income of various age groupings of the elderly population are sparse. Table 1–7, however, presents data for 1992 that illustrate the income differences between age groups by looking at younger versus older units. The data in Table 1–7 might be interpreted as indicating that the economic status of older individuals declines

Table 1–8

Median Income of Age Units Age 65 or Older, by Race, Hispanic Origin, and Gender, 1996

	All	Married Couples	Males	Females
White	$16,954	28,392	14,300	11,205
Black	9,649	20,464	10,050	7,286
Hispanic[a]	8,854	16,406	7,725	6,791

[a]Hispanic persons may be of any race.

Source: Social Security Administration (SSA), *Income of the Population 55 or Older, 1996* (Washington, D.C.: SSA Office of Policy, 1998).

as they grow older. This is not always the case, however. Ross et al. (1987) show, for example, that the average incomes of cohorts of older persons, when in the same retirement and marital situation, did not decline over the 1950 to 1980 period. They find instead that incomes changed significantly (usually dropped) when aged units *moved into retirement* and especially when someone *became widowed*—often increasing thereafter. This is consistent with the findings of Burkhauser et al. (1988); their study of older persons in the 1970s indicates that the highest risk of becoming poor is during the period just after becoming widowed.

Demographically, one of the fastest growing groups among the elderly is the "oldest old" (Suzman et al., 1992). All evidence to date shows this group (age 75–80 and older) to be economically less well-off than the younger aged. Radner (1993a) finds, for example, that the median cash income of family units with persons 85 and older in 1990 was 63 percent of those age 65–69—with the poverty rate for the group more than double that of the younger group. When data for the oldest old were separated into three subgroups (widows living alone, other females, and males), the median income for the widows was half that of the other females and 60 percent of income for males.

Black-White and Gender Differences

Differentiation of the aged population by various socioeconomic characteristics must also be made. The Social Security Administration (1998) reports that only a small proportion of the elderly population in 1996 received public assistance payments; however, this proportion included a much larger percentage of the black elderly (18 percent) than whites (5 percent). Other data showing differences in median incomes by sex among whites and nonwhites are presented in Table 1–8.

The plight of the minority aged has been characterized by some writers

Figure 1–4
Measures of Low Income by Race and Gender, 1996

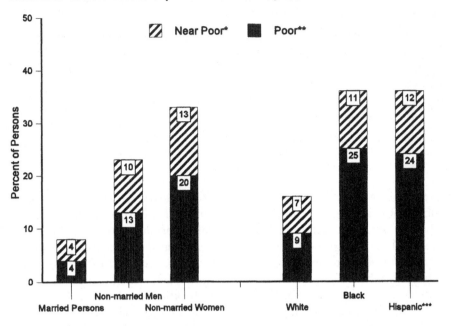

*The near poor are defined as having income between the poverty line and 125 percent of
    the poverty line.
**Based on family income of aged persons in relation to the official poverty index.
***Persons of Hispanic origin may be of any race.
Source: Social Security Administration (SSA), *Income of the Aged Chartbook, 1996* (Wash-
    ington, D.C.: SSA Office of Policy, 1998).

as one of "double jeopardy" or "multiple hazard" (Jackson, 1970). Data
on aged blacks, Mexican Americans, and whites living in Los Angeles
County and New York City provide insight on this issue. Dowd and
Bengtson (1978) investigated differences across and within ethnic categories. Their analysis supported the double jeopardy characterization, especially with regard to income and self-assessed health. Cantor and
Brennan (1993) report similar findings for New York in the 1990s.

Figure 1–4 shows differences by race and gender for the elderly with
low incomes. Poverty among the black and Hispanic aged is nearly three
times that of whites.

As we will discuss later in this chapter, poverty is also a serious problem
among older women, and it is a more serious problem for them than for
men (see Figure 1–4).

Table 1–9 shows the income distribution of nonmarried older women,
categorizing them by whether they were never married, widowed, or divorced. Widowed and divorced older women are much more likely to

Table 1–9
Differences in Income among Nonmarried Older[a] Women, 1992

Money Income	Never Married	Widowed	Divorced	Total[b]
Less than $10,000	48%	56%	55%	56%
$10,000 - 29,000	43%	38%	37%	38%
$30,000 or more	9%	6%	9%	6%
Total percent	100%[c]	100%	100%	100%
Median	$10,436	$9,073	$8,892	$9,042
Number (in thousands)	795	8,578	1,054	10,720

[a]Age 65 or older.
[b]Includes those separated or married but living apart from spouse.
[c]May not add to 100 percent due to rounding.
Source: Based on Susan Grad, *Income of the Population 55 or Older, 1992* (Washington,
    D.C.: U.S. Department of Health and Human Services, 1994), Table iii.7.

have low income than women never married. Later in this chapter we
present estimates of poverty rates among older women and show that
the highest rates of poverty are among "separated women" (not tabulated
separately in Table 1–9).

Dual Pensioners

We discuss in later chapters the fact that a high proportion of wage
and salary workers in private industry are *not* covered by private pensions. The result is that many people reaching retirement age have to rely
solely on social security pensions. Table 1–10 illustrates the income dis-
parity between aged units with dual pensions and those receiving only
social security. In 1996, the median income of couples with social security
and a private pension, for example, was much higher ($28,141) than
couples not receiving a second pension ($16,220).

In later chapters we will discuss further this divergency of economic
status among one- and two-pension families. One major policy issue currently being discussed is the extent to which government policy promotes
a growing "pension elite" (i.e., dual pensioners with high pension income) while at the same time large numbers of aged have, essentially,
only their social security income to rely on.

THE IMPACT OF TAXATION, ASSETS, AND IN-KIND
INCOME

Thus far we have looked only at the distribution of *money income*
among the aged. Three other factors have an important impact on the

Table 1–10
Total Median Money Income of Nonworking Aged,ª 1996

Retirement Benefits	All Units	Married Couples	Nonmarried Persons
Social Security onlyᵇ	$9,934	$16,220	$8,765
Only Social Security and a Private Pension	$21,398	$28,141	$15,996
Three or More Benefits	$34,500	$38,559	$26,505

ªAged units 65 or older. Excludes units with no benefits; private, railroad retirement, or
    government pensions only; and social security and government pensions only.
ᵇRetired worker, dependent and survivor benefits; disability benefits; those transitionally
    insured; and special age 72 benefits.
Source: Based on data in Social Security Administration (SSA), *Income of the Population 55
    or Older, 1996* (Washington, D.C. SSA Office of Policy, 1998).

economic status of elderly people. First, there is the extent to which the
income is actually available to meet current needs (what economists call
disposable income); some of one's income usually goes to the government in taxes. Second, we need to assess the size, type, and distribution
of assets held by older persons. And, finally, not all income is *money*
income; sizable amounts of *in-kind* income are received by the elderly,
improving their economic status.

Taxation

Most income distribution statistics look at the pretax distribution of
income. Because taxes affect people differently, we would expect the
after-tax distribution to be different. In 1980, for example, nonaged
households in the United States paid taxes averaging about one-quarter
of their yearly income to federal, state, and local governments.[4] In contrast, persons age 65 or older paid on average only 13 percent of their
income in taxes (U.S. Bureau of the Census, 1983). These tax differences
were largely a result of special federal and state income tax laws that
favored the elderly.

Over the years, however, federal tax treatment of the elderly has become much less favorable. Until 1984 all social security benefits were
exempt from federal income tax; starting in that year, however, half of
benefits became taxable for individuals with very high incomes (see Chapter 5). Currently, nearly 40 percent of elderly income is not subject to
the federal income tax (primarily as a result of the special treatment of
social security income).

Another change in the federal income tax law eliminated the *double*
"personal exemption" that persons age 65 and over could claim. How-

ever, every person who is blind or over age 64 is now entitled to an addition to the federal income tax "standard deduction." (In 1999 this additional deduction was $850 for each married person and $1,050 for an unmarried person—the amount being raised periodically to reflect increases in the Consumer Price Index.) In addition, there is a nonrefundable federal tax credit available to certain individuals 65 and older who have retired on permanent and total disability and a one-time $125,000 capital gains tax exclusion on the sale of an owner-occupied residence (starting at age 55).[5]

Given the distribution of elderly income, together with these special tax provisions, about 46 percent of individuals age 65 and over paid no federal income taxes in 1993.[6] Figure 1–5 compares the *average* federal income tax rates of aged and nonaged persons filing tax returns in 1990. These estimates are based on computer simulations using the Price Waterhouse Income Tax Model. "Average tax rates are about two and one-half times as great for the under-age-65 single populations as for the single seniors, and nearly twice as great for the married filers under 65 as for the married seniors" (Gist and Mulvey, 1990).

At the state level, there are a variety of special tax provisions benefitting the elderly. Income taxes are a major source of revenue for state governments. Many states provide income tax relief in two major ways: (1) exclusion of social security and other pension income and (2) additional personal exemptions, credits, or standard deductions. Four states allow the elderly to exclude from personal income some of their dividend and interest income (Mackey and Carter, 1994), and nine states have provisions that refund or offset the cost of paying sales taxes on food and prescription drugs (or both).

Property tax reductions are now granted in all states for elderly persons. One common type of reduction is a "circuit breaker." Tax relief under this mechanism is tied to need, as defined by taxpayers' income levels in relation to their property tax liabilities. The amount of relief declines (or phases out) as taxpayer income rises, using a formula that avoids a sharp drop in relief at some arbitrary income level; typically, the circuit breaker comes into play when the property tax burden exceeds 3 to 5 percent of household income. Income ceilings or rebate limits vary from state to state, and some states do not give tax relief to elderly renters. In 1994, twenty-two states used this mechanism for the elderly, and eleven states used it for property owners of all ages (Mackey and Carter, 1994).

Another method of state property tax relief (used by twenty-four states) is the "homestead exemption." Under this mechanism, a state excludes before the tax rate is applied a portion of the assessed value of a single-family home from total assessed value. Some states allow deferral of property taxes until after an elderly owner dies or sells his residence, and a

Figure 1–5
Average Tax Rates of the Elderly and Nonelderly, by Income Class

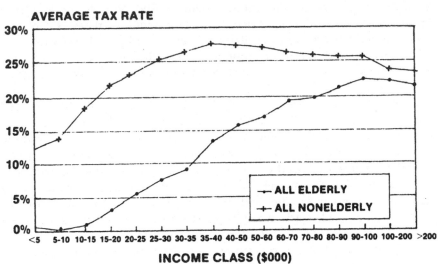

INCOME CLASS ($000)

Married Couples

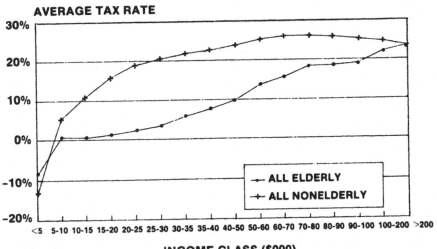

INCOME CLASS ($000)

Source: J. R. Gist and J. Mulvey, "Marginal Tax Rates and Older Taxpayers," *Tax Notes* (November 5, 1990): 679–694. Reprinted with the permission of the American Association of Retired Persons.

few freeze the tax rate at the rate in force when the aged person reaches a certain age, usually 63 or 65.

Despite these tax reduction programs, a study (Reschovsky, 1994) concludes that "most elderly homeowners face higher tax burdens than the nonelderly."

Assets

In addition to current income, many of the aged own assets that provide housing, serve as a financial reserve for special or emergency needs, contribute directly to income through interest, dividends, and rents, and generally enhance the freedow with which they spend their available income. Most assets can be sold and thereby converted to money that can be used to buy goods and services. But one should distinguish between liquid assets and nonliquid assets. Fortunately, most published statistics on assets do make such a distinction.

Liquid assets are relatively easy to convert into goods and services or money (the most liquid of assets). These consist generally of cash, bank deposits, and corporate stocks and bonds. *Nonliquid assets* usually require more time to convert. The two major types of nonliquid assets are equity in housing and equity in a business.

Assets (or savings) are held by individuals because they perform a number of very useful economic functions. They are used as a precaution against unexpected economic need in the future. One puts money aside so that it can be drawn upon should the need arise. This saving might be viewed as self-insurance. Assets are also accumulated in anticipation of known or planned large expenditures in the future; for example, because of a worsening illness one might anticipate going into a nursing home, or one might save in order to take a round-the-world retirement cruise. Still another reason for saving is to leave an inheritance to one's children or to other people.

One of the most important reasons for saving is to smooth out the irregularities in the flow of income coming to an individual over his or her lifetime. People are becoming increasingly aware of the fact that (given current life expectancies) there is often a ten- to thirty-year period of living in retirement after earnings from work have stopped. Thus, individuals must decide how to deal financially with this nonwork period of life and whether to provide through asset accumulation economic resources to supplement pension income.

However, assets put aside as a precautionary measure or for anticipated major expenditures in old age are not available for meeting immediate needs. If you are worried, for example, about having high medical expenses that Medicare will not completely cover, if you expect that you might have to go into a nursing home, or if you anticipate that property

Table 1–11
Homeownership Rates by Age, 1991

Age of Householder	Percent Homeowners
Less than 35	38%
35 - 44	66
44 - 54	75
55 - 64	80
65 and older	77
All ages	64

Source: U.S. Bureau of the Census, "Homeownership: 1989 to 1991," Statistical Brief (Washington, D.C.: U.S. Bureau of the Census, June 1992).

taxes will increase dramatically in your city or town, you must accumulate additional assets to provide for such events. Thus, some studies (e.g., Danziger et al., 1982–1983; Menchik and David, 1983; Torrey and Taeuber, 1986) show that contrary to predictions by economists based on the lifecycle hypothesis, the elderly as a group tend to save, not dissave; it is only among the very old that widespread dissaving occurs. However, other economists (e.g., Hurd, 1990) come to the opposite conclusion— that significant dissaving is taking place. Currently, there is no agreement among economists on the matter.

Similarly, if you have nonliquid assets such as housing, as long as you are determined to keep that housing and not sell the property, that asset is not convertible into income to be used for day-to-day living. In effect, the asset is "locked in."

A high proportion of older people own a home or have equity in it. The U.S. Bureau of the Census (1992) reports that in 1991, 77 percent of elderly "householders" lived in an owned home; Table 1–11 shows how ownership varied with age. The amount of mortgage debt on those homes is usually very low; in fact, about four-fifths of elderly homeowners own their homes free of any mortgage. Thus we find that many older persons have a sizable asset accumulation in home equity, but often most of it is not available for day-to-day living expenses.

Until recently in the United States there was no available financial mechanism that would permit people to sell the equity in their home, get back money over a period of time, and still be able to live in the house. In contrast, in France a home annuity plan called *viager* has been in existence for many years. A viager arrangement is negotiated by the homeowner with a buyer and results in the buyer paying an agreed down payment and a monthly payment to the owner for the rest of the owner's life (in return for the property at death). The amounts paid are mutually agreed, with the age and health of the owner taken into account. The arrangement, to a certain extent, represents a gamble on the part of both parties. The buyer, however, can go to an insurance company and take out an actuarial insurance plan to help offset the payments promised in the resulting legal agreement.

Since January 1, 1979, the Federal Home Loan Bank Board (FHLBB) in the United States has allowed federally chartered savings and loan associations to offer *reverse annuity mortgages*. Under this type of mortgage, a homeowner continues to live in the home but sells some of the financial equity in the house, receiving in return a fixed monthly sum based on a percentage of the current market value of the house. Reverse annuity mortgages are potentially available in all states, but each federal savings institution's program has to be approved by the FHLBB. Thus far, the spread of this option has been very slow.

There are two basic kinds of reverse mortgages: term and tenure. Term loans pay out for a pre-specified number of years. The amount of the monthly payment depends on the interest rate, the term length, the property value, and the allowable loan to property value ratio. Since the loan must be repaid at the end of the term, careful planning is required for the homeowner's protection. Term loans are most useful for homeowners who need high monthly income payments (e.g., people needing home care or other expensive health services) or for homeowners who plan to remain in their homes a relatively short period of time.

Currently, the other type, the *tenure* reverse annuity mortgage, is the type most frequently chosen. Tenure loans allow homeowners to stay in their homes until they die or decide to move. The monthly payment size depends on the borrower's life expectancy, the expected property appreciation, and the same factors mentioned for term loans. Thus, other things equal, younger borrowers receive smaller monthly payments than older borrowers.

Scholen and Chen (1980) and Venti and Wise (1990) give a good introduction to the complex set of issues that must be satisfactorily resolved before "unlocking home equity" becomes commonplace. The slow acceptance is in part a result of the newness of the mechanism, but more important are the risks involved and the small amount of income for the elderly that often results. In a move to deal with the risks, Congress recently authorized the Federal Housing Administration (FHA) to insure (for homeowners age 62 or older) up to 25,000 reverse mortgages over a five-year period. The insurance guarantees that lenders will get all their money back and that borrowers will get their monthly payments, even if the lender goes broke.

Another problem that has arisen is the cost of getting one of these special mortgages. Reverse mortgages can be very costly, especially if terminated early or if payments to be received are small. To begin with, all borrowers must pay closing costs, typically $3,000 to $5,000. In addition, financial institutions often charge origination fees, insurance premiums, annuity premiums, and "mortgage servicing fees." These additional costs may add up to as much as $9,000. On top of these fees, some tenure plans take a share of any house value appreciation that may occur. All these up-front fees can be financed through the mortgage loan, but that then reduces the amount of available equity.

It is clear that deciding whether to take out a reverse mortgage is extremely complicated. It involves making estimations or judgments about many unpredictable future events: How long will I live? How long can I live independently? How long will I remain healthy? Will future interest rates rise or fall? How will the value of my house change?

Because of the complexity of decision making and the danger of scams, experts in this area generally agree that people should seek help from reliable professional counselors, and many government-sponsored programs in this area require some amount of counseling.

But finding good advice is not easy. Impartial counselors are not widely available. Moreover, scams involving people pretending to give good advice have now appeared across the country.

In addition to private sector reverse mortgages, there are also programs operated solely by state and local governments. The most important one is reverse mortgages to allow deferral of property tax payments. State programs currently operate in California, Illinois, Maine, Oregon, Washington, and Wisconsin. "Local option" programs operate in Colorado, Connecticut, Florida, Georgia, Iowa, Massachusetts, New Hampshire, Texas, Utah, and Virginia (AARP Public Policy Institute, 1991). However, a very high proportion of all current tax deferral accounts are in only two states—California and Oregon.

Net Worth

Gustman and Juster (1995), reviewing a number of different data sets on wealth and the elderly, summarize the data as follows:

Wealth is highly unevenly distributed among the older population. . . . Married couples have substantially higher levels of wealth, even after implicit correction for household size, than single men or single women; the disparities are substantially larger for **net worth** less housing equity than for total net worth, since housing equity itself is somewhat more evenly distributed than most other assets; minority households have substantially fewer assets than whites by an order of magnitude of four or five to one in mean values, and an order of magnitude more like ten to one for net worth less housing equity.

Table 1–12
Distribution of Median Household Net Worth by Age, 1991

Quintile[a]	Total Net Worth	Net Worth Minus Home Equity	Proportion of Age Group in Each Quintile
	Age 55-64		
Lowest Income Quintile	$16,959	$1,406	18%
Second Income Quintile	52,660	$10,580	19%
Third Income Quintile	77,439	24,382	20%
Fourth Income Quintile	135,458	42,586	20%
Highest Income Quintile	212,660	95,692	22%
	Age 65+		
Lowest Income Quintile	$32,172	$3,577	35%
Second Income Quintile	90,635	29,152	28%
Third Income Quintile	154,203	68,372	17%
Fourth Income Quintile	225,594	121,154	11%
Highest Income Quintile	424,721	299,679	8%

[a]Quintiles based on monthly household income. Upper quintile limits for 1991 were; 1st quintile, $1,071; 2nd, $1,912; 3rd, $2,914; 4th, $4,454.
Source: Based on U.S. Bureau of the Census, *Household Wealth and Asset Ownership, 1991* (Washington, D.C.: U.S. Government Printing Office, 1994), Table E.

Table 1–12 shows the net worth of the aged in 1991. We see that the net worth of many aged units is quite high when we add together financial assets, real estate (own home, rental property, vacation homes, and land holdings), any business holdings, and the value of motor vehicles.

Table 1–12 divides households into five groups. Ranking *all* households on the basis of their total monthly income, the 20 percent of the households with the lowest income are grouped together and constitute what we call the lowest income quintile. The median net worth of two subgroups is reported in Table 1–12, with and without home equity included. In 1991, 35 percent of aged households were in the lowest income quintile and had a median total net worth of $32,172. But if home equity is excluded, the median net worth drops dramatically to only $3,577.

If we look at the third quintile, or middle group of households, we find that 17 percent of aged households were in that group and that their median total net worth in 1991 was $154,203. Again, with home equity removed, the net worth figure drops to $68,372.

Table 1–12 also gives similar statistics for the 55–64 age group. Its net worth is, in all cases, significantly lower.

Radner (1989) has calculated the percentage of households that have *financial* assets greater or less than a specified number of months of income. This measure gives us a good impression of the protection against income loss that is provided by assets. Radner found that among persons age 65 and over in 1984, 41 percent had financial assets that covered less than 6 months of their income, and about half had financial assets covering at least 12 months.

Again, a note of caution is in order. As we discussed earlier in this chapter, it is difficult to get *accurate* statistics on income and assets. Large surveys to determine asset holdings of individuals have been undertaken very infrequently in the United States, and those attempted have been plagued by the problem that many people underreport their assets. Although surveys on the amounts and kinds of income also have under-reporting problems, the amount of underreporting is greater when attempting to ascertain assets. In this regard, Juster, who is an expert on survey data, comments: "While my judgment is that we know remarkably little about saving in the aggregate, except for a few components of saving that are well-measured and well-understood, what we know at the macrolevel represents a solid concrete-and-steel edifice compared to what we know at the microlevel" (Juster, n.d.).

In-Kind Income

In-kind income consists of goods and services available to the aged without expenditure of money or available at prices below their market value. When family members raise much of their own food or own a house, rather than rent,[7] they gain economically. Government programs also provide in-kind benefits. For example, special housing programs for the elderly provide apartments at rates below the normal market price, a subsidy being paid by the government. The federal food stamp program issues coupons that can be used in place of money to purchase food in retail stores. Another large program provides "energy assistance" to the elderly. The largest in-kind programs, Medicare and Medicaid, provide the elderly with various health care services. A major problem in estimating the impact of in-kind benefits on economic status is determining

Table 1–13
Aged Poverty When the Income Definition Is Changed, 1992

Definition of Income	Percent in Poverty
Income before taxes:	
1. Traditional money income measure	12.9
Income after taxes:	
2. Money income (less means-tested cash benefits) less state and federal income taxes and payroll taxes	14.8
3. Definition 2 plus the value of Medicare	12.9
4. Definition 3 plus means-tested cash transfers	11.5
5. Definition 4 plus the value of Medicaid and all other means-tested programs	10.4
6. Definition 5 plus net imputed return on equity in own home	6.2

Source: U.S. Bureau of the Census, *Measuring the Effect of Benefits and Taxes on Income and Poverty: 1992*, Current Population Reports, P60-186RD (Washington, D.C.: U.S. Government Printing Office, 1993), Table J.

how best to value these benefits. As Schmundt, Smolensky, and Stiefel (1975) have noted, the value that the recipients themselves place on some in-kind goods may be substantially less than the market price.

In recent years, the Census Bureau has calculated income after major taxes and has also estimated the monetary impact of certain in-kind benefits. Table 1–13 shows how the poverty rate rises two percentage points when money income is reduced by taxes but drops again when a value for Medicare is added. Homeowners (with home equity) receive income in the form of housing services, but that income is usually omitted from income distribution estimates. The Census Bureau makes a crude estimate of this in-kind income by calculating a rate of return (i.e., an interest rate) for estimated home equity using the average rate on high-grade municipal bonds. Table 1–13 shows a big drop in poverty when that estimate is included in the definition of income.

Interfamily and Intrafamily Transfers

Another issue to be considered is the impact of transfers among various members of the family. While we know relatively little about the magnitude and nature of these transfers, available data indicate that it is a decreasing but still important means of support for some elderly.

Numerous studies have documented the fact that the elderly in this country prefer to live apart from their children. In 1989, only 13 percent of the aged were living with their children or with another nonspouse relative (*Aging America*, 1991). For most older people, moving into a household with relatives remains an act of financial or social necessity rather than preference (Soldo, 1981). In an effort to enable an elderly person who is otherwise functioning well to remain in his or her home or apartment, relatives may often provide economic assistance to supplement public transfers. However, the greatest transfers go to unmarried older people who for one reason or another have been forced to move in with relatives (Morgan, 1978).

Transfers within families take many forms, however, and go both ways (in terms of age); however, they typically go to the less well-off family members (McGarry and Schoeni, 1997). They include the provision of (1) emergency money, loans, or services; (2) regular support over relatively long periods; (3) child care; (4) gifts; (5) food; and (6) shelter. Morgan (1983) concludes that "the family is by far the most important welfare or redistribution mechanism even in an advanced industrial country like the United States with extensive public and private income maintenance programs." However, in his analysis of American intrafamily transfers based on data from the Michigan Panel Study of Income Dynamics, Morgan concludes that one finds relatively little help is given on a regular basis *in the form of money*. And, to the extent that money transfers do take place, there is far more giving from older people to their children than from children to their parents.

Indeed, the minor role played by financial transfers between family members is underscored by the decrease in the proportion of elderly parents who have received cash contributions from their children. In the United States in the early 1950s, for example, 5 to 10 percent of the aged received cash contributions from children. Data from the Survey of Income and Program Participation (SIPP) show that by 1985 only 918,000 aged parents (roughly 3 percent) received any *financial* support from one or more of their children (U.S. Bureau of the Census, 1988).

If the number of aged recipients of family transfers is low, it is also true that the average amount of money exchanged is relatively low. The same SIPP survey found that the average amount of support given by children making such transfers in 1985 to their parents was only $1,484 per person.

The small proportion of the aged receiving money from their children needs to be placed in perspective, however. Morgan (1983) points out that there are many more people who feel that potential family help is available if it is ever needed than the number who report actual transfers. Figure 1–6 summarizes, for example, the views of persons age 45 and older regarding sources of help that are *potentially available if needed*.

Figure 1–6
Parent Views on Sources of Potential Help from Children, 1979

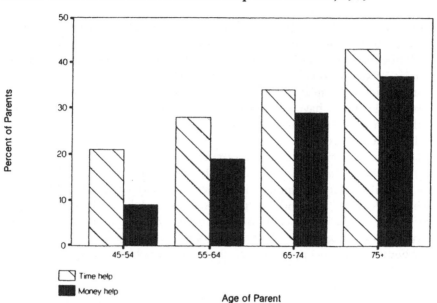

Source: Based on Figures 1.9 and 1.11 in G. Duncan and J. Morgan, eds., *Five Thousand American Families*, Vol. 6 (Ann Arbor: Survey Research Center, University of Michigan, 1983).

Two sources of potential help are depicted: (1) nonmonetary assistance in the form of giving of one's time to help out; and (2) emergency monetary assistance given on an irregular basis. The responses clearly show that many Americans feel that help will be there if they ever need it.

THE ADEQUACY OF INCOME IN OLD AGE

In 1976 a task force of government experts reviewed ways of measuring poverty more accurately. In their final report, members emphasized the fact that assessing income adequacy necessitates standards that are *relative*:

Poor persons living in the United States in the 1970s are rich in contrast to their counterparts in other times and places. They are not poor if by poor is meant the subsistence levels of living common in some other countries. Nor are most poor like their counterparts in this country fifty or one hundred years ago. This country is concerned about poverty, its causes and correlates. It is willing to relieve the poverty of some of the poor, and it wants to measure the effectiveness

of its efforts to do so. None of this can be done without some idea of who is to
be considered poor and who is not. (Poverty Studies Task Force, 1976)

In this section we look at various measures of adequacy in relation to
the income of older persons. In early times nations had little choice but
to define basic needs in terms of survival. But for the more affluent
nations of the world today, "need" becomes more relative and, hence,
more difficult to measure. A large number of different approaches to
measuring poverty have been proposed over the years. Good discussions
of the various options can be found in Poverty Studies Task Force (1976)
and Ruggles (1990).[8]

The most common measure of poverty in America today is the government's poverty *index*.[9] Developed in the early 1960s by the Social Security Administration, it gained prominence in President Johnson's declared
"War on Poverty." The index continues to be widely used today, despite
the fact that the Nixon administration—very early in its first term—
strongly discouraged government agencies from using the index, arguing
that because of conceptual and measurement problems it was a misleading and unreliable measure.

A succinct description of the Social Security Administration's poverty
index was presented in testimony by Wilbur Cohen before the U.S. House
Committee on Ways and Means (1967):

The starting point for the SSA poverty index is the amount of money needed to
purchase the food for a minimum adequate diet as determined by the Department
of Agriculture. The food budget is the lowest that could be devised to supply all
essential nutrients using food readily purchasable in the U.S. market (with cus-
tomary regional variations). The poverty line is then calculated at three times the
food budget (slightly smaller proportions for one- and two-person families) on
the assumption—derived from studies of consumers—that a family that has spent
a larger proportion of its income on food will be living at a very inadequate level.
The food budgets and the derivative poverty income cutoff points are estimated
in detail for families of differing size and composition (62 separate family types)
with a farm/nonfarm differential for each type. This variation of the poverty measure in relation to family size and age of members is its most important distin-
guishing characteristic.

Because the level of living implied by the poverty index is lower than we think
most people would regard as an appropriate measure of adequacy of income for
retired persons or disabled workers and their families or widows and children,
we have also developed a slightly higher index. We call this the low income index,
and it is definitely low income.

It is an interesting fact that in actual practice, the low-income index
has rarely been used for policy evaluation purposes. Instead the poverty

index has almost exclusively dominated the discussions of how many nonaged and aged are in economic difficulty and what policies are needed to deal with these difficulties. It is important, therefore, to understand how the poverty index is calculated and its limitations.

Calculating the Poverty Index

Because of its wide use and importance, let us run through step by step the construction of this poverty measure. First, as was indicated in Cohen's statement above, an amount of adequate food for the family unit is determined, and then the cost of that food at prevailing prices is ascertained by sending people out to record the prices for it in various retail stores.

For decades the Department of Agriculture has produced "food plans" that meet the nutritional standards set out by the National Research Council. While these plans meet nutritional standards, they also try to make the quantities and types of food chosen compatible with the general preferences of American families, preferences determined by food-consumption studies. Thus it is not simply a matter of giving poor people only beans to eat; general eating habits and preferences are taken into account.

Therefore, in constructing a food plan, an attempt is made to respond to the fact that most people prefer meat to beans, although in terms of protein you can get more or at least as much protein from beans as you can from meat. The fact remains, however, that most of the protein in such plans is provided by the cheaper nonmeat products.

It is also important to note that the food plans were originally devised for *emergency periods only* and that no one is expected to have to live over a long period of time on these very minimal food amounts. This implies that these food diets could be detrimental to your health over an extended period.

Finally, the Department of Agriculture makes no pretense of assuming that all families can skillfully budget or that they are willing to eat the foods specified in the plans. These assumptions need not be made, given the purpose of the plans. They were developed simply as a device to provide social welfare agencies with a needs standard that was not completely subjective in determining how much money poor people needed to avoid serious malnutrition.

The next step in developing the poverty measure is to construct food budgets for different types of families. There is not one poverty index; rather, there are many. The poverty indices (or "poverty thresholds") are currently based on family units with different combinations of the following characteristics[10]:

1. Age of head over or under age 65
2. Size of family (two to nine or more)
3. Number of related children under age 18
4. "Unrelated" family units

The final step is to multiply the cost of the various food plans by three. As explained by the Social Security Administration:

The Agriculture Department evaluated family food consumption and dietary adequacy in a 1955 survey week and reported for all families of two or more—farm and nonfarm—an expenditure for food approximating one-third of money income after taxes. Two-person nonfarm families used about 27 percent of their income for food and families with three or more persons about 35 percent. A later study made in 1960–61 by the Bureau of Labor Statistics found for urban families that nearly a fourth of a family's income (after taxes) went for food. There is less variation by size of family than might have been anticipated, ranging between 22 percent and 28 percent. . . . The earlier relationship based upon the Department of Agriculture's study was adopted as the basis for defining poverty—that is, an income less than three times the cost of the economy food plan for families of three or more persons. (U.S. House Committee on Ways and Means, 1967)

Thus we see that the "three" used to calculate the poverty level is based upon a survey of the ratio of food consumption to income of *all* families in the United States. Averaging all families, the Agriculture Department came out with an estimate of three, and this was the number used to calculate the index. The Bureau of Labor Statistics' estimate of four was ignored by the Social Security Administration, in part because of data quality issues (Fisher, 1992).

How Good a Measure?

Reflecting on the adoption of the poverty index, Mollie Orshansky (its major architect) observed:

The utility of the SSA poverty index owes much to an accident of timing: it appeared when needed. The link to nutritional economy and food-income consumption patterns endowed an arbitrary judgment with a quasi-scientific rationale it otherwise did not have. And, the fact that adjustments for family size and composition produced about the same results as the . . . [1964 Council of Economic Advisors' $3,000 poverty level for a family of two or more], even while it permitted more meaningful comparisons of group vulnerability, was perhaps the chief reason for its acceptance. (Orshansky, 1988)

Over the years the poverty index has been criticized frequently. For example, one congressional committee asserted: "To tout a 'poverty line' based on a starvation diet and an outdated concept of a family's budget as an adequate measure of what is necessary to humanely survive is indefensible" (U.S. House Select Committee on Aging, 1978). More recently, economist Robert Haveman (1992–1993) has stated: "The poverty cutoffs [i.e., current poverty levels] are tenuous. They have no reliable scientific basis."

In a major study of how to measure poverty, Patricia Ruggles (1990) concludes that the measure *originally* did a reasonably good job of identifying people "with truly inadequate access to consumption." However, since the index was first estimated, the only major modification made over the years has been to adjust the index numbers upward for inflation.[11] No adjustments have been made for any changes over the decades in: consumption behavior, tax laws, the (higher) living standards of the general population, family living arrangements, the mix of consumer products (and services) available, or the expanded range of government social programs giving benefits to the poor. Yet all of these factors have changed, in some cases dramatically, since the index was constructed.

Ruggles (1990) argues that the obsolete consumption data underlying these measures result in a poverty line that "is no longer realistic as a standard for minimally adequate consumption." As indicated above, the ratio of food to other expenditures is a key factor in constructing the poverty index. The higher ratio suggested by the early Bureau of Labor Statistics data was not adopted when the index was first constructed. However, other data that have become available since 1955 also suggest that a higher ratio is appropriate. Tabulation of the 1965 Food Consumption Survey produced a 3.4:1 ratio. "More significantly, the Consumer Expenditure Surveys of 1960–61 and 1972–73 seem to indicate that the ratio exceeds 5:1" (Poverty Studies Task Force, 1976).

A related issue is the measurement of the minimum food requirements used to estimate food costs for the ratio. The current index uses a measure of adequate diet based on the Department of Agriculture's 1963 Economy Food Plan. In 1975 the Department of Agriculture replaced this food plan with a new Thrifty Food Plan. The Thrifty Food Plan reflects revised allowances for essential nutrients and newer data on family food selections. However, it was not adopted for the index.

The index's principal architect, Mollie Orshansky, pointed out as early as 1978 that the new food plan implies poverty income thresholds that are about 40 percent higher than current levels. Testifying before Congress, she estimated that "shifting to the more realistic update . . . would just about double the number of aged poor to include nearly a third of all persons 65 or older, and the number either poor or near poor would embrace approximately two in every five" (Orshansky, 1978). The more recent study by Ruggles (1990), using the Orshansky approach, estimates that updated consumption standards indicate that the poverty levels should be at least 50 percent higher than the official levels currently in use.

One highly controversial aspect of determining who is in poverty is the question of how and what income is measured. Most "off the books" income is missed. Large amounts of public cash transfers (such as welfare payments) are not reported to survey interviewers. And most important, argue many economists, is the fact that in-kind income, wealth, and tax payments are currently ignored in the official estimates.

But dealing with these issues is difficult. As Radner (1993b) points out, with regard to in-kind income, it is necessary to consider *both* the "needs" and "income" sides when trying to deal with noncash income in a poverty measure. The clearest and most important example is in trying to incorporate Medicare benefits into the poverty measure. If the common recommendation is followed to include a value for Medicare benefits in the income of the elderly and medical needs are ignored, "then groups that are 'sicker' (i.e., have greater medical needs) could be estimated to be 'richer.' . . . The elderly as a group are relatively 'sicker' than the nonaged are and therefore could be estimated to be relatively 'richer' on this basis" (Radner, 1993b).

Another problem is taxes. In developing her poverty estimates, Mollie Orshansky used Current Population Survey (CPS) data, because it was the only good source of nationally representative income data available at the time. This created a problem. The CPS reported *before-tax* money income. But the poverty indices were developed using the *after-tax* money income concept used in the Department of Agriculture's survey from which the critical food to other needs multiplier (3:1) was derived. According to Fisher (1992):

From the beginning, Orshansky was aware of the inconsistency of applying after-tax thresholds to before-tax income data, but there was no other alternative. She reasoned that the result would yield "a conservative estimate" of poverty. At that time, and for some years thereafter, most families and individuals at the poverty level had little or no Federal income tax liability.

Still another problem involves not counting low-income persons as poor if they are institutionalized or living with relatives. In 1976 there were over a million "hidden poor" (mostly unmarried women) who were living with relatives because their low incomes did not permit independent living (Orshansky, 1978). A more recent estimate of the extent of this measurement problem is provided using statistics developed by Grad (1985). In 1984, 10 percent of the aged (65 and older) units (couples and nonmarried persons) living with other family members were in families where the *total family income* was below poverty. If we look at *only the income of these aged units*, however, we find that not 10 but 34 percent of these aged had "own income" below the poverty level. Most of these poor aged are missed in the official poverty statistics.

The NAS Recommendations

At the request of Congress, in 1992 the National Academy of Sciences (NAS) appointed a study panel on poverty measurement. This panel issued its recommendations in 1995 (Citro and Michael, 1995). Agreeing with prior experts that the current poverty measure was very defective, the panel made three major recommendations:

- That there should be a change in how income was measured;
- That the "poverty thresholds" should be changed; and
- That the government's "Survey of Income and Program Participation" (SIPP) should be the statistical data base for estimating poverty.

Regarding the first two recommendations, NAS proposed adding certain "in-kind" benefits to the measure of income and subtracting taxes, work expenses, child support, and out-of-pocket medical expenses from income. They also proposed new poverty thresholds based on more than food—recommending that these thresholds be updated annually for not just inflation but also for the growth in median national expenditures on "basic goods."

The heart of the NAS panel's revision of the poverty measure is to set a minimally adequate standard of living based on a *commodity bundle of basic needs*. Basic needs would be specified with regard to food, clothing, shelter, and utilities—allowing a small additional amount of income for other needs (such as personal care and household supplies).

Researchers at the U.S. Bureau of Labor Statistics (Garner et al., 1998) have estimated the impact of switching to the NAS procedures. Table 1–14 compares poverty rates using the current methodology and an alternative using one of many possible bundles of basic needs commodities. For the elderly, the incidence of poverty more than doubles, using the recommended alternative.

While the researchers found poverty rates to be generally higher across subgroups of the population (and also for different years back to 1990), they also found changes in the relative composition of poverty. They concluded: "Does the new poverty measure change our view of who is poor? . . . It is clear that, as we have interpreted the Panel's proposal, the composition of the poverty population changes quite a bit."

Table 1–14
Poverty Measure Reforms: Old and New Rates, 1995

Sub-Groups	Poverty Rates	
	Current Methods[a]	An Alternative[b]
All Persons	13.8%	21.1%
Whites (all ages)	11.2	18.7
Blacks (all ages)	29.3	35.3
Hispanics (all ages)[c]	30.3	45.8
Female Householders (all ages)	35.5	42.9
Elderly (65 and over)	**10.5**	**24.2**
Children (under 18)	20.8	27.7
Persons age 18–64	11.4	17.7

[a]Based on the current methodology used to calculate the official poverty index.
[b]Based on the National Academy of Science recommendations, using their most conservative "base bundle" of commodities.
[c]Can be of any race.
Source: T. Garner, K. Short, S. Shipp, C. Nelson, and G. Paulin, "Experimental Poverty Measurement for the 1990s," *Monthly Labor Review* (March 1998): 39–61.

The following groups of persons make up a *smaller* percentage of the poor when the new approach is used:

• Children
• Blacks
• Hispanics
• Persons living in families with no workers
• Persons living in households headed by women

In contrast, the groups with a *larger* percentage of poor are:

• The elderly
• Persons living in married-couple families
• Persons living in families where at least one worker is present

To date, no official action has been taken by Congress on the NAS proposal.

Poverty Index Statistics

Figure 1–7 shows the change that has occurred in the official rate of elderly poverty over the 1967 to 1997 period. In 1998 the official gov-

Figure 1–7
Poverty Rate by Age, 1967–1997

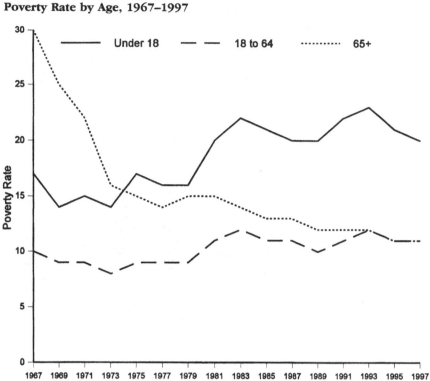

Source: U.S. Bureau of the Census, "Measuring 50 Years of Economic Change Using the March Current Population Survey," *Current Population Reports*, P60-203 (Washington, D.C.: U.S. Government Printing Office, 1998).

ernment poverty index level for a two-person family with head age 65 or more was about $10,000; the one-person level was about $8,000. (The level for a *nonaged* person family was about $17,000.) Figure 1–8 shows that there are wide differences in 1989 poverty rates among subgroups of the elderly. For example, while the poverty rate for the married aged was about 5 percent in 1989, it was six times more for the black aged.

As Figure 1–8 indicates, aged poverty is concentrated among ethnic minorities and women. Table 1–15 looks at poverty among women, dividing them into five marital status groups. The table also shows the poverty rates at different ages, beginning at age 45. Table 1–16 shows more recent data.

As one would expect, at any age all of the subgroups of nonmarried women have substantially higher poverty rates than those of married women. After age 62, the incidence of poverty among *divorced* older women is as high or higher than that of widowed or never married

Figure 1–8
Percent of Elderly Poor or Near-Poor by Selected Characteristics, 1996*

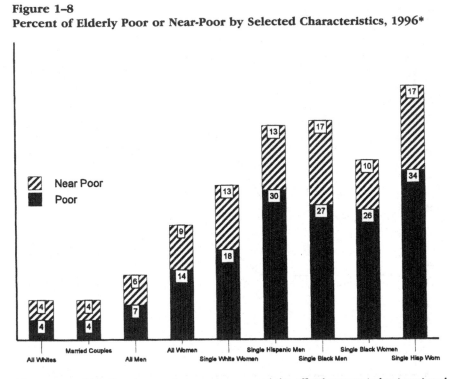

*Persons age 65+, Based on total money income and the official poverty index (poor) and
    125 percent of the poverty index (near poor).
Source: Based on data in Social Security Administration (SSA), *Income of the Population 55
    and Older, 1996* (Washington, D.C.: SSA Office of Policy, 1998).

women. However, the incidence of poverty among *separated* older
women is much higher than that of any other group of unmarried older
women—including divorced women. This results in large part from the
very high concentration of minority older women in the separated group
(Crown et al., 1993).

Maintaining Living Standards

Today older workers are retiring at increasingly early ages (see Chapter
2). Following their departure from the labor force, they are faced with
the prospect of expenditure needs that do not decrease as much as many
would like to believe. In the retirement period there are usually rising
health expenditures, increased leisure activities, and increased need for
supportive services. There is also a continuing need for the basic essen-
tials of food and housing. Moreover, the retired quickly become aware
of any rise in the living standards of nonretired families as these younger

Table 1–15
Poverty Among Older Women Age 45 and Over, 1989

	Age 45-61	Age 62-74	Age 75+	All
Married	5%	5%	9%	6%
Widowed	22	16	21	19
Never Married	24	17	22	19
Divorced	17	23	28	24
Separated	36	38	*	42

*insufficient sample size.
Source: William H. Crown, Phyllis H. Mutschler, James H. Schulz, and Rebecca Loew, *The Economic Status of Divorced Older Women* (Waltham, Mass.: Policy Center on Aging, Heller School, Brandeis University, 1993), Table 2.

families share in the general, long-run economic growth of the country. Such increases no doubt generate a desire among many of the aged to "keep up."

It is this ability to keep up that we will now focus on. In addition to the aged who find their income near or below the poverty level, there are other aged whose earnings during the working period allowed them to maintain a comfortable living standard but whose retirement incomes have dropped far below their pre-retirement levels. This decline in living standards in retirement has become increasingly unacceptable in the United States. It is a generally accepted goal of retirement planning (see Chapter 3) to provide enough income in retirement to prevent living standards from dropping significantly. The President's Commission on Pension Policy (1981) expressed the goals this way:

Individuals should be able to maintain their preretirement standard of living during retirement years. Retirees should not have to experience a sudden drop in their standard of living. These goals should be accomplished by using income from all sources, including benefits from retirement programs as well as from income derived from individual efforts.

In later chapters we discuss in great detail the extent to which pensions replace preretirement earnings and the use of replacement rates to assess pension income adequacy. In anticipation of that discussion, one key statistic from a study by the Social Security Administration (Grad, 1990) is given here to show the magnitude of the problem. Of those couples who began receiving social security benefits in the early 1980s, a little over 90 percent received total pension income (social security plus employer pension benefits) below the amount necessary to maintain their preretirement living standard at levels associated with their *highest* earnings prior to retirement. Thus, even among the better-off elderly,

The Economics of Aging

Table 1–16
Poverty Status,[a] by Age, Sex, and Marital Status, 1996

Age	Married Persons	Nonmarried Men	Nonmarried Women
	Percent Poor		
65–69	4	13	19
70–74	4	10	18
75–79	5	11	21
80–84	5	17	20
85 or older	5	15	21
	Percent Poor or Near Poor[b]		
65–69	8	24	30
70–74	8	24	30
75–79	9	16	35
80–84	10	24	33
85 or older	9	27	34

[a]Based on family income of aged persons in relation to the official poverty index.
[b]The near poor are defined as having income between the poverty line and 125% of the poverty line.
Source: Social Security Administration (SSA), *Income of the Aged Chartbook, 1996* (Washington, D.C.: SSA Office of Research, Evaluation, and Statistics, 1998).

there were many who found themselves faced with a sharp decline in income relative to their preretirement levels and a consequent decline in their living standards. (We have much more to say about this problem in later chapters.)

Equivalency Scales

One often sees the median (or mean) income of the aged compared with the medians for other age groups. These crude comparisons are somewhat misleading, however. Elderly households are on average much smaller than those of other age groups (except the very young); for example, households whose heads are ages 34 to 54 are on the average twice as big. This means that elderly incomes are generally supporting fewer people, with more income potentially available to each person. Because we often want to compare the adequacy of aged income with that of other groups, we need to take account of these size differences.

One common adjustment for comparison purposes is to divide each family's income by the number of people in the household, thereby obtaining a per capita measure. Danziger et al. (1984) point out the weaknesses of this approach:

> The per capita measure is easy to understand and mathematically convenient but has little else to recommend it. Its use implies, for example, that people who marry spouses with no income or earnings potential are cutting their economic well-being in half. The per capita measure also ignores all economics of scale and specialization within households and is especially inappropriate for households that derive a large share of their full income in the form of leisure or production of home services.

There is an alternative approach to comparing different groups. One can develop an index that takes account of differences in family size and composition, health status, age, sex, and other relevant characteristics when determining the level of income necessary to achieve a given level of economic well-being. This measure is called an **equivalence scale**.

The basic approach in calculating an equivalence scale is to develop an objective way of determining equivalent levels of consumption for families of varying composition. Historically, measures based on food–income relationships have been most common. As we saw previously, the current official poverty index embodies an equivalence scale based solely on food consumption needs.

Danziger et al. (1984) have estimated an equivalence scale for a wide range of family types, based on expenditures on all types of consumption goods and services. Table 1–17 presents some of these estimates to illustrate some of the differences they found. For example, Danziger's estimates indicate that an elderly couple needs income that is about 64 percent of the income of a four-person family (age 35–54, children ages 12 to 17) to achieve a similar or equivalent level of well-being. And an older woman living alone needs about half the income of an aged couple to achieve a similar equivalency.

The principal advantage of this approach to comparing adequacy is its seeming objectivity. It can be calculated directly by direct measurements of actual consumer behavior of different groups. We must remember, however, that such measures do not take into account all of the factors that affect the consumption levels of families differing in size and stage in the life cycle. Moreover, as with other measures, underlying the calculations are certain assumptions that are essentially arbitrary—what consumption to measure, how to define different groups, how to interpret differences in savings rates, and so forth. While many scholars have constructed equivalence scales, their results differ significantly. There is currently no agreement among experts on the best way to take account of family size differences when making comparative judgments about the economic well-being of various groups.[12]

Table 1–17
Equivalence Scale

Consumer Unit Composition	Age of Head			
	35	35–54	54–64	65+
One person (female)	50	53	46	37
Two persons (man and wife)	77	80	73	64
Four persons (couple, two children):				
Age of children				
Under age 6	83	87	80	71
Ages 12–17	97	100	93	84
Ages 18 and over	101	105	97	89

Source: Based on data in Sheldon Danziger, J. Van der Gaag, E. Smolensky, and M. K. Taussig, "Implications of the Relative Economic Status of the Elderly for Transfer Policy," in H. J. Aaron and G. Burtless, eds., *Retirement and Economic Behavior* (Washington, D.C.: Brookings Institution, 1987), Table 3.

Who's Doing Better—the Young or the Old?

We now come back to a question raised at the beginning of this chapter. In recent years, many policymakers have made statements about the improved economic situation of the aged and the fact that the elderly are now economically better off than younger age groups. What is the basis for these claims—which, we argue, are an exaggeration of the elderly's improved status?

A common assertion one often hears is that the elderly are now better off because the percentage of aged in poverty is now lower than the rest of the population. Using the official poverty index, it is true that the percentage of the aged in poverty is slightly below the nonaged, but to conclude from this statistic that "the elderly are better off" is simply wrong.

When the poverty index was first constructed, a lower spending threshold was set for people age 65 and over. It was argued that the needs of the elderly were less—less food, lower mortgage expenditures, no expenses associated with transportation and clothing for work, and so on. Others point out, however, that when you get old, you have higher expenses in other areas—health care, home maintenance and taxes, special dietary needs, and so on; and one should not assume, it is argued, that the elderly just want to sit at home in their rocking chairs, ignoring social and travel opportunities.

Ruggles (1990), after reviewing the research to date on expenditure patterns, concludes that "it is difficult to justify the continuing use of a lower poverty standard for this population [age 65 and over]." Moreover, according to her estimates, if identical thresholds were used for both the aged and nonaged, the poverty rate for the elderly would have been almost three points higher than the official level in 1987; *and instead of the elderly having a poverty rate that was below the nonaged* (12.3% vs. 13.7%), *their rate would have been over a point and a half higher* (15.3% vs. 13.7%).

Over the last 15 years or so there have been a number of studies by economists that have documented the improving situation and contrasted the economic status of the aged to the nonaged.[13] An early study by the Institute on Poverty at the University of Wisconsin–Madison focused on the economic status of the elderly relative to the nonelderly (Danziger et al., 1984). The researchers took the money income of the elderly and made three adjustments. The aged are more likely than their younger counterparts to own their own homes and other consumer durables (except cars). The study estimated the value of the contribution these durables made to family income (for example, the amount not spent for rent by owning a home). Since the aged have special tax advantages, they also adjusted incomes for federal and state income tax and local property taxes. Finally, adjustments were made for differences in household size.

Danziger et al. applied these adjustments to a national sample of families in 1973. In that year the average money income of the aged was only 49 percent of all other families. The Danziger estimates indicated, however, that when the adjustments enumerated above were made, the relative income of the aged was 90 percent of the rest of the population. By adding in-kind income, the situation would be significantly better. Reporting on the Danziger findings, the Institute on Poverty at the University of Wisconsin–Madison (1983) concluded, "Thus it can be safely said that today the aged are *at least* as well off economically as the rest of us." Based on more recent data for 1986 (U.S. Bureau of the Census, 1988), Smeeding et al. (1990) reached a similar conclusion: "The elderly *as a group* are now as well-off as are the nonelderly *as a group*."

Another study on this question has been carried out by the U.S. Congressional Budget Office (U.S. House Committee on Ways and Means, 1991). The study looks at the income of families and unrelated individuals in 1989 but first *deducts* federal income and payroll taxes and adds in estimates for food stamps, school lunches, and government housing benefits. The Congressional Budget Office estimated that the mean income of family units with an *aged* head was 94 percent of the mean for *all* family units and below all other age groups except the group under age 35:

Age Group	Ratio Age Group Average to Average All Families
Under Age 35	0.79
Ages 35–49	1.06
Ages 50–64	1.24
Ages 65 and over	0.94

If the study had imputed some income for Medicare coverage, home ownership, or wealth, the relative economic status of the aged would appear
even better. Hence, as we stated at the beginning of this chapter: *As a
group, the economic status of the elderly in the United States looks, on
average, a lot like the rest of the population—but not significantly better.*

We must also remember, however, that this finding does not mean all
or most of the elderly are well-off. As we have already shown, there are
still quite a few elderly people (and people at other ages) who are economically disadvantaged. The studies summarized above (and others) do
not refute that fact. Rather they show that the aged as a group are not—as
in years past—an exceptionally or uniquely disadvantaged group.

These studies also caution us in our use of the poverty index. We can
use poverty index statistics as an indicator of changes in the economic
status of the low-income population. But such measures should be used
with great caution and sensitivity to their many limitations. For example,
what about the many "nonpoor" elderly whose income is not far above
the poverty level (often called the near-poor or the "tweeners")?

The "Tweeners"

Thus far we have looked primarily at income and assets (and adjustments to them) as a measure of economic status and security for the
general elderly population. Many people argue, however, that other
measures are more appropriate. For example, Holden and Smeeding
(1990) argue that instead of just looking at current income and asset
measures, one should take account of "the *security* of those assets and
income *relative* to the economic and health-related hazards that the elderly are likely to face." They focus on the aged who are neither poor nor
rich—a low-income group (which they call the "tweeners") that falls between the "safety net" of public programs and the supplemental security
protection provided by private income programs. They identify five potential sources of economic insecurity that are special problems for many
in this group: (1) lack of supplemental medical insurance; (2) few financial resources to cover the expenses of long-term care; (3) ineligibility for
SSI if forced to rely on social security income alone; (4) housing costs as
a high percentage of income; and (5) higher living costs due to significant

Table 1–18
Sources of Insecurity among the "Tweeners"

Type of Insecurity	Percent with This Insecurity
Lack of SSI protection[a]	76
Lack of supplemental medical insurance[b]	70
Long-term care cost vulnerability[c]	57
High housing costs[d]	32
Disability[e]	25

[a]Those with more than 65 percent of total income from OASI who would not be eligible for SSI based on OASI alone.
[b]Lack of any health insurance subsidy beyond Medicare.
[c]Sufficient assets are not available to cover the cost of a median (two-year) nursing home stay.
[d]Unsubsidized renters and homeowners who have below $36,000 in net equity and are already paying more than 33 percent of income for housing.
[e]People needing help getting in or out of bed, getting meals or doing housework, and/or needing assistance with personal needs (such as eating or dressing).
Source: Based on data in K. C. Holden and T. M. Smeeding, "The Poor, the Rich, and the Insecure Elderly Caught in Between," *Milbank Quarterly* 68(2) (1990): Table 10.

physical disability. Defining the tweeners as those elderly with money income (plus food stamps) that is between the poverty level and twice the poverty level, they estimate (for 1984) what proportion of the 4.5 million elderly in that group faced these five sources of economic insecurity. Table 1–18 shows the high prevalence of insecurity so defined among the tweeners, leading Holden and Smeeding to conclude that "economic insecurity among the elderly in the United States today is a problem of greater magnitude than is poverty status."

THE IMPACT OF INFLATION

Economic instability, causing unemployment and inflation, creates insecurity for families and individuals of all ages because of the uncertainty of when and how it will strike. For those actually affected, inflation or unemployment can have a major impact on their economic situation by changing the real value of their wealth or affecting their earning power.

The phenomenon of inflation is without doubt one of the least understood of economic occurrences. We can go only briefly into the economics of inflation in this book. Readers interested in a relatively nontechnical but more extensive discussion on the issue should read Solow (1975).

Almost everyone feels harmed by inflation; yet the truth is that some people and institutions *gain* from inflation. One person's loss is typically somebody else's gain. The result is a redistribution of wealth and income that can be both quite drastic and quite haphazard.

Inflation is a general and widely diffused increase in the level of prices. In any period the prices of some goods are declining; for example, calculator and computer prices have fallen dramatically over the past twenty years. When there is inflation, however, the quantity of goods and services with rising prices far outnumbers those with declining prices.

The most commonly employed measure of inflation is the Consumer Price Index (CPI). Until January 1978, the CPI measured changes in the prices of goods and services purchased by urban wage earners and clerical workers (CPI-W). In 1978, however, the Bureau of Labor Statistics began publication of a new version of the CPI for all urban consumers (CPI-U). This new index takes into account the expenditures not only of wage earners and clerical workers but also salaried professionals, technical and managerial workers, the self-employed, retirees, and the unemployed. As a result, it covers approximately 80 percent of the total noninstitutional civilian population—about twice the coverage of the old CPI-W index.

The CPI is a weighted aggregative index with fixed weights; it seeks to represent the annual consumption patterns of various individuals. Consumption patterns in the population are measured by the Survey of Consumer Expenditures. Based on this survey, a "market basket" of about 400 goods and services is randomly selected and weighted. Prices for the CPI market basket are then obtained monthly, mostly by personal visits (statistically selected) to thousands of stores and service establishments.

While inflation affects people of all ages, we will restrict the discussion that follows to the older population. There are five principal ways older people can be affected adversely by inflation:

1. If net creditors, assets that do not adjust in value for inflation will depreciate in value, reducing the *net worth* of the individual or family.

2. If recipients of **transfer income** (pensions, unemployment benefits, and so on) or other income, adjustments in these various income sources may lag behind inflation, reducing real income.

3. If employed, adjustments in earnings levels may lag behind inflation, reducing real wages.

4. If taxpayers, the real burden of federal and state income taxes may increase if the tax brackets specified in the laws are defined in **money** rather than **real** terms.

5. If inflation is concentrated among items, such as health care, that constitute a larger proportion of elderly persons' budgets, the older age group may be differentially affected—especially if indices used to measure and adjust various sources of income do not correctly reflect aged buying patterns.

Wealth

With regard to the first item, the impact of inflation on the wealth position of the elderly, the evidence is most clear. As we indicated earlier in this chapter, substantial financial assets are held by some of the elderly; these assets are highly concentrated, in the possession of a relatively small number of the aged. On the other hand, tangible assets—such as homes, automobiles, and the like—are held by a large proportion of the aged population.

In general, the money value of tangible assets tends to increase with inflation, leaving the real value of this portion of the aged's wealth unaffected. The value of most *financial* assets does not adjust in any consistent fashion with changes in the general level of prices. Persons holding bonds, checking accounts, savings accounts, and insurance policies often find the real value of these assets falling with inflation; in contrast, persons with debts—such as an outstanding mortgage on a home—find the real value of these debts also falling (which is to their advantage).[14] Stock prices fluctuate greatly in the short run but generally increase over long periods.

A number of studies have investigated the effect of unanticipated inflation on the distribution of wealth among households. They have found that when households are grouped according to age of head, the largest decline in wealth occurs among families headed by elderly persons. In contrast, the largest increase in wealth occurs among those age 25 to 34 who tend to be net debtors. It is the minority of the aged with substantial nonadjusting financial assets who are most severely affected. That is, for those aged fortunate enough to have substantial savings, inflation is often a serious problem.

Transfer Income

With regard to the second item, lagging **transfer income** (e.g., social security and social assistance benefits), again the impact is relatively clear, but in a way that will surprise some readers. Because persons living primarily on relatively fixed incomes are clearly hurt by rising prices and because the aged are so heavily dependent on pensions, the aged traditionally have been cited as the major group harmed by inflation. While this was a major problem for the aged in years past, recent developments have substantially moderated it. The major source of retirement income, the social security program, now adjusts benefits automatically for inflation using the CPI-W index.

As we discuss in later chapters, concern about rising pension costs caused Congress in 1983 to delay for six months the inflation adjustment due that year. Congress also passed legislation that, starting in 1985, the automatic benefit adjustment would be based on the increase in the CPI *or average earnings*, whichever is less. However, this latter provision is to go into effect *only* if the combined social security pension reserves fall to a specified low level, and "catch-up" benefit payments are to be made when the reserve situation improves.

Thus, we see that social security benefits are generally well protected against inflation. Unfortunately, many people do not realize this, including some older people currently receiving benefits. A survey by Peter D. Hart Research Associates (1979) for the National Commission on Social Security found that there was a significant lack of understanding about this aspect of social security. Over half of those interviewed did not think (or were not sure) that "social security benefits go up automatically to match the rise in the cost of living." Quite surprising was the fact that 24 percent of retirees receiving benefits thought the statement was not true.

The social security pension programs are not the only programs indexed for inflation. The federal Supplemental Security Income (SSI) and food stamps programs also adjust fully for inflation. Civil service and military pensions adjust almost fully. And many state and local pension plans are adjusted automatically; these automatic increases, however, are typically limited to a 2 percent to 4 percent maximum per year.

The three major income sources that do *not* adjust *automatically* are veterans' pensions, private pension benefits, and most supplemental state payments under SSI. Also, the levels of allowable income determining eligibility for SSI, food stamps, and some Medicaid programs are not changed automatically.

Overall, then, we see that the bulk of aged retirement income is currently adjusted for inflation with a relatively short lag. The significant number of elderly who depend heavily on income from assets and/or private pension income are much more vulnerable.

Earnings and Tax Brackets

Earnings and tax brackets share the common characteristic of being very difficult to predict with regard to inflationary impact. While earnings generally increase over time, partly in response to inflation, earnings in particular firms or industries may lag behind inflation. Some of the aged still working will find this to be a problem. In general, however, few are affected because not many of the elderly continue to work full time and because not all that do are employed in firms where earnings lag behind inflation.

Similarly, many aged do not pay income taxes because their incomes are low and social security income is exempt from federal taxes for all but those with higher incomes (see Chapter 5). In the past, those who did faced two problems. Some of the added income to compensate for inflation was taxed away. Moreover, it was taxed away under a **progressive federal income tax** structure at progressively higher marginal rates. Starting in 1985, however, the federal tax law has operated to index the brackets for inflation, thereby eliminating the problem. However, the income exemption ceiling below which social security is *not* taxed is not indexed (Chapter 5). Therefore, as inflation tends to push the various sources of elderly income higher, more and more people will find some of their social security benefits subject to federal income tax.

Expenditure Patterns and Cost-of-Living Indices

During inflationary periods, the prices of various goods change by different amounts. Because the expenditure patterns of individuals and families differ, any particular pattern of inflationary price increases will have a varying impact, depending on the particular expenditure patterns of the individuals. For example, if medical and housing prices go up faster than other goods and services and if the aged spend a larger share of their income on food and housing, the result is a larger increase in prices paid by the aged than the nonaged.

Thus, there is concern that the CPI used to measure inflation and adjust social security benefits does not accurately reflect the aged's buying patterns. Over the years certain organizations and individuals have advocated, for example, that a separate price index for the elderly be established; and in 1987 the U.S. Senate passed legislation to create such a special index, but the proposal was not agreed to by the House of Representatives.

Numerous studies over the years have investigated the need for such an index.[15] Rarely has there been such agreement among economists on research findings. *All studies have found that the differences between the CPI and a special aged index are likely to be very small.* Table 1–19 shows the results of a recent U.S. Bureau of Labor Statistics study to compare the current indices with an experimental index for persons age 62 and older. The experimental index rose only slightly faster over a six-year period (Amble and Stewart, 1994).

"Given the absence of solid evidence that . . . [a multiple price index system] would yield different indexing outcomes over the long haul, we should probably leave special group indices alone" (Minarik, 1981). Instead of a special index for the aged, a better approach would be to continue improving the existing CPI. Measuring general price changes accurately is a very difficult task. The most serious problem is a general upward bias in the CPI. This is due primarily to a lag that occurs in the introduction of new products and quality improvements in old products into the index (see Gordon, 1981). With regard to quality change, for

Table 1–19
An Experimental Consumer Price Index for the Elderly, Percent Changes from 1987–1993[a]

Component	CPI-U[b]	CPI-W[c]	"Aged Index"
All items	26.3	25.5	28.7
Food	24.8	24.8	25.0
Housing	23.1	22.4	25.1
Apparel and upkeep	17.7	16.6	16.6
Transportation	22.8	21.9	25.0
Medical care	54.2	53.3	59.4
Entertainment	25.9	25.0	28.2
Other	47.0	46.2	41.8

[a]Aged experimental consumer price index based on expenditures of persons age 62 and over.
[b]All Urban Consumers Index.
[c]Urban Wage Earners and Clerical Workers Index.
Source: N. Amble and K. Stewart, "Experimental Price Index for Elderly Consumers," *Monthly Labor Review* (May 1994): Table 4.

example, the CPI usually does not take into account improvements in product performance when prices of a product go up. Thus, the prices of motor oil, tires, light bulbs, appliances, and so forth have increased, but the service life of many such products has also increased; and, thus, in an important sense not all the price increases are inflationary.

The Bureau of Labor Statistics periodically does try to update the index. The bureau has changed, for example, the way owner-occupied housing is handled. This item in the index had become particularly troublesome when interest rates, including mortgage rates for housing loans, rose to unprecedented levels over the 1969–1972 period. The old way of handling the item in the index did not distinguish between homeowners who took out mortgages some years ago at much lower rates and those who had purchased housing recently.

Many problems with the CPI remain. Given the amount of indexing that now occurs based on this index, the government continues to study ways of improving the index.

The Highly Vulnerable Elderly

As we pointed out above, most retirement income is fully or partially inflation protected. However, there are two major sources of elderly income that are still highly vulnerable to inflation: financial assets and private pensions. Most financial assets—bonds, checking accounts, savings accounts, and insurance policies—do not adjust when the general level of prices changes. Others, which have at times adjusted better, require considerable financial sophistication or have much higher associated risk: real estate, corporate stock, and gold. The recent development of money market funds and similar financial securities offers some help for the small saver but again does not offer complete security from inflation over any particular short-run period.

As the numbers of elderly grow who have incomes just above the poverty level but far below what is adequate, we are developing a new class of vulnerable elderly: the very big proportion of the elderly who live on incomes not very far above "official poverty." In 1992, for example, 13 percent of aged persons had incomes below the poverty level; 29 percent were above that threshold but below twice that threshold.

Large numbers of older people fall between the "safety net" of public programs and the supplemented economic protection provided by private income programs. Many of these elderly families depend on their financial savings and their private pensions to provide the margin of support necessary for a modest but more comfortable lifestyle. But inflation is a major threat. How can these people be helped?

Purchasing Power Bonds

Some people have argued that saving, particularly personal saving, is discouraged by the uncertainty of not knowing future rates of inflation. Another way of saying this is that people are discouraged from saving by the certainty of knowing that inflation is bound to take place at some rate and that their savings are likely to become devalued over time.

Various proposals have been made for the creation of a different type of financial asset—an **indexed** bond providing constant purchasing power. These bonds would be sold by the government to people to protect their savings from inflation. The basic idea of constant purchasing power bonds is that people should be able to buy these bonds from the government to save for retirement or other purposes. They might or might not receive interest from them. Economist James Tobin has argued, for example, that many people might even be willing to buy these bonds at a zero rate of interest—as long as there was a firm guarantee that their value would not depreciate from inflation. Having been purchased for a stated amount, the bond would be redeemable at some point in the future for that amount, adjusted for any inflation that took place over the intervening period. Thus, the value of the bond would remain constant in real terms and actually increase if there was a rate of interest associated with it.

Henry Wallich (1969), himself an advocate of the bonds, summarized the *opposition* to them as follows:

The case against purchasing power bonds every good official can recite in his sleep. If you escalate government obligations, people will say that you are throwing in the towel against inflation. Investors will stop worrying about inflation if they are protected. And the government with its unlimited resources would be competing unfairly with private borrowers who could not take the risk of assuming this kind of open-ended debt.

Milton Friedman (1971) argues against this sort of reasoning:

The government alone is responsible for inflation. By inflation it has expropriated the capital of persons who bought government securities. Often at the urging of high officials who eloquently proclaimed that patriotism and self-interest went hand-in-hand (the good old government savings bond). The right way to avoid this disgraceful shell game is for the government to borrow in the form of purchasing power securities.

Over the years, the principal opposition to purchasing power bonds was centered in the Treasury Department. In addition to the reasons cited by Wallich, the Treasury worried about possible destabilizing effects on the bond markets of introducing this new type of bond, and the possibility of making more difficult the government's debt financing. In this particular area—debt management and federal debt issue—the Treasury is politically very powerful.

Finally, however, the Congress passed legislation authorizing the creation of price indexed government bonds, and the U.S. Treasury began issuing such bonds in January 1997. Called Treasury Inflation-Indexed Securities (TIIS), they pay a constant interest rate. However, the principal (i.e., face value) of the bonds is index adjusted semi-annually by the CPI-U. In addition, the dollar amount of interest paid in any year (as a specified percentage of the principal) reflects any increase in that principal.

With the availability of government indexed bonds, an attractive private investing option has become available. It is now possible for investment and mutual fund companies to offer "inflation-linked bond accounts." These funds are designed to track an inflation index. Like conventional bond funds, the principal or interest (depending on how the bonds are structured) are adjusted periodically to reflect changes in an inflation index. These funds invest in indexed bonds offered by the Treasury, other U.S. agencies, private corporations, and indexed bonds offered by foreign governments and corporations (especially in the United Kingdom, Australia, and Canada).

Almost no private pension plan *automatically* adjusts **pensions** during retirement for increases in the Consumer Price Index. Some plans adjust benefits on an ad hoc basis every few years, but these adjustments usually lag far behind the rise in prices.

Some people have recommended "retiree bargaining" as a way of dealing with this problem. However, the Supreme Court ruled in 1971 (*Allied Chemical and Alkali Workers v. Pittsburgh Plate Glass*) that retirees are not "employees" within the meaning of the National Labor Relations Act and, therefore, that benefits for retirees are not mandatory subjects of union bargaining. This means that if a company does not want to discuss increases in retirees' pensions, there is no way a worker or union can legally force it to do so. Thus, for example, in the late 1970s major companies in the electrical manufacturing industry refused to bargain with unions seeking to improve what they saw as the serious financial plight of many retirees (Fitzgerald, 1978).

It is not likely that many private plans will ever voluntarily adopt full indexing provisions similar to social security. The uncertainties involved in funding such provisions are extremely high, and the costs of such provisions would make private plans unattractive to both employers and workers.

CHAPTER 1 HIGHLIGHTS

We have tried to show in this chapter that attempts to assess the economic status of the elderly as one group are not very meaningful. Mindful of this danger of overgeneralizing about the aged, let us now summarize some of the major observations presented in preceding sections:

1. The economic status for a large segment of the elderly has improved significantly in recent years—primarily as a result of rising social security, private pension, and government employees' pension income.

2. Great caution is in order in generalizing from available statistics on income and assets. Both underreporting and the lack of disaggregation cause serious problems.

3. The major source of elderly income is social security, but earnings still represent a large proportion of the total—going to the minority of aged still working.

4. Statistically, the economic status of the elderly *as a group* is now very similar to the rest of the population—a dramatic change from their disadvantaged position in the past.

5. Expanding the analysis of economic status to include such factors as in-kind income, special tax provisions, and household size narrows the differences considerably between the young and old. In fact, many researchers and policymakers now say there are no significant differences!

6. The official poverty index used in the United States is out-of-date and understates the number of poor people.

7. Poverty among the aged, when measured by this index, is now much lower than in past years.

8. Economic deprivation and insecurity still exist on a large scale among the elderly. Poverty level incomes are common among the oldest old, ethnic minorities, and older women.

9. Large numbers of the elderly whose incomes are above the poverty index have incomes that are clustered not far above the poverty level—incomes that make them extremely vulnerable, for example, to the rising costs of health care. And many people in old age still experience a large drop in living standard when they retire (i.e., comparing pre- and postretirement income).

10. Contrary to popular belief, the aged have a large measure of protection from inflation. Those heavily dependent on financial assets and private pensions are most vulnerable.

SUGGESTED READINGS

Blank, Rebecca M. *It Takes a Nation.* Princeton, N.J.: Princeton University Press, 1997. An excellent overview of American poverty at all ages and discussions of past and future policies to deal with it.

Coward, R. T., G. R. Lee, J. W. Dwyer, and K. Seccombe. *Old and Alone in Rural America.* Washington, D.C.: Public Policy Institute, American Association of Retired Persons, 1993. One of the few publications to focus on the rural elderly.

Crystal, Stephen. "Economic Status of the Elderly." In Robert H. Binstock and Linda K. George, eds., *Handbook of Aging and the Social Sciences*, 4th ed. New York: Academic Press, 1995. A succinct, up-to-date overview.

Holden, Karen C., R. V. Burkhauser, and D. A. Myers. "Income Transitions of Older Stages of Life: The Dynamics of Poverty." *Gerontologist* 26 (June 1986): 292–297. This study examines the risk of poverty among a sample of elderly couples and widows interviewed over a ten-year period. One of its many interesting findings is that a far larger percentage of the elderly is subject to the risk of poverty over their lifetime than is suggested by studies measuring poverty at a particular point in time.

Holden, Karen C., and Timothy M. Smeeding. "The Poor, the Rich, and the Insecure Elderly Caught in Between." *Milbank Quarterly* 68(2) (1990): 191–219. Measures are provided of the aged population "at risk," or those who face significant economic insecurity. Measures of insecurity for people with incomes *above* the poverty level are presented.

Hurd, Michael D. "Research on the Elderly: Economic Status, Retirement, and Consumption and Saving." *Journal of Economic Literature* 28 (June 1990): 464–637. A comprehensive review of the economics literature on these topics.

Morgan, James N. "The Redistribution of Income by Families and Institutions and Emerging Help Patterns." In G. J. Duncan and J. N. Morgan, eds., *Five Thousand American Families—Patterns of Economic Progress*, Vol. 10. Ann Arbor, Mich.: Institute for Social Research, University of Michigan,

1983. Given the dearth of information in this area, this article is a research goldmine of important findings.

Ruggles, Patricia. *Drawing the Line*. Washington, D.C.: Urban Institute Press, 1990. An excellent and very readable discussion of all the major issues related to measuring poverty and various proposed changes to the "outdated" measure currently used in the United States.

Smeeding, Timothy M. *Social Security Reform: Improving Benefit Adequacy and Economic Security For Women*. Policy Brief No. 16/1999. Syracuse, N.Y.: Center For Policy Research, Syracuse University, 1999. Female poverty and what to do about it.

Social Security Bulletin. Washington, D.C.: U.S. Government Printing Office (quarterly). This journal reports changes in social security and other similar legislation. It also publishes the results of research studies by the SSA (and SSA-sponsored research projects), various survey findings, and international social security developments.

U.S. Senate Special Committee on Aging. *The Supplemental Security Income Program: A 10-Year Overview*. Washington, D.C.: U.S. Government Printing Office, 1984. A classic collection of papers reviewing past and current SSI operations, policies, and issues.

Yelin, Edward H. *Disability and the Displaced Worker*. New Brunswick, N.J.: Rutgers University Press, 1992. This book argues that disability "take-up" is concentrated among workers in contracting industries, using disability benefits as a buffer to unemployment.

Chapter 2

To Work or Not to Work

Everyone is in favor of keeping older people in the labor force except the unions, government, business, and older people.

So commented a participant at a conference on the roles of the elderly in society (Mothner, 1985). The observation astutely summarizes the paradox of retirement policies in the United States over the years. Everyone talks about permitting and even encouraging older people to work. Yet until recently, fewer and fewer did. And, in fact, public and private actions, compared with words, have been instrumental over the years in biasing the work-retirement choice toward retirement.

THE RIGHT TO RETIRE

As observed by Donahue, Orbach, and Pollak (1960), "retirement is a phenomenon of modern industrial society. . . . The older people of previous societies were not retired persons; there was no retirement role." A number of developments, however, changed this.

Even before public and private pension systems were widely established, large numbers of older persons were not in the labor force. As early as 1900, for example, almost one-third of all men age 65 and over were "retired," in large part because of health problems. Prior to the institution of **pension**[1] systems, however, older persons not in the labor force had to rely on their own (often meager) resources, help from relatives, or public and private charity. Over the years recognition spread that complete reliance on these sources of old age support was unsatisfactory. *Public pensions were, in part, a reaction to the need for more rational support mechanisms to assist older persons unable to work.*

Industrialization created a new problem. In contrast to the farm, where people could almost always "work" (even if it was at reduced levels), industry was characterized by a large amount of job insecurity. Recurrent **recessions** and **depressions** and shifts in employment opportunities created competition for the available jobs. Job obsolescence was a constant threat, as technology continued to change rapidly. *Thus, another motivation for establishing pensions was to facilitate and often encourage older workers to leave the work force—creating jobs (it was hoped) for younger workers.*

But probably most important of all, industrial growth—fueled by the rapid technological change—resulted in vast increases in economic output. As we discuss in the next section, economic growth provides an expanding option for greater leisure with a simultaneous increase in living standards. That is, the rapid economic growth of the 20th century made it possible to more easily support older people who could not or did not wish to work. *Retirement became more economically feasible.*

Thus, we see the institutionalization of retirement arising as a result of and reaction to:

• the needs of large numbers of elderly unable to work;
• changing employment opportunities for both the young and the old; and
• expanding national economic output over the long run.

Pension programs were developed that "provided compensation based upon years of service rather than upon need per se. They were to emerge as an 'earned right' and were to become instrumental in defining a retirement status as appropriate for the older worker" (Friedman and Orbach, 1974).

THE WORK-LEISURE TRADE-OFF

Every individual during his or her lifetime makes important choices regarding his or her use of time, including the type and amount of work to be undertaken. The Institute for Social Research at the University of Michigan (Herzog et al., 1989) has estimated that people in the United States average 1,348 hours per year of *paid* work but 1,638 hours of *unpaid* work. Thus, each of us chooses some combination of work in the paid labor force, together with housework, personal care, and leisure (Juster and Stafford, 1991). Most economists emphasize the trade-off be-

Figure 2–1
Distribution of Unpaid Work, 1986

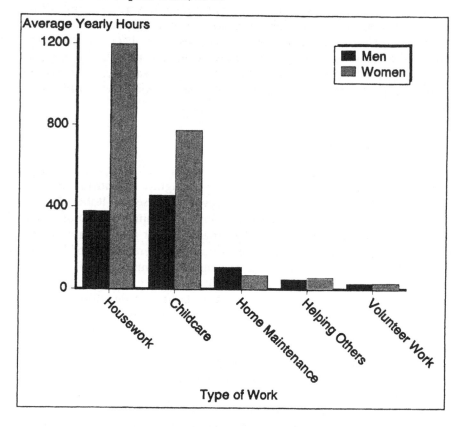

Source: Based on data in A. R. Herzog et al., "Age Differences in Productive Activities,"
Journal of Gerontology 44 (July 1989): Table 1.

tween paid work and leisure. Paid work produces goods and services and results in **income** necessary to buy the goods and services produced by others. Leisure, also useful and valuable, is unobligated, discretionary time spent in nonpaid activities that the individual does not consider work. Thus, individuals can adjust their time utilization to get more leisure, but often only at the expense of less money to buy goods and services.

Paid employment results in the economic output—**gross national product**—measured by **national income accounting** techniques and reported regularly by government statistics. *Nonmarket work* (see Figure 2–1 is not included by economists in the national income accounts but adds significantly to total output. Nordhaus and Tobin (1973) estimate that in 1965, for example, nonmarket work was equal to nearly half of our (counted) gross national product (see also Eisner, 1989).

Not working translates into a given amount of leisure over one's lifetime. However, the work-leisure dichotomy is not as simple as we make it seem. After reviewing the literature, Robinson et al. (1984) conclude that "the greatest difficulty in dealing with leisure in retirement stems from the lack of consensus on its definition." For example, leisure often takes on aspects of employment (e.g., volunteer work and hobbies that earn money).

"Productive Aging"

In recent years some people working in the field of aging research have attempted to deal with the work/leisure ambiguity by introducing the concept of "productive aging." The term was first used by Robert Butler, currently head of the International Longevity Center at Mount Sinai School of Medicine. Butler wanted to make it clear that aging and productivity do not necessarily describe totally different stages of life. According to Butler, it is a myth that the aged are unproductive. "In fact, in the absence of diseases and social adversities, older people can and do remain productive and actively involved in life," writes Butler (1989).

The concept of productive aging developed in part as a reaction to economists' limited view of work. Given present ways of measuring the gross national product, many of the activities and contributions people make before and after retirement are not counted in the official government statistics measuring *economic* activity.

Why would anyone care how government statistics classify various activities of life—economic or noneconomic? Because such statistics have an important impact in the political arena. The concept of productive aging, as originally developed in the United States, was motivated in large part by a perceived need to provide a *political* response to *political* attacks on the elderly.

As Bass and Caro (1992) put it, "productive aging is a concept that refocuses the political debate and discussion about social welfare and programs for the elderly. It provides a different perspective from which to view the elderly and their needs. It changes the way we think of aging and our images of older people." Thus, it is no accident that the origins of the concept coincided with a change from a public image of the elderly as a group of "deserving poor" *unable* to work—to a much more negative image of "greedy geezers" who are *unwilling* to work (see Chapter 8).

Apart from its political origins, the concept of productive aging has served to stimulate a debate on the changing roles of older people in an industrial society. Sociologist Matilda White Riley argues, for example, that the focus should not be on whether or not people are productive. Rather, Riley sees economic growth in industrialized societies *providing an opportunity* for nations to reallocate the ever-growing leisure of retirement over all ages. As output and leisure increase, older people (Riley argues) can assume some of the work responsibilities of the middle-aged. Younger people, as a result, would be released from some of the stress that arises from the overwhelming pressures of their labor force and family roles.

In this regard, Bass and Caro (1992) point out that "over the last decade in the United States, there has been a growing interest in involving older people in significant economic and social roles"—what they call "elder engagement." That is one reason why many aging advocates give a lot of attention to the barriers that prevent elderly roles from evolving—such things as age discrimination, lack of training opportunities, punitive pension provisions (like the Social Security retirement test), and the need for more part-day work opportunities.

The concept of productive aging helps to expand the ways in which both the general public and the scientific community think about the *potential* of older people. But immediately there arises the question of how one defines "potential." In general, the common approach is to include traditional market and nonmarket economic activities that result in the production of goods and services. Proponents of productive aging seek to expand this view by adding activities that *help to develop the capacity* to produce these goods and services (e.g., attending educational or training programs). But most definitions of productive aging exclude "important and constructive activities undertaken by the elderly, such as worshiping, meditation, reflection, reminiscing, reading for pleasure, carrying on correspondence, visiting with family and friends, traveling, and so forth" (Bass et al., 1993).

Not everyone agrees with this approach of focusing discussions about the worth of the aged solely on their *economic* potential. As philosopher Harry Moody (1993) points out:

By insisting on the productivity of the old, we put the last stage of life at the same level as the other stages. This transposition implicitly sets up a kind of competition or struggle (who can be the most productive?) which the old are doomed to lose as frailty increases. By celebrating efficiency, productivity or power, we subordinate any moral claim for the last stage of life in favor of values that ultimately depreciate the meaning of old age.

As Moody correctly points out, the productive aging debate is much more than a matter of semantics. It deals with a most important question: What is later life for? Moody calls for a wider vision of late-life productivity, a vision that includes altruism, citizenship, stewardship, creativity, and the search for faith. That is a view of productive aging very different from what was originally proposed.

Confusing Policies toward Work in Later Life

We have shown in the first part of this chapter that there is great confusion with regard to the economic roles of people in later life. It is not surprising then that government and business policies relating to work in the later years are similarly confused. Figure 2–2 illustrates the historical continuum of policy options that have shaped the past and present behavior of employers and older workers. At the extremes are policies that, on the one hand, *require people to work* and, on the other hand, that *prohibit people from working*. Policies promoting both extremes have existed in American history.

There were, for example, the early American welfare policies with work requirements patterned on the **British "Poor Laws."** In fact, the recent federal welfare "reform" law "to end welfare as we know it" reintroduces many of the rules of those colonial days.

There were also (at the other extreme) the mandatory retirement rules (discussed below) that were very common during the middle of the 20th century (and now illegal). In addition to these extremes, there are a whole range of policies that to a greater or less degree either *encourage* or *discourage* work in the later years. Figure 2–2 lists only a few for illustrative purposes.

Figure 2–2 also reminds us that policies determine options and influence behavior not just in the formal labor force but also in the informal sector. On the one hand, federal and state governments and foundations have financially supported programs to encourage older persons to help others in need and to provide services to the community. On the other hand, there are the attitudes of different segments of the population against "working for nothing"; and there are inhospitable neighborhood environments (particularly transportation and crime problems) that discourage older people from going out into their communities to provide services.

The ambiguity toward the labor force participation of the elderly is not likely to be resolved—ever! As in many policy areas, it is in large part the product of conflicts in values and goals that are themselves not resolvable. In the next section, we discuss the work/leisure trade-off further and discuss projections by economists Kreps and Spengler. Their work helps us understand that in a basic sense, the nation does not necessarily need the elderly to be productive, given its ever-growing economic potential. Rather, it is a matter of choice as to how we want to divide up the nation's growth potential between goods and services and greater nonparticipation in other forms of positive life activities.

Figure 2–2
Work Policies for Older Workers, United States

Formal Labor Force

Encourage Work				Discourage Work			
"Poor Laws"	Partial Retirement Options	Age Discrimination in Employment Act	Job Training Partnership Act	Social Security Retirement Test	Employer Age Discrimination	Special Early Retirement Programs	Mandatory Retirement Rules
No help for family caregivers	Senior Community Service Employment Program	Experience Corp	Americans with Disabilities Act	Union attitudes toward volunteerism	Inadequate public transportation	Age discrimination	Materialistic society discourages altruism

Informal Labor Force

Require — Work

Prohibit — Work

Source: Author.

Retire at Age 38!

Paid work patterns vary significantly among individuals; however, a few generalizations can be made. Measuring work in terms of hours per week, it begins at a zero level in early childhood. At some point the individual might start a paper route, do some baby-sitting, or engage in some other part-time work. In the teenage years, part-time work may increase, and some begin full-time work. Others go to college full time and "stop work." Through the middle years most men and a majority of women work in the labor force full time. Nearly three-quarters of all women ages 25 to 54 are employed full or part time. After age 55, paid work stops abruptly for many individuals. For some, however, there is a period before full retirement of what has been called "postcareer or bridge employment"—typically characterized by new occupations, lower pay, frequent job changes, and often part-time or temporary work (Doeringer, 1990). With retirement, individuals undertake more nonpaid work and increasing amounts of recreational and other leisure activities.

This brief summary approximates the work pattern of the typical American worker today. Granted, of course, there are many variations in this pattern.

Should this pattern be changed? Back in 1966, economists Kreps and Spengler developed estimates of the economic growth-leisure trade-off confronting the United States between 1965 and 1985. Although their projections are now relatively old, they still illustrate well some of the options a nation and its workers face as they look to the future. Figure 2–3 presents their projections of the various possibilities of additional gross national product (GNP) and/or leisure available over the twenty-year period. As the various factors influencing economic growth (technological change, **investment**, rising quality of labor, and so forth) increase **productivity**, new opportunities for increased leisure and/or increased consumption arise.

With regard to the possible future growth in leisure and its probable distribution . . . at one extreme, assuming no change in working time, per capita gross national product could rise from $3,181 in 1965 to $5,802 in 1985, or by about 80 percent. At the other extreme, if one supposes that all growth is taken in leisure time except the amount necessary to keep per capita GNP constant at $3,181, the possible changes in working time would be as follows: the workweek could fall to 22 hours, or the workyear could be limited to 27 weeks per year, or retirement age could be lowered to 38 years, or almost half the labor force could be kept in retraining programs, or additional time available for education might well exceed our capacity to absorb such education. (Kreps and Spengler, 1966)

If we took all the increased growth potential in the form of greater per capita output, Kreps and Spengler estimated (in 1966) that by the year

Figure 2–3
Alternative Uses of Economic Growth per Capita Gross National Product and Hours Worked, 1965–1985

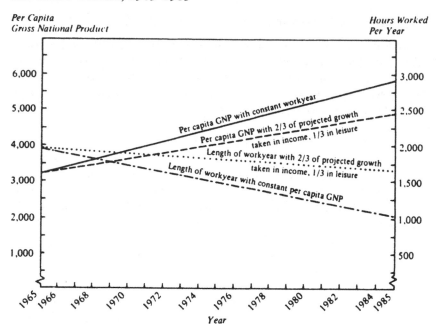

Source: Juanita Kreps and Joseph Spengler, "The Leisure Component of Economic Growth," in National Commission on Technology, Automation and Economic Progress, *The Employment Impact of Technological Change*, Appendix Vol. II (Washington, D.C.: U.S. Government Printing Office, 1966), pp. 353–389.

1985 we could have almost double the level of 1985 per capita output. By lowering economic growth a little, however, we could also increase leisure; and, in fact, their projection is close to what actually happened. Average weekly hours have declined moderately from 39 to 35 hours per week in the nonagricultural sector of the economy; and at the same time, real GNP (i.e., adjusting the statistics for **inflation**) has increased by about two-thirds.

Projections like those of Kreps and Spengler assume that there are no "costs to growth," an assumption increasingly questioned by economists. Also, the projections assume that the government encourages the potential growth by use of appropriate **monetary** and **fiscal policy** and that the assumptions about future changes in technology and the growth of capital based on past occurrences are correct. Accepting these qualifications, we can extrapolate from Figure 2–3 into the future. One major option available to the nation is a sizable increase in the future real standard of living of individuals in the society. Alternatively, we can choose fewer goods and services but more leisure.

The Pattern of "Nonwork"

In addition to the choice between work (more output) and leisure, there is the question of when leisure (or "nonwork") is taken. The increases in leisure experienced early in this century came primarily in the form of shortened workweeks and longer vacations. In contrast, most of the new leisure in recent decades has been allocated to the end of the lifespan.

Suppose that a country wants to hold constant the total amount of work and leisure over the lifespan but wishes to alter the way in which they are currently distributed. One procedure would be to determine at what point in the life cycle it might be appropriate to taper off weekly hours of work, if the option were available. Providing more leisure by reducing hours of work means, however, that some people *must work more* at some other time—later or earlier in their lives. Providing a significant increase in leisure without a significant drop in lifetime income probably means working longer when older.

Of course, historically, increases in the productivity of workers have permitted *both* leisure and income to increase simultaneously. But it is important to see that a different mix (both in amount and timing) was possible in the past and will be possible in the future.

Why do many professionals advocate changes in our present mix of work and leisure? Why do some urge, for example, that we stop the trend toward earlier retirement?

Matilda White Riley argues that "tremendous numbers of capable and potentially productive older people cannot long co-exist with empty role structures, while younger adults are struggling under overweening role demands. Something will have to give. A 21st century revolution in age structure seems inevitable" (*Productive Aging News*, 1993b); other researchers, however, think that "role loss" is not a major problem among older people and that a quick adjustment is made by most of the aged to the new retirement realities (see the discussion later in this chapter).

A number of physicians have asserted that some people die earlier, partly as a result of the change from an active to a more sedentary lifestyle (Bradford, 1979), although there is little but anecdotal evidence to support such claims (Ekerdt, 1987).

Many economists worry about the problems of financially supporting a growing retired population with its accompanying rise in public and private pension costs; others argue that "no strong economic reason exists to resist the trend toward early retirement" (Burtless and Munnell, 1990; see also Quinn, 1993).

Some analysts, anticipating a possible future shortage of workers brought about by low fertility and rising retirement, call for incentives to keep people working longer; others argue that it is unlikely there will be a general labor shortage, given the many ways nations can adapt—increased capital, immigration policy, cross-national production, and so on (Schulz et al., 1991; Mishel and Teixeira, 1991). We discuss this issue again in Chapter 8.

Finally, it can be argued that greater lifetime satisfaction would be achieved if leisure were not bunched at the end of the lifespan. However, almost no information exists on how workers feel about this issue. One survey carried out in 1978 asked local government employees in California their preferences. The survey found a strong desire among these workers for lifetime work/leisure patterns that were significantly different from those that are now dominant (Best, 1978). More than 80 percent of the workers interviewed responded favorably to hypothetical options that would redistribute some of the leisure now taken in the retirement years into the middle years of life. Moreover, workers were also asked whether they preferred to work more at their present pay rate—earning more. The study found that 21 percent of respondents indicated a preference for more leisure, even if it meant less total income from their job.

While gerontologists and advocates on behalf of the elderly have been almost unanimous in calling for more flexibility in retirement age policies, much of the movement has been in the opposite direction. There is a major reason for this—one often ignored in academic discussions. We show in later chapters that public and private pensions have been carefully and deliberately designed to *encourage* retirement to help deal with America's chronic unemployment problems. In 1977, economist Juanita Kreps summarized past and current practices; we think her views are as applicable today as they were then.

Retirement, a relatively new lifestage, has quickly become a . . . device for balancing the number of job seekers with the demand for workers at going rates of pay. Insofar as retirement practice is used to drain workers from the labor force, a reversal of the downward pressure on retirement age would seem to be possible only if labor markets tighten. Extensions beyond the usual retirement age are granted when there is a demand for specific talents. Given current levels of unemployment, however, there is no incentive to prolong worklife in general. (Kreps, 1977)

Legislation passed to prohibit mandatory retirement based on age is a step in the opposite direction; but, as we argue later in this chapter, the impact of such laws has been minimal.

The Economics of Aging

Figure 2–4
Labor Force Participation of Older Men and Women

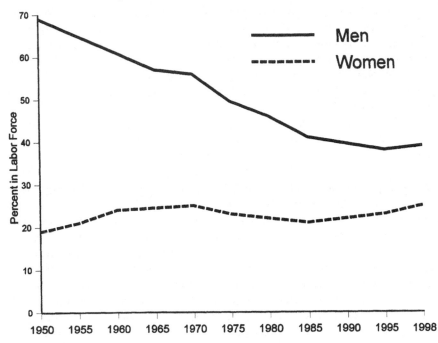

Source: Based on data in Sara E. Rix, "The Older Worker in a Graying America," in R. N. Butler, L. K. Grossman, and M. R. Oberlink, *Life in an Older America* (New York: Century Foundation Press, 1999), Table 9.1.

Changing Labor Force Participation

There is general agreement that one of the most important labor force developments of recent decades has been the dramatic decline in labor force participation by older men. Figure 2–4 shows trends by gender in labor force participation after age 54 over the 1945–1998 period. The labor force participation rate for men over 64 has dropped from 46 percent in 1950 to only 17 percent. But perhaps even more striking is the relatively recent decline in participation at earlier ages. The labor force participation rate for men age 55 to 64 has also fallen dramatically. And what is truly amazing is that, currently, nearly half of older men are totally out of the labor force *before* age 65 (and about one-fifth are out at age 55 to 59).

In contrast, the proportion of females in the labor force has risen sharply in almost *all age groups*, with an overall increase from 26 percent in 1940 to 58 percent in 1990. The labor force participation rate for women age 55 to 64 has risen rapidly, from 27 percent in 1950 to above

50 percent in 1998. For women over age 65, participation has been relatively stable—at about 9 percent.

Black men in the later years are not as likely to be in the labor force as white men. In December 1993, average annual participation rates were (U.S. Bureau of Labor Statistics, 1994):

Age	White	Black
65–69	27%	22%
70–74	15%	9%
75+	7%	6%

Part-time work is most common among the very young, women workers, and the elderly. Over half (56% in 1992) of employed civilian persons over age 64 worked part time (EBRI, 1994). Much of this part-time work is concentrated in the service and retail trade industries where wages tend to be low. Some older persons work part time out of necessity; others do so by preference. For example, some need to supplement other income sources—primarily pension income. Others are forced by health limitations to cut back on the hours they work, and others become unemployed—forced to take stop-gap jobs. Some employed workers prefer a gradual withdrawal to an abrupt stop. Finally, there are no doubt many who want more leisure but still value highly the various social and monetary benefits arising from some amount of labor force attachment.

There are probably many more workers who would like to work **part time**—moving gradually from work to retirement. Most workers, however, face rather limited choices, given current job options. "Someone approaching retirement who wants to retire gradually from a career-type job will have to change jobs, losing job-related skills, and [will have] to compete for low-paying, easy-entry jobs. Faced with that option most retire completely" (Hurd, 1993a). (We discuss this issue again in the last section of this chapter.)

Compared with other industrialized countries, United States labor force participation by the aged falls in the upper range. Only Japan has higher participation rates. In Japan, *current* pensions are low and many work because of financial necessity.[2] Others work because so-called "lifetime employment" jobs end at early ages, but institutionalized alternatives (usually lower-wage jobs) have been created to accommodate part-time preferences and/or lower worker productivity (Schulz et al., 1989; Rebick, 1993).

Are Participation Rates for Men Rising?

After many years of declining participation rates among *older men*, the trend downward seems to have stopped. Since the mid-1980s, the rates

have leveled off. Assessments by some observers, however, that participation rates are actually *rising* seem to be premature. As Figure 2–4 indicates, there has been no clear upswing in the labor force participation
rates for men in the 1990s.

There are many factors that may be operating to cause the change in
participation rates. Articles by Joseph Quinn (1999) and Sara Rix (1999a)
list the following possible explanations:

- Changes in social security and employer-sponsored pensions that discourage
  early retirement (discussed in Chapters 4, 5, and 7).
- An end to mandatory retirement rules.
- A favorable labor market as a result of an expansive economy extending over
  many years.
- "A new social attitude toward work late in life." (Quinn, 1999)

While these factors may play a role in the evolving participation trends,
research to date indicates that we should not expect their impact to be
large. Computer simulation studies of the changes in public or private
pension provisions have estimated a relatively small labor force impact.
As we explain below, mandatory retirement rules were never a big im-
pediment to older worker employment, so abolishing them has had little
effect. The boom economy of the 1990s has raised the demand for labor
but has also been accompanied by rising insecurity for older workers.
And, as we discuss later in this chapter, the attitude surveys that indicate
more people want to work in the later years are highly suspect.

Two additional explanations for the change in trends can be mentioned. First, "early retirement incentive programs" were a major mechanism for inducing workers to leave employers at very early ages. In the
1980s (as we discuss below), almost every major company in the United
States had such a program; many provided two or more special early
retirement offers to their employees over the space of a few years. In the
1990s, the availability of these early retirement bonus pensions to workers declined significantly—in part as a result of the vibrant economy but
also because companies have "trimmed out" their older workers and have
achieved their goal of a younger workforce.

At the same time, companies responded to pressures from growing
global competition and to the less favorable economic conditions
throughout much of the 1980s. Many companies engaged in massive
downsizing and, often for the first time, laid off middle and upper management. This sent a shock wave through the companies, as surviving
employees felt a new sense of insecurity. Not only did they see co-
workers losing jobs, they also heard how difficult it was for many of these
unemployed people (especially older workers) to find new jobs. As a

result, it is quite possible that employees have developed new attitudes, not about wanting to work longer but about the dangers of leaving a job early.

Until more research is carried out, the reasons for the change in older men's labor force participation rates will be unclear. What does seem to be clear, however, is that the dramatic decline in participation rates over the past decades among men has not been reversed.

ECONOMIC PROBLEMS OF OLDER WORKERS

Most workers do not hold one job throughout their career. In fact, American workers, on average, have had ten jobs by the time they reach the later years (Mitchell, 1993). There has been increasing recognition that a variety of special job problems may face middle-aged and older workers: (1) age discrimination in hiring; (2) job obsolescence; (3) changing job-performance capabilities; and (4) adverse work rules, institutional structures, and managerial policies. In addition, older workers, while often protected by seniority against job loss, generally find themselves as vulnerable as younger workers to plant shutdowns and many of the dislocations arising from mergers and government spending cutbacks. Not only do these problems create immediate difficulties for workers and their families, but they often have an economic impact on their situation during the retirement years. Long-term unemployment, for example, makes saving for retirement difficult if not impossible. Moreover, periods of unemployment often result in lower pension benefits.

These special employment problems associated with age are part of a larger set of factors influencing individuals in their decisions to work or not to work. In this regard, economists study factors influencing labor force participation and seek to understand the choices made in the relative amounts of time allocated between work and leisure. We emphasize in this section the institutional pressures and constraints placed on individuals in their determination of *when* to retire. We begin with a discussion of the retirement decision.

An important distinction in terminology must be kept in mind here. Throughout most of the book, when we talk about the aged or older persons, we are usually referring to people in their sixties (often age 65 or older). In this chapter we talk about older workers but are not focusing exclusively or even primarily on persons over age 65. Rather, the major focus of this chapter is on workers who have reached middle age and those approaching retirement age (generally, the 45–64 age group).

Unemployment

In 1989, Louis Harris and Associates conducted telephone interviews with 3,509 men and women between the ages of 50 and 64. Based on the survey, it was estimated that over eight million people (38 percent) in this age range were *not working*, and of these nearly two million were "ready and able to work" (McNaught and Barth, 1991). Why weren't they working?

Prior to the late 1960s the official **unemployment rates** for men 55 and over tended to be slightly *higher* than for those ages 25 to 54. This relationship began to change in the 1970s. By the 1980 recession, the rates for men 65 and older were well below those age 25 to 54. But Rones (1983) shows that these statistics underestimate the problem. Using data from the Current Population Survey, Rones estimated the number of workers who report that they want a job but are not looking because they believe they cannot find one—that is, they are what we call "discouraged workers."

The Bureau of Labor Statistics (BLS) estimates the number of discouraged workers in the United States. They count workers who (a) want a job, (b) have searched for one in the previous year, and (c) say they are available for work. Using these criteria, BLS estimated for 1998 that less than 1 percent of nonworking men and women over age 54 could be classified as discouraged workers.

Rix (1999a) argues that the BLS definition is probably too restrictive. She points out that many older workers are reluctant to even start a search, given the negative reception they expect to encounter from many employers. However, if we include persons out of the labor force who would like a job (regardless of whether a search was undertaken), the proportion of discouraged workers rises to only 2.2 percent (800,000 men and women).

As we mentioned above, another important phenomenon of recent years has been the widespread restructuring and downsizing of American companies. This too has had a major effect on older workers.

The Bureau of Labor Statistics (Hipple, 1999) has also carried out a number of important studies to determine how many and which workers have suffered "job dislocations" in the last two decades.[3] The studies focused on job losses where it was unlikely that the worker would ever be "hired back." In such cases, workers face a major change in employment opportunities and are often forced to shift to a very different job (if they find one).

In the 1980s, one study (U.S. Department of Labor, 1988) found that about 5 percent of the civilian labor force (age 20 and older) had experienced such a dislocation over a five-year survey period. Older workers age 55 to 64 had the highest dislocation rate (6.2%); and once dislocated, these workers experienced higher unemployment and longer periods of unemployment.

In the more economically prosperous years of the 1990s, the risk of job loss fell for most major age groups (Hipple, 1999). However, the displacement rates for older workers (age 55 and over) have fluctuated. They fell from a high of 4.5 percent in 1991–1992 to 3 percent (1993–1994), only to rise again to 3.3 percent in 1995–1996.

Job Discrimination

Another problem that arises is that there has been a clear bias in private and public employment policy against older workers; they are discriminated against in job hiring. Moreover, work and job structures have been made relatively inflexible, making midcareer adjustments very difficult. Various policies have encouraged or forced workers to retire from their "regular jobs." They are then discouraged or prevented from returning to the work force in new jobs.

The nation was first made aware of the extent and nature of discrimination toward older workers in 1965, through a report issued by the Department of Labor. This report documented that, at that time, more than 50 percent of all available job openings were closed to applicants over age 55 because of employers' policies *not* to hire any person over that age. Moreover, about 25 percent of the job openings were closed to applicants over age 45.

Since its passage in 1967, the federal **Age Discrimination in Employment Act** has attempted to protect individuals from age discrimination in hiring, discharge, compensation, and other terms of employment. This law originally covered (with some exceptions) persons between the ages of 40 and 65. It was amended in 1978 to include workers up to age 69 and again in 1986 to prohibit mandatory retirement at any age.

As a result of this legislation, the more blatant signs of discrimination—such as newspaper ads restricting jobs to younger persons and forced retirements—have virtually disappeared. *However, it is difficult to determine the total extent to which actual discrimination has in fact lessened, for little comprehensive evidence exists on the matter.* The much longer duration of unemployment for older men is one indicator that serious problems still exist (see Figure 2–5). Another crude indicator of the problem is the number of workers who formally file age discrimination charges with state agencies or the federal Equal Employment Opportunity Commission (EEOC).[4] The EEOC reports that complaints have not declined over the years. Instead, they have been fairly steady over the past decade—fluctuating between 24,000 and 26,000 each year.

In 1993, the Fair Employment Council of Greater Washington (financed by the American Association of Retired Persons) mailed the job resumes of equally qualified older and younger job-seekers to almost 2,000 companies and employment agencies across the country. "The applicants were in fact 'testers'—fictitious job-seekers who applied for these jobs for the sole purpose of testing for bias" (Lewis, 1994). The overall re-

Figure 2–5
Percent Unemployed 15 Weeks or More, 1991 and 1992

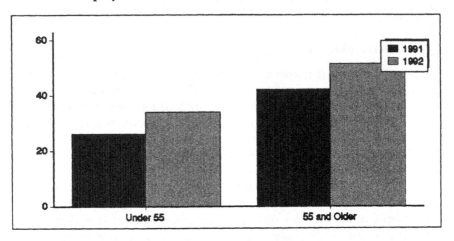

Source: Based on data in U.S. Bureau of Labor Statistics, *Employment and Earnings* (January 1992 and 1993).

sponse rate of companies to receiving a resume in the mail was very low (for both younger and older workers), and 90 percent of the replies were negative (to both ages). Only 79 companies out of 1,860 showed any interest. In 27 percent of these cases, however, the older applicants *were treated less favorably*.

Older Workers and the "Global Economy"

Many people think that the employment environment in the United States has recently changed in a fundamental way. Politicians point the finger at the growing economic interdependence between the United States and other countries—both industrialized and less developed. The pressures of international competition, together with the sluggish growth of the 1980s and the 1989–1993 recession, caused a great deal of corporate downsizing and restructuring. Many workers lost jobs, but, unlike in past periods, middle-aged and older workers have been affected in unprecedented numbers.

A study by James Medoff (1993) found that middle-aged workers (ages 35 to 54) were 45 percent more likely during the 1980s to be unemployed due to permanent layoff or job loss than was true during the 1970s (and 55 percent more likely in the 1990s).[5] According to an article in the *New York Times* (December 12, 1993), "One abiding lesson of the [1989–1993] recession is that many employers seeking lower costs and increased productivity through computers and high technology, can get

Figure 2–6
The New Way to Fire People (Minimizing Possible Legal Recourse)

"We regret to inform you that due to a recent reorganization, your job no longer exists. We have made every effort to find a place for your skills in the new organization, but have been unable to do so. This decision is not a reflection on your job performance or skills, but the result of business change. It has been reviewed at the highest levels of the organization and will not be reversed.

"You will be escorted to your desk and allowed to pack your personal belongings. You are to be off the premises within one hour and are not to return. Should you have forgotten any personal belongings, they will be mailed to you.

"The company has provided an outplacement center at another location to which it is suggested that you report at 8 am tomorrow.

"Your supervisor will provide you with a packet that explains your severance pay and benefits. Included in that packet is a letter of final settlement (absolving the company from any further liability) which you must sign in order to receive your severance pay. If you choose not to sign it at this time, please be aware that this offer of severance pay expires at the end of business today."

Source: Alan Downs, "Tale of a Reformed Corporate Executioner," *The Christian Science Monitor* (March 15, 1994): 8. Reprinted with permission.

the work they need from a 25 year old engineer or business school graduate, rather than a company veteran, and do so at a far lower salary."

A 1994 article in the *Christian Science Monitor* (Downs, 1994) gives us an insider's view of the termination process as it has been, and continues to occur in many companies. The view is shocking and scary. Alan Downs, a personnel manager in a San Francisco Bay–area 400-employee company, describes the secret planning session leading up to the "termination day":

We had to plan for every possible contingency imaginable: In case of violence, we had security guards; in case of shock or temporary insanity, we had counselors; in the event of employee vindictiveness, we had all [computer] system passwords terminated the precise moment of the lay-off. We even identified the closest exit to facilitate whisking the affected employee out of the building with the least disruption.

Figure 2–6 shows what was told to each individual employee.

Why couldn't the company and the terminators show any concern, comfort, or compassion? Why was the process so inhuman? Downs says that the company's attorney warned terminators against saying any more than the words shown in Figure 2–6, lest they make some promise that might be supported in a court case. What an unexpected consequence of our admittedly litigious society and its legal system, developed to "protect" individuals.

Other Problems

This longer average duration of unemployment is not all caused by age discrimination. Often older workers lack the necessary skills to qualify for available jobs or are not living in areas where job opportunities exist. Competing for jobs in the growing electronics and computer industries, for example, is difficult for many older workers, given their educational backgrounds. Often skills developed in the old established industries cannot be readily used in the new, high-technology industries. And, although evidence exists to indicate older workers can learn new skills, no large-scale programs exist in the United States to provide older workers with the newer skills often required.

Moreover, the problems arising from this incompatibility of skills have been aggravated by shifts in industries from their traditional locations in the Northeast, Middle Atlantic, and North Central states to the Southeast, Southwest, and West. Many older workers with usable skills (reluctant to leave communities where they have established roots) have been left behind with little hope for suitable new employment.

Many economists think that "the costs" of older workers create serious employment problems for older workers. For example, nonmoney employee benefits, a growing part of workers' total compensation, contribute to the reemployment problems of older workers. Some managers are reluctant to hire older workers because they believe it is more costly to provide such workers with many of these benefits.[6] For example, the higher costs of **defined benefit pensions** for older workers (discussed in Chapter 7) result primarily from two factors: (1) a shorter work history over which employer pension contributions must be made and thus lower investment income arising from the pension contributions; and (2) a declining probability with age of employee withdrawal (job turnover) between hiring and retirement. That is, the later the age of job entry, the shorter the period over which contributions can be made, the shorter the period over which interest is earned on pension funds, and the less likely the worker will die or leave the plan before qualifying for full benefits.

Another benefit that probably influences many employer hiring decisions is the provision of health care financing plans. While employers generally assume older workers' health care benefits cost more, relatively little research on the question has been done to date. Two studies (U.S. Senate Special Committee on Aging, 1984; Stapleton et al., 1993; Clark, 1994) conclude, however, that claim costs rise as the age of the employee increases. Rix (1999a) points out, however, that we do not know "the extent to which older workers' salaries are increased less sharply than those of younger workers to compensate for the higher [benefit] costs."

In addition to costs, a recent study sponsored by the American Association of Retired Persons (1995) reports that of growing importance are two big obstacles to the hiring and training of older workers. Employers perceive them to be less flexible and less adaptable with regard to new technologies—qualities that businesses see as vital in an era of change and global competition.

Finally, evidence indicates that older workers have difficulty finding new jobs because of their "job-seeking" behavior and the lower priority given to them by various manpower agencies. Sobel and Wilcock (1963) in a study of 4,000 job seekers found that older workers displayed less willingness (1) to change types of work methods or methods of looking for work; (2) to engage in job retraining; (3) to adjust salary expectations; and (4) to move to areas of higher employment opportunity. Sheppard and Belitsky (1966), in a study of 500 workers in one locality, found that older workers were also "more restrictive" in their job search techniques and less persistent in their activities (see also U.S. Office of Technology and Assessment, 1985). Rones (1983) reports that in 1981 only about one-half of discouraged workers age 65 and older indicated plans to look for work during the subsequent twelve-month period. In contrast, two-thirds of persons ages 55 to 64 and six out of seven ages 25 to 54 were looking.

What evidence there is indicates that older workers often get lower priority from government agencies set up to aid the unemployed. A 1973–1974 study by the National Institute of Industrial Gerontology reaffirms earlier findings of the Sheppard and Belitsky study: there are no age differences in the proportion of unemployed persons seeking job assistance from the employment service but there is differential treatment by age (Heidbreder and Batten, 1974; Pursell and Torrence, 1979). Significantly fewer older workers were (1) tested, counseled, or enrolled in training; (2) referred to employers for job interviews; or (3) actually placed in a job.

Life-long Learning

Life-long learning is one of those ideas that many people talk about but few people take seriously. It is very much like early retirement where, again, everyone voices concern about its harmful aspects and then goes on to ignore them.

The lack of serious commitment to life-long learning and the great enthusiasm about early retirement are intimately related. Government and businesses think it is cheaper to terminate workers at early ages than to retrain them for the new jobs being constantly created.

Economic efficiency (i.e., the allocation of economic resources to maximize production and consumer satisfaction) means that various jobs are constantly made obsolete. *Technological changes* typically result in a demand for workers with different skills and make old jobs in various industries obsolete. *Shifting preferences* of consumers as a result of new products and shifting relative product prices also make some jobs obsolete. Moreover, changes in the competitive advantage of different individuals, regions, or countries (what economists call **comparative advantage**) change labor demand in various regions and countries. Together these three sources of change (technology, consumer preference, and comparative advantage) mean no job is really secure. No worker can predict what will happen in his or her lifetime, nor can workers easily shield themselves and their families from the insecurities generated.

When factories and machines become obsolete, we discard them. But what do we do when humans become obsolete?

The 1998 hit movie *The Full Monty* dramatized the social, economic, and psychological impact that can occur when people lose their jobs. The movie focuses on the desperation of a group of men—old and young—who cannot find work after the local steel mill shuts down in a small British town. The magnitude of their shame and desperation after fruitless job searches pushes these men ultimately into becoming strip-teasers and executing "the full monty"—that is, revealing "it all." The inability to find a job in their community causes them to overcome the strong inhibitions and embarrassment of being seen naked in public (especially by friends and neighbors). The movie graphically shows the powerful forces that caused these men to turn, first, to crime, and then to stripping.

Governments, however, can provide some protection from the insecurity that arises from market forces; and history shows that both workers and business owners subjected to strong competitive threats are often quick to turn to government for help. A task confronting all countries is to provide reasonable economic security to populations without sacrificing too much economic growth. The most appropriate policies to do this are not obvious. Hence the debate continues all over the world with regard to appropriate trade and tariff policies and the extent to which workers and businesses hurt by "free trade" should receive some sort of assistance.

As Robert Reich has pointed out, however, "a national economic strategy that puts people first is not an outgrowth of ideology or a continuation of campaign sloganeering. It is a hard-nosed response to economic reality. U.S. competitive strategy must be based on the American workforce because the people are the only resource that remains in any meaningful sense 'American' " (Reich, 1994).

When workers are asked to rank the most important factors that influence their decision to stay or move from a job, the opportunity to learn new skills is generally at the top of their list, and the amount of money to be received from a job usually ranks lower. Thus, it seems appropriate to focus on education. Individuals need to learn skills that can be used as they move from one job to another and that will help minimize the disruption of job changes—such skills as writing, entrepreneurship, computer operation, financial planning, and good health practices. As Rosabeth Moss Kanter (1994) and others have argued, companies need flexibility in hiring and firing policies, but at the same time there needs to be an explicit commitment to actions in the workplace that focus *not* on promoting "narrow skills to fill today's slots" but on providing abundant learning opportunities to promote *increased* competence with age.

There seems to be general agreement in the United States that we need to do a better job of educating youth for entry-level jobs. *There is less agreement on the need to commit nationally to updating those skills over time*, especially in the later work years. "Back to basics" should be available to people of all ages. Research to date clearly shows that people have the ability to learn at any age and that education is a major asset in seeking reemployment at "living wages."

TRAINING OLDER WORKERS

In 1993, the federal government spent $18 billion on 126 different, and often duplicative, training programs run by six different agencies. While no age group is well served by these programs, experience indicates that the elderly face special problems. While older workers constitute a large proportion of the long-term unemployed, they have always been an almost insignificant proportion of the persons trained under the various manpower training programs operated or financed by federal and state governments. Steven Sandell (1987) argues that this situation should be changed. Summarizing the findings of a major research project on older worker issues conducted by the National Commission for Employment Policy, Sandell writes: "Although employer actions are essential to the improvement of the employment situation of older workers, many older workers have a need for training and other services that cannot be adequately addressed by employers alone. Thus, government has an important role to play" (see also Moore, 1996)

Despite the evidence to the contrary, most government officials and employers do not consider it worthwhile or cost effective to train older persons (compared with younger persons) because of the expectation of shorter work tenures, lower levels of education, and a belief that learning abilities decline with age. As a result, the Comprehensive Employment and Training Act (CETA), a major federal program until 1983, did little to help older workers (Schram and Osten, 1978). Kalman Rupp (1983) reports that in 1980 only 1 percent of the approximately seven million persons age 45 and older who were eligible for CETA training actually participated.

The Job Training Partnership Act (JTPA) of 1982 established a nationwide network of job training programs, some of which are targeted specifically to older workers. JTPA legislation established two principal training programs. The first of these, Title II, was targeted toward disadvantaged youths and adults (but had no upper age limit). The second, Title III, was targeted toward dislocated workers, including long-term unemployed older workers. (As discussed later, Title III was restructured in 1988.) In addition, under Section 124 of JTPA, states were required to set aside 3 percent of their Title II-A allocation for the training of economically disadvantaged workers age 55 and older. JTPA programs are meant to be jointly administered by local governments and private agencies. Thus, JTPA programs provided an appropriate focal point for state and local policy in developing employment programs for older workers.

JTPA targeted persons who were "economically disadvantaged." JTPA regulations gave states wide latitude in the use of the 3 percent set-aside money. General guidelines permitted a wide range of services—including, for example, job search assistance; job counseling; remedial education; basic institutional, on-the-job, and advanced career training; surveys; work habit development; literacy training; and job development. Between July 1992 and June 1993, only 8,423 older workers were involved in *regular* JTPA programs and 27,800 were participants in special "set-aside" programs (U.S. Department of Labor, 1994).

Workforce Investment Act of 1998

Once again, a major program has been legislated by the federal government to deal with employment problems. The Workforce Investment Act has been described by some of its supporters as a radical overhaul of the country's job-training system. The legislation aims at empowering individual workers by giving them greater choice of, and control over, their training and retraining. Unlike prior programs, this one explicitly seeks to be accessible and support workers throughout their entire work lives.

At the heart of the new program are "one-stop career centers" promising comprehensive, easy-to-access information on training and employment opportunities.

These centers, of which there are already more than 800, are intended to foster a customer-driven integrated workforce delivery system that makes available in one location all the information that workers of all ages need to find or retain employment. They will offer such core services as job search and placement assistance, career counseling, labor market information for identifying job vacancies and necessary skills for occupations in demand, initial assessment of skills and needs, and information on available services and programs. (Rix, 1999b)

Unfortunately, older workers are barely mentioned in the new legislation. Moreover, they are never singled out as an underserved population.

Older Worker Employment Programs

In 1969 a demonstration project was funded to promote useful part-time opportunities in community service activities for unemployed, low-income older persons. The success of this project was followed by statutory financing in 1973, and in 1978 the Senior Community Service Employment Program (SCSEP) was legislated as Title V of the Older Americans Act (amended).

Persons participating in the SCSEP must be age 55 or older, unemployed, and at an income level that is not more than 125 percent of the official poverty level. The legislation requires that priority be given to persons age 60 or older, and regulations promulgated by the U.S. Department of Labor (the administering authority) give priority to "the most needy" and individuals applying for reenrollment following termination from the program due to illnesses or placement in unsubsidized employment (O'Shaughnessy, 1985).

The SCSEP program employs older persons in a wide variety of part-time community services: health care, nutrition programs, home repair, weatherization and beautification, fire prevention, conservation, and restoration efforts. Program participants work an average of 20 hours per week in schools, hospitals, parks, community centers, and in various other government and private nonprofit facilities. From July 1989 to June 1990, participants in the SCSEP program were: 71 percent women, 81 percent with incomes below the official poverty levels, and 43 percent ages 55 to 64 (U.S. Department of Labor, 1991).

While general administration of the program is carried out by the U.S. Department of Labor, this department delegates the actual operation of state and local programs to a number of national sponsoring organizations and government agencies (such as the National Council on the Aging and the U.S. Forest Service).

Although regulations permit contractors to provide training to participants, few financial resources are devoted to this activity. Most of the efforts go into *creating* community jobs for participants and *matching* participants with existing jobs that are unsubsidized by the program. The major occupational functions performed by participants were clerical work, maintenance, and services such as recreational, health, or social aides (Centaur Associates, 1986).

The SCSEP has been a popular program in the U.S. Congress. It is one of only a few government social welfare programs that has received higher allocations of funds during the tight federal budget environment of the 1980s. However, given the total number of older workers *eligible* for this program and the JTPA special older worker program, the number of older workers *actually involved* in these programs is quite minimal (about 80,000 people in fiscal 1993). In 1993, almost 82 percent were age 60 or older; about 58 percent were 65 or older; almost 75 percent were female; and all were "economically disadvantaged" (U.S. Department of Labor, 1994). Studies show that less than 1 percent of those eligible are able to participate in the SCSEP, and less than 0.4 percent participate in JTPA (Miranda, 1988). Given these limits, the Department of Labor in recent years has used portions of the available funds to encourage and promote unsubsidized private-sector employment of eligible workers.

There are also a number of private agencies specializing in job services for older persons seeking employment. Studies by Rosenblum and Shepard (1977) and Doctors et al. (1980) indicate that significant numbers of older workers have been placed in jobs by these agencies. However, older workers using these services are typically not hired in jobs that utilize their existing skills and abilities to any high degree. Instead, they are most likely to be placed in low-skill and part-time positions, usually with small employers in various low-paying service occupations.

A few private companies have made *special* efforts to hire older workers. A study by the Commonwealth Fund (1991) looked in-depth at the experiences of three major companies: Days Inn of America (hotels/motels), The Travelers Corporation (insurance and other financial services), and B&Q plc (a chain of do-it-yourself stores in Great Britain). The study provides additional empirical evidence that older workers can work effectively, learn new technologies, and be cost-effective in a variety of service-providing settings.

However, Hirshorn and Hoyer (1994), based on a national sample of private-sector employers with 20 or more employees, found little "purposeful" hiring of older workers in the United States. They found that the hiring of retirees in 1991–1992 was widespread and common; over 46 percent of firms interviewed hired retirees. But few firms "targeted" older workers for their special qualities, that is, undertook any *special* efforts to recruit such workers. Not surprisingly, most firms that did in fact hire older workers did so because they possessed certain desired skills or backgrounds. However, Hirshorn and Hoyer also report that many companies that wanted to hire retirees because of their experience, skill, reliability, and so forth felt they did not know how to find them in the job market.

Table 2–1
Primary Reason for Older Men Leaving Their Last Jobs[a]

Reason	Age[b]	1941-42	1968		1982	
		65+	62-64	65+	62-64	65
Employer-initiated		56%	17%	57%	17%	20%
Health problems		34	54	21	29	17
Worker-initiated		10	29	22	54	63
Total Percent		100%	100%	100%	100%	100%

[a]Nonemployed men receiving retired-worker benefits from OASDI. (For 1968 and 1982, the self-employed on the last job are excluded.)
[b]Age at entitlement to benefits in the 1941–1942 and 1968 surveys and age at receipt of first benefits in the 1982 survey.
Source: Virginia P. Reno and Susan Grad, "Economic Security, 1935–85," *Social Security Bulletin* 48 (December 1985): Table 20.

THE RETIREMENT DECISION

Interviews of older men soon after they claim social security benefits reveal dramatic changes since the early 1940s in stated reasons for leaving their last job. Table 2–1 contrasts the reasons given in 1941–1942, 1968, and 1982. In the early 1940s, only 10 percent of the men said their departure was voluntary; most left because of employer-initiated action (56 percent), such as mandatory retirement, or because of health problems (34 percent). In 1982, however, 63 percent said that they themselves initiated their departure. Perhaps even more interesting is the finding that more than half of nonworking men ages 62 to 64 (i.e., early retirees) reported that *they initiated* the decision to leave their last job.

The term "voluntary" or self-initiated retirement, as used here, is meant to convey the basic idea of more freedom in making the decision. One should remember, however, that these decisions are often influenced by health limitations and by subtle (and sometimes not so subtle) threats and economic incentives from employers and social pressures from co-workers. Scott and Brudney (1987), for example, present a variety of case studies documenting the sometimes shocking ways older workers are "forced out" of their jobs.

What are the implications of retirement? In view of traditional work-oriented values in the United States and the importance of income derived from work, retirement is one of the most important lifetime decisions made by persons. Aging in general, and the retirement decision in particular, involve more complex choices than just deciding between more or less income. The amount of income and assets available is certainly one of the major considerations in deciding when to retire, but there are other, *personal considerations*. For example, the individual must consider his or her health and evaluate the physical and emotional difficulties of continued employment on a specific job vis-à-vis the benefits and problems of alternative employment or of leaving the workforce.

Poor Health Encourages Retirement

Deterioration of health, which Burtless (1987) has shown varies systematically among different occupations and industries, is one of the most important factors encouraging early retirement. Some persons are unable to continue working because of disabling illness. Even those persons who, despite health problems, could continue to work in their current job, or perhaps in a less demanding one, may decide to retire early if there is alternative income available from one or more pensions.

Many studies have documented the importance of health in the retirement decision. An especially important one is the 1966–1981 National Longitudinal Survey (NLS) of men, initially ages 45 to 59. The survey found, for example, that, other things being equal, men with health problems in 1966 were twice as likely to have retired between 1966 and 1971 as those who were free of health limitations (Andrisani, 1977).

The NLS findings are of particular interest because they measure the influence of health problems *before* retirement on *subsequent* withdrawal from the workforce. Most other studies have asked people *after* they retire why they retired. Some social scientists worry that a high proportion of those who cite health may be giving what they consider to be a socially acceptable reason for retirement, rather than reflecting serious health limitations.

Later years of the NLS also included a series of questions inquiring about the extent of particular physical or mental impairments—such as difficulty in standing, walking, and dealing with people. From these questions an **index** of impairment was constructed. When this index was related to labor force participation or hours worked (controlling statistically for other factors), a strong relationship was found between health and participation. "For instance, an average blue-collar worker with even a moderate degree of impairment is 9% less likely to be in the labor force and works 9% fewer hours per year than a comparable individual with no impairments" (Parnes, 1981).

More recently, Quinn (1999) has analyzed data from the Health and Retirement Study, a newer longitudinal survey. Quinn looks at retirement behavior on "career jobs" (defined as jobs held for at least ten years) for men and women ages 51 to 61 in 1992. Again, health status was found to significantly affect people's work decisions. The worse the health status of the workers, the less likely they were to continue working on their career jobs.

The Big Retirement "Carrot"—Pensions

The potential availability of significant **public or private pension** income is a powerful influence on the retirement decision. Moreover, many researchers have pointed to the growing role of social/demographic and institutional factors that interact with the availability of pension income. For example, as we just discussed, workers with poor or declining health are more likely to retire than those whose health remains good. And early retirement decisions are not as likely if children are still living at home (Sheppard, 1977). Various *institutional realities* also affect the individual's retirement decision—factors that, in part, are beyond the person's own control.

Does Social Security Encourage Retirement?

Prior to 1962, men could not get social security benefits before age 65. In that year, the law was changed to allow men the same option granted to women in a 1956 amendment—early retirement at ages 62 through 64 with actuarially reduced benefits. The result was an immediate and major increase in the number of men accepting early retirement benefits.

Some workers apparently retire before age 65 because they can afford to, often supplementing their reduced social security benefits with a private pension or other income. There is another group of workers who have already stopped working before reaching age 62. The Social Security Administration's Survey of New Entitled Beneficiaries provides information on this group of workers. "Forty-one percent of the nonworking men entitled [i.e., becoming beneficiaries] at age 62 had been out of work for six months or more; 33 percent had not worked for at least a year; and 17 percent had been out of work three or more years" (Reno, 1971). These statistics support the findings of the studies cited earlier that document the difficulties older workers face in finding employment.

The extent of the impact of various social security provisions on labor force participation is currently being hotly debated in the pension literature (Leonesio, 1993; Quadagno and Hardy, 1995; Ruhm, 1990). There is no agreement among researchers on the impact of the earnings test, payroll taxes, the early and delayed retirement benefit adjustment provisions, disability regulations, and the asset value (or wealth effect) of future benefits. Studies generally indicate, however, that historically, social security has probably encouraged workers to retire earlier than they would have otherwise. But most projections done to assess the impact of congressional action to raise the future social security retirement age, liberalize the retirement test, and improve benefits through the delayed retirement credit (see Chapter 4) indicate that these actions are not likely to raise retirement ages significantly (see, e.g., Burtless and Moffitt, 1984; Fields and Mitchell, 1984).

The Major Impact of Employer-Sponsored Plans

While many people think that the availability of social security benefits facilitates and encourages retirement, fewer people realize the powerful, perhaps greater, impact of employer-sponsored pensions. In recent years it has become common practice for employers to encourage earlier retirement by setting the age of normal retirement specified by the pension plan below age 65. In addition, employers have provided "early retirement options," often absorbing all or most of the added costs of paying pensions out over a longer period to time. This practice allows workers to retire early without major penalties in the form of significantly lower pension income. Workers who *continue* on the job, however, are often severely penalized. In fact, Kotlikoff and Wise (1989), using data on pension plans in 1979, report that it was not unusual in that year for the reduction in pension benefit accruals at later retirement ages to equal the equivalent of a 30 percent reduction in earnings!

More recently, employers have encouraged early retirement using another device, the "early retirement incentive program." Workers eligible for pensions are offered credits to increase their pension levels or a lump-sum payment (typically equal to one-half to two years' salary) in addition to their regular pension.

In the 1980s, early retirement incentive programs swept the country; there was hardly a major company that did not use this mechanism as a way of adjusting the size and age structure of its labor force. The mechanism continued to be used by many companies in the 1990s but at a more moderate rate.

Concern has been voiced (AARP, 1987; NOW, 1987) that older workers are increasingly expected to bear the major burden of staffing adjustments in companies. In the 1990s, continued corporate consolidations, buyouts, mergers, and restructuring (in response to shifting demand, global competition, and "financial entrepreneurship") have caused cuts in the workforce of many companies. Particularly hard hit, for the first time, have been managerial and professional workers, many of whom are at older ages.

"Bridge Jobs"

There is increasing evidence that many workers do not go from a "full-time career job" to full-time retirement. Many workers, instead, take transitional jobs—often referred to as "bridge jobs."

Using data from the Health and Retirement Study, Quinn (1999) looked at older men and women who had been on a job for ten years

Table 2-2
Job Transitions by Older Workers,ᵃ 1996

	Still on Career Jobᵇ	Moved to Bridge Job	Moved to No Job	Don't Know
Gender				
Men	44%	25%	28%	4%
Women	51	23	24	2
Type of Work				
Wage and Salary	46	22	28	3
Self-employed	46	35	16	3

ᵃWorkers who were ages 51 to 61 in 1992.
ᵇA job held for ten or more years.
Source: Based on J. F. Quinn, *Retirement Patterns and Bridge Jobs in the 1990s*, EBRI Issue
   Brief 206 (Washington, D.C.: Employee Benefit Research Institute, 1999), Table 3.

or more. As shown in Table 2-2, about half were no longer working at
that job. Of these, about half had moved to bridge jobs.

Some of the transitional shifts are voluntary. But as Doeringer (1990)
points out, many are probably otherwise:

There is evidence that career jobs for workers in their fifties and sixties are ending
before such workers are ready to retire. When the career jobs end, these workers
experience substantial job changing, lost earnings, and reduced job status. Instead
of retirement at the end of a career job, there is an extended period of work in
the twilight zone of bridge jobs between career jobs and retirement.

MANDATORY VERSUS FLEXIBLE RETIREMENT OPTIONS

There used to be a stigma to going out. He was over the hill. But now it's a
looked-for status. Those retirement parties, they used to be sad affairs. They are
darn happy affairs now. The peer pressure is for early retirement.

This observation (Flint, 1977) is by Victor M. Zink, who was director
of employee benefits at General Motors Corporation. For many years,
early retirement among workers has been increasing, and workers' attitudes toward retirement have changed dramatically. The statistics show
the average age of retirement dropping rapidly in many companies.

At the same time, many gerontological studies show retirement to be
less traumatic than was initially perceived.[7] Atchley (1976) observes, for
example, that "the general trends very definitely contradict the myth that

retirement causes illness. . . . It appears that retirement is a welcome change for couples in good health who enjoy middle or upper socioeconomic status."

Paradoxically, as retirement ages decline and retirement living is becoming increasingly popular, public policy has taken a big step toward allowing workers to continue longer on their jobs. A bill amending the Age Discrimination in Employment Act swept through Congress in 1977. The House passed legislation abolishing mandatory retirement with only four dissenting votes. The Senate quickly followed with only seven dissenting votes. The resulting law extended protection against age discrimination to nonfederal employees up to age 69 and eliminates the upper age limit entirely for most federal workers.

In October 1986, the Age Discrimination in Employment Act was again amended. The new provisions prohibit job termination on the basis of age, *at any age*. The only employees excluded were those working in private businesses with fewer than twenty employees and labor unions with fewer than twenty-five.[8]

Congressman Claude Pepper (who before his death in 1989 was the oldest member of the U.S. Congress and a leader in the fight against mandatory retirement) hailed the new law. He saw mandatory retirement as "a mean and arbitrary indignity imposed on our senior citizens when they, though of sound mind and sound body, are told they are too old to earn a living" (Lawrence, 1986). In contrast, two prominent University of Chicago economists argued the opposing view this way:

These [mandatory retirement] rules surely hurt some elderly persons who continue to be productive, but they are not motivated by a desire to discriminate against productive older workers. Rather, these rules are a recognition both of the decline in the health and productivity of a significant fraction of elderly workers and of the inability of most large companies to pick and choose among their older workers in order to retain only the productive ones. (Becker, 1986)

Young workers are paid less than they are worth and old workers are paid more. By doing this in a way that keeps the *present value* of lifetime *productivity*, incentives are provided to workers that would be absent if they were to be paid a wage that followed life-cycle productivity more closely. . . . The efficient wage arrangement requires an upward-sloping wage profile to provide motivation against shirking, and it also requires mandatory retirement since workers facing a rising wage profile will not choose to leave at the efficient age, when the value of leisure exceeds their productivity. (Lazear, 1991; emphasis added)

What was the impact of the now illegal mandatory retirement provisions? How many older persons want to work? Will the continued employment of older workers interfere with the employment opportunities of younger workers? Data are available to help answer these questions.

Mandatory Retirement Practices

Research findings indicate that the overwhelming number of retired workers were not directly affected by mandatory retirement rules (Parnes and Nestel, 1979; Clark et al., 1979). To understand more clearly why so few workers' jobs were actually terminated by mandatory retirement rules, it is useful to break down the retirement population into categories. First of all, many workers were not subject to mandatory retirement rules because they worked for establishments without such provisions; and, of course, all self-employed persons were unaffected by such provisions.

Next, it is important to realize that many workers potentially subject to such rules left establishments *before* reaching the age maximum. Early retirement has become a normal occurrence in recent years, while retirement at or after the normal retirement age has become less common. Furthermore, as Streib and Schneider (1971) have documented, "not *all* persons subject to retirement at a certain chronological age are reluctant to retire; some welcome the step." And, of those who do *not* want to retire, a certain proportion are encouraged by health or physical condition to accept mandatory retirement and do not try to reenter the work force. Finally, some of those able and willing to work do, in fact, seek and find new jobs on a part-time or full-time basis. Figure 2–7 illustrates these various alternatives.

The percentage estimates shown in Figure 2–7 are based on a 1968–1970 survey of social security beneficiaries and exclude those not covered by social security (e.g., federal and certain state and local government workers). The data show that about two out of five males (age 65 or less) *who reached a compulsory retirement age* were able and willing to work but were not working. As the figure shows, however, these workers represented less than 10 percent of the total cohort of retired males.

The Economics of Encouraging or Forcing Retirement

Each year before 1986 there was a small but significant number of workers forced to retire who would have preferred to continue working. The overwhelming proportion of workers, however, were unaffected by mandatory retirement provisions.

Far more important than mandatory retirement over the years has been the design of pension and other financial inducements to encourage workers to leave their jobs at increasingly early ages. As we discussed earlier, throughout this century, and especially over the past two decades, employers have used financial retirement incentives as a major way of dealing with issues of labor redundancy, promotion policy, and concerns

Figure 2–7
The Incidence of Mandatory Retirement

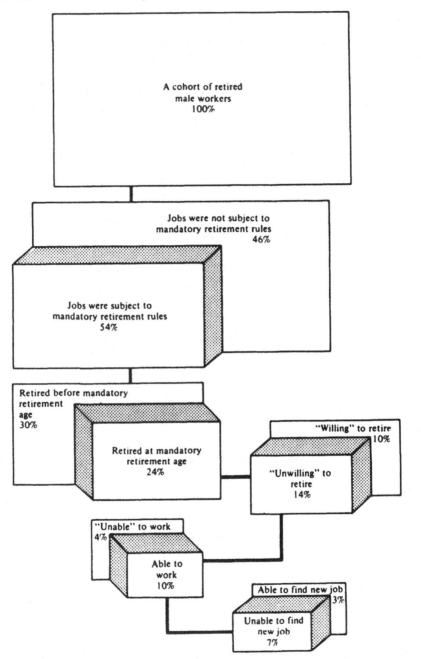

Source: James H. Schulz, "The Economics of Mandatory Retirement," *Industrial Gerontology* 1(1), New Series (Winter 1974): 1–10. Reprinted by permission of The National Council on the Aging, Inc.

about worker productivity (see also Chapter 7). What are the economic implications of these developments?

Whether the firm gains economically from arbitrarily terminating older workers at some specified age depends in large part on the **productivity** and earning levels of those terminated versus (1) those of workers hired as replacements (in the case of constant or expanding output) or (2) those of other employees of the firm who would be otherwise terminated (in the case of contracting output). The question is not easy to answer because of the great difficulty in measuring the productivity of particular workers.

It has often been asserted that mandatory retirement provisions can increase the productivity of a business. Similar to the two economists quoted above, a leading pension authority, Dan McGill, states that one of the most important reasons that private pensions with mandatory retirement provisions were introduced was the desire of management to increase levels of workforce productivity.

The available evidence, however, on the question of whether retiring older workers raises productivity indicates that one should be cautious about generalizing. The results of a relatively large number of research studies bearing on this issue are available, but the findings are far from conclusive. Here is the way a number of survey articles summarize the research:

Collectively, leading studies on various aspects of the effects of aging document the conclusion that chronological age *alone* is a poor indication of working ability. Health, mental and physical capacities, work attitudes and job performance are *individual traits* at any age. Indeed, measures of traits in different age groups *usually* show *many* of the older workers to be superior to the average for the younger group and many of the younger inferior to the average for the older group. (U.S. Department of Labor, 1965)

(1) While some declines with age in productivity have been observed in certain industries (e.g., clerical, manufacturing, sales), older workers are more productive than younger workers. (2) There are wide differences in productivity within age groups. (3) There are some declines with age in physical capacity, but environmental conditions are important in mitigating the effects of decline. . . . (4) Older employees score well or better than younger employees on creativity, flexibility, facility of information processing, absenteeism, accident rates, and turnover. (Robinson, Coberly, and Paul, 1984)

It is apparent from a number of well-designed studies that age often has no real influence on performance. Wide individual differences exist and experience often counteracts any age effects. Where age differences are found, it appears they may be caused often by psychosocial factors, such as reduced work commitment because of limited career advancement opportunities. (Sparrow, 1986)

The general finding is that on average productivity falls but only marginally as workers age through their 50s and early 60s. The evidence is of three kinds: surveys of managers, opinions of experts, and studies of physical productivity. (Hurd, 1993a)

[Reviewing many studies reveals] an exceedingly weak relationship between age and performance. In other words, a worker's age is of little value in predicting job performance. While this observation may be complex-intuitive, the large number of individuals on which the studies are based and the consistency of the results across reviews allows one to place substantial confidence in it. (Sterns and McDaniel, 1994)

Factors working against older workers are (1) their on-average *formal* education deficit compared with younger workers (which may or may not be offset by their greater on-the-job experience); (2) their greater risk of chronic illness and the possibility of declining physical and mental capacity; (3) some degree of work assignment inflexibility due to the interaction of work rules, seniority systems, and pay scales; and (4) generally higher levels of compensation.

It is probably reasonable to assert that most employers recognize that the productivity of some of their older employees is as high as or higher than that of younger workers. These employers argue, however, that it is difficult (and costly) to identify such workers and that older workers are often higher paid workers. Thus, they argue, retirement rules and pensions provide (in dealing with these complex matters) a practical administrative procedure that is objective, impersonal, and impartial.

Mandatory retirement rules avoided charges of discrimination, favoritism, or bias in the termination process. Without mandatory retirement, employers are faced with either allowing workers to decide when to retire or undertaking potentially expensive activities for "sorting out" (given pay levels) the insufficiently productive older workers. More important, the employer must justify these termination decisions so that general worker morale will not be adversely affected. Historically, employers have been reluctant to terminate workers solely on the basis of age—especially given past levels of social security old age pensions. But with the establishment of supplementary private pension plans, management (especially in larger firms) apparently felt such practices were much less inequitable. With the passage of legislation prohibiting employers from using age as a basis of job termination, there has been renewed interest among management in techniques of measuring performance. (However, the "pension carrot" still remains the principal management tool to encourage retirement.)

DO THE AGED WANT TO WORK?

A Louis Harris poll in 1974 was devoted to "the myth and reality of aging in America." One of the most widely publicized findings from that survey related to the number of older persons wanting employment. For example, *Newsweek*, in a cover story on "The Graying of America," reported the Harris poll finding that "nearly a third of the nation's over-65 retirees said if they could they still would be working" (28 February 1977). (Another Harris poll in 1979 reporting on the high proportion of people desiring to work in old age also received national publicity.) When this finding was cited, it was almost invariably (as in the *Newsweek* story) a part of a discussion examining the importance of work to the aged and the problems caused by mandatory retirement. Yet earlier in this chapter we presented data for the late 1960s that indicated that less than 10 percent of those approaching retirement were forced to retire because of mandatory retirement provisions. Are the two findings compatible?

Why People Who "Would Like to Work" Don't

What most discussions of the Harris survey on this issue failed to report were the answers to a related question asked in the surveys. Those older persons not working who said they would like to work were asked, "What's keeping you from working?" The answers broke down as follows (NCOA, 1975):

Poor health	57%
Too old	28%
No work available; lack of job opportunities	15%
Lack of transportation	10%
Other interests	8%
Would lose pension benefits or pay too much in taxes if worked	4%

As we discussed previously, the high number of people giving health as a reason for not working is difficult to interpret; some people may use this answer as an excuse in place of less socially accepted reasons—although existing research indicates that the number who do is relatively small. It is clear, however, that there is a wide range of reasons that people who would like to work do not work. Thus, when those aged who were retired or unemployed were asked if they would come back to work or take on a new job that "suited them well," only 11 percent responded that they would definitely consider it. Moreover, only 12 percent of the retirees reported in the survey that they had some skills they would like to use but that no one would give them a chance to use the skills.

Still another survey by Louis Harris in 1989 focused on 50- to 64-year-olds who were out of the labor force. Based on the responses received, the Commonwealth Fund (*Americans Over 55*, 1993) estimates that there were about a million women and men "most willing and able to work." In this survey, many questions to test the work commitment of respondents were inserted into the survey to get a better measure of interest in working. Again, however, the result indicates that only a small percentage of nonworkers in this age group were out of the labor force against their will.

Retirement Expectations Change

Again, a 1979 Lou Harris poll (Johnson and Higgins, 1979) reported that nearly half (48 percent) of workers ages 50 to 64 said they intended to continue working instead of retiring at the usual time. Harris concluded that in the future more people will want to defer retirement.

But a study by Goudy (1981) indicates that work expectations change dramatically during the preretirement years (see also Morgan, 1980; and Burkhauser and Quinn, 1985). Using data from the Longitudinal Retirement History Survey, Goudy discovered that survey findings like those from the 1979 Harris poll can be unreliable predictors of actual practices. His study indicates that retirement "attitudes are relatively volatile; many change within two or four years, and *large numbers retire shortly after they've stated that they never expect to stop working for a living*" (emphasis added).

Who Doesn't Retire?

An econometric analysis of factors associated with continuing work identified six that were statistically highly significant. "Labor market activity is positively related to good health, level of education attained, both measures of strength of work ethic,[9] and having a wife who is also working. It is negatively related to age and level of income in the absence of work" (Parnes and Sommers, 1994).

Once retired, most older persons adapt quickly to their new life situations and indicate a high degree of satisfaction with their lives. As we previously noted, a variety of studies over the past two decades have documented that a high proportion of the elderly are relatively satisfied with their lives after retirement. Those who express dissatisfaction often perceive themselves in poor health and/or without adequate income, but these persons are a small minority, with most elderly expressing general satisfaction with their health and income (Liang and Fairchild, 1979). In 1981, another NCOA/Harris survey asked retired people: "Do you now think you made a right decision to retire when you did; did you retire too early; or do you now think you retired too late?" The responses were (NCOA, 1981):

Made the right decision	90%
Retired too early	6%
Retired too late	1%
Not sure	3%

The evidence is now very clear that most older workers want to retire as soon as financially possible, and that once retired, they adjust well to their new situation in society and enjoy their increased leisure. Thus, increasing numbers of workers are looking forward to the retirement period—retiring at increasingly early ages and raising their expectations about retirement living standards. The issue of planning financially for the retirement years, therefore, moves right to the top of the decision-making agenda for most older workers. That is the subject of the next chapter.

CHAPTER 2 HIGHLIGHTS

Given the increasing numbers of people no longer working in the later years, much attention has been given to understanding the various factors influencing older workers' choices between work and retirement. Some of the important points made in this chapter are:

1. *When an economy is growing and is at a full-employment level*, a choice must be made on how to divide the higher productive potential between more leisure and/or more income (i.e., more goods and services). But when there is high unemployment, nations often encourage and facilitate more leisure through retirement mechanisms—attempting to deal with the unemployment problems by encouraging older workers to retire.
2. A minority of Americans are still working after age 65, and most of those still employed work only part time.
3. While many factors *interact* to influence the work/retirement decision, health and potential retirement income are probably the two most important factors. Thus, the growing amounts and availability of public and private pension income have had a significant influence (negatively) on labor force participation rates.
4. Even though their productivity does not necessarily fall as they grow older, most older workers face a variety of barriers to reemployment when they become unemployed and receive relatively little help from private and government organizations in dealing with the problem.
5. Historically, few workers were "forced" to retire; currently, mandatory retirement policies are illegal at any age.
6. Most workers retire as soon as they think it is financially feasible and, once retired, usually adjust well to their new situation.

SUGGESTED READINGS

Commonwealth Fund. *The Untapped Resource*. New York: The Commonwealth Fund, 1993. The final report of the fund's Americans Over 55 at Work Program.

Crown, William H., ed. *Handbook on Employment and the Elderly*. Westport, Conn: Greenwood Press, 1996. A comprehensive collection of articles on all important aspects of this topic.

Doeringer, Peter B., ed. *Bridges to Retirement: Older Workers in a Changing Labor Market*. Ithaca, N.Y.: IRR Press, 1990. The book contains a large amount of new information and discusses the "transition" to retirement and ways to promote more jobs for older workers.

Freedman, Marc. *Seniors in National and Community Service*. Philadelphia, Pa.: Public/Private Ventures, 1994. A review of programs and issues.

Graebner, William. *A History of Retirement*. New Haven, Conn.: Yale University Press, 1980. The best book available on the historical relationship between pensions and the employment policies of management, unions, and the government.

"Older Persons in Employment." A special edition of *Ageing International* 13 (Autumn/Winter 1986). A collection of articles on older workers—looking at job performance, ways to prolong work life, job matching, and experiences in foreign countries.

Parnes, Herbert S. et al. *Retirement Among American Men*. Lexington, Mass.: Lexington Books, 1985. A collection of articles presenting findings from the National Longitudinal Survey of Older Men. This book is the sixth publication in a series of reports and covers the first fifteen-year period of the survey cohort, from 1966 through 1981.

Quinn, Joseph, R. V. Burkhauser, and D. A. Myers. *Passing the Torch: The Influence of Economic Incentives on Work and Retirement*. Kalamazoo, Mich.: W. E. Upjohn Institute for Employment Research, 1990. The best book to date summarizing the research on why American older workers are retiring at increasingly earlier ages.

Rix, Sara E. "The Older Worker in a Graying America." In R. N. Butler, L. K. Grossman, and M. R. Oberlink, eds., *Life in an Older America*. New York: Century Foundation Press, 1999, pp. 187–216. An up-to-date review of the literature.

Scott, Hilda, and Juliet F. Brudney. *Forced Out*. New York: Simon and Schuster, 1987. An eye-opening study of older workers driven from their careers. Based on interviews of over 100 people between the ages of 50 and 70, the book explores the (often shockingly) difficult problems encountered by many older workers who lose their jobs and then try to find new ones. Also discussed is the limited help provided these workers by most public and private employment agencies.

Weaver, David A. *The Work and Retirement Decisions of Older Women: A Literature Review*. ORS Working Paper Series, No. 61. Washington, D.C.: Social Security Administration, 1994. This review summarizes thirteen major studies in the area of women and retirement decision-making.

Chapter 3

Retirement Planning

We now turn from employment problems and the retirement decision to the issues of financial provision for retirement. A 1994 national survey of Americans approaching retirement (ages 45–59) found many who had not done any *individual* preparation for retirement ("Fear of Future . . . ," 1994). While 70 percent had started to save for retirement, 28 percent had not, and about half of those with income below $30,000 had *not* started to save.

There are various ways in which individuals can provide income for the retirement years, when normal income received from work declines or stops. Table 3–1 lists the major mechanisms and institutions available in the United States today for providing economic support in retirement. These are divided into two broad groups—private and public. The private mechanisms are either individual preparation or preparation undertaken by the individual as a part of group action. For the public mechanisms it is important to distinguish between two major categories: those mechanisms for which there is a means test and those without a test.

In this chapter the focus is primarily on private mechanisms, especially the task that faces individuals who want to prepare for retirement. In the absence of *group* mechanisms, both public and private, what must the individual do to have adequate retirement income?

We begin with this focus or emphasis not because this is the principal way that preparation for retirement is currently being carried out, or because it is the most important way that we would expect it to be carried out in the future. Rather, beginning with individual preparation is a use-

Table 3–1
Options for Retirement Income Provision

Private		Public	
Individual Provision	Collective Arrangements	Means Tested	Not Means Tested
Physical assets	Family gifts & transfers	Medicaid	Medicare
Insurance claims	Private pensions	SSI	OASDI
Other financial intermediary claims	Group Savings Plans	State property tax reductions*	Special federal tax benefits
Direct financial investment claims	Charity assistance	Veterans' benefits (nonservice-connected disability)	Veterans' benefits (service-connected disability)
	Help from friends and neighbors	Housing programs	
		Food stamps	
		Government financed elderly services*	

*Some elderly tax reductions and services are not means-tested.

ful way of developing a good understanding of many of the concepts and issues involved in providing adequate income in old age. By starting at this level, it is easier to show some of the personal options, the major problems, and the magnitude of the task the individual faces. This allows us to obtain some needed perspective on the whole problem.

RETIREMENT PROVISION BY INDIVIDUALS

First, let us list some of the problems faced by nonaged people in preparing systematically for retirement:

1. One doesn't know with certainty when she or he will die.
2. One doesn't know exactly what the future preretirement income flow (e.g., earnings) will be.
3. One doesn't know what basic retirement needs will be or what lifestyle will be ultimately preferred for that period.
4. One doesn't know the age of retirement.
5. One cannot easily predict the future rate of inflation, which, if it occurs, will depreciate the value of those retirement assets that do not adjust fully and reduce the buying power of income from those assets.
6. One cannot easily predict the rate of economic growth, which is likely to affect one's economic position relative to the working population.

The number and magnitude of problems listed above indicate that individual retirement planning is a very difficult job. There is no doubt that the personal decision-making process involved in preparation for retirement is a very complex one. First, not knowing when you (or maybe a spouse) are going to die is a major complicating factor in ascertaining the amount of money needed for retirement. To plan for adequate income the individual needs to know the number of years for which income is required. Thus arises a major justification for not providing for retirement entirely by *individual* actions alone; one can simplify the decision-making process and reduce uncertainty by entering into an insurance arrangement, either public or private, that provides collective protection by grouping those who live short, medium, and long lives. (This "insurance principle" is discussed later in the chapter.)

The second problem is the uncertainty of the earnings and other income flows that the individual will receive over his or her working life. The problem here arises from an inability to work as a result of child-bearing, ill health, or disability (either short term or long term). Problems are also created by unemployment during recessions, job obsolescence, and unequal economic opportunity for various groups in the labor market. Recurrent periods of **recession** (and **inflation**) are outside the control of the individual and are very difficult to predict; yet these factors have a significant, if not dominating, impact on the flow of earnings, the total amount of income individuals receive over their lifetimes, and the purchasing power when it is spent.

A third problem arises from not knowing what retirement needs will be. A major factor here is the great uncertainty that exists with regard to the state of one's health when one gets old. Will chronic or serious illness develop? Will nursing care be required? Will institutionalization be necessary? Not only is health status directly related to medical costs, it also affects retirement mobility—influencing recreation and transportation expenditures.

Yet another difficulty arises if one is married. There is uncertainty as to whether the family unit will break up (divorce) and uncertainty about how long each spouse will live. Pension benefit rights often change if the eligible worker dies. Thus the amount of money a *spouse* will need or will have in retirement depends to a major extent on their lifetime marital history and, therefore, is essentially unpredictable as far as the individual is concerned. This is one of the major factors involved in the current high rate of poverty among unmarried older women.

A fifth problem occurs because of the variability in the age at which people retire. Although individuals have a large measure of control over when they retire, in some cases the decision is based on factors they do not control. Such factors as deteriorating health, pension rules, the growth of early retirement options (sometimes accompanied by management and/or union pressures to retire), and discriminatory practices in hiring and promoting older workers often dominate.

Perhaps one of the most difficult retirement preparation problems is dealing with the unpredictable inflation that will occur before and during retirement. To the extent that an individual accumulates assets (or pension rights) for the retirement period that do not automatically adjust in value for inflation, he or she is faced with the possibility that these assets may shrink in value—perhaps being of little worth in the retirement period.

Finally, individuals preparing for retirement may be concerned about changes in their *relative* economic status in retirement. After one retires, the real incomes of the working population will continue to rise over the years. If the retiree wants to keep up with the general rise in living standards, he or she will have to make some estimate of the economic growth that will occur during retirement. Additional funds must then be provided before retirement that can be drawn upon to keep a person's economic status rising along with that of everybody else. Some people will decide that they do not want to bother dealing with this issue; they will be content just to keep their retirement standard of living constant. Some may even prefer to allow it to decline. Nevertheless, this is an important issue that should not be overlooked in retirement planning. There is a choice to be made, and it should not be made passively because individuals are unaware of the nature of that choice.

What Must I Save for Adequate Retirement Income?

To see the retirement preparation issues clearly, let us *assume* certain answers to most of the questions listed above in order to answer the following question: Suppose an individual (on his or her own) wants to save a sufficient amount for retirement; how much should the person save? To put the question another way, suppose you were a preretirement counselor and someone came to you and said, "I'm 25. I don't have much confidence in the present pension mechanisms available to prepare for retirement; I just don't trust them. Instead, I want to sit down and work out a financial plan for myself that will provide me with adequate income in retirement. How much should I save?"

The answer to this question depends on a great many factors. Most important are the following:

1. The standard of adequacy chosen
2. The number of years one plans to be in retirement
3. The number of years one plans to work and the earnings (and other income) that will be received over that period
4. The yield one can anticipate on one's savings and investments
5. The rate of inflation that is expected over the period

Let us look first at the standard of adequacy. In Chapter 1, we focused on the Social Security Administration's poverty index. But a retirement counselor would probably argue (we think correctly) that the poverty index is not the best measure for most people to use. Instead, it is common to propose that nonpoor individuals choose a standard of adequacy based upon the concept of "income replacement." *An income replacement standard seeks to provide the individual with income in retirement that is a certain specified percentage of his or her income prior to retirement.* Immediately, a key question arises. What should that replacement goal be; what rate should be chosen—100, 80, or 50 percent?

Replacement Rates

The amount of financial resources needed in retirement depends upon the standard of adequacy used. One reasonable goal is to keep one's living standard not too different from what one has been accustomed to in the not-too-distant past. If the retired person's living standard is to be related in some way to a standard of living experienced just before retirement, sources of retirement funds must enable the person to replace a certain proportion of the earnings lost when work stops.

It is generally agreed that a number of expenditures in retirement will be somewhat lower than before retirement and, hence, that 100 percent income replacement is not necessary. There are likely to be differences in (1) pre- and postretirement tax liabilities; (2) work- and age-related expenditures; and (3) savings rates. For example, payroll taxes are eliminated for those fully retired. Similarly, work-associated expenses (e.g., transportation, dues, clothing, and lunch costs) go down, while health care expenditures may go up; and saving needs for children's education and future retirement are no longer a necessity. In a recent study, Palmer (1989) estimated that a hypothetical couple retiring in 1988 with preretirement gross earnings of $25,000 would have: $4,769 less in taxes, $1,622 lower savings, and a $738 reduction in age- and work-related expenses. In 1981, the federal income tax marginal tax rates were lowered significantly, and in 1984, social security income became taxable for some higher-income individuals. Both change target replacement rates. Table 3–2 shows a set of target rates estimated by Palmer.

Table 3–2 shows that the replacement rate targets vary between 82 and 66 percent over the $15,000 to $80,000 earnings range. How can that much income be provided in the retirement years, if people stop working? One option is to provide it out of savings accumulated *before* retirement.

Table 3–2
Target Replacement Rates Needed to Maintain Preretirement Living Standards[a]

Gross Preretirement Earnings[b]	Before-Tax Income Needed at Retirement for Same Living Standard[c]	Target Replacement Rate[d]
(A)	(B)	(C)
$15,000	$12,276	82%
20,000	15,087	75%
25,000	17,872	71%
31,250	21,380	68%
40,000	27,055	68%
50,000	33,189	66%
60,000	39,720	66%
80,000	54,464	68%

[a]Assumes a married "one-worker" couple with retiree age 65 and spouse age 62, retiring in 1988.
[b]Final earnings.
[c]Takes account of differences in (1) pre- and postretirement taxes, (2) work- and age-related expenditures, and (3) savings rates.
[d](C) = (B) ÷ (A).
Source: Based on information in Bruce A. Palmer, "Tax Reform and Retirement Income Replacement Ratios," *Journal of Risk and Insurance* 56 (December 1989): 702–723.

How Much Would I Need to Save?

Using the appropriate replacement rate target, one can calculate the saving rate necessary to achieve a specified living standard in retirement. That is, one can determine what amount must be saved every year out of income up to the point of retirement. The year one begins saving can vary. One could decide to start saving at, say, age 25, or one could decide to postpone the task until age 45 and then save more over a shorter period. However, the longer one waits, the more difficult the job becomes.

Let us assume, for example, that one begins to save a certain percentage of annual income starting the first year of work and that one saves the same proportion of income throughout one's whole lifetime. Assume a life expectancy equal to the average life expectancy and retirement at age 65 and an investment return on savings of 4 percent.

Suppose one's goal is to provide retirement income equal to 60 to 70 percent replacement of average earnings during the last five years prior to retirement. *To do this, one would have to save about 20 percent of one's earnings each and every year.*[1]

An individual might desire, however, to save at a lower rate in the earlier years when earnings are relatively low compared to anticipated earnings later in his or her career. In this case, later savings rates would have to be much higher, and disposable income in the years prior to retirement would be lower.

Not everyone agrees that the most appropriate replacement rate adequacy standard is *the years before retirement*. In his book on social security, economist Michael J. Boskin (1986) argues that "with some intertemporal borrowing and saving going on, it does not make sense to compare a flow of income during retirement to a particularly biased small subset of years prior to retirement." Instead, Boskin argues that one should use the average of real (i.e., adjusted for inflation) earnings throughout the entire work career of the individual. But the standard of living measure resulting from *averaging* earnings over a lifetime will be much lower and, for most workers, would mean a sharp drop in living standards upon entering retirement. That is the major reason so many retirement planners and pension analysts reject such a measure.

THE ROLE OF PENSIONS

Our estimate of required individual savings assumed that one saved for retirement without the help of either public or private pension plans. In reality, pensions in the United States play a major role—we will argue, a dominant role—in providing retirement income. Before looking at the operation of the social security program and other pensions in the United States, we first need to understand the basic rationale behind their development.

The Great Depression of the 1930s went a long way toward exposing the great political lie of American welfare debates: that poverty was generally the result of the laziness or personal unworthiness of particular individuals. In the 1930s it became painfully obvious to everyone that this was not the case. Millions of jobless workers and their families suffered severe financial problems because of an economic catastrophe caused by factors unrelated to their own personal activities. Moreover, the cures for their problems lay almost entirely outside the range of their individual reactions.

Until this depression there had been a great deal of controversy in the United States with regard to the role of (and need for) some sort of public **pension** system. Many other countries had already followed the example of Germany, which established the first comprehensive social insurance program in the 1880s. But in the United States there was no widespread public support for public pensions until the economic upheavals of the

Great Depression. And although there was a scattered handful of employer-sponsored pensions provided by governments and private firms in existence during the first half of the 20th century, the significant expansion of these pension programs occurred in the relatively recent years of the 1950s and 1960s (see Chapter 7).

Thus, the social institution of pensions has had a relatively short history in the United States, and there has been continuing discussion and debate over just what are the appropriate roles to be played by both public and private pensions. We now look at this question and discuss some of the important goals for a good pension program; in later chapters we look at social security and employer-sponsored pensions as they currently operate in the United States.

Why Pensions?

Some of the debate over pensions has revolved around the advantages and disadvantages of public versus private pensions, but there are two more basic questions that first need to be discussed: Why is there a need for *any kind* of pension program, and should individuals be compelled (either by the government or an employer) to join a particular pension program?

Pensions can be an efficient and effective way of dealing with various sources of economic insecurity and risk. You will recall that earlier in this chapter we listed and discussed a number of uncertainties confronting individuals making economic preparations for retirement on their own. The first problem was that the individual does not know exactly when he or she will die—that is, how long a period to provide for. This means that any person (or family) preparing for retirement must assume the "worst"—a long life—and put aside enough money to take care of that eventuality; or one must be prepared to rely on private or public charity if one lives "too long" and one's own economic support is exhausted. But deciding how much to save is not enough. Another big question is how to manage the money and deal with financial risks. "The array of investment choices offered by financial institutions and markets often bewilders the ordinary citizen who is untutored in the fundamentals of finance" (Bodie, 1990). Moreover, private financial markets, because of problems of "adverse selection" (discussed later in the chapter), generally do not offer to individuals suitable retirement securities or offer them at disadvantageous prices.

A pension program managed by experts provides an attractive option—grouping individuals and money and utilizing a basic principle of insurance. If the number of individuals in a pension program is sufficiently large, mortality tables of life expectancy can be constructed that show estimates of average **life expectancy** at particular ages. Retirement preparation costs can then be geared to *average* life expectancy, with the "excess" payments of individuals who die before the average age going to those who live beyond it. The result is that no one has to pay more than they would need to put aside personally if it were known with certainty that they would live for a period of years equal to the average life expectancy, and the problems of adverse selection can be minimized.

The second problem discussed earlier in connection with individual retirement preparation is the lack of predictability of future income. For example, unexpected chronically low earnings, ill health, or periods of unemployment (as a result of a variety of factors) may make sufficient saving for retirement very difficult or even impossible. Also, health or employment problems may force an individual to retire unexpectedly and much earlier than was originally planned.

Collective arrangements to deal with this problem are not new. Since earliest times people have attempted to mitigate or eliminate economic insecurity by banding together in groups—families, tribes, associations, or guilds. Especially important has been the family. Throughout history individuals have relied heavily on family ties to provide protection from economic insecurity in old age. Even today in the United States, the family still remains an important source of economic and social support for many older persons when they become seriously ill; and in some other countries—particularly those less industrialized—the family still remains the major source of economic protection and security in old age.

The major problem with the family (and many other group associations) for sharing risk is that the number of people involved is relatively small. As Kenneth Boulding (1958) has observed, "it is when the 'sharing group' becomes too small to ensure that there will always be enough producers in it to support the unproductive that devices for insurance become necessary. When the 'sharing group' is small there is always a danger that sheer accident [illness, crop failure, unemployment, etc.] will bring the proportion of earners and nonearners to a level at which the group cannot function."

The commonly held view that in earlier America most of the aged lived in rural communities together with, or in close proximity to, adult children who provided financial support in the later years is not supported by the facts (Tibbitts, 1977). Nuclear parent-child families have always been the more common family type in the United States, and the three-generation family has been relatively rare.

Thus, the need for better collective arrangements to deal with the economic problems of old age has probably always been with us. The earliest available statistics on the economic status of the elderly prior to the establishment of pensions indicate that most of the aged in the United States were poor and that, in fact, many were completely destitute. The reasons that pension programs were not developed sooner are not en-

tirely clear, but various writers have pointed to the *relative* economic
prosperity throughout America's history, the country's decentralized gov-
ernmental structure, and (most important) the individualistic ethic of
much of the population.

Why Compulsory Pensions?

Individual self-reliance and voluntary preparation for retirement—together with family interdependence—dominated the early discussions of
old age security provision. It is now generally accepted, however, that
this is not the appropriate cornerstone of an income maintenance policy
for the aged. Instead, there is widespread support for relying on compulsory pensions. Pechman, Aaron, and Taussig (1968), in their classic
book on social security, give one reason:

There is widespread myopia with respect to retirement needs. Empirical evidence
shows that most people fail to save enough to prevent catastrophic drops in postretirement income. . . . Not only do people fail to plan ahead carefully for retirement, even in the later years of their working life, many remain unaware of
impending retirement needs. . . . In an urban, industrial society, government in-
tervention in the saving-consumption decision is needed to implement personal
preferences over the life cycle. There is nothing inconsistent in the decision to
undertake through the political process a course of action which would not be
undertaken individually through the marketplace.

Action to respond to the myopic behavior of individuals (i.e., their lack
of foresight and their poor planning) is often referred to as the *pater-
nalistic* rationale for compulsory pensions. However, it can be argued
that compulsion is also appropriate from a *self-interested* point of view.
A number of prominent American economists have pointed out a "free-
rider" issue. Boulding (1958) states the argument this way:

[If an individual] were rationally motivated, [he] would be aware of the evils that
might beset him, and would insure against them. It is argued, however, that many
people are not so motivated, and that hardly anyone is completely motivated by
these rational considerations, and that therefore under a purely voluntary system
some will insure and some will not. This means, however, that those who do not
insure will have to be supported anyway—perhaps at lower levels and in humiliating and respect-destroying ways—when they are in the nonproductive phase
of life, but that they will escape the burden of paying premiums when they are
in the productive phase. In fairness to those who insure voluntarily, and in order
to maintain the self-respect of those who would not otherwise insure, insurance
should be compulsory.

Laurence Kotlikoff (1989) expresses it in yet another way:

Suppose each person in society is altruistic and cares about the welfare of all other individuals. While each individual may be altruistic towards everyone else, those who fare better economically will end up transferring resources to those who fare poorly. Since each individual can anticipate such transfers in the event of bad luck, each individual will have an incentive to free ride on the generosity of others in considering how much to save.

Two empirical studies of this issue have been carried out, by Peter Diamond (1977) and Kotlikoff et al. (1982). Both studies conclude that without social security (or its equivalent), a substantial fraction of the population would be inadequately prepared for retirement. The data analyzed in both studies indicated that large numbers of the population, if left on their own, are likely to undersave for old age. Similarly, Bernheim (1993) concludes that most members of the Baby Boom generation are currently not saving enough to provide adequate income to supplement social security during retirement.

Legislating Mandatory Social Security

J. Douglas Brown, who helped draft the original social security program for the United States, writes in his book on the history of social security that the drafting group never seriously considered anything other than a compulsory program. The drafting group did worry, however, about whether a national compulsory program would be constitutional.

Hoping that it might be possible to avoid a court test of the constitutionality of social security, the drafting group did consider briefly a plan that would have permitted elective social security coverage by states and various industrial groups, but rejected it. According to Brown, the plan was "so cumbersome, ineffective, and actuarially unsound that no further attempt was made to avoid a head-on constitutional test of a truly workable system" (Brown, 1972).

As it turned out, during the debates that followed, the principal argument for compulsion was a financial one. It was argued that an optional coverage program would make it actuarially impossible to project both benefits (costs) and revenue. It was feared that this problem would create financial instability and make it difficult to guarantee adequate, equitable, and improved benefits as social security developed.

The original Social Security Act required participation by all workers in commerce and industry except those working for railroads. Railroad workers were exempted because similar legislation on their behalf had already been enacted in 1934. Although this original legislation was later declared unconstitutional, new (and still separate) railroad pension legislation was enacted in 1935 and 1937.

A number of groups, however, were specifically excluded from coverage—the major groups being farm workers, the self-employed, and government employees (including military personnel). Over the years, as coverage was extended to these groups, optional coverage was introduced for certain specific groups: employees of nonprofit institutions, state and local governments, and most clergymen. But in each case, coverage was not optional for the individual, depending instead on the collective decision of the organizational unit. Today almost all these groups are covered mandatorily by social security (see Chapter 4).

The decision of the United States to have a compulsory pension program is in no way unique. There is only one country in the world with a social security old age pension program that has designed a large amount of voluntary coverage into the program. In Great Britain workers must participate in a basic social insurance plan that provides a flat-rate benefit, but employers and/or individual workers can opt out of a second-tier earnings-related national pension (see Schulz, 1991 and 2000). Like the United States, many countries have special public pension programs for certain groups of workers (especially government employees), and many exclude from coverage certain groups (such as farm workers, the self-employed, or employees of very small firms). Some countries—for example, Ghana, the Federal Republic of Germany, Kuwait, Liberia, Peru, Uganda, and Zambia—have voluntary coverage, but these noncompulsory provisions *are all limited* to certain (usually small) groups in the country.

If we shift our attention from public pensions to *private* pensions in the United States, we find that the situation is not very different. Most of the workers who are covered (or not covered) by private pension plans have *not* achieved that status by personal election. Not all firms have established private pension plans for their employees, but almost all private pension schemes that have been set up are compulsory. Typically, once a worker joins a firm, he or she automatically becomes a member of the pension plan—sometimes after a short waiting period. There are a few private plans, however, that provide for an employee contribution out of salary; such plans sometimes make coverage optional.

In summary, we see that the usefulness of pensions in helping to provide for economic security in old age is generally accepted and that compulsory coverage remains a feature of both public and private programs.

PUBLIC OR PRIVATE?

While the overwhelming proportion of compulsory pension programs throughout the world are public, there are some countries that rely heavily on mandatory private provision. Australia has no social insurance program, relying instead on a relatively generous means-tested public program, together with mandated private pensions. Switzerland combines a first-tier social insurance program with mandatory employer-sponsored plans with specified minimums. Chile terminated its social insurance program for "new hires" in the early 1980s and mandated that 10 percent of every worker's earnings be deposited for retirement purposes into private investment institution accounts (regulated by the government).

If one wants to choose between mandating public or private plans (or evaluate a pension program or a pension proposal), what factors should be considered? With an institutional arrangement as complex as pensions, one can generate a long list of plan features that might be studied. Opinions differ widely as to which of these are most important. Moreover, there is little agreement on the relative weights that should be assigned to each feature when making an overall judgment about a particular pension plan. There are some important characteristics of pension plans, however, that would probably appear on everyone's list.

The Adequacy of Pension Benefits

Any discussion of a particular pension plan's adequacy must explicitly recognize the variety of means available to the individual (or society) in achieving a particular level of income in old age. A mandated pension plan is rarely designed to be the sole source of such income. Thus, in evaluating the adequacy of any particular pension benefit, it is necessary to relate such analysis to a general framework for evaluating individuals' general economic status and the variety of means available to achieve or change that status. How much are individuals expected to accumulate for their old age through personal savings? Are all individuals *able* to save for old age? What noncash programs (such as health insurance) are available to provide economic support? How large are both public and private pension benefits; who is currently covered by each; who should be covered?

There will never be complete agreement about the appropriate roles for the various means of providing income in old age—collective pension schemes are only one major way (see Table 3–1). Rather, it is almost certain that there will be continuing political debate and private discussion among bargaining groups over these matters. Out of such discussions come decisions on legislation, employment contracts, and employer policies in the area of pensions. As these decisions are made, it is possible to evaluate their economic implications for retirement income adequacy, estimating the contribution the resulting pensions will make to a particular individual's or group's goal.

The Certainty of Benefits

In addition to estimating or projecting the size of pension benefits, one can examine particular pension plans and estimate the degree of uncertainty associated with the *promised* benefits. At least five major contingencies should be evaluated:

1. Plan termination: what provisions can be established to ensure that the plan will survive economic or political adversity, such as a change in government (public pensions) or bankruptcy of the firm (private pensions)?
2. Political risk: Are the levels of benefits promised so high that it is unlikely that the promise can be kept in later years, given conservative **actuarial** projections?
3. Investment risk: to what extent will benefits ultimately paid out be dependent on the financial performance of invested funds and the skills of the investors?
4. Inflation: how well can the workers' future benefits and the pension recipients' actual benefits be protected from general increases in the level of prices?
5. Job termination: what happens to pension rights if a worker involuntarily or by choice stops working or changes jobs?
6. Survivor options: Are survivor benefits automatically provided or can they be elected? Who makes the decision (the worker or both the worker and the spouse) in cases where coverage is optional?

Flexibility and Discretion for Varying Conditions or Preferences

The larger the pension program in terms of people covered, the greater the differences in the circumstances and preferences of these participants are likely to be. It is generally desirable for pension plan provisions and rules not to be too rigid. The introduction of greater flexibility, however, usually results in greater administrative costs (see the section on administrative costs, below); and by complicating the program, flexibility often makes it more difficult for participants to become knowledgeable and to understand their pension program.

Adequate and Nondiscriminatory Coverage

The determination of eligibility for pension coverage is a very complex but an important factor in assessing pension options. Most people would agree that individuals in similar circumstances (e.g., working for the same employer) should not be arbitrarily excluded from coverage under a pension plan or excluded because of age, sex, race, and so forth. But the actual determination of who should be included is often difficult because of a variety of administrative, technical, political, and economic considerations. For example, should workers be excluded from protection because they do not (or cannot) work full time or work at home?

Equity

Whether a pension program is perceived as fair depends in large measure on how the program treats different individuals and how these individuals think they *should* be treated. The major issue around which equity questions usually cluster is financing: how much do the benefits received cost the individual in contrast to other benefit recipients and, possibly, nonrecipients (see Chapter 5)? Some pensions emphasize "individual equity," where benefits received are closely related to payments or taxes paid. Other pensions, especially public pensions, are designed to also redistribute some income among recipients to provide additional help to those more needy (often referred to as promoting "social adequacy").

Administrative Costs

Apart from the benefits paid out by a pension program, the level of administrative expenses can significantly influence the amount of benefits ultimately paid out. These costs can be separated into the following categories:

- **Customer Acquisition**: advertising, sales commissions, and other marketing expenses.
- **Fund Management Charges**: expenses associated with financial research, market analysis, remuneration to financial managers, transaction fees, profit returns to financial management firms, etc.
- **Business Maintenance Costs**: record keeping, client communication and reports, and general administrative expenses.
- **Adverse Selection Contingency Charges**: costs imposed on annuity purchasers, assuming that "adverse selection" will occur (i.e., that persons with low life expectancy will be more likely to take out annuities).
- **Costs of Switching**: charges that result from switching money from one fund account to another, early plan termination, investing in multiple funds, maintenance of inactive funds, etc.

Thus, Boulding (1958) has argued that one valid criterion for choosing between private and public programs is whether there can be significant economies of scale in their operation:

If there are these economies—that is, if the cost of administering the insurance declines with every increase in the amount of insurance written—then a state monopoly will almost inevitably be cheaper than a number of competing private companies. . . . We may venture a hypothesis that where the operations of insurance are fairly routine, the case for state or national monopoly is stronger than where the operations involve great difficulties of definition of rights.

There is now a large literature that documents the high administrative costs of private pension plans (for example, James et al., 1999).

Simplicity and Ease of Understanding

It is important that individuals know whether they are covered by a pension plan, what the conditions of entitlement are, what benefits they (or their family) can or will receive, what the risks of losing benefits are, and various other facts about the plan. Over the years a large amount of evidence has accumulated that indicates a great lack of knowledge and much misinformation among workers in the United States with regard to their own expected pensions, both public and private. As the number and variety of pension programs grow and many of these programs become more complicated, this problem will also grow. Therefore, in reviewing existing programs or proposals for pension changes, the complexity of the program should be considered. An assessment should be made of the resultant impact on the employees' ability to understand the pension program and to incorporate it realistically into their preretirement planning.

Integration

A particular pension plan is almost always only one of a number of collective programs operating to provide economic security. It is not sufficient to view a particular pension program in isolation from these other programs. For example, eligibility or benefit determination under one program is sometimes related to benefits received from another program (Schulz and Leavitt, 1983). The value of social security pension benefits to the elderly is affected by the fact that some benefits received by beneficiaries with high incomes are subject to the federal income tax (see Chapter 5). Employer-sponsored pensions paid to workers are sometimes reduced as a result of the social security benefits they receive.

Economic Impact

While primary concern is generally on the impact pensions have on individuals, attention also needs to be given to their impact on the economy as a whole. Major concerns are the impact pensions have on saving, work incentives, government fiscal burdens, and international competition.

One issue, for example, has received a lot of attention in recent years. With the aging of the population (see Chapter 8), there is concern that the social security pension program decreases saving and impacts negatively on economic growth. Economists have long theorized that people would accumulate savings for old age and then spend down most or all those savings before the end of life (the "**lifecycle hypothesis**"). If true, the aging of a population should be associated with a reduction in aggregate saving (all other things held constant), decreasing investment, and collective programs like social security might add to the problem by discouraging the amount of personal saving (discussed further below).

Some people (including many economists) make statements that seem to argue that the impact of population aging and social security on saving is the most, or one of the most, important considerations in evaluating policy options relating to growth (e.g., Gramlich, 1997). But personal saving is only one of many sources of national saving, and there are many other factors, as important or more important, determining how fast a nation grows—technological change being one of them (Schulz, 1999).

WHAT MIX OF PUBLIC AND PRIVATE PENSIONS?

Despite the fact that the first pension plans were established about a century ago, there is still controversy about the relative virtues of public versus private pensions and what the ideal combination of the two types should be. There is great diversity in the mix of pensions in various countries, but there are fewer countries where private programs assume a major role than there are countries that rely primarily on public pensions.

In the United States, the well-known conservative economist Milton Friedman has been a consistent critic of social security and one of the few academics to advocate complete abolition of public pensions. He argues, "Social security combines a highly regressive tax with largely indiscriminate benefits and, in overall effect, probably redistributes income from lower to higher income persons. I believe that it serves no essential social function. Existing commitments make it impossible to eliminate it overnight, but it should be unwound and terminated as soon as possible" (Cohen and Friedman, 1972).[2]

There has been very little public support for Friedman's extreme position. Instead, the more common negative view toward social security advocates a smaller role for it and, consequently, seeks to limit any future growth of the program—either by expansion of real benefits or by adding additional functions.

ARGUMENTS AGAINST AND FOR SOCIAL SECURITY

Over the years concern about further expansion of the role of social security and raising social security benefits has not been the major issue raised by critics. Rather, most of the concern and criticism has centered on the way benefits have been financed. In the chapters that follow, we discuss many of the issues connected with social security financing and evaluate their merits. In general, critics assert:

1. That social security places a heavy tax burden on the poor and near-poor (see Chapter 5).
2. That there are very great differences in contributions paid in versus benefits received among different socioeconomic groups and between current and future generations (see Chapter 5).
3. That individuals lose control over money put aside for old age and could earn higher rates of return if allowed to invest it privately (see Chapter 5).
4. That current benefit levels are unsustainable in future years and are currently a major reason that federal budget deficits cannot be eliminated (see Chapters 5 and 8).

On the positive side, six major arguments have been advanced in its favor:

1. That social security can more readily redistribute income ("target" income) to those most in need without the problems arising from means-testing.
2. That lifetime **annuities** can be offered more easily and more cheaply, overcoming the "adverse selection" problem of private markets and protecting the individual (and often the spouse) from running out of money if they live an exceptionally long period of time.
3. That the (per capita) nonbenefit costs of social insurance are much lower than the costs for private pension administration, fund investment, mobility, disclosure to recipients, supervision and regulation, and reinsurance.
4. That it is easier to make social security pensions both inflation-proof—adjusting for inflation at and during retirement—and adjustable for economic growth.
5. That it is relatively easy to cover all workers and provide complete portability of credits under social security, whereas private pensions present formidable problems in this regard (unless coverage is mandated by the government).
6. That **defined benefit plans** like social security pensions place on the sponsoring organization—not the individual—the risks involved in the investment of funds, the inflation protection of reserves, and the providing of adequate (or expected) benefits.

Redistribution

It is generally agreed that it is a legitimate role of government to adjust the distribution of income in response to the society's general values, equity considerations, and perceived needs of special population groups (such as the poor). Social security programs often embody explicit redistributional goals. Thus, the 1937–1938 Advisory Council on Social Security (1939) emphasized in its report "the need to revise the existing old-age insurance program in the direction of fitting the structure of benefits more closely to the basic needs of our people." And the legislated amendments based on that report introduce a number of redistributive mechanisms still with us today (e.g., spouse, children's, and widow benefits).

One of the most important decisions made when social security was first legislated in the United States was to redistribute income through a public program from people in the labor force to retired workers who had contributed very little into the program (see Chapters 4 and 5). President Roosevelt and the Congress were reacting to the high unemployment of workers at all ages and the existing poverty among both older workers and the elderly already retired. The result has been large transfers that exceed payroll taxes for almost all individuals who have retired since payments began in 1940.[3]

It is common for writers to ignore the fact that historically many private pensions also have redistributed income. Typically, when **defined benefit plans** were started by employers, older workers received "past service credits" for years worked before the plan was introduced. The result was much higher benefits for these workers, paid out of the lower take-home pay of those workers still on the job.

Annuities and Adverse Selection

We discussed previously the problem that individuals do not know exactly when they will die and how this complicates retirement planning. Annuity contracts can be purchased from private companies that promise a specified amount of money until one's death (and, optionally, the death of a designated survivor). However, there is a tendency for people who have higher-than-average life expectancies to be more frequent buyers of such policies if they are optional. This "adverse selection" problem results in annuity purchase terms that are highly unfavorable to many individuals. In fact, Friedman and Warshansky (1988) conclude that private market annuities are not a good buy for the average individual.

Social security (and compulsory collective private plans) offer an effective way to deal with the adverse selection problem. By requiring everyone to participate, the adverse selection problem is avoided. If participation in social security were optional, as some people have advocated, it would greatly complicate the financing issue—as the early policymakers were quick to point out when the basic form for social security was being debated.

Administrative Costs

Although the structure of social security in the United States is far from uncomplicated, there are many aspects of its operation that are relatively simple. Consequently, the collection and benefit payout process permits the extensive use of computers. This in turn permits the handling of large numbers of claims in a way that allows significant economies of large-scale operation to be realized. Administrative expenses were around 1 percent of payroll contributions for the old age and survivors program (OASI). These costs are in sharp contrast to private life insurance costs, which are 12 to 14 percent of annual benefits (American Council of Life Insurance, 1992).

The low expenses associated with OASI are far different from public perceptions. A Roper opinion poll found that only 2 percent of those interviewed thought that social security administrative costs were less than 10 percent of contributions collected (U.S. Social Security Administration, 1981). Amazingly, the median respondent estimate was 52 percent!

Comparing costs between social security and private pensions is complicated by the fact that social security financing in the United States is essentially on a pay-as-you-go basis, whereas American private pensions are nearly always funded (see Chapter 7). Private pension funding costs generated as a result of financial investment on behalf of employers (and, in part, indirectly benefiting the economy) have no analogous counterpart in the U.S. social security program. Also, another difference between the two types of pensions is the fact that employers and the Department of the Treasury give many "free" administrative services to the social security system.

Pension Adjustments for Inflation

Another important argument made in favor of public pensions is their ability, in contrast to private plans, to deal with the need to respond to inflation and economic growth. The problem of inflation has plagued pension programs since their inception. All countries have had to struggle with this problem, continually adjusting pension programs and benefits to offset increases in price levels. Inflation has varied, for example, from the catastrophic rate in post–World War I Germany (which completely wiped out the monetary value of that country's social security reserves and benefits) to the relatively mild price increases averaging less than 2 percent in the United States during the 1958–1968 period, to the much higher rates in later years (including double-digit inflation in 1974 and 1979–1980).

Gradually, most industrialized countries (including the United States in 1972) have introduced some sort of automatic benefit adjustment mechanisms into the social security program to deal more effectively with the inflation problem. In contrast, private pension plans, with few exceptions, virtually ignore the need for *regularized* adjustment mechanisms (see Chapter 7). This results, in large part, because of employers' unwillingness to make financial commitments based on guesses about future price levels and the fear that the cost of these adjustments may be too high. In addition, most private pension analysts feel that it is very difficult, if not impossible, for private companies to devise an acceptable inflation-proofing mechanism without government assistance (see the differing views in Munnell, 1979; Bodie, 1990).

It is much easier for governments to deal with the inflation problem, given their inherent taxing powers and their ability to minimize the size of the monetary fund necessary to guarantee the financial soundness of the pension program. A pay-as-you-go system, for example, makes it easier to increase revenues to pay for inflation-adjusted pensions because the earnings base is also rising with inflation. In contrast, many securities in a reserve fund will not adjust upward in value with the inflation.

The actual history of social security programs in various countries dealing with inflation supports that conclusion; even after runaway inflations, countries have been able to adjust pensions to the current price level. In addition, public pension programs have shown an ability to devise equitable ways of permitting retired persons to share systematically in the real growth of the country. Social security programs in some countries—such as Belgium, Canada, Norway, and Germany—provide for automatic or semiautomatic adjustments in *real* benefit levels. Still others adjust systematically by various ad hoc processes.

Coverage

It has proven to be a relatively easy matter in all *industrial* countries to extend social security coverage to large segments of the labor force. Coverage of agricultural workers and the self-employed has presented problems, especially in developing countries. Coverage in industrialized countries, however, is now virtually universal.

In contrast, as we discuss in Chapter 7, extension of private pension coverage beyond current levels presents serious problems. It has been especially difficult to extend coverage to workers in small firms. As a result, a sizable proportion of the workforce in countries with private pensions is not covered by such pensions and is not likely to be covered.

One possible solution to the coverage problem is for the government to require that all employers provide private pension benefits. In fact,

Holzmann (1991) concludes his review of experience worldwide by stating: "International evidence suggests that, unless mandated, massive tax preferences are required to induce the establishment of complementary [private] schemes on a large scale."

Some countries have used the mandating approach (e.g., Switzerland and Australia). As we noted earlier, in Great Britain employers or individuals themselves must provide pension protection at least equal to a government earnings-related scheme or participate in the government program. In 1981 the President's Commission on Pension Policy recommended mandatory private coverage for the United States, but the recommendation received little support in Congress.

Who Assumes the Risks?

One type of pension that has become increasingly popular in the private sector is **defined contribution plans**. These are discussed at length in Chapter 7. Here, however, we want to emphasize the difference between these plans and others with regard to risk.

A typical defined contribution plan sets up an *individual account* for each person, with contributions from the employer and/or the individual going into that account. Pension benefits are then determined solely by the amounts contributed and the investment return on that money. As with other types of pension plans, good financial planning requires that someone make estimates of how much total contribution is required to insure an adequate income in retirement. But once a plan accumulation target is estimated, many things can happen between the years of accumulation and the time when the funds will need to be used. Inflation, unemployment, job change, financial market fluctuations, "bad investments," and so on can result in missing the retirement income target.

In defined *contribution* plans, the individual must assume these risks. In defined *benefit* plans, the risks are assumed by the sponsor. If the stock market "crashes," it is the employer (in the latter case) who must put more money into the plan to pay benefits—unlike the *individual* responsibility built into defined contribution plans. When the Soviet Union collapsed, the new Russia (and other eastern European countries) was hit by a hyperinflation that doubled and tripled prices daily. Individual Russians saw the value of their savings in banks evaporate. But it was the government that had the responsibility to keep paying pensions to retirees, adjusting these defined benefit plans to compensate for the now much higher price levels.

As Lawrence Thompson (1998) observes:

When unforseen problems do arise, prospective retirees under defined benefit plans are usually not required to absorb the entire impact of any necessary adjustment. . . . Typically, the impact of correcting the imbalance [that results between receipts and expenditures] is spread among current retirees, future retirees and other contributors, with each absorbing a fraction of the total impact. In contrast, under the funded, defined contribution approach, all unanticipated economic changes are reflected fully in changes in the retirement assets and future retirement income of each participant.

ARGUMENTS IN SUPPORT OF PRIVATE PENSIONS

There are two major arguments supporting the existence and expansion of private pensions[4]:

1. That social security, because of its broad coverage, must remain very uniform in its benefit provisions, while private pensions are more flexible and can be tailored to meet differing situations and conditions (e.g., hazardous conditions) of various industries, particular firms, or different occupational groups
2. That private pensions are vital to ensure the saving necessary to provide sufficient investment in a growing economy.

Flexibility

On the one hand, a private pension can be a flexible management tool. As Charles A. Siegfried (1970) of the Metropolitan Life Insurance Company has observed, "A pension plan can be devised to attract and hold employees or it can be devised to facilitate the separation of employees from employment." On the other hand, pension objectives may vary to accommodate different employee wishes and aspirations, these being determined by decisions of the employers (unilaterally or in consultation with workers) or by collective bargaining.

The late Edwin S. Hewitt (1970), a well-known pension consultant, arguing the case for private pensions before the Senate Special Committee on Aging, emphasized the flexibility factor:

It is extraordinary how flexible an instrument for providing adequate security the private plan has proved to be. There are two kinds of flexibility and perhaps this fact is underrated when we oppose what private plans are doing.

First is their flexibility in terms of adapting to different needs. Very real differences in security problems exist among different companies, different industries, different age groups. . . .

The second dimension is the flexibility between periods of time. Private plans have exhibited amazing flexibility to make their provisions meet the different needs that a group may have at different times.

The initial job of most pension plans when first established is to concentrate on retirement income for the older worker, hence the importance of *past service benefits*. As plans become better funded, they tend to branch into other areas.

Variety increases as plans are able to spend more money and give attention to tailormade benefits to meet specific needs. (emphasis added)

Pension Saving and Capital Formation

A much more controversial argument made in favor of private pensions is their role in the mobilization of national saving for economic investment and growth (see the critique in Schulz, 1999). Charles Moeller, an economist for the Metropolitan Life Insurance Company, argued the positive aspects this way:

The key to any nation's economic growth is its ability to direct substantial portions of its output into real investment, i.e., to defer current consumption of output through saving and to permit investment in *productive* facilities for use in future production processes. . . . In effect, what pension funding operations and other forms of contractual saving do is to improve the efficiency and stability of the capital markets. . . .

The importance of the saving function for private pension plans cannot be too strongly emphasized. The need for encouraging the accumulation of individual saving flows and for recirculating these funds back into the economy through the investment process has been spotlighted by the dramatic events of recent years including the "crunch" of 1966 and the "liquidity crisis" of 1970. (Moeller, 1972)

It is a common misconception that there is a direct relationship between the personal saving of individuals (for retirement and other reasons) and economic growth. While there is a need for saving to facilitate investment in the economy, there is a variety of ways such saving can be accumulated. Hence, there is no agreement on the need or importance of any one accumulation process, such as through personal saving or private pensions.

In the key growth sector of *corporate* production, the overwhelming majority of funds needed to finance new investment comes from the *internal* funds saved by the corporations themselves. "If you subtract housing investment from total capital investment funds, more than 99 percent of real capital investment funds took the form of corporate *retained earnings* or *depreciation allowance* in 1973" (Thurow, 1976; emphasis added). That result would not be very different today.

Other possible sources of savings are unincorporated business, individuals, and government budget surpluses. Moreover, there is disagreement over the extent to which there is any insufficiency of saving in the United States relative to investment opportunities and the willingness of business to undertake investment. Economist Arthur Okun (1975) observed that "the specter of depressed saving is not only empirically implausible but logically fake. . . . The nation can have the level of saving and investment it wants with more or less income redistribution, so long as it is willing to twist some other dials."

A *New York Times* article reviewing this issue during a recession period reiterated the caution of many economists that even if the savings rate rises, this will not necessarily increase investment, productivity, and growth. Quoting economist Robert M. Solow, the article stated that "increasing savings only matters when what is limiting investment is capacity, and that is not the case now. The problem affecting investment now is one of profitability. How will more saving make the automobile or steel industry more profitable?" (Arenson, 1981).

Franco Modigliani (1987), recipient of a Nobel Prize in economics, states, "one of the interesting implications of the **life-cycle theory** [of savings] suggests that when a country needs capital to drive rapid growth, capital will be forthcoming." Modigliani was echoed by the *Wall Street Journal* (1990) in an article titled "Investment opportunities create their own saving."

Currently, there is also disagreement among economists about the impact of social security on personal savings. Economists Martin Feldstein (1974) was the first to present statistical evidence indicating that growing social security benefits may have reduced total personal savings in the United States. A great deal of additional research and debate followed Feldstein's original article. For example, Barro (1978) argued that evolving social security has changed the pattern of voluntary intergenerational transfers (from parents to children and vice versa). Barro presented statistical evidence (disputed by Feldstein) indicating that this changing pattern of family transfers offsets the savings impact of social security. Lesnoy and Leimer (1981) then demonstrated a serious error in Feldstein's original study and reached the opposite conclusion from the same data. Reviewing these and other studies, Munnell (1982), Aaron (1982), and the U.S. Congressional Budget Office (1993) conclude that *there is little evidence that the pay-as-you-go social security system has significantly depressed personal saving in the United States.* Feldstein (1994), however, continues to hold to his original position.

Finally, it should be noted that the generation of savings through pensions is not limited to private pensions. Public social security reserve funds can also be generated. For example, there is a debate in the United States currently over whether to allow the OASDI trust funds to grow dramatically over the next two decades investing some of the reserves in the stock market (see Chapter 5). In Sweden the financing rates for the social security program were deliberately set high enough to help generate savings in the Swedish economy. In fact, public pension reserves may be a particularly attractive means of mobilizing savings in developing countries where private pensions are virtually non-existent.

THE PENSION MIX IN VARIOUS COUNTRIES

If we look at the pension programs currently existing in various industrialized countries, we find that there is a tendency to rely heavily either on public pensions or on some sort of private/public combination *with extensive regulation of the private sector* (Schulz and Myles, 1990). In countries that rely heavily on private pensions, the tendency is for the private and public pension programs to be closely coordinated by a large number of complex legislative and administrative mechanisms and regulations. In France, for example, it is difficult to make a distinction between social security and the widespread private pension programs, given the elaborate coordinating mechanisms that have been established.

In the United States, both public and private pension plans have assumed a growing share of responsibility for providing retirement income needs. The indications are that reliance on this collective approach is not likely to diminish in the future. But it is not yet clear how this collective responsibility ultimately will be divided between public and private institutions.

PLANNING FOR RETIREMENT

President John F. Kennedy once remarked that "it is not enough for a great nation merely to have added new years to life—our objective must also be to add new life to years." For those approaching retirement, the challenge is to take advantage of those years in a creative and fulfilling manner. There is little doubt that preretirement planning by individuals can help many achieve this end.

As we see in this chapter, however, the problems involved in preretirement planning are very complex. Most people seem to have a natural inclination to live for today and avoid thinking about old age and death. Hence, they give very little systematic thought to the financial issues of old age until they come face to face with them—when it is usually too late. The flood of criticism about the adequacy, financial viability, and equity of social security and private pensions (regardless of their merits) creates confusion and distrust among workers—further discouraging early thinking about retirement preparation.

As we have emphasized, even if you want to plan, the task is very difficult. Moreover, with the growth of personal retirement savings through employer-sponsored pensions and a variety of savings schemes encouraged by government tax incentives (discussed in Chapter 7), increasing numbers of individuals must make major investment decisions about large sums of retirement money. Ready to help with those decisions are growing numbers of investment salesmen, brokers, and financial counselors.

It is common to hear in the media about frauds that have wiped out the personal retirement savings of older people. However, at 1993 hearings by the U.S. Senate Special Committee on Aging, the securities administrator for the state of Maine, Stephen Diamond, pointed out that focusing on the frauds that get media attention ignores a much bigger and more basic problem. Diamond (1993) argued that "investment abuses are not always the work of con artists who are engaged in criminal fraud. . . . In Maine, the elderly lose more money from abuses committed by licensed persons selling lawful products. Much of this results from what I call . . . soft-core fraud, or from broker incompetence." For example, over 23,000 investors were sold $250 million worth of unsecured bonds in the Lincoln Savings/American Continental scandal (Cohen, 1993). Many were elderly persons investing retirement savings.

FINDING SOMEONE YOU CAN TRUST

Finding a good, reliable financial advisor is not an easy task. However, there are a number of key steps that can be taken that will dramatically reduce the possibility of major problems:

- One must be willing to take the time necessary to find a good person; one should not simply follow the suggestion of a relative or friend. Asking people for suggestions is a reasonable place to a begin but is no substitute for an in-depth investigation of a variety of options.

- One should interview more than one advisor. The first person a person talks to is almost certainly going to sound good, especially since one has no basis for comparison.

- A list of questions should be prepared. A potential advisor should be asked about his or her investment philosophy, their planning approach, the methods that will be used, the extent of their training, whether they are "certified" (and by whom), the final product that will be provided, and the fees the client will have to pay.

- A planner's prior work should be assessed by asking to see copies of plans done for other people and talking to some of the planner's recent clients. (Although the planner is not going to refer you to dissatisfied clients, you will find it useful to learn what prior clients see as the planner's strong and weak points.)

- The background of an advisor should always be investigated thoroughly, checking for prior legal or certification problems. A copy of both parts of Form ADV (the background materials that most advisors file with the Securities and Exchange Commission) should be requested.

- Before talking to a financial planner, clients need to do some preliminary organization of their financial information and particular situations, and they also need to think about their financial goals. For example, preparing a list of current assets and liabilities is a must.

Women and Financial Planning

Although studies show (e.g., Alcon, 1999) that both men and women lack knowledge about financing retirement, it is particularly hard for women to manage the financial planning challenge. Adequate income in retirement is especially difficult for women to achieve because of traditional sex biases in the workplace, the complexity of women's roles, their longer life expectancy, lower pension coverage, inadequate survivors' benefits, and a long tradition of women not "managing the family finances."

Midlife and older women are at a special disadvantage. Given traditional gender roles over their lifetimes, they have had less income and accumulated less wealth. Often they have left managing the money to someone else and have made the care of others a higher priority than planning and saving for their own future. When women become involved in issues of investing and financial planning, whether by choice or necessity, some become profoundly uncomfortable and feel unprepared.

A survey of 500 women ages 50 and older (National Center on Women & Aging, 1998) found that women do not feel knowledgeable about "the investments that count." They were asked about seven types of financial assets and how they rated their understanding of them (see Table 3–3). While comfortable with CDs and savings bonds, they reported low understanding with regard to the others. For example, mutual funds were designed to allow people with even small amounts of money to invest in a greater range of investment opportunities, while reducing risk and the amount of sophistication required to make sound decisions. Yet less than one-third of the women indicated they had significant understanding of them.

In many companies today there are 401(k) plans requiring workers to make individual investment decisions. To make informed decisions related to the money going into these plans, workers obviously need to understand the various trade-offs between return and risk among various investments. However, Table 3–3 indicates that most of the older women surveyed felt that they lacked the personal expertise to perform this critical task.

Employer Assistance

In recent years, the major efforts to deal with this problem have shifted from the individual to private and public collective efforts. Business managers, labor leaders, and gerontologists all bring different perspectives to the question of how we should deal with and improve preretirement planning. Their primary goal, however, is similar: to generate a greater awareness among workers and their spouses of the problems and poten-

Table 3–3
Older Women's Knowledge of Various Financial Assets

Financial Options	Not at All Knowledgeable 1	2	Scale (1-5) 3	4	Extremely Knowledgeable 5	Total Percent
Bank Certificates of Deposit (CDs)	14	11	22	26	27	100%
U.S. Savings Bonds	14	12	21	27	26	100
Mutual Funds	27	20	24	21	8	100
Stocks	34	19	24	16	7	100
401(k/403(b)	40	18	19	15	8	100
Annuities	41	18	22	12	7	100
Corporate and Municipal Bonds	48	25	18	7	2	100

Source: National Center on Women & Aging, *Financial Challenges for Mature Women* (Waltham, Mass.: Heller Graduate School, Brandeis University, 1998). Reprinted with permission.

tials of approaching old age and to assist where appropriate in the preparation for successful retirement. For example, 67 percent of large
companies surveyed by Charles D. Spencer & Associates had some kind
of program designed to ease the transition to retirement (Taplin, 1989).

Many employers, however, offer little more than booklets with retirement and benefit information. Other employers, however, organize programs that often last two or more days and cover company benefits,
health care cost issues, social security, legal considerations, and topics
on financial planning (taxes, investments, and estate issues). The Spencer
survey (Taplin, 1989) found the **median** length of time for an ongoing
company program was 10 hours and often covered (in addition to the
economic topics listed) issues related to nutrition, housing alternatives,
leisure activities, postretirement employment, and psychological adjustment to retirement.

The challenge is (1) to increase the availability of preretirement education to persons seeking such information; (2) to improve the quality
of available programs; and (3) to encourage people to begin preparing
for retirement at a relatively early age. Unfortunately, a number of studies
have reported that minorities and those with less education are not as
active in preparing for retirement. As Ferraro (1990) points out, "Those
who might benefit most from such planning are among those least likely
to pursue it."

Individual financial planning for retirement is a difficult and complex
matter. Planning shortly before retirement (even ten or fifteen years before) is usually too late. In the chapters that follow, we look at the options
for dealing with this dilemma.

CHAPTER 3 HIGHLIGHTS

What are the mechanisms available for providing economic support in
retirement? How should choices be made among the alternatives? In this
chapter we emphasized the following points:

1. While there are many ways of providing for retirement, a major choice is between personal saving and collective pension programs (both public and private).

2. Planning for retirement by individuals is complicated by (1) a variety of uncertainties, such as future health and employment possibilities; and (2) the
   need to take action far in advance of the actual event.

3. A reasonable planning goal for a *middle-income* worker is retirement income
   equal to about 65 to 80 percent of preretirement income—the percent depending on the level of preretirement income.

4. The principal arguments for making pension coverage compulsory are myopic
   behavior and preventing the "free rider" situation.

5. Assessments of pension alternatives should be based on differences in adequacy, the certainty of receipt, flexibility, coverage, equity, costs, simplicity, integration mechanisms, and economic impact.

6. Greater flexibility in the design of private plans is one of this mechanism's major assets.

7. Advocates for social security emphasize its ability to redistribute income, deal with adverse selection, compensate for inflation, and provide widespread coverage and portable benefits.

8. A more controversial criterion for assessing pension alternatives is the impact of particular types of pensions on national saving.

SUGGESTED READINGS

Bernheim, B. Douglas. *The Vanishing Nest Egg: Reflections on Saving in America*. New York: Priority Press, 1991. A very readable discussion about low savings rates in the United States and how this country compares with other countries. Factors influencing savings behavior are reviewed, and proposals to change policies are presented.

Blinder, Alan B. "Why Is the Government in the Pension Business?" In S. M. Wachter, ed., *Social Security and Private Pensions*. Lexington, Mass.: Lexington Books, 1988, pp. 17–34. Blinder reviews arguments in three areas: (1) correcting market failure, (2) redistributing income, and (3) paternalism.

Cates, J. R. *Insuring Inequality*. Ann Arbor, Mich.: University of Michigan Press, 1983; Jill Quadagno, *The Transformation of Old Age Security, Class and Politics in the American Welfare State*. Chicago: University of Chicago Press, 1988; and C. L. Weaver, *The Crisis in Social Security*. Durham, N.C.: Duke Press Policy Studies, 1982. Three very different views regarding the origins of social security in the United States.

Chilton, David. *The Wealthy Barber: Everyone's Common-Sense Guide to Becoming Financially Independent*, 2nd ed. Waterloo, Ontario, Canada: Prima Publishing for Financial Awareness Corp., 1996. The place to start for personal retirement planning.

Esping-Andersen, Gostta. *The Three Worlds of Welfare Capitalism*. Princeton, N.J.: Princeton University Press, 1990. An excellent comparative discussion of the origins of social security in Europe and the United States and differences in the resulting "welfare states."

Modigliani, F. "The Role of Intergenerational Transfers on Life Cycle Saving in the Accumulation of Wealth"; and L. Kotlikoff, "Intergenerational Transfers and Saving." *Journal of Economic Perspectives* 2(2) (Spring 1988): 15–40, 47–58. Two excellent articles providing literature reviews and assessments of empirical studies in the areas of personal and intergenerational saving.

National Center on Women & Aging. *Financial Challenges for Mature Women*. Waltham, Mass.: Heller School, Brandeis University, 1998. Findings from a survey of 500 women on financial knowledge, financial planning, and experience with "financial planners."

Schulz, James H. "Saving, Growth, and Social Security." In R. N. Butler, L. K.

Grossman, and M. R. Oberlink, eds., *Life in an Older America*. New York: Century Foundation Press, 1999. Discusses the impact of social security and population aging on economic growth.

Schulz, James H., and John Myles. "Old Age Pensions: A Comparative Perspective." In Robert H. Binstock and Linda George, eds., *Handbook of Aging and the Social Sciences*, 3rd ed. New York: Academic Press, 1990, pp. 398–414. This article provides an international overview of public and private pensions' origins and characteristics.

Chapter 4

Social Security: Old Age and Survivors' Benefits

The first American social security benefit ever paid was $22.54 a month and was received by Miss Ida Fuller, a retired law firm secretary, in early 1940. Miss Fuller (who died in 1975) lived to be over 100, paid into the program less than $100, and over the years received an amazing $22,000 in social security benefits.

Ida Fuller's experience with social security dramatically illustrates one of the major benefits of public pensions discussed in Chapter 3. One of the reasons Miss Fuller received much more than she paid into social security was that she lived far beyond the average **life expectancy**; pensions are designed to pay more to those who live an "unexpectedly" long life.

As we discuss further in Chapter 5, there is another reason that many Americans like Ida Fuller have received *significantly more in benefits than they have contributed*. Because the income of most of the elderly was so low, Congress decided to reduce in the early years of the program the eligibility requirements (i.e., the required length of the work/tax payment period) to help deal immediately with the widespread poverty. As a result, while the eligibility requirement was rising, most individuals received benefits that far exceeded the **payroll taxes** they paid.

Created in 1935, the United States social security system has grown over the years to be one of the biggest operations of the federal government. This chapter focuses on the benefit structure for retirees and survivors; the next chapter discusses how the benefits are financed; and Chapter 6 looks at the federal Medicare, disability, and SSI programs.

THE CHANGING SOCIAL SECURITY SYSTEM

The Social Security Act of 1935 established the basic federal old-age benefits program (OAI) and a federal-state system of unemployment insurance. Various key events occurred in succeeding years. In 1939, survivors' and dependents' benefits were added (OASI). In 1956, social security was expanded to include disability insurance to protect severely disabled workers (OASDI). In 1965, Medicare was added, establishing a comprehensive health program for the elderly (OASDHI).[1] In 1972, automatic cost-of-living increases were introduced, and **indexing** of earnings used to compute benefits was legislated in 1977. Total annual OASDHI expenditures have grown from less than $1 billion in 1950 to over $700 billion in 1998. Between its inception and today, over $8 trillion has been paid out in benefits.

Encouragement of Retirement

Paradoxically, the major motivating force behind the passage of the Social Security Act in 1935 was probably not the provision of adequate retirement income but the creation of jobs. Passed in a period that at one point witnessed more than a quarter of the labor force without jobs, the social security legislation was one of many New Deal laws seeking to respond to the need for job creation and relief for those out of work. The 1935 legislation encouraged the creation of state-administered unemployment insurance programs to help unemployed workers find work and to provide them with financial support while they looked. Old-age pensions were promised in future years to help the elderly financially but were also legislated to *encourage older workers to leave or remain out of the workforce*. Old-age benefits to otherwise eligible persons age 65 or over were made conditional on meeting a "retirement test." In the original 1935 act, benefits were *not* to be paid to persons receiving any "covered wages from regular employment."

Regular employment, however, was not specifically defined in the 1935 act. In the 1939 social security amendments, the retirement test was made less ambiguous; it specified that no benefits would be paid to anyone earning more than $14.99 a month in covered employment. Over the years the earnings exemption rules have varied by age, and the level has been increased periodically by specific increments. Currently the test only applies to persons younger than age 65.

Changes

Over the past three and a half decades there have been a great many adjustments in the social security system. However, except for the introduction of disability insurance in 1956, medical insurance (Medicare) in 1965, and automatic cost-of-living benefit adjustments in 1972, there have been few, if any, major programmatic changes. Three other historical developments are of particular importance, however.

First, as a result of a series of legislated liberalizations there was an expansion of persons covered by the system. Over the years successive major groups of workers have been brought into the system: certain self-employed, farm, and domestic workers and employees of charitable, educational, and religious organizations (1950), most other self-employed (1954), members of the uniformed services (1956), Americans employed by foreign governments or international organizations (1960), physicians (1965), new federal employees (1983), and state and local government employees not under a state or local pension (1990). Currently, the only major groups of gainfully employed workers not covered are: (1) federal employees hired before 1984[2]; (2) about 20 percent of state and local government employees[3]; (3) farm and domestic workers who do not earn or work "enough"; and (4) self-employed persons with very low net earnings (generally less than $400 per year) or ministers who opt out for religious reasons.[4]

Second, adjustment of the pension formula's preretirement earnings using a **wage index** was introduced in the 1970s to stabilize the earnings replacement rates provided by benefits. The objective of this indexing was to provide the same **replacement rates** at the time of retirement to successive cohorts of workers with equivalent average monthly earnings over their working lifetimes (relative to the average earnings of the economy). At the same time, cost-of-living adjustments were introduced to protect benefits from inflation occurring during retirement. (Benefit payments are adjusted every December to reflect increases in the Consumer Price Index.)

Finally, "higher income" beneficiaries since 1984 have been required to pay income tax on a portion of their social security benefits (see Chapter 5).

Financing

Although there is a detailed discussion of financing in Chapter 5, some initial remarks are appropriate here. From the very beginning, social security was never completely funded. President Roosevelt called for an almost fully funded social security system, but this approach was not accepted by Congress (Leonard, 1986). Congress recognized from the start that this was not necessary because (1) mandatory participation resulted in the involvement of a large part of the employed population; (2) a mandatory, public pension system could be assumed to operate indefinitely; (3) the taxing power of the government ultimately stood behind

the system; and (4) building up a fund is **deflationary** and often economically unwise during periods of high unemployment.

Congress opted for a system of partial funding. As initially enacted in
1935, legislated social security contribution rates were expected to provide the money for a fairly large trust fund as payments came in over the
years. But as this reserve fund began to accumulate and **actuarial** projections predicted that it would grow much bigger, congressional leaders
began to argue that there was no reason for the fund to grow so big.
Instead, the decision was made in 1939 (and years thereafter) to liberalize
the system and to use the scheduled increases in contributions to pay
for these liberalizations.

Historically, as coverage increased and payroll tax receipts rose, an almost completely pay-as-you-go funding policy facilitated the liberalization
and improvement of the system. New groups were added to the system,
sometimes with liberalized eligibility and benefits not based on any prior
payroll tax payments. Cost-of-living increases in benefits were legislated
periodically, and, in 1972, a major increase in real benefits was provided
to current and future participants in the system.

The historical evolution of social security financing is important to keep
in mind. Some argue that the program's financial problems of the recent
past and those projected for the 21st century are, in part, a result of
overly liberal expansion decisions made in earlier years. In response, others argue that Congress deliberately legislated benefits considerably in
excess of contributions to keep millions of elderly out of almost certain
poverty; the aim was to deal with the problem through a program that
avoided the stigma of needs-tested public assistance programs (see Chapter 6). In the opinion of the latter group, the future costs of this approach
are to be expected and should not be viewed with alarm. In fact, the
original designers of social security in the 1930s called for later government contribution out of general revenues to meet the costs of providing
benefits to the several initial generations who had not contributed very
much into the system. As we discuss later, this proposal has never been
implemented.

THE PRINCIPLES OF SOCIAL SECURITY

The social security legislation that was accepted by President Roosevelt
and the Congress was based on a number of principles. First, participation was to be *compulsory* and ultimately *universal*.[5] Workers could not
opt out of the system, and persons with either high earnings or high total
income were not excluded.

Second, social insurance was set up as an *earnings-related* program.
When this decision was made in the 1930s, it was not at all obvious that

social security should be based upon an earnings-related principle. At the time, many countries in Europe had flat-rate pensions. Dr. Francis E. Townsend, a California physician, had proposed in 1933 a flat pension of $200 per month for all persons age 60 and over—resulting in the Townsend movement of 7,000 clubs with two million people.

The decision against the flat rate is explained by J. Douglas Brown (1972), one of the architects of the system: "It was early recognized that a single flat rate of benefits for a country as diversified as the United States would fail to meet the needs of those living in the high-cost urban areas of the Northeast while being unduly favorable to those in the rural South." Moreover, a *high* flat pension for *all* the aged would have been very costly and more than most government decision-makers thought was financially feasible.

Third, *social adequacy* was to be emphasized in the determination of benefits for various recipients, and *income redistribution* was to take place. A weighted benefit formula that favored workers with lower earnings was established. Also, a contribution cutoff point (the maximum contribution ceiling) was established; the earnings was above the ceiling of highly paid earners were excluded. The intent was to focus the program on those people with the greatest problems and with the greatest need for a public benefit (while allowing all eligible earners to participate).

Fourth, it was decided that social security should be only *one of many sources* of economic protection and that further supplementation, either through group or individual means, would be needed to maintain an adequate standard of living in retirement. In the early years, social security was often referred to as providing "a floor of protection."

Fifth, it is *contributory and self-financed*. Funds for operating the program were to come from earmarked payroll taxes called contributions. Social insurance was to be "a cooperating institution taken over by the state [national government], but still a reflection of the responses of workers who are willing to contribute from their earnings today to protect themselves and their families from the hazards of tomorrow" (Brown, 1972).

Sixth, social security benefits were to be *a matter of right* through participation by all workers (rich, middle-class, and poor); there was to be no means test. All Americans were to "earn" their benefits through workforce participation and financial contributions to the program. The system was to be self-supporting through these worker contributions, together with so-called employer contributions.[6]

Seventh, as indicated above, *a retirement test* was established. Pension benefits were viewed as "insurance" against the many difficulties of working during old age. To keep costs down, benefits were to be withheld if a person earned above a specified amount.

RETIREMENT BENEFIT PROVISIONS

To be eligible for retirement benefits under the old-age and survivors insurance program, a worker must have worked in covered employment for the required number of calendar quarters. Prior to 1978 a quarter of coverage was defined as a calendar quarter in which the worker in covered employment was paid at least $50. In 1978 the reporting of social security wages was changed from a quarterly basis to an annual basis (to reduce administrative costs). Currently, therefore, the number of quarters credited depends on annual earnings, one quarter (up to four) credited for each $740 (in 1999) of wages paid. (The amount is adjusted annually using an index of average national earnings.)

The number of quarters required for eligibility has varied by date of birth, to make it easier for older workers to achieve eligibility during the early history of the program. The original 1935 legislation required covered work for only five years, but the number of required quarters has increased over the years. The gradually increasing work requirement has now reached the legislated maximum level: Persons attaining age 62 in 1991 *or later* will need credit for ten years of work (40 quarters) in covered employment.

The various types of benefits paid under the old-age and survivors insurance program to *eligible* workers and their spouses are first briefly listed and then discussed in more detail.

1. The *basic benefit*, based on a "normal retirement age" of 65, is based on a worker's average indexed monthly earnings (AIME) in covered employment. It is derived from a legislated benefit formula that is weighted to provide workers with lower average earnings a relatively greater percentage of earnings replacement than workers with higher earnings. Credited earnings (and hence benefits) are limited by an "earnings ceiling"; workers do not receive credit (or pay taxes) on earnings above this ceiling. Only taxed earnings below this ceiling enter into the calculation of the average monthly earnings used in the benefit formula. (Also, total family benefits are limited by prescribed maxima.)

2. A *minimum benefit* is provided only to workers (and their survivors) who attained age 62 before 1982 and who would otherwise be eligible for very low basic benefits. Available to some workers with extensive earnings histories is a *special minimum benefit*, paid if larger than the regular benefit; its amount is increased annually by the Consumer Price Index. However, it is available only to workers with relatively low annual earnings who have many years of covered earnings above specified minimum levels—the size of the benefit being dependent on the number of "years of coverage" in excess of ten and up to a maximum creditable limit of thirty years.

3. *Early retirement benefits* may be paid to beneficiaries at ages 62 to 64, but these benefits are **actuarially** reduced (by 20 percent at age 62) to take into account the longer period over which they will be paid.

4. *Delayed retirement credits* are given to workers age 65 or older who continue working and, as a result, do not receive their entitled benefits. An additional amount is added to benefits (for those reaching age 62 in 1979 or later) for each year between ages 65 and 70 that they delay benefit receipt. The delayed retirement credit is gradually rising from 3 percent per year in 1989 to 8 percent in the year 2008.

5. *Spouses' and children's benefits*, equal to 50 percent of the worker's basic benefit, may be paid to a spouse and to each child under age 18 (and elementary or secondary school students under age 19), subject to the "family maximum." Benefits for some spouses, however, are reduced by federal, state, or local pensions payable to the spouse based on earnings in noncovered employment. Disabled adult children and divorced persons may also receive a benefit if certain specified conditions are met.

6. *Survivors' benefits* are payable to a surviving spouse beginning at age 60; or, if disabled, at age 50; or, if he or she is caring for a disabled adult child or a nondisabled dependent child under age 16, at any age. This benefit equals 100 percent of the basic benefit (see 1) for widows age 65 or over or for a widow with a child in her care. Reduced benefits are paid to widows and widowers ages 60 to 64 and to disabled widows and widowers ages 50 to 59. Unmarried minor children and disabled adult children, dependent parents, divorced wives, and remarried widows are also eligible for survivors' benefits of various levels when meeting certain specified conditions. Benefits for surviving spouses are partially reduced for receipt of a government pension based on noncovered employment income (see 5).

7. *An earnings test* reduces benefits paid to nondisabled beneficiaries under age 65 who earn more than a certain amount. The exemption ceiling was $10,080 in 2000, and benefits are reduced by 50 percent of earnings over the ceiling.

Table 4–1 lists the major steps in the benefit calculation process. Each of the components listed or mentioned in the table are discussed in more detail.

Benefit Levels

Benefits generally are based on *all* years (except as noted later) of earnings after the year 1950—even those years a person has zero earnings as a result of not working. Only earnings resulting from work covered under the social security program are counted, and credited earning are limited to amounts below a legislated maximum earnings ceiling ($72,600 in 1999). Each year's earnings up to age 60 are adjusted upward based on historical changes in average wages throughout the whole economy. The adjustment process is called wage **indexing**. Generally, 35 years of earnings after 1950 are used to calculate the benefit (based on five less than the number of years elapsing after the year one attains age 21 and before the year one attains age 62).

Table 4–1
Major Steps in the Old-Age Benefit Calculation Process

1. Check eligibility (required "quarters" of coverage).
2. Calculate average monthly indexed earnings (modified "lifetime earnings").
3. Determine primary insurance amount (from benefit formula or table).
4. Check if eligible for a minimum benefit:
   (a) Regular minimum or
   (b) Special minimum.
5. Reduce benefit if "early retirement."
6. Raise benefit if "delayed retirement."
7. Apply retirement test if age less than 65.
8. Calculate spouse benefit if married (and compare with spouse's own benefit).
9. Determine if other family benefits apply.
10. Check to make sure total benefits do not exceed family maximum.

The actual years selected for the computation period are the years of highest indexed earnings after 1950, including any years before age 22 or after age 61 (and the year of disability or death, if applicable).[7] The resulting total earnings are averaged to produce a measure called "average indexed monthly earnings" (AIME).

The law specifies a formula to determine the amount of benefit based on the worker's calculated AIME. The benefit formula for those reaching age 62 in 1999 was 90 percent of the first $505 of AIME, plus 32 percent of AIME over $505 and through $3,043, plus 15 percent of the AIME over $3,043. The AIME dollar amounts in this formula change each year as part of a mechanism to stabilize replacement rates over time (see Chapter 5).

One of the best ways of evaluating the resulting level of social security benefits is to look at **pension replacement rates**. You will remember from Chapter 3 that a pension replacement rate specifies the proportion of a worker's prior earnings that is replaced by the pension he or she receives.

Table 4–2 shows the amount of earnings replacement provided a couple by social security at various earnings levels. Given the target rates (also shown in Table 4–2), we see that social security provides some, but not all, of the income required. The last column of the table shows the gap between the replacement rates necessary to maintain living standards upon retirement and the replacement rates provided by social security retirement benefits.

The Social Security Administration (SSA) now annually provides information on employer-reported earnings recorded in the SSA files and an estimate of future retirement benefits. This information can be used to

Table 4–2
How Much Income Replacement Is Provided by Social Security for an Elderly Couple Retiring in 1988?[a]

Gross Preretirement Earnings	Target Replacement Rate Goal	Social Security Replacement	Gap
$15,000	82%	61%	21%
20,000	75	56	19
25,000	71	50	21
31,250	68	42	26
40,000	68	34	34
50,000	66	28	38
60,000	66	23	43
80,000	68	17	51

[a]Assumes a married "one-worker" couple with retiree age 65 and spouse age 62, retiring in 1988.

Source: Based on information in Bruce A. Palmer, "Tax Reform and Retirement Income Replacement Ratios," *Journal of Risk and Insurance* 56 (December 1989): 702–723.

check the accuracy of the SSA records and to estimate the need for supplemental retirement, survivor, and disability coverage.

To get information immediately, an individual can go to www.ssa.gov on the Internet or fill out Form SSA-7004, which can be obtained by telephoning the Social Security Administration's toll-free number (800–772–1213). In four to six weeks, SSA sends a statement with a summary of the individual's credited social security covered earnings and an estimate of: (1) monthly retirement benefits at ages 62, 65, and 70; (2) survivors' monthly benefits if the person were to die during the year; and (3) disability benefits if the individual were to qualify.[8]

Minimum Benefits

For most of its history, the old-age pension program has had a minimum benefit. In the original legislation, the guarantee was $10 per month. Over the years the original minimum benefit has been periodically increased and is currently $3,000 per year but is only available to beneficiaries who have attained age 62 before 1982.

Writing in the 1960s, Pechman, Aaron, and Taussig (1968) summarized the major problem that caused Congress to eliminate for future retirees this minimum in favor of an alternative:

If minimum and low benefits were paid exclusively to aged householders with little or no other money income, the case for sharply increasing the minimum would be overwhelming. In the absence of an income test, however, many beneficiaries receive minimum or low benefits because they have had limited attachment to occupations covered by social security, not because they have had low lifetime earnings. Former employees of federal, state, and local governments can enter covered employment late in life and acquire insured status sufficient to entitle them to low or minimum benefits.[9]

Recognizing this problem, Congress created a special minimum for long-term workers; in 1977 it froze the regular minimum for future beneficiaries; and in 1981 it eliminated eligibility for the regular minimum if an individual reached age 62 after 1981.

The elimination of the minimum was highly controversial. In the spring of 1981 the Reagan administration proposed a number of social security amendments. These proposals included *complete* elimination of the minimum benefit. The administration argued that "the main beneficiaries of the minimum . . . [were] those with a modest work history in employment covered by social security." In response to this proposal, Congress passed legislation terminating the minimum. It restored the provision almost immediately, however, for "the current aged"—reacting to intense lobbying and a growing awareness that a significant number of low-income beneficiaries would be harmed seriously by the elimination.

Under the provisions of the special minimum, persons with more than ten "years of coverage" under social security have a guaranteed level equal, in 1998, to approximately $27.90 per month times the years of coverage in excess of ten years and up to thirty (but not exceeding $567 per month). The special minimum is adjusted automatically over time for increases in the cost of living. Relatively few workers have earnings that are consistently so low that the special minimum is higher than their regular benefit (about 190,000 beneficiaries in 1994).

Early Retirement

Until 1956, workers could not receive their old-age benefits until they reached the age of 65. The selection of age 65 for the receipt of benefits was a somewhat arbitrary decision of those who drafted the legislation. In large part the decision was simply to copy the age provisions of existing public and private pension programs, almost all of which used age 65.

In 1956 the social security law was changed to permit women workers to receive reduced benefits between the ages of 62 and 64; and in 1961 this option was extended to men. In both cases the reduction was to be the full actuarial amount. That is, persons receiving benefits before age 65 were to receive over their remaining lifetime amounts that—based on

Table 4-3
Social Security Worker Beneficiaries[a] Receiving Reduced Early Retirement Benefits

	Men		Women	
Year	Number[b] (000s)	Early Retirement[c] %	Number (000s)	Early Retirement %
Prior to 1970	274[d]	05[d]	115[e]	08[e]
1970	2,758	36	3,308	59
1975	4,465	49	4,904	66
1980	5,889	56	6,307	69
1985	7,166	61	7,553	71
1990	8,391	65	8,607	73
1996	9,532	68	9,581	69

[a]OASDI benefits in current payment status.
[b]Number of individuals receiving reduced benefits.
[c]Percent of all beneficiaries receiving reduced benefits.
[d]1961.
[e]1956.
Source: U.S. Social Security Administration, *Social Security Bulletin*, Tables Q2, C3.

average life expectancy—would not exceed (on average) the total amounts received by those retiring at age 65.

From the very beginning, the early retirement option was exceedingly popular and has been exercised by the great majority of workers. The Social Security Administration reports that over half the men awarded initial retirement benefits each year since 1962 have received reduced benefits. Table 4-3 shows the rise in the proportion of social security beneficiaries receiving reduced benefits. Almost 70 percent of women and men do not receive full benefits.

Delayed Retirement

In 1939 the calculation of the social security pension was changed to include a 1 percent increase in benefits for each year that credited earnings were at least $200. "This provision thus gave an individual who postponed his retirement after 65 a larger benefit when he retired than if he began to draw his benefits at 65. This provision was the subject of much controversy and was repealed in the 1950 law" (Cohen, 1957).

In 1972 a provision was again added to the social security law that raised benefits for those who delayed retirement beyond age 65. Between 1950 and 1972, persons who continued to work beyond age 64 lost the value of all pension benefits potentially available while they worked. The 1972 provision reduced the loss somewhat but did not totally eliminate it. For there to be no loss in the actuarial value of a worker's benefit requires that the benefit level be increased by about 8 percent a year, instead of the 3 percent adjustment in effect until 1990. In 1983 Congress moved to achieve that result, legislating future liberalizations in the delayed retirement credit. The credit is gradually increasing from 3 to 8 percent over the 1990–2008 period.

Benefits for Family Members

In 1939 the social security program was amended to provide dependent benefits for wives age 65 or older and for children under age 16. Successive legislation liberalized these provisions and extended benefits to students ages 18 to 21, disabled children age 18 and over, divorced wives, and "dependent" husbands meeting various eligibility conditions. In 1977 the Supreme Court further liberalized benefits by ruling unconstitutional the social security provision that men must prove they were financially dependent on their wives in order to get dependent benefits. As a consequence, widowers can now qualify for benefits based on their deceased wives' records without demonstrating "dependency."

As indicated above, eligible family members can receive a benefit based on the related worker's earnings and work history. Spouses who also work and become qualified for benefits based on their own work experience can receive a benefit based only on their own work history. However, if their spouse's benefit is larger, they receive their own pension *plus the difference* between the spouse's benefit and their own worker's benefit. That is, in effect they receive either the benefit based on the spouse's earnings or a benefit based on their own work history, whichever is greater.

Survivors' Benefits

We are apt to forget that social security provides more than worker retirement benefits. For example, about one-fifth of all OASDI benefits being paid are to survivors—totaling over 7 million pensions in 1992.

When a worker protected by social security dies, a modest $255 lump sum payment is made to the surviving spouse who was living with the worker or who is eligible for a survivor benefit (or if there is no such spouse, to an eligible child). Qualifying widows, surviving divorced wives, children, and dependent parents may also be eligible for monthly benefits. Conditions for receipt of a survivor's benefit vary considerably.

The two most important categories are widows (5 million) and children (2 million). A widow who was married to a fully insured worker for at least nine months and who has reached age 60 may be entitled to a benefit. This benefit equals 100 percent of the worker's age-65 pension if payments begin at age 65 and is reduced if benefits begin at an earlier age (71.5 percent at age 60). Benefits are also subject to reduction if earnings exceed the retirement test exempt amount. Younger widows with eligible children, unmarried dependent children under age 18, and disabled adult children may also be entitled to a benefit equal to 75 percent of the deceased's basic benefit amount. Special benefits are available for disabled widows ages 50 to 59.

Supreme Court decisions in 1975 and 1977 struck down provisions of the Social Security Act that prohibited men from receiving survivor benefits based on their wives' earnings. The number of widower benefits received by men remains relatively small, however. For example, in 1994 there was one widower receiving benefits for every 127 widow beneficiaries. The main reason for the relatively small number of widower beneficiaries is (1) that most men are entitled to higher benefits based on their own earnings records than the benefits based on the earnings of their wives; and (2) that most men die before their wives.

The monetary value of survivors' benefits is often very large—$12.1 trillion in 1993 (Ball, 1994). Ball also reports that a male worker and wife (age 27) with two children ages 2 and less than 1 year, would have social security survivors' protection equal to $700,000.

Until 1983, one of the major factors resulting in low (and often inadequate) benefits for widows and widowers has been the way earnings were indexed to calculate benefits. A survivor benefit was based on the amount of benefits that would have been payable to the deceased worker, as determined by applying a benefit formula to the worker's covered earnings. These earnings were indexed by a wage index reflecting the national wage trend. However, this wage indexing was applied to reflect nationwide wage increases only through the second year before the death of the worker. The resulting benefit amount was then adjusted by a price index only—beginning with the year the widow or widower attained the age of eligibility.

In cases where the worker died long before retirement age, the benefit for which the widowed spouse ultimately became eligible in old age (or at disability after age 50) was based on outdated levels of wages and prices. Thus, the spouse who became widowed at a relatively young age but who did not become eligible for benefits for many years was deprived of the worker's unrealized earnings, as well as the economy-wide wage or price increases that occurred after the worker's death.

The Social Security Amendments of 1983 changed this calculation procedure. For newly eligible widows and widowers after 1984, deferred survivors' benefits are wage indexed until the year the deceased worker would have been age 60 (or indexed up to two years before the widow(er)'s own eligibility, if earlier). This significantly increases benefits for many survivors.

The Retirement Test

Over the years officials of the Social Security Administration have acknowledged that this test generates the most questions and the most criticisms among people covered by the social security program. Further evidence of the controversy is that in every session of Congress since 1940, numerous bills have been introduced to eliminate or liberalize the test. In 1987 the then commissioner of social security called for elimination or major liberalization of the test. This was the first time any commissioner of the program called for such an extreme change in the test.

Critics argue that the test significantly discourages work by confronting potential workers with a high **marginal tax rate**. Not only must workers pay payroll and income taxes on their earnings, they must also pay the 33⅓ or 50 percent retirement test "tax." Thus, the test distorts labor supply decisions. Abolishing the test would also treat older workers more equitably, they argue, just as abolition of mandatory retirement stopped one type of discrimination against older workers.

The arguments in favor of the test relate to means-testing, high costs, inequity, and the macroeconomic issue of unemployment. A past Advisory Council on Social Security (1975), for example, gave the following rationale for the test:

The Council has reviewed the provisions of the retirement test and believes that the test is consistent with the basic purpose and principles of social security: to replace, in part, earnings lost because of retirement in old age, disability, or death. Complete elimination of the retirement test is inadvisable. The retirement test has been criticized because it does not take into account a beneficiary's income from such nonwork sources as dividends, rent, or pension payments. If the test took account of income other than earnings from work, it would no longer be a retirement test but an income test. If it became an income test, the fundamental idea that social security benefits are intended as partial replacement of earnings from work would be diluted or lost.

While the reasoning advanced by the Advisory Council has also been the official position of the Social Security Administration, it is important to recognize two other arguments that are frequently made in support of the test.[10] First, because there are still many workers age 62 or older who do not receive social security benefits and because many of them work full time, repeal of the retirement test would be relatively expensive and benefit most those who need help the least. For example, about 93 percent of the increased benefits resulting from the liberalizations in the earnings test legislated in 1977 went to individuals at the top or in the middle of the earnings distribution (Esposito, Mallan, and Podoff, 1980). In 1989, 14 percent of beneficiaries affected by the test earned more than $48,000; in contrast, only 6 percent of workers of all ages had earnings above that level (Bondar, 1993).

Second, given the fact that relatively high rates of unemployment have been a frequent phenomenon in the American economy, the retirement test encourages older workers to retire; until low unemployment is a more common historical phenomenon, policymakers are likely to see the test as a relatively compassionate way to shift "unemployment" from the young to the old (and change its name to "retirement"). Moreover, unions have argued that the test discourages older workers from competing with younger workers for jobs by offering their services at wages below prevailing levels.

Whereas complete elimination of the retirement test would be costly and benefit many high earners, it can be argued alternatively that the test should be liberal enough to encourage and allow those people with low or moderate pension incomes to work in retirement. Various proposals have been advanced that would effectively exclude people with high earnings from the receipt of benefits but would not penalize low earners who wanted or needed to supplement their pension income.

The second argument—that older workers should be encouraged to retire to make room for younger workers—raises a number of very complex issues. Ideally, an appropriate mix of monetary and fiscal policy by the government could promote an expansionary economy with jobs for almost everyone, thereby avoiding the dilemma of the older versus younger worker trade-off. The problem that arises, however, is that as the economy approaches full employment, inflationary factors tend to push up the general level of prices. Economic policymakers feel they are faced with the unpleasant trade-off of less employment to prevent more inflation. In addition to having to choose between inflation and unemployment (sometimes referred to as the problem of "fine-tuning" the economy), there is the problem of the recessions and depressions that have occurred throughout the century. The result of these has been millions of unemployed workers.

The causes of downturns in the economy are varied. While it is generally agreed that increased economic sophistication now provides nations with the necessary tools to prevent or moderate economic instability, the application of this knowledge has been far from perfect. Given, then, the recurring instability and joblessness that have characterized the

American economy, it is not surprising to find workers and unions supporting policies that promise to moderate the situation. The retirement test appears to be one policy that falls into this category.

Over the years there have been numerous studies attempting to estimate how many individuals would work more (or less) if the retirement test were abolished (see, for example, Burtless and Moffitt, 1984; Gustman and Steinmeier, 1986; Honig and Reimers, 1989; Packard, 1990). Most have concluded there would be very little change, indicating that the labor force disincentives of the test are not as great as critics suggest. The most recent study (Friedberg, 1999) reaches a different conclusion. Friedberg, using a different methodology from others, concludes that elimination of the test would produce "a substantial boost to labor supply . . . at a minimal fiscal cost."

Responding to intense political pressure to completely abolish the test, Congress has instead retained it but has enacted over the past two decades four liberalizations:

1. It reduced the maximum effective age for the test from age 72 to 70, effective in 1983.
2. It increased the annual exempt amount and wage-indexed the amount.
3. It changed the reduction in the "take-back" rate after the "normal retirement age" from 50 to 33⅓ percent, effective in 1990.
4. In the year 2000, it eliminated the retirement test entirely for individuals attaining the "full retirement age"—which is currently age 65 (but scheduled to rise in future years).

The latest change was passed in an election year, sweeping through both houses of the Congress with little debate and no opposition. Argued Republican Bill Archer, chair of the House Ways and Means Committee, "Why in the world would we want to discourage any American—whether they're 17 or 67—from working? Americans are living longer now. Older Americans can work, they want to work and they shouldn't be punished by an outdated law if they choose to work" (Stevenson, 2000). Lawmakers ignored the fact that the action was expensive ($22 billion over the first ten years) and that the new benefits would go primarily to the relatively well-to-do elderly.

The new retirement test eliminates the test in and after the month in which a person *attains* full retirement age. However, in the calendar year that the beneficiary attains that age, the test is still applied for the months prior to *attainment*—reducing benefits ($1 for every $3) above the exempt amount. No change was made in the test for those younger than 65.

The earnings ceiling in the calender year of attainment (for pre-attainment months) is $17,000 in the year 2000, $25,000 in 2001, and $30,000 in 2002. The ceiling for those younger than age 65 is $10,080 in the year 2000.

Only one *restrictive* provision has been enacted in recent years. The 1977 social security amendments eliminated the monthly exemption test (except for one month, generally the year of entitlement). Under this monthly measure, a beneficiary who did not earn over the specified monthly exemption or render substantial services in self-employment in a month received a benefit for that month regardless of the level of his *annual* earnings. Now only an annual test applies.

SOCIAL SECURITY PENSION REFORMS

Criticism of the old-age and survivors program has centered on seven major issues:

1. The adequacy of benefits
2. Separating welfare from social security
3. The relative roles of the public and private sectors
4. The treatment of women
5. The retirement age
6. Administering the social security system
7. Financing current and future benefits

The last of these issues will be discussed in Chapter 5. In this section we discuss the other six.

Benefit Adequacy

Are benefits too low or too high? Until recently nearly everyone thought social security benefits were too low. A national survey by Peter D. Hart Associates, Inc. (1979) for the National Commission on Social Security found "most Americans neither extremely satisfied nor totally dissatisfied with Social Security." The most frequent complaints, however, were about benefit levels. Although most respondents recognized that social security was intended to supplement other sources of retirement income, *most felt that social security alone should provide enough income to meet the basic needs and obligations of retirees.* A representative survey of 1,209 people in 1986 found that 57 percent wanted benefits increased, and 40 percent wanted levels to remain the same, adjusted only for inflation (Cook, 1989). There were few differences in support for social security across different age groups, and 71 percent said they would be willing to pay more taxes to maintain or increase benefits. (Similar opinions are reported in YSW, 1985.)

Increasingly, however, arguments are made that social security benefits are now adequate—maybe even too large. The current controversy over benefit levels centers around the changes legislated by Congress in 1972.

Early in his first term (1969) President Nixon sent a message to Congress proposing changes in social security. The key recommendations were, first, a 10 percent increase in benefits; second, and more important, a proposal that the Consumer Price Index be used to adjust future benefits automatically and that a wage index be used to adjust the contribution and benefit base.

At the same time that the president proposed changes in social security, he proposed a welfare reform bill—the Family Assistance Act. The House Ways and Means Committee and the Senate Finance Committee held hearings that *simultaneously* considered both the social security and welfare reforms. The major focus of these hearings, however, was on welfare reform and not on social security. Therefore, most of the testimony did not even mention the social security proposals.

At about the same time, a Social Security Advisory Council issued its report. This council had been appointed in the early part of the first Nixon administration. Nixon took the position that aside from the changes recommended in his social security message, he would make no other legislative suggestions until the Advisory Council made its report. He argued that it would be premature for the administration to propose legislation while this blue-ribbon group, which was given the job of surveying the whole situation, was still deliberating. This position, of course, set up expectations that something significant would come out of the council's report. Nothing did. The council looked at a number of incremental changes, mostly equity changes, and rejected most of the major benefit proposals people had made.

Instead, the initiative for a major change in benefits took place in the Senate. Without prior committee action, the Senate passed an unusually large benefit increase (20 percent) proposed by Senator Frank Church on the floor during debate. Surprisingly, this dramatic increase, when it reached the House, was supported by the very conservative and then powerful chairman of the House Ways and Means Committee, Wilbur Mills. (Mills was at the time a presidential hopeful and hence very anxious not to antagonize the aged and other social security supporters.)

The Advisory Council's only important recommendations were in the area of financing. Its report argued strongly in favor of keeping an essentially "pay-as-you-go system" and argued that only a "one-year reserve" was needed. The council also strongly recommended changes in the static actuarial assumptions in use for projecting benefit outlays and contributions. It called for introducing *dynamic* assumptions, arguing that one should expect earnings levels to rise over time, that the contribution and benefit base would increase as earnings rose, and that benefits would be increased as prices rose. Both recommendations made the large benefit increases that were eventually legislated appear feasible without any increase in the payroll tax. However, the council itself never recommended any increase.

The increased benefit levels and indexing enacted in 1972 have caused some pension experts to argue that there is little need for future retirees to supplement social security. For example, Robert Ball, a former commissioner of Social Security, writes: "At average wages, the [social security] replacement rate for the couple is approaching adequacy" (Ball, 1978). Similar opinions have been voiced by other pension experts (see, for example, Bassett, 1978).

Perhaps the strongest view on this point came from prominent conservative economist Martin Feldstein. Feldstein (1977) asserted that the high earnings replacement rates resulting at retirement from public and private pensions are "quite inappropriate for middle and higher income couples." Feldstein argued that retiring on social security income now brings little decline in an average family's standard of living and that, furthermore, workers often receive additional income from employer-sponsored pensions. It is important to see how Feldstein reaches this debatable conclusion, because it is a view shared by others.

Feldstein and some other discussants of social security reform focus on the replacement rate for an "average (male) earner"—that is, a hypothetical worker *who earns the average annual wage each year of the working period*. The social security benefit formula provides a retiring worker who has earned (each year) an amount equal to the average wage with a retirement benefit equal to about 42 percent of earnings just prior to retirement.[11] But if the worker has a nonworking spouse, the replacement rate jumps to 63 percent as a result of the additional spouse benefit. Given estimates that around 60 percent to 70 percent of gross earnings for nonpoor families allows these families to maintain their living standards in retirement (see Chapter 3), it looks as though social security has the potential of providing most of the normal retirement needs for these so-called average workers.

For those who are eligible we must then add the contribution of private pensions to retirement living. These formulas are designed to provide 25 percent to 35 percent earnings replacement for hypothetical *long-service* workers (U.S. Bureau of Labor Statistics, 1991).

Combining the replacement rates from social security with those from private pensions raises the average pension replacement rate for the "average" one-worker couple to almost 90 percent to 100 percent. Can there be any doubt that we are over-pensioning some workers today?

The truth is that the over-pensioning characterization suffers from a number of major limitations. There is no doubt that severe economic deprivation faces far fewer retiring persons—at least as long as they stay well and avoid institutionalization. But the picture is not as rosy as the replacement rate percentages usually cited would suggest.

The statistic for average earnings before retirement selected by Feldstein (and others) for the hypothetical earnings calculations is an average for both part-time and full-time workers at all stages of their earnings career (i.e., for all age groups). In estimating pension replacement adequacy, do we really want to use an average that, in effect, turns out to be the earnings of a worker about 30 years of age? Such a measure of preretirement earnings for a worker who is currently retiring is not appropriate. In fact, workers close to retirement have earnings that are much higher than the chosen statistic and, consequently, much lower replacement rates from social security.

In addition, the couple replacement rates of 63 percent (social security alone) and nearly 100 percent (with a private pension) are for a couple with one worker earning median wages, retiring at age 65. But most people retiring today do not fall into that particular category. First, more than half of married women approaching retirement age are in the labor force. The relevant replacement rates for many two-worker couples are very different from those for one worker; the combined higher earnings of the couple *are not replaced proportionately* by higher social security benefits. In fact, if the spouse doesn't earn enough to become entitled to a benefit greater than 50 percent of the other worker's benefit, there will be no increase in social security benefits at all! Thus, the pension replacement rate from social security for an "average" two-worker family will often be much lower.

An equally important consideration in the determination of actual (rather than potential) replacement rates is the age at retirement. The dramatic rise in the numbers of workers retiring before the retirement age of 65 has made early retirement the norm. Once again, because of the actuarial reduction provisions in social security (and reductions in some private pensions), the actual replacement rates of a great many retirees will be lower than the percentages originally cited.

While no individual is required to retire before age 65, and many retire early because they want to, numerous studies have shown that there is also a sizable group of early retirees without a meaningful option. These workers have little or no potential to engage in substantive employment activity because of poor health or structural unemployment problems.

Finally, as we discuss in Chapter 7, the private pension supplement that boosts the replacement rate significantly for some is not available to many; large numbers of workers are never covered or lose pension credits before retiring. Failure to meet **vesting** requirements and plan terminations, for example, result in lost service credits for many workers.

Table 4–4
Total[a] Replacement Rates for Workers Retiring in the Early 1980s

Replacement Rates	Men	Women
Highest Earnings[b]		
Less than 25%	26	21
25–49%	59	59
50–66%	9	12
67% or more	6	8
	100	100
Last Earnings[b]		
Less than 25%	4	2
25–49%	47	44
50–66%	26	24
67% or more	23	30
	100	100

[a]Old-age insurance benefits plus employer-sponsored pensions (if any).
[b]See text for definition.
Source: Susan Grad, "Earnings Replacement Rates of New Retired Workers," *Social Security Bulletin* 53 (October 1990): Table 10.

Inflation erodes those benefits that are vested. Even those that are covered long enough to receive a pension often do not achieve the *long* periods of service required for large private pension benefit amounts.

If we look at *actual* replacement rates for retiring workers, we see how all these considerations affect pension adequacy levels. An important study by Susan Grad (1990) provides estimates of actual replacement rates for a sample of persons who first received social security retirement benefits in the early 1980s. Grad calculates the proportion of total preretirement earnings replaced by pensions (both social security and employer-sponsored plans). Two measures of wage-indexed preretirement earnings are used: (1) the average of the five years of *highest* earnings over the career; and (2) the average earnings during the *last* five years before benefit receipt. The median worker replacement rate for social security benefits is only 28 percent of "highest earnings" and 40 percent of "last earnings" (Table 4–4). Replacement rates for couples are 30 percent (highest earnings) or 49 percent (last earnings).[12] This contrasts with the hypothetical 60 percent to 70 percent rates cited by Feldstein and others. Even when private and government employer pension income is taken into account, actual replacement rates fall far below that level necessary to maintain living standards in retirement. Table 4–4 shows that only 6 percent to 8 percent of new retired workers replaced at least two-thirds of their *highest* earnings (23 percent to 30 percent when last earnings are considered). The Grad data indicate that, despite improvements over the years, a gap still exists between the retirement income goals of most retirees and the benefits they get from pensions.[13] We will return to this issue in Chapter 7, when we discuss the role of private pensions.

Separating Welfare from Social Security

Pechman, Aaron, and Taussig argue in their book *Social Security: Perspectives for Reform* (1968) that the aged should be eligible for either an earnings-related pension or welfare payment, whichever is the greater. They argue further that the earnings-related pension should have a replacement rate that is roughly the same at all earnings levels between subsistence and the level of median earnings. They also recommend that there be no spouse benefits but that pensions be based on total family earnings instead.

A "Negative Income Tax"

Their major point is that the social security system *should not operate both as a welfare system and a pension system*. If a person receives income in old age (including a social security pension) that places her or him in a taxable bracket, they feel that such a person should pay taxes (regardless of age). On the other hand, if the elderly person's income is too low, they argue, she or he should be eligible for a negative income tax:

The advantage of the dual system [both social insurance and negative income tax benefits] is its efficiency and flexibility. . . . The present system supplements income regardless of the income status of the beneficiaries. In many instances higher minimum benefits would be paid to individuals with adequate income. Under the proposed system the earnings related benefit could be set at any desired percentage of past earnings. Negative income tax allowances to those with low earnings histories would be sufficient to keep income above the poverty level. Thus, policy makers and the public could identify immediately the cost of performing the two distinct functions of the system. (Pechman, Aaron, and Taussig, 1968)

The advantage Pechman et al. (and various other economists) see in separating the two issues is considered a drawback by others (for example, Brown, 1972). Some writers argue that separating the two groups (clearly identifying who is being helped) makes it very difficult to get sufficient political support for improving the situation of the poor. They argue that the only way one can get help for the poor is to piggy-back it onto help for middle- (and even upper-) income groups. For example, Wilbur Cohen (who helped to develop American social security) argued:

In the United States, a program that deals only with the poor will end up being a poor program. There is every evidence that this is true. Ever since the Elizabethan Poor Law of 1601, programs only for the poor have been lousy, no good, poor programs. And a program that is only for the poor—one that has nothing in it for the middle income and the upper income—is, in the long run, a program the American public won't support. This is why I think we must try to find a way to link the interests of all classes in these programs. (Cohen and Friedman, 1972)

The "Double-Decker"

Still another approach to the matter is the "double-decker." The 1979 Social Security Advisory Council seriously considered but rejected a double-decker social security plan. Under this plan each aged, disabled person, and surviving child would receive a flat grant of money (paid out of general revenue) that would be the same for all. In addition, as in the present system, a "second deck" benefit would be paid that was directly proportional to the past covered earnings of social security contributors. However, this second benefit would not be paid to dependents or survivors. (Variants of this type of plan are currently operating in Canada, New Zealand, and Scandinavian countries.)

In rejecting the plan on a split vote, the majority of the Advisory Council stated in their report that they believed the current system performed its functions well. They saw "no need for the kind of radical changes embodied in the double-decker plan." Their specific objections to the plan included:

1. The resulting reduction of benefits for many dependents and survivors
2. Fear that the lower deck (financed out of general revenue) would not be adjusted over time for rising earnings and an eventual result would be lower benefits than under current law
3. The high costs of the lower deck and hence the large burden on general revenues
4. Fear that the lower deck would eventually be means-tested
5. Difficult coordination issues related to federal, state, and local pension plans

Four prominent members of the 1979 council (all economists) strongly supported the double-decker approach. They felt that the major objections raised by the majority of council members were attributable to the specific form of the double-decker that was used as a model, rather than to the principles of such a scheme. In their supplementary statement to the report, they argued that a double-decker plan: (1) could effectively separate the adequacy and equity elements of the present system and permit separate adjustments of the two components; (2) would prevent high earners with limited coverage from qualifying for benefits on more favorable terms; (3) would reduce reliance on the means-tested SSI program; and (4) would help solve some of the adequacy and equity issues arising in connection with female and disabled workers.

The Relative Roles of the Public and Private Sectors

One of the most important, and continuous, debates in American history has been about defining the balance between individual (private) and government (public) responsibility. In this context, it is important to understand that "the passage of Social Security not only changed people's lives, it changed our views about the role of government" (Bryce and Friedland, 1997). Like no other program, social security created a major role for government in dealing with one of the most important individual needs—economic support.

Debates over the years about eligibility and benefit levels have been indirectly about that public/private balance. In recent years, however, the debate has changed dramatically. Proposals to radically shift retirement provision through private means, sharply cutting back social security, are now being given serious consideration. This is often referred to as the "privatization debate."

In recent years, various privatization approaches have been tried or proposed in various countries. The four major approaches are (1) tax incentives to increase private plans, (2) "opting out," (3) mandatory individual savings accounts, and (4) mandatory occupational pensions.

Approaches to Privatization

Mandatory private savings accounts to completely replace social security programs were first tried in 1981. In that year, Chile instituted a government-mandated retirement saving program for almost all workers (the military was a conspicuous exception). Subsequently, several other Latin American countries have instituted similar but less radical programs. In general, these schemes require workers to deposit a certain percent of their earnings into personal pension accounts managed by private-sector financial managers.

No industrialized country has adopted the mandated savings account approach. Instead, one of the most common forms of pension privatization is providing government tax incentives. These incentives are designed to encourage private employers or financial institutions to offer (and individuals to participate in) special savings or pension programs. Thus, for example, tax laws have been deliberately liberalized in many countries to encourage the expansion of union or employer-sponsored pensions. In addition to encouraging such plans, some governments have passed legislation to create special savings plans for retirement, again using liberalized tax laws to encourage participation. In the United States, for example, there is now a wide variety of such plans (see Chapter 7).

Mandated pensions are another option. For example, the Australian government's shift to privatization places major emphasis on group funds with individualized accounts. These plans are developed and supervised by employers and/or unions. The Australian "Superannuation Guarantee Charge" program started in 1992 requires employers to make retirement contributions on behalf of individual workers. The contribution rate is 9 percent of an individual worker's wages and deposited into an industry (rather than employer) fund that was privately managed.

The United Kingdom has developed a different approach to privatization, known as "opting out." An individual can opt out of part of the public pension system and set up a "Personal Pension" plan. Alternatively, an individual can opt out by participating in a qualifying private pension plan set up by his or her employer. (The UK approach is discussed in more detail below.)

American Privatization Proposals

The 1994–1996 Advisory Council on Social Security gave major attention to social security financing issues and the desirability of some form of privatization. The Council could not reach any agreement on these matters, however. Instead, the members divided into three groups, each supporting a different proposal:

- A **Maintain Benefits Plan**, which would keep social security essentially as it is, with minor tax increases and benefit reductions. With regard to privatization, the proposal suggested the possibility of investing some of the social security trust fund assets in the private equity markets.
- An **Individual Accounts Plan**, which would add a new mandatory 1.6 percent payroll tax to social security, to be used to fund "individual investment accounts" *managed by the federal government.*
- A **Personal Savings Account Plan**, which would partially privatize social security by diverting a portion of the payroll tax into individual equity accounts *managed by the private sector.*

These proposals were followed by a variety of other proposals, many by members of the Congress. For example, House Ways and Means Committee chairman Bill Archer, joined with a Republican colleague, Clay Shaw, to offer a variant of the "personal savings account plan." At the time this edition was written, however, no proposal had achieved widespread support—let alone legislative success.

Lessons from Privatization in the UK

The eleven-year experience of Britain counsels caution with regard to pension privatization. Prime Minister Margaret Thatcher's decision to privatize in the 1980s produced horrendous problems, most of which remain unresolved even today.

As with all reforms, the British political rhetoric at the time sounded good: bigger benefits, lower government outlays, greater individual control, investment flexibility, and use of more "efficient" private companies. But the reality has turned out to be much less.

Today most of the British people are disenchanted. A recent government review of the situation concludes that they have "lost faith in all parts of the pension system" (Secretary of State for Social Security, 1998). Many people have discovered that they will do less well under the private approach, and they have learned that they cannot trust many of the experts giving financial advice.

In 1988 an individualized pension, called the Personal Pension, was added to the British pension system. This pension allows workers some control over retirement investments—primarily by choosing among various kinds of privately administered plans.

Ineptness, fraud, and disinformation have dominated the history of the British Personal Pension. Perhaps the biggest shock to the nation came with the 1993 revelation that financial institutions were using unethical procedures to encourage workers to opt out of employer-sponsored plans into Personal Pensions. Many salespersons performed inadequate analyses for clients, provided biased information, and encouraged people to make wrong decisions.

In reaction to this pension scandal, the British Securities and Investments Board mandated reviews of suspected mis-selling cases—numbering in the millions. The potential cost of the mandated reviews and compensation to clients wrongly advised is estimated to be over £11 billion (around $6.6 billion)!

But as even the financial industry admits, no amount of rules and regulations can overcome a fundamental contradiction. Typically, salespeople are not paid to give people good advice; they are paid to sell their product. Thus, despite greater regulatory efforts, mis-selling continues. For example, investigators from *The Guardian* recently found salespeople from Prudential were still giving bad advice (Levene, 1998). Posing as clients, the investigators found that salespeople were selling the pension plans that maximized earnings for themselves and their companies—rather than recommending what was best for customers.

Complexity is the British pension system's most basic problem. Complex provisions and numerous regulatory rules accompany the Personal Pension option (and the other three major pension programs operating in Britain today). The mis-selling scandal is just one result of this complex retirement planning reality. Most individuals are "ripe for the picking"—looking for quick and easy answers or finding it difficult to evaluate in an informed way the advice they receive.

The administrative costs associated with Personal Pensions pose an equally serious problem. Providers can charge whatever they want to recoup expenses and make a profit. It was hoped that market forces would keep the charges down. In fact, charges have been very high, and there is no indication that they are declining significantly with competition and time.

Charges, however, vary enormously from company to company. Unfortunately, it is practically impossible for an individual to compare the costs of competing plans. Charges are imposed in a bewildering variety of ways—often disguised or presented in a misleading fashion.

Another problem occurs at retirement. Personal Pension holders are required to convert most of their plan assets into an annuity at retirement. The size of the resulting annuity payment depends fundamentally on the value of the pension assets at the time of conversion. But these values, especially those of assets with the highest potential return, fluctuate with changes in securities markets. For example, an individual with a Personal Pension in equities—retiring at the time the stock markets "crashed" on October 30, 1987—would have received an annuity benefit that was *30 percent less* than if he or she retired a week earlier.

Given these and other issues, how adequate will the British Personal Pensions be? No one knows—least of all the individual pension holders. Personal Pensions promise no guaranteed benefit at retirement. The amount of pension ultimately received depends on premiums paid (and at what age), administrative costs, investment performance, the retirement date, and the type of annuity chosen (to name only a few).

Women and Social Security

There is widespread agreement that social security provisions related to women need to be reformed but no consensus on how to do it. The social security benefit structure reflects a pattern of marital life and family obligations which is no longer typical in the United States. Benefits (and payments) are designed to provide family protection under an assumption that there are just two major family types: single workers and married couples consisting of lifelong paid workers and lifelong unpaid homemakers.

A number of important social trends have made that assumption increasingly unrealistic. First, female participation in the paid labor force has increased dramatically. Moreover, increasing numbers of married women spend part of their lives solely as homemakers and another part in the paid labor force.

Second, there is a changing perception of roles within families. A government report (U.S. HEW Task Force, 1978) described these changes as follows:

As more married women work and have broader employment opportunities, the homemaker role is more frequently viewed as a career choice in itself; the decision to have a spouse at home full-time is viewed as a conscious decision rather than a foregone conclusion. The idea that the homemaker role has economic value—though difficult to measure—is gaining acceptance. . . . Both the rising labor-force participation of married women and the changing perceptions of the homemaker role tend to lead toward a view of marriage as an interdependent relationship between spouses.

Third, there is a rapidly rising number of women who are divorced, separated, or widowed. The United States has one of the highest divorce rates in the world, and there are currently about five widowed women for every widowed man in the United States. Studies investigating the economic consequences of families breaking up have found that the economic status of former husbands improves while that of the former wives deteriorates (Weitzman, 1985). Under social security, divorced persons do not achieve eligibility for a spouse or widow's benefit for marriages briefer than ten years. This results in significant periods of marriage (often with perhaps little or no earnings) and consequent low benefits at retirement, and in past years many of the women becoming widows have found their income falling below the poverty line.

In reaction to the many new issues that have emerged, attention has been given to changing the way social security programs treat women. A number of other countries have already instituted major reforms, and many countries have legislative proposals actively under consideration. Canada, for example, has passed legislation at the federal level for a "child-rearing dropout" provision and "credit splitting" (both provisions are discussed below). Optional credit splitting at the time of a divorce is also available.

In the United States, discussion has centered on four issues: the equity and adequacy of spouse and survivor benefits, fairness of coverage of one-earner versus two-earner couples, coverage of homemakers and divorced persons, and the impact of proposed privatization.

Spouse Benefits

The original Social Security Act did not provide benefits to spouses; these were added in 1939. At a time when only about a quarter of women over age 15 were in the labor force, this seemed like a reasonable way to make benefits for couples more adequate. Given changing attitudes and women's roles, however, the question arises as to whether the spouse benefit should be eliminated. "Since many women are contributing significantly to family income, a spousal benefit inaccurately conveys a notion of economic dependency. It is argued, therefore, that women who have earned entitlement to an old age pension based on their earnings should receive only a retired-worker pension" (O'Grady-LeShane, 1993). But as Ferber (1993) points out, "Whether any Social Security benefits should be provided for spouses, and if so what kind, is a complex and emotionally charged issue. On the one hand, most homemakers and secondary wage earners need such payments in order to attain a modicum of security. On the other hand, these benefits provide incentives for married women to remain out of the labor force."

A spouse (usually the wife) may pay social security taxes without adding to the family's retirement income. If a husband and wife both work, the working wife has several advantages not available to the nonworking wife. She can retire and draw benefits at 62 or over even if her husband works on. Survivors' benefits—lump-sum, children's benefits, and parents' benefits—may be paid on her earnings record. Also, before age 65 she may draw disability benefits on her own record.

The problem is further aggravated by the fact that the working husband and wife are treated as separate taxable units and consequently may collectively pay more social security taxes than a family with only a single worker earning the same amount. This occurs as a result of the taxable earnings ceiling that limits the taxed earnings of the single-earner family to the ceiling but taxes each earner of the dual-earner family up to the maximum.

Table 4–5 provides examples of the differences that can arise. The table shows four retiring couples and the benefits they would have received in 1987 if they had four different combinations of earnings. The first three examples show couples with equal *total* earnings that are divided differently between spouses. The fourth case shows a couple with more earnings (earned by the wife) but with no greater benefits.

As with the weighted benefit formula and the minimum, the justification for the spouse benefit is made on social adequacy grounds: on a given earnings history, two people are less able (than one person) to provide for retirement and need more income in retirement. Pechman, Aaron, and Taussig (1968) argue, however, that the greater amount a couple receives (currently 50 percent more than the single worker) is too large: "The benefits of single workers should be raised substantially, relative to those of married couples. A smaller increment than 50 percent is justified because, at any given earnings level, single persons now receive smaller benefits relative to their previous standard of living than do married couples."

Table 4–5
1987 Benefits for Four Retiring Couples[a]

	Couple A	Couple B	Couple C	Couple D
Earnings				
Husband	$24,000	$12,000	$16,000	$24,000
Wife	0	12,000	8,000	8,000
Monthly Benefits				
Husband	797	499	606	797
Wife	398	499	393	398
Total Benefits	1,195	998	999	1,195

[a]Benefits are calculated assuming individuals begin benefits at age 65.
Source: Technical Committee on Earnings Sharing, *Earnings Sharing in Social Security: A Model for Reform* (Washington, D.C.: Center for Women Policy Studies, 1988), Table A-1.3.1.2.3.

Other arguments against the spouse benefit are (1) that a majority of women (but not all) in the future will be covered by social security on the basis of their own earnings, (2) that since few husband-wife families are poor, the spouse benefit is an extremely inefficient way to channel money to low income families, and (3) that with rising female earnings, most families are now characterized by the mutual economic dependence of husbands and wives (Munnell, 1977).

Three reforms are often proposed:

1. To eliminate the spouse benefit and split the combined earnings of the husband and wife for purposes of calculating benefits.
2. To increase the worker benefit level and/or the survivor benefit and, at the same time, reduce the spouse benefit.
3. To extend coverage and benefits directly to nonsalaried household workers (as is done, for example, in Germany).

Survivor Benefits

A retired couple has combined social security income based on "the worker's" benefit and 50 percent of that benefit for the spouse—with some having a combination of their own and some portion of the spouse benefit. But when the retired worker dies, the benefit is cut by one-third (i.e., 100 percent of the worker benefit). The surviving spouse of a couple that was living just above the poverty line will often find that his/her income is below the poverty level specified for a single individual. This is one reason official statistics show that the poverty rate for women is very high.

As we discussed above, there is general agreement that the 50 percent survivor benefit is too high if differences in living costs between one- and two-person families is the only consideration. Therefore, some argue it should be reduced and the money be shifted, say, to survivors. Various proposals have been made for ways to increase survivor benefits. For example, Burkhauser and Smeeding (1994) propose that the survivor benefit be calculated as some specified percent of the couple's combined benefit; and Robert Ball, former Commissioner of Social Security, has in fact proposed that we reduce the spouse benefit and, at the same time, raise the basic benefit; he sees this as a way of making the program more adequate for survivors.

Homemaker Credits

One proposed option to the spouse benefit is to make provision for "homemaker credits." Persons who stay out of the paid labor force to raise children or maintain a household currently accumulate no earnings credits for that period of their lives and do not receive benefits if they become disabled. If they later take a job outside the household, they find their average lifetime earnings depressed and hence receive lower social security benefits. Furthermore, American homemakers who never work outside the home must depend entirely on the earnings records of their spouses for any social security benefits. Consequently, the divorce, disablement, or death of a spouse (especially in the early years) can result in the homemaker receiving very meager benefits or no benefits at all. Alternatively, the death or disability of the homemaker deprives the household of valuable services, but lack of homemaker coverage precludes any social security compensation.

Homemaker credits are used in several countries. In the United Kingdom, Germany, and Japan, voluntary contributions by homemakers to the social security system are permitted. In Japan, where the system provides benefits in excess of the value of contributions paid, 80 percent of eligible homemakers participate (Lapkoff, 1981).

In the United States, it has been proposed (AARP, 1991) that "caregiving credits" be given in determining eligibility for the special minimum benefit. This would help to increase benefits for those with long work histories who drop out of the labor force to provide family care. (Several other proposals have been introduced in Congress that would provide general social security credits for people performing homemaker services in the family.)

In his campaign for the presidency, Al Gore proposed to allow parents (men and women) to take credit for up to five years of earnings, if they use the time for raising young children. Such a credit is estimated to increase an eligible woman's social security retirement benefit by about $600 a year (Gore, 2000).

A number of issues and problems have been raised in connection with these proposals. Disagreement arises over how these benefits will be financed: by general revenue, by a special earmarked tax, or by the covered person. Another issue is the difficulty in determining how much credit the homemaker should receive. Some have suggested that the Secretary of the Department of Health and Human Services should determine the value; others advocate using the median wage for all paid workers (or all women workers). Another issue to be resolved is deciding who would be eligible and determining how to insure proper reporting of homemaker services. Still another issue pointed out by Ross and Upp (1993) is that homemaker credits and childcare drop-out years "acknowledge the non-market contributions of some women but not others. Mothers who must work for pay also have homemaker and childcare responsibilities." Finally, there is a serious "targeting" issue. The findings of various research studies indicate that a homemaker credit provision is likely to primarily benefit higher-income families (see, for example, Holden, 1982). "Is this a good use of our social security dollars?" ask the critics.

Earnings Sharing

The homemaker credit approach has received little political support over the years (see U.S. House Committee on Ways and Means, 1985). An alternative reform approach—earnings sharing—has received much more attention but, again, little support in Congress. This reform would divide social security earnings credits of married couples equally between spouses. Retirement credits could be split and credit given on three alternative occasions: (1) as the credits are earned; (2) only in case of a marriage dissolution; or (3) at the time of retirement or disability. Although earnings sharing is a new idea for social security, the concept has been in use for a long time in community property states, especially with regard to divorce settlements.

Over the past twenty years various earnings-sharing proposals have been developed and evaluated. The National Commission on Social Security gave major attention to this option. It concluded in 1981 that the most serious problem was that most earnings-sharing schemes that have been proposed would lower benefits for a significant number of future beneficiaries, even for some whom the plan was designed to help: "It was the sense of the Commission that changes which erode the adequacy of the system do not help women. The Commission concludes that such changes could not be supported unless the unintentional disadvantages could be remedied at a cost which was deemed reasonable. To be fair to some women at the cost of reducing the protection of others does not achieve fairness" (National Commission on Social Security, 1981).

Instead, the commission chose "to concentrate on the incremental improvements" that it considered most urgent. It proposed that the special minimum benefit now available for long-term, low-wage workers be computed on a maximum of 35 years of coverage and allow credit for up to ten childcare years. A bill that allowed up to two additional years to be dropped from the earnings history of persons leaving the workforce to care for a child under age 3 was passed by the Senate in 1983. The provision was dropped, however, in the conference agreement between the House and Senate. The commission also recommended that the earnings of deceased workers be wage-indexed for purposes of calculating survivor benefits. This recommendation was legislated in 1983 and significantly increases benefits for many widows.

The earnings-sharing approach has continued to receive study and discussion over the years. A study by the U.S. Congressional Budget Office (1986) concluded that "the key issues for the Congress . . . are whether it wants to make changes in the social security benefit structure that would raise some people's benefits, and, if so, how it wishes to pay for them." Cost estimates for various earnings sharing approaches have ranged from *saving* $600 million a year to *spending* an additional $16 billion (Forman, 1987).

With congressional concerns focused on budget issues, few people expect much attention in the short run to this or any other major reform to improve the situation for women covered by social security. The Technical Committee on Earnings Sharing, a private group seeking to improve women's treatment under social security, worked for over five years to design an earnings-sharing scheme that would deal with all the major technical problems and still be acceptable to a broad spectrum of political interests. Its proposal (which was designed to be implemented over a 45-year period) would result in *increases* going to those with lower benefits under current law; decreases would be experienced primarily by those with higher benefits (Fierst and Duff, 1988). To reduce opposition from "the losers," the committee devised a declining individual guarantee to insure beneficiaries who became eligible for benefits during the transition period a lifetime benefit equal to a high fraction of their current law benefit (if it were higher).

Writing in 1990, one of the plan's chief architects describes the general political response to the plan:

[It] is the story of a failure. . . . [We] found that the world had no interest in . . . [our] product. Indeed, many of . . . [the committee's] own members walked away from their own recommendations. . . . The proposal is so well balanced that no one is willing to fight for it. The winners and losers are individuals, not groups.

Thus, while most working wives would be better off, not all would be. While most widows of two-earner couples would get higher benefits, those whose earnings are substantially lower than their husband's would not. . . . Not even the most likely group, married women with higher earnings, would all be gainers. Instead, in order to prevent the cost of social security from skyrocketing, the plan retains the current maximums on survivor benefits, thereby depriving this group of major incentives to fight for earnings sharing. . . . Thus, there is no readily ascertainable group whose members would be so much better off that they will organize and lobby for this change. (Fierst, 1990)

Thus, the Technical Committee's experience echoed (one decade later) the concern expressed in the 1981 National Commission on Social Security's report—that the biggest obstacle to social security reform for women is the inability to devise a reform plan at reasonable cost without lowering benefits for some retirees. Ross and Upp (1993), both with many years of research and policy experience in this area, comment that "these conflicts appear insoluble."

The Social Security Retirement Age

Currently, age 65 is the "normal retirement age"—the age when workers can retire and receive an *unreduced* social security retirement benefit. Over the years, however, there has been increasing support for raising the age. Increasing the retirement age beginning around the turn of the century was recommended by three major commissions: in 1981 by the National Commission on Social Security and the President's Commission on Pension Policy and in 1983 by the Republican-appointed majority of the National Commission on Social Security Reform.

The major reasons given to support this change are:

1. Americans are living longer, and many are healthier.
2. Older workers will be in greater demand in future years.
3. Rising pension costs (especially in the next century) can be partially offset by reversing the trend toward earlier retirement.

Those arguing against an increase in the social security retirement age argue that:

1. While life expectancy in later life is increasing, there is no evidence that general health and ability to work at later ages are improving (Markides, 1993).
2. A large proportion of people retire involuntarily (due to poor health, obsolete skills, and lack of job opportunities) and will not be able to respond to changes in social security eligibility requirements by working longer (Packard and Reno, 1988).

3. The presumption that the economy in the future will be *unable* to support retirement at the current retirement ages is questionable (Schulz et al., 1991; Hurd, 1993b).

It seems clear that the predominant factor that has motivated those favoring an increase in the age is a desire to reduce the long-term costs of social security retirement pensions. Faced with a serious shortfall in social security funds in the short run and large projected deficits beginning around the year 2010, Congress began (in the early 1980s) a search for ways to bring the system into financial balance. One part of the solution voted by Congress in 1983 was a future increase in the retirement age. Under the new law, workers starting in the year 2027 will have to be age 67 before receiving a full benefit. Individuals will still be able to retire as early as age 62 but will suffer a 30 percent reduction in their benefits. The effects of this change will be felt even earlier, however. The change is scheduled to occur gradually, beginning in 2003 and achieving its full impact in 2027.

SSA: Just Another Bureaucracy You Can't Trust?

In its early years the Social Security Administration (SSA) developed the reputation of being different from the rest of bureaucratic government. It was seen as dependable (always getting the checks out on time), efficient (a leader in data processing and the newest administrative methods), and client-oriented (it really tried to help people get benefits). Today public confidence in SSA may be at an all-time low. What happened?

SSA's problems began in the 1970s. At least four major problem areas brought SSA into the media headlines and gave concern to citizens and policymakers alike. First, as we discuss in the next chapter, for the first time in its history there were big fears that various social security programs might run out of funds. By 1979 a Louis Harris survey reported that more than four out of five workers did not have confidence that social security would be able to pay the benefits due them when they retired. These fears were compounded when various administrations in Washington were charged with manipulating the social security accounts to deal with the budget deficit problem and to mask the true size of the deficits.

The second development that undermined confidence in SSA was a variety of problems that arose in connection with the start-up of the Supplemental Security Income program (SSI) in 1974. In large part because of SSA's excellent reputation, Congress assigned it the job of administering this new means-tested program for the aged, blind, and disabled (discussed in detail in Chapter 6). SSI was seen by the Congress as a better way of dealing with the poor; the hope was to eliminate the invasive and

degrading welfare practices existing in many of the states under the Old
Age Assistance programs. But SSA had very little time to prepare administratively for the new program. Yet it was asked to take over from the
states most of the task of administering what turned out to be a very
complex set of regulations governing welfare to the destitute aged, blind,
and disabled. To make matters worse, many of the SSA staff were actively
hostile to working in an agency dealing with "the poor" and having to
oversee a program where benefits were means tested rather than received
as a matter of "right" (as a result of working). And to make matters even
worse, the SSA leadership seriously underestimated the manpower
needed to administer the program and the transition time needed to start
it up. As a result, the early years of SSI were plagued by wrong payments,
work backlogs, crowded and unresponsive field offices, low morale, poor
training of staff, and a huge outpouring of administrative regulations
(many of which became obsolete quickly).

The third problem arose out of administering the social security disability program (discussed in Chapter 6). During the 1970s the disability
rolls grew rapidly and became very large. Motivated by mushrooming
costs and claims of widespread cheating, Congress required in 1980 that
the SSA review all disability recipients (except the "permanently disabled") once every three years. The new Reagan administration saw the
"disability review" mandate as consistent with its cost-cutting and antifederal views and pushed the review forward with a vengeance. Hundreds
of thousands of disability recipients were declared ineligible, and benefits
were terminated before any appeal could take place. A great many people
(some close to death) were wrongly terminated and had to go through
a long and agonizing process before their benefits were restored. The
disability review process lasted until the spring of 1984. "By then opposition was so powerful and the chaos was so complete that the administration was compelled to suspend the review and wait for Congress to
try to restore order with new legislation" (Derthick, 1990). In 1993, there
was still a backlog of more than half a million disability claims! No longer
was SSA viewed by many people as a bureaucracy trying to help people,
given the negative publicity resulting from this new hostile and adversar-
ial activity and widespread administrative delays.

A fourth problem arose when SSA instituted a toll-free telephone system to replace its traditional information dissemination through a network of local social security offices around the United States. During
1990, the first year of nationwide operation, the lines were constantly
busy. People were unable to easily reach the SSA, and when they did,
they often got wrong information:

A GAO [U.S. General Accounting Office] study commissioned by the Committee
[Senate Special Committee on Aging] found that 43 percent of callers who were

evaluated got wrong answers. One in five got wrong answers that could affect their benefit amounts. In addition, it was revealed that busy signal rates above 50 percent were commonplace. . . . Amid growing congressional criticism of the toll-free system, SSA began detailing staff out of Social Security field offices and into the teleservice centers to help answer calls. According to GAO, some of these staff were unqualified to do so, while the accompanying drain on field staff jeopardized the ability of those offices to serve the public. . . . When callers of the toll-free line realized that they could no longer speak with staff in a local SSA office, many became upset and reluctant to discuss their financial affairs with a stranger. More-over, callers cannot reach the same person twice over the toll-free line when a problem arises that requires more than one call to settle. (U.S. Senate Special Committee on Aging, 1991)

While SSA was trying to deal with these four problems (and others), it was also faced with a crisis of leadership and staffing. Hostile to means-testing, many very competent people left SSA when it assumed respon-sibility for the SSI program (Derthick, 1990). Much more serious was the fact that 17,000 SSA personnel were cut during the Reagan administra-tion. On April 20, 1990, the *Washington Post* published a story reporting a warning by retiring Deputy Social Security Commissioner Herbert R. Doggette, Jr. (Rich, 1990). In a memorandum to Social Security Com-missioner Gwendolyn S. King, Doggette warned, according to the *Post* article, that there were signs of a serious "deterioration in levels of ser-vice" and that the agency could be "overwhelmed" as a result of employee cutbacks. In 1993, the U.S. Senate Special Committee on Aging (1993) reported that congressional testimony and GAO reports continued to re-veal that severe stress from increasing workloads was contributing to a deterioration of overall staff effectiveness. Yet in October 1994, SSA, un-der pressure from budget cutters, announced it would cut 5,000 jobs over five years.

While all this has been going on, SSA was subjected to frequent changes in leadership at the top. Robert M. Ball was commissioner of Social Se-curity for eleven years, from 1962 to 1973, and is widely acknowledged as having been extremely effective in administering the agency and help-ing promote the strong positive image existing before the 1970s. Over the next eighteen years, there were ten new commissioners and no visible continuity of leadership.

One reaction to all these problems was that SSA has lost much of its historical autonomy. "Courts and the presidency have become much more vigilant and intrusive. Congress has become more critical. And the SSA has become a more vulnerable and inviting subject of scrutiny as its programs have run into financial and administrative trouble" (Derthick, 1990). What is probably even worse, to many of the public SSA has be-come just another government bureaucracy not to be trusted.

Congress has sought to respond to these developments. The disability review process discussed above was modified by new federal law. Congress created new rules—known as the "fire wall" procedures—designed to make it more difficult to diminish the social security reserves that are currently being built up. Congress ordered the agency to publish phone numbers in telephone directories so that people could call, as an option, their local social security offices (instead of the 800-number), and the agency has taken action to reevaluate its administrative needs and policies.

Another suggestion proposed by members of Congress was to insulate SSA from political manipulation by taking it out of the Department of Health and Human Service and making it an independent agency. Advocates of this approach argued that this would shield the agency from short-term partisan politics and bureaucratic infighting, promote administrative independence, and provide a more continuous, consistent leadership—which would enhance public confidence in SSA. In 1989 House and Senate bodies approved bills aimed at achieving this objective. Final enactment was stalled. In 1994, however, President Clinton announced his support of the independent agency concept and it was legislated into law.

While the public has been concerned with social security financing and how the system has been administered in recent years, numerous opinion polls over the years have indicated that Americans strongly support the programs and want the system to continue (Sherman, 1989; Friedland, 1994). If participation were optional, about three-fourths of the population say they would stay in, and almost all see social security as the government's "most important" program (96 percent) and "a successful" program (92 percent).

CHAPTER 4 HIGHLIGHTS

The Social Security Act passed in 1935 is considered a landmark in social legislation. This chapter—focusing on the old-age and survivors' program—explained the major provisions and changing nature of the program as it has evolved over time:

1. OASDI is a universal, compulsory, earnings-related, contributory program that seeks to provide protection against common problems confronted by the whole population.

2. In responding to the economic problems of old age, Congress decided to emphasize a "universal scheme" that avoided the need to put most individuals through a means-testing screening device—an approach that was designed to garner widespread political support.

3. To reduce the number of people who would have to rely on needs-tested public assistance, Congress incorporated into OASI a large number of provi-

sions that made it easy to qualify for benefits in the early years, raised the adequacy of benefits for low earners, and created dependent benefits. Critics today argue that these early decisions now create serious issues of equity and cost. (This point is discussed more extensively in Chapter 5.)

4. Important changes in OASI have occurred over the years with regard to coverage, benefit levels, eligibility ages, the retirement test, indexing, and the taxing of benefits.

5. Despite increased benefit levels, there is still a large gap for most workers between OASI benefits and the income needed to maintain living standards in retirement.

6. Social security is not just a program for old people. It helps millions of the nonaged who are unemployed, disabled, or the survivors (both adults and children) of workers who have died.

SUGGESTED READINGS

Ball, Robert M. *Straight Talk about Social Security: An Analysis of the Issues in the Current Debate*. New York: Century Foundation Press, 1998. The views of a former commissioner of social security and a staunch advocate for its improvement and continuance.

Dixon, John. *Social Security in Global Perspective*. Westport, Conn.: Praeger, 1999. A discussion of all major aspects of social security with program provisions and statistics from around the world.

Employee Benefit Research Institution (EBRI). *Assessing Social Security Reform Alternatives*. Washington, D.C.: EBRI, 1997. A collection of conference papers on benefits, financing, and proposed privatization reform.

Kingson, Eric R., and Edward D. Berkowitz. *Social Security and Medicare: A Policy Primer*. Westport, Conn.: Auburn House, 1993. The authors provide an excellent survey of the topic, avoiding a complex, technical approach that can bewilder nonspecialists.

Kingson, Eric R., and James H. Schulz, eds. *Social Security in the 21st Century*. New York: Oxford University Press, 1997. Chapters by experts on all major areas of social security except medical care financing—including benefit levels, women's equity, work incentives, administrative issues, and means testing.

Lubove, Roy. *The Struggle for Social Security, 1900–1935*. Cambridge, Mass.: Harvard University Press, 1968. An interpretive, historical analysis of the passage of the 1935 Social Security Act.

Myers, Robert J. *Social Security*, 4th ed. Philadelphia: University of Pennsylvania Press, 1991. An authoritative review of history, concepts, program provisions, and statistics.

Rimlinger, Gaston. *Welfare Policy and Industrialization in Europe, America, and Russia*. New York: Wiley, 1971. Where did American social insurance come from? Rimlinger provides a history and comparative analysis of earlier social security systems in Germany, Russia, and Britain, comparing them with the origins of the programs in the United States.

Schulz, James H. *Older Women and Private Pensions in the United Kingdom*. Waltham, Mass.: National Center on Women and Aging, Brandeis University, 2000. A detailed review of the British pension privatization experience.

Steuerle, C. Eugene, and J. M. Bakija. *Retooling Social Security for the 21st Century*. Washington, D.C.: The Urban Institute Press, 1994. A critical look at social security with much information and detail. It provides a highly authoritative discussion of various reform issues, providing, for example, an in-depth discussion of the redistribution impact of social security.

Thompson, Lawrence H. *Older and Wiser: The Economics of Public Pensions*. Washington, D.C.: The Urban Institute Press, 1998. This book examines major social security issues from an economic perspective, focusing on various criticisms and the current reform debate.

U.S. Social Security Administration (SSA). *Annual Statistical Supplement, Social Security Bulletin*. Washington, D.C.: SSA, published annually. The first place to look for information on chronological changes in the social security law. Also provided is a wide range of statistical data.

William M. Mercer, Inc. *Guide to Social Security and Medicare*. Louisville, Ky.: William M. Mercer, Inc., published annually. A succinct summary of OASDHI provisions, written for nonexperts.

Chapter 5

Social Security Financing:
Who Pays? Who Should Pay?

In an article titled "The Young Pay for the Old," journalist Edwin L. Dale, Jr. (1973) wrote:

A funny thing happened to your taxes on the way to 1973. Congress passed the biggest federal increase since the Korean war (and that one was temporary), and hardly anybody peeped except a few intellectuals. This was happening at the same time of the "taxpayers' revolt" at federal, state, and local levels. . . .

Before anyone wonders whether he missed some important news development, or has been somehow bamboozled, it is best to explain the mystery. The paradox is resolved in two words: social security . . . a $7 billion tax increase enacted in 1972 with scarcely a voice of protest.[1]

In 1977 Congress again found it necessary to schedule further increases in social security payroll taxes. "President Carter and Congress have a bear by the tail," wrote Hobart Rowen (1978). "Having decided . . . [in 1977] that the only way to rescue the social security system from bankruptcy was to raise an additional $227 billion in payroll taxes over the next ten years, they now have discovered—big surprise!—that this isn't very popular with the voters."

The 1978 report of the Board of Trustees of the social security trust funds stated that the payroll tax increases included in the 1977 social security amendments would "restore the financial soundness of the cash benefit program throughout the remainder of this century and into the early years of the next one." But by 1982 the assets of the OASI fund (after taking into account the taxes to be received in the year) was less than the amount needed to pay benefits for the year, and interfund borrowing from the disability insurance and hospital insurance trust funds began. In 1983 Congress had to pass another major social security financing package, including—for the first time—taxation of certain social security benefits (discussed later).

Then suddenly in the late 1980s the discussion reversed. Social security deficits disappeared and huge surpluses loomed. Reacting to another scheduled increase in the payroll tax, Robert Myers (1987), former chief actuary of the social security system, asked in the *Washington Post* (1987): "Are these increases desirable or necessary? The answer is clearly 'no.' " In reply, former Commissioner of Social Security Robert Ball argued: "I disagree completely. . . . Let's make sure we have a safety margin for the immediate future" (Ball, 1987). Controversy over this matter came to a head in the early 1990s when Senator Daniel Patrick Moynihan proposed that the Congress roll back payroll tax levels, thereby largely eliminating the projected excesses of income over payments. Congress ignored his initiatives.

For the public, one of the most important aspects of pension policy is the way these programs are financed; yet until recently there has been little controversy over these matters. Why in recent years has pension financing become front-page news?

RISING PENSION EXPENDITURES AND GROWING CONTROVERSY

Few people realize the magnitude of the expenditures involved in pension programs and hence the huge amount of funds that must be raised annually through taxes, worker "contributions," returns on pension reserves, and employer allocations for pension purposes. In 2000, $411 billion in OASDI benefits were paid to Americans.

In recent years there has been a sharp increase in criticisms of the approach used to finance pensions—especially those used for social security. Pension financing involves many complex issues, and, no doubt, part of the recent controversy arises because of the confusion and misunderstanding that generally prevails. Is the social security system "bankrupt," as is frequently charged? Will younger workers get back less than they contribute to social security? Does the burden of financing social security fall disproportionately on the poor and treat racial minorities and women unfairly?

We will divide the discussion of social security financing into three broad aspects: (1) current social security financing practices and short-term versus long-term issues; (2) the equity of present practices; and (3) a review of various proposed changes in social security financing.

Table 5-1
Maximum Taxable Earnings and Payroll Tax Rates, OASDI for Selected Years

Year	Maximum Taxable Earnings	Combined Payroll Tax Rate[a]
1937	$3,000	2.00%
1940	3,000	2.00%
1950	3,000	3.00%
1960	4,800	6.00%
1970	7,800	8.40%
1980	25,900	10.16%
1990	51,300	12.40%
1995	61,200	12.40%
2000	76,200[b]	12.40%[c]

[a]The tax is split equally between employee and employer payments. The amount shown here combines the two. The hospital insurance tax is not included. Rates for the self-employed are different up to 1990 and not shown.
[b]The amount in the years that follow is automatically determined by law on the basis of the annual increase in nation-wide employment average earnings in prior years, increasing the prior year's amount by the rate of the earnings increase.
[c]The combined rate is not scheduled to change in future years.

FINANCING SOCIAL SECURITY

The OASDHI program is financed by a **payroll tax** that requires the self-employed and workers in covered employment (regardless of age) to pay a percentage of their earnings into the program and employers to pay an equal percentage based on their employees' earnings. In all cases the percentage paid is limited to earnings up to a specified annual maximum. In the original legislation (and up through 1950) this maximum, called the *earnings base*, was $3,000. Between 1951 and 1972 the earnings base was increased periodically on an ad hoc basis. Then in 1972, legislation was passed that set the earnings base at $12,000 in 1974 and specified that the base was henceforth to rise *automatically* as average earnings rose.[2] By 1999 the earnings base for OASDI—through a combination of ad hoc and automatic increases—had reached $72,600.[3]

Table 5-1 shows past and future increases in the payroll tax. As legislated by the Social Security Amendments of 1983, the OASDI combined tax rose to 12.4 percent in 1990. An additional tax of 2.9 percent is currently levied for the hospital insurance program under social security (Medicare). Self-employed persons pay a tax rate of 15.30 percent.

The Reserve Funding Issue

It is important to understand that in the past most of the revenues generated each year by these payroll taxes were used to pay benefits to nonworkers *in the same year.* If there is a surplus of revenue over expenditures, it is maintained as part of the reserves for future needs and is deposited in one of the three social security trust funds: the OASI, Disability, or Hospital Insurance trust fund. However, during much of social security's history, the size of these trust funds has not been very large relative to future obligations.

Concerning reserves, J. Douglas Brown (1972) writes that "as originally enacted the old age insurance system would have accumulated in time a reserve of $47 billion, more than the outstanding debt of the government in 1935." While President Roosevelt favored substantial reserve financing, a coalition of both liberals and conservatives opposed this approach. In 1935, for example, Republican presidential candidate Alf Landon charged that billions of dollars would be raised and wasted by Washington politicians and bureaucrats—echoing similar views of the AFL, the U.S. Chamber of Commerce, and the *New York Times* (Lopez, 1991).

The 1937–1938 Social Security Advisory Council spent a great deal of time examining this issue and finally recommended that only a "reasonable contingency reserve" be maintained. Congress subsequently postponed the scheduled 1940 payroll tax increase and others scheduled for later in the 1940s—embarking on a partial funding approach for the next 50 years.

Over the years there has been considerable controversy over whether adequate financing of social insurance programs requires the accumulation of large financial reserves. Much of the discussion has centered on the extent to which public insurance programs need to follow financing practices conforming to the traditional tenets of actuarial soundness associated with *private* insurance.

The term **actuarial soundness** refers to the ability of insurance programs to provide sufficient (i.e., legally obligated) payments to eligible recipients at the time they come due. A private insurance company, for example, must necessarily operate on the basis that it will not sell any new policies in the future. Therefore, it should always have sufficient assets on hand to meet its obligations for existing policyholders, even if they all surrender their policies at once. Similarly, private pension plans generally try to maintain (or build up over time) reserve funds sufficient to meet contracted obligations.

This involves putting aside money for **accrued benefits** based on employment *after* the plan is initiated. However, it also involves payments (often spread out over a period of years) for the costs of unexpected new obligations or benefits provided for employee services rendered *before the pension plan began operation.*

The Partial Funding Approach

There is now widely accepted agreement among pension specialists that social security programs do *not* require the accumulation of large amounts of reserves to be actuarially sound (see, for example, Myers, 1991). It is recognized that the taxing power of the government guarantees the long-run financial integrity of such programs and that, unlike private insurance, it is appropriate to assume that the programs will operate indefinitely—with a consequent continuous flow of revenue. Moreover, the fact that public insurance is usually compulsory and covers most of the population avoids the financing problems arising from an unexpected fluctuation in the number of participants.

Until the social security amendments in 1977 and 1983, relatively few reserves had been accumulated in the trust funds. This way of financing social security is commonly referred to as the "pay-as-you-go" method. However, because some significant amount of reserves has always been maintained, it is more correct to refer to the financing of social security as a "partial reserve" approach. Benefits, to a large extent, are paid to the current aged out of the payroll tax contributions of the current working population. In return, members of the working population know that they are promised benefits when they become eligible, financed out of the taxes of future workers.

Thus, while OASDI reserves have increased in 48 out of 60 years (1937–1998), total reserves in recent years have been equal to about two years' disbursements. Given this small reserve, some people have argued (erroneously) that social security is a bankrupt program that does not have the money to pay its obligations. Without necessarily characterizing the situation as bankruptcy, others have seriously questioned the financial soundness of the program.

In answer to critics of a small partial reserve financing approach, five former secretaries of the Department of Heath, Education, and Welfare and three former commissioners of social security issued on February 10, 1975, a statement emphasizing why they thought that the government did not need to amass vast reserves to keep social security financially sound. In part, they argued:

By earmarking the proceeds of social security taxes for the payment of benefits and depositing them in a trust fund for this purpose, by entitling the system insurance, by continuing actions to assure its financial soundness, and by innumerable pronouncements of congressional committees and individual spokesmen, Congress has made clear beyond question its pledge to the American people that the social security commitment will be honored. (Ad Hoc Advisory Committee, 1975)

Thus, we see that *the main argument for nonfunding rests on the quality of the pension promise made by the government*. To fulfill this promise requires that Congress insure that over the long run the flow of funds remains in a "satisfactory actuarial status." But what constitutes satisfactory actuarial status? An expert Panel on Social Security Financing, composed of economists and actuaries, argued that this means being able to predict with reasonable confidence (1) that future scheduled flows of income and expenditures will be in harmony and (2) that future scheduled taxes required to support the program be within the limits of practical acceptability to the population paying the social security tax (U.S. Senate Committee on Finance, 1975).

Reviewing the financing experience of social security in the past and research on "reserve adequacy," Munnell and Blais (1984) conclude that:

[Social security] balances should be equal to at least 75 percent of annual outlays plus the additional 10 percent that is required to pay benefits on a timely basis. Somewhat higher balances, however, may be desirable to give Congress more time to act in the wake of back-to-back recessions. In short, trust fund balances somewhere between 85 percent and 145 percent of annual outlays should provide an adequate contingency reserve.

Other experts have called for 100 percent to 150 percent of annual outlays; none has called for full reserves to protect social security finances.

A Benefit Bonanza?

As we indicated in the previous chapter, social security's unfunded liability results from a decision by Congress not to operate a funded system. Most important is the fact that, historically, *both* private employers and government have opted to grant significant pension benefits to persons reaching retirement age during the initial years (or start-up) of pension programs—benefits "not paid for."[4]

To become eligible for social security benefits, an individual must have a certain number of calendar quarters of coverage based on employment. Congress initially set the required quarters low for the older worker group, which resulted in their receiving benefits that far exceeded what could be "actuarially purchased" from their relatively few years of contributions.

Thus, ever since the social security system began, the vast majority of retirees have received far more retirement benefits than they ever paid contributions into the program. New groups that were covered in the 1950s and 1960s also were granted these "windfall gains," and with subsequent liberalizations in the benefit structure, most new retirees will also experience these gains—and for many years to come.

Why did Congress grant these generous benefits (relative to payroll contributions) for early participants in the system? First, because most of the early participants needed the benefits. Without them, a majority of the aged would have had incomes below the poverty level. Many had seen their lifetime savings disappear or decline dramatically during the Great Depression. Congress, aware of their economic plight, sought to ameliorate it *without forcing people to confront the stigma of needs-tested public assistance.*

Second, as we discussed in Chapter 4, Congress at the time was confronted with historically high unemployment rates. It initially set benefit eligibility very low to encourage older workers to leave the labor force and to avoid drawing funds out of a depressed economy, and continuing unemployment during downturns in the postwar period again encouraged Congress to expand coverage and liberalize eligibility requirements.

Finally, the growing social security coverage itself and the general economic growth of the post–World War II years resulted in revenues exceeding outlays for the system. These actual and projected short-run surpluses made it politically and economically easier for Congress to improve benefits.

The resulting policy—*not* to exclude persons with relatively few years of participation in the program and *not* to make them "pay their way"— was financed on an essentially pay-as-you-go basis out of the rising earnings of the working population, with only modest increases in taxes. But it has also added to the future "unfunded" liabilities of the social security program.

Long-Term Financing

Actuarial projections of future benefits and taxes are made annually by the Social Security Administration's Office of the Actuary. The projections and a general assessment of financial status are submitted in a report by the Social Security Board of Trustees to Congress each year. In the early years these reports expressed little concern about any long-term financing problem. In the 1974 report, however, the actuarial projection forecast a significant actuarial deficit over the 75-year period 1974–2048. This projected deficit, higher than any previously forecasted, was *almost doubled one year later* when the trustees issued their 1975 report! This was the beginning of concern about the serious financial problems that plagued the system over the next decade.

The long-term financing concerns of that decade were the result of three major factors: (1) expanding benefit expenditures, including costs arising from the automatic cost-of-living adjustment mechanism legislated in 1972; (2) rising future costs of the post–World War II baby boom; and (3) declining revenues due to a projected lower rate of economic growth and a dramatic decline in the American birth rate.

Problems with Indexing

Projected deficits were in large part related to the particular way the Social Security Amendments of 1972 specified the **indexing** of pension benefits. Soon after this legislation was passed, various experts demonstrated that the particular indexing adjustment mechanism used could have major unintended effects. Under certain economic conditions (with regard to the relationship between price and wage changes), the mechanism could produce steadily increasing social security replacement rates for workers retiring in future years. The greater the rate of inflation and/ or the smaller the rate of growth in real wages, the greater the increase in real benefits, and hence the greater the future financial burden on social security.[5]

The result of what was generally acknowledged to be a mistake in indexing procedures was a dramatic change in *projected* benefits. The social security benefit structure promised (given forecasted inflation rates) to provide future generations of retiring workers with social security benefits that replaced much larger proportions of preretirement income than were originally intended. These replacement rates were projected to get bigger for successive cohorts of retiring workers. Thus, the replacement rates for some retirees in the 21st century were projected to be well above 100 percent of preretirement earnings.

Naturally, the cost of these high benefit levels was also projected to rise. As a result, actuarial assessments of the financial status of the social security system projected sharply rising system deficits in the next century and the need for greatly increased payroll tax levels.

Congress acted in 1977 to correct the indexing procedures and to roll back for future retirees most of the real benefit increases resulting from the "over-indexing" procedures that had occurred over the five-year interim period. This corrective action is the origin of the so-called "notch" issue. The cut-back in benefit levels for those working beyond age 62 and born after 1916, below the benefit levels for those just preceding them, produced public cries of inequity. The inequity, however, was that those born before 1917 (who worked well beyond age 62) received benefits larger than Congress had intended (i.e., windfalls)—not that those born after 1916 received too little. Two authoritative studies of this issue (National Academy of Social Insurance, 1988; U.S. General Accounting Office, 1988) have advised against making any changes related to the notch situation.

Thus, in 1977 the projected deficits were significantly reduced by eliminating the unintended indexing increases. But projected deficits in the long term were not eliminated, given two other key factors: the baby boom and declining fertility.

The Future Costs of the Baby Boom

The steady rise in births after World War II (reaching a peak in 1957 of 4.3 million) will cause a future rise in the retirement age population relative to the working age population (see Chapter 8). This will begin around the year 2010, when this baby boom population begins reaching old age. The drop in births that followed the postwar increase has caused the rise in the ratio to be even sharper, because the falling number of births reduces the number of persons who are in the future working population. The result is a large rise in social security retirement benefits that come due in the 21st century, without as rapid an increase in payroll tax revenues from workers, whose numbers will be increasing more slowly.

Congress took major steps in 1983 toward eliminating the projected deficits of the next century. The social security amendments in that year contained a number of provisions designed to have a positive impact on long-term financing. We discuss below a major provision of that legislation to gradually increase the normal retirement age (currently age 65). This will have a favorable long-term financial impact. However, the transition to this higher age will not be completed until the year 2027. Tax revenues are also increasing significantly in the long run as a result of the mandatory coverage of workers in the nonprofit sector and new federal employees, and an increase in the payroll tax for self-employed persons.[6]

The most unexpected action by Congress in 1983, however, was to impose for the first time federal income taxes on part of social security benefits for beneficiaries with incomes over specified levels. Exempted from taxation on benefits are couples with income below $32,000 and single persons with income below $25,000. There is a special definition of income used in connection with this provision: "adjusted gross income" (as defined in the federal income tax laws), plus interest on tax-exempt bonds, plus certain foreign-source income, plus 50 percent of social security income.

In the initial law (1983), persons with "income" above the exemption levels were subject to federal income tax on 50 percent of their social security benefits. Beginning in 1994 the law was changed to tax more. In general, higher-income beneficiaries now pay 50 percent of all income in excess of $25,000, plus an additional 35 percent of the income in excess of $34,000 (if any).[7]

Currently, this provision affects relatively few elderly persons, because

Figure 5–1
Projected OASDI Outgo and Income^a in Constant 1999 Dollars, 2000–2030

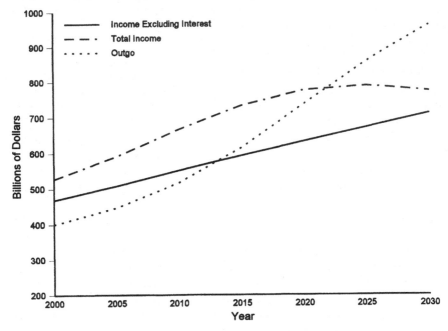

^aProjections are "intermediate assumptions" of the SSA Office of the Actuary.
Source: Based on data in Social Security Administration (SSA), *1999 OASDI Trustees Report*
    (Washington, D.C.: SSA, 1999), Table III.B2.

most have income levels below the exemption. In 1994, an estimated 20
percent of beneficiaries paid higher taxes as a result of this new tax provision (Pattison and Harrington, 1993). Eventually, however, real and
inflation-induced income increases will push a significant number of
future elderly persons into the taxable range, given that the exemption
level is not indexed. The result will be more revenue for the social security system in future years, because the 1983 amendments specified
that the tax revenue from social security income is to be transferred to
the social security trust funds.

However, it was clear in 1983, as it is today, that social security financing will need to be adjusted in future years. Figure 5–1, based on the
current law and assumptions about demographic and economic trends,
indicates that the current surpluses of income over outgo are expected
to disappear around 2025. Initially, ear-marked federal revenues ("interest") based on trust fund reserves will make up the difference. But ultimately, unless benefits are reduced, there is almost certain to be a need
for higher social security taxes or lower benefits.

Slow Growth

Unlike the rapid growth period of the 1960s, the years that followed witnessed a dramatic slowdown in productivity and associated economic growth (Denison, 1979; Baumol et al., 1989). In contrast to the rise in real average earnings that occurred in the United States from 1947 to 1973, average earnings (in real terms) declined in the late 1970s and rose slowly in the 1980s (Myers, 1990).

With lower growth and lower earnings come lower payroll tax revenues (discussed further below), and given this experience, projections of economic growth and social security revenues for future years were lower, contributing to the pessimistic actuarial projections that began to appear in the 1970s.

A great deal of the current debate about social security's financial future involves disagreements over what these future growth rates will actually be. The vibrant economy of the 1990s and a dramatic rise in productivity have resulted in more optimistic projections. But, as Figure 5–1 indicates, changes to bring OASDI in balance will have to be made. (We discuss options later in this chapter.)

An Uncertain Future

The lesson from our past experience is clear: unforeseen circumstances and constantly changing economic, political, and demographic considerations make it impossible to plan social security's financing future with complete certainty. As observed by Morrison (1982), for example, "As long as Social Security payments are financed by intergenerational transfers instead of by the contributions of the recipients themselves, the system will be vulnerable to demographic shifts—for example, unforeseen swings in future fertility—that legislation cannot fully anticipate."

We should not worry excessively about this, however. What is also clear from past history is that attention is constantly being given to the evolving finances of social security. The activities of various government groups (some mandated by law), numerous interest groups, academics, think tanks, and the Congress itself result in continuous monitoring of the situation. When long-term problems arise, we are likely to quickly know about them, providing us with an opportunity to take appropriate corrective action.

The Short-Term Scares of the Recent Past

In 1979 a survey by Louis Harris Associates (Johnson and Higgins, 1979) reported that more than four out of five workers did not have confidence that social security would be able to pay the benefits due them when they retired. Perhaps more startling was the finding that about 40 percent *had hardly any confidence at all* that they would receive their entitlement.

These were startling statistics, but later surveys have produced similar results. For example, the 1991 Advisory Council on Social Security conducted a survey similar to the 1979 Hart survey. As Reno and Friedland (1997) report, the survey also found "that many seemed to doubt that Social Security would have the money to pay their benefits; just 46 percent of those not receiving benefits agreed with the statement: 'Social security will have the money to pay benefits to me when I retire.' " However, Reno and Friedland point out that "more in-depth surveys of retirement expectations, in contrast with opinion polls, find that the same workers who express little confidence that Social Security will be there, when later asked about their expected sources of retirement income, almost always say they expect to get Social Security; in fact, many expect it to be a major source of retirement income." Moreover, the 1991 survey found that 73 percent of Americans had favorable impressions of social security, and 77 percent said that they did not mind paying social security taxes to support it.

What produces such pessimism about future benefits? Clearly, media stories about the indexing problem in the 1970s and the specter of the baby boom generation eventually retiring have contributed to the anxiety many people have about the security of their promised social security benefits. It is probably the financing problems of the 1980s, however, that created an aura of crisis that has scared the American public. Off and on over a period of thirty years, the American public have been told that the social security system was about to run out of money. If we want to understand the anxiety existing among Americans today, we must understand why social security finances in the 1970s and 1980s seemed to bumble along like those of a small corner grocery store on the verge of bankruptcy.

Starting in the mid-1970s, both high inflation and high unemployment rates rocked the American economy. As far as social security was concerned, there was both a decline in expected payroll taxes and an increase in benefit obligations. The result was unexpected funding deficits, with payment obligations exceeding revenue by billions of dollars. A Social Security Administration study (Thompson and Van de Water, 1975) of these unexpected short-term deficits concluded that the deficits were "due almost entirely to unforeseen adverse economic circumstances."

In later years the situation became even worse. The nation, during the late 1970s and early 1980s, was battered by poor economic conditions that were unprecedented in our postwar economic history. There was double-digit inflation, record levels of agricultural and industrial bankruptcy, the near-destruction of whole industries, the agony of millions suffering long-term unemployment, and turmoil in financial markets.

These economic problems resulted in financial problems plaguing our public and private pension programs. In fact, the pension problems were basically a result of the other problems (unemployment and inflation) and the fact that prices rose faster than wages. Rising prices meant that more revenue was needed to pay benefits indexed for inflation, while slower rising wages meant less revenue than anticipated was coming into the system from the payroll tax on wages. Social security reserves over this period continued to dip, despite various congressional actions.

As we discussed previously, social security has never historically accumulated more than minimal partial reserves. The reserves that accumulated were, in fact, there to be nearly exhausted. That is, their function was to provide a cushion against adverse economic conditions that can never be fully and accurately anticipated by Congress and the actuaries who advise Congress. The adverse economic situation of this period was not anticipated, and hence the emergency reserves were needed to meet the drains on the system.

While the short-term social security financing problems in the 1970s and 1980s were real and serious, they were not unsolvable and were not a result of some basic flaw in the concept of social security. Yet many critics of social security seized on this situation to proclaim disaster and call for major changes in the system, and the media saw the social security "crisis" as big news. Reacting to the critics, Henry Aaron (1981), one of the most knowledgeable persons in the field of social security today, argued that "it is intellectually dishonest, though it may be politically convenient, to use the short-run problems as the basis for making changes in the system that are more relevant to the long-run problem." In assessing the viability of social security in delivering promised benefits, it is important to keep the distinctions between short- and long-term development clearly in mind. But unfortunately this period of financing history (together with the long-term issues) seems to have left the American public with very skeptical attitudes about future financing and the long-term credibility of the social security "benefit promise."

SOCIAL SECURITY AND THE FEDERAL BUDGET

Social security was included in the federal budget for the first time in 1969. This inclusion of the operations of the social security trust funds in the federal budget has been criticized by many social security experts. They argue that social security operations were put into the budget primarily for political reasons. The surpluses being generated in social security during the 1960s and early 1970s had the effect of helping to balance the budget. In fact, when the accounting procedure was introduced in 1969, the expected social security surplus for that year permitted President Johnson to take credit for sending a "balanced budget" to

Congress, instead of one with a deficit. In the recent past, when social security sometimes ran a deficit, some government officials tried to blame the very much larger *total* federal budget deficit on "out of control" nondiscretionary programs like social security. As we discussed previously, operating on a partial funding basis, social security taxes and expenditures must be kept in close balance. *Unlike the federal budget, there is little possibility that social security will generate large deficits over long periods of time.*

Critics of what is called the "unified budget" argue that these "artificial" and sometimes manipulative accounting procedures actually hinder the budgetmaking process. The 1981 National Commission on Social Security recommended that the social security trust funds be removed from the unified budget. This recommendation was accepted by the Congress, and the Social Security Amendments of 1983 scheduled social security's removal from the annual budgeting process by fiscal year 1993. Later congressional action, however, as part of the Gramm-Rudman-Hollings (GRH) procedures to promote a balanced federal budget, accelerated the timetable to 1987 but introduced a more complicated arrangement. Under the GRH provisions, social security's income and outlays were excluded from budget documents, budget resolutions, and budget reconciliation legislation. However, the system's projected surpluses over the next couple of decades were still taken into account in the calculation of the "budgeting targets" called for by the GRH process. Thus, social security continued to serve the needs of those in Washington seeking to avoid the politically difficult decisions of budget cuts or tax increases. Observed the U.S. Senate Special Committee on Aging (1987): "Were it not for the inclusion of the large Social Security surpluses, then the [overall federal] budget deficit would have to be cut by an additional $50 to $60 billion in order to meet the targets set for the final years of . . . [GRH]."

Finally, Congress incorporated into the 1990 Omnibus Budget Reconciliation Act a provision to completely remove the social security trust funds from the GRH deficit-reduction calculations. Despite this provision (and others), the debates continue about how to "protect" social security. It remains unlikely, given social security's current size, that officials in Washington will be willing or able to disentangle the actual economic impact of social security from the day-to-day politics of the budgetary process.

The Growing Surplus

Ironically, the Social Security Amendments of 1983 and demographic trends have combined to create a very different financing issue for the near future. The social security *deficits* of the recent past are now *sur-*

pluses. But unlike the modest surpluses of the past, legislated payroll tax levels and demographics are projected to send future surpluses in the OASDI trust funds skyrocketing. A 1993 estimate by the Board of Trustees of OASDI indicated that reserves would grow by the year 2020 to about $4.4 trillion (yes, trillion!) in 1999 dollars. Reserves are projected to then decline very rapidly as the baby boom generation retires.

The new situation has triggered a growing debate. Some argue the surpluses will *cause* problems and should not be allowed to accumulate. Others think the surpluses will *solve* problems and don't want to change current policy. Still others think we need to change the way we record these surpluses in the national accounts, and still others advocate a change in the way the surpluses would be invested.

The main argument for lowering future surpluses is a political one. Many people (especially conservatives) fear that as the "assets" pile up in the form of government Treasury bonds, Congress will be tempted to liberalize social security (thus compounding long-term future financing problems) or increase other types of federal spending. Another fear is that if the government were to invest the surpluses in the private sector (rather than buying government bonds), this might introduce undesirable interference in the control and operation of private businesses—resulting, in some cases, in government ownership of companies. Others argue that these surpluses are being used to hide the true size of the federal budget deficits in the general, discretionary account. Still others believe that it is unfair to have the current general budget deficits financed by payroll taxes, which they view as regressive (but see our discussion in the next section).

Another view (favored by many economists) is that these surpluses, if not offset by dissaving elsewhere, could increase the nation's saving rate. The United States, not a big saver in recent years by international standards, has seen personal saving plummet to record lows. Thus, larger surpluses are viewed as an opportunity to counteract the nation's habit (both public and private) of deficit spending. Higher saving and the investment it supports, some argue, could result in a higher level of output and consumption during the next century than would otherwise occur.

But as argued in Schulz (1999), the connection between saving and actual economic growth is tenuous. Economic growth is determined by many factors in addition to saving (e.g., technological change and education of the workforce). Thus, while saving and investment are necessary, they are not sufficient to insure that the rate of growth will be adequate to achieve any specified set of goals. As economist Richard Nelson (1997) has observed, "the key intellectual challenge to formal growth theory . . . lies in learning how to formally model entities that are not easily reduced to a set of numbers, such as the character of a nation's education or financial system or the prevalent philosophy of management."

Another view of the surpluses relates to the future demographic situation and equity issues related to financing. As we discuss below, the distributional equity of social security financing is a very complicated and controversial question. The "future surpluses" issue complicates the matter further. The surpluses are consistent with the need for the very large baby boom group to pay into social security while working to help pay for the huge expenditures that will be necessary when they reach retirement ages. Not increasing payroll taxes now, it is argued, will mean a shift of the baby boom financing burden from the "baby boomers themselves to their children, who, because they are a smaller generation, would find the burden heavier" (Rauch, 1987b). Alternatively, the accumulation of surpluses through social security, argues economist Alicia H. Munnell, results in "shifting consumption away from a relatively poorer to a relatively more affluent generation" (Clark, 1985). Moreover, others see payroll taxes that weigh heavily on lower- and middle-income workers as a poor way to raise national savings rates, given the many alternatives.

But as economist Lawrence Thompson (1990) points out:

If a surplus is desired over the next 15 to 20 years, . . . running it in the Social Security account does have several real advantages. First, the tax rates necessary to produce that surplus are already in place. It is a lot easier to deal with rates already in place than to try to get new rates. Second, since the demographic shift changes the burden imposed by the aged, using Social Security surpluses to help offset the increased burden does have a definite appeal, a certain plausibility. Although it is not . . . [necessary] economically, it fits nicely with the kind of moral statements that "we ought to be doing this anyway." In large part, then, due to these two propositions, it may well be easier politically to run a surplus in the Social Security account than to run a surplus in the rest of the budget.

However, as mentioned above, many fear that any large surpluses in social security will lead to offsetting increases in other parts of the federal budget. "In fact, many members of Congress contend that the inclusion of the surpluses [in the federal budget] has disguised the enormity of the nation's fiscal problems and delayed true deficit reduction" (U.S. Senate Special Committee on Aging, 1991).[8]

In the early 1990s, Senator Daniel Patrick Moynihan headed a group in Congress that wanted to eliminate the surpluses by lowering employer and employee payroll taxes from 6.2 percent to 5.2 percent by 1996. (Also, Moynihan proposed that the taxable ceiling for social security be raised significantly to raise more of the money from higher earners.) Moynihan argued that the surpluses were being used to further "budget trickery" and that a payroll tax cut would help deal with the 1990–1991 recession, while promoting a more equitable tax system for the lower and middle classes. On April 24, 1991, the Senate, on a procedural vote of 60 to 38, defeated a motion to consider a version of the Moynihan proposal. The "unexpectedly lopsided vote was a stinging setback," according to the *Washington Post* (Kenworthy, 1991).

As the contingency reserve grows, it may help to restore public confidence in social security's ability to pay promised benefits. As we discussed in the previous section, the economic chaos of the post-OPEC period (and the social security deficits associated with those bad economic times) left the nation with widespread fears regarding the future. Many people lost confidence in social security's ability to deliver on its future obligations.

Presumably, we have learned an important lesson from that experience. Social security reserves accumulated to meet unexpected economic bad times should never again be allowed to fall as low as those resulting from our social security policies in the 1960s and early 1970s. Former Social Security Commissioner Robert Ball (1987) argues that we need to allow reserves to accumulate, at least in the short-run: "In its 50-year history, Social Security has had two financial crises, one in the mid-70s and one in the early '80s. In both cases, the short-term crises were caused principally by inadequate reserves and reliance on economic assumptions that turned out to be too optimistic. We cannot afford to take a chance on a third mistake of this kind."

FINANCING EQUITY

Rising costs of social security now and in the future increase the importance of developing financing methods considered fair by the population. Our first question in assessing the equity of social security is: Who pays? In the United States, payroll tax revenue now exceeds all other federal, state, and local types of taxes except the federal income tax. Thus, it is important to look at who pays the tax and the relationship between those taxes paid and the benefits ultimately received.

Who Pays?

Determining "tax incidence," or who ultimately bears the burden of any tax, is one of the most complex issues in economics. Although the general population thinks it knows who pays taxes, economists disagree—especially about who actually bears the corporate income tax, sales taxes, and the property tax. Most people have assumed the worker bears the burden of *his or her* payroll contribution, but there has been great disagreement over the employer payments.

A variety of economic studies indicate that most of the employer tax is ultimately (i.e., in the long run) paid by the worker in the form of wages that are lower than what they otherwise would have been (or, to a smaller extent, by consumers in the form of higher prices). In an early study of the question, for example, economist John A. Brittain concluded that the worker generally bears all the tax. He argued that given a particular level of *productivity*, the higher the employer payroll tax rate, the lower the basic real wage—the wage rate being lower by the same amount as the payroll tax increase (Brittain, 1972). Not all economists, however, agree with the Brittain findings (e.g., Feldstein, 1972; Leuthold, 1975).[9]

After reviewing the research, Chen and Goss (1997) conclude:

It is a reasonable assumption that an employer will attempt to shift his taxes onto someone else, either forward to the consumer by means of higher prices, or backward to the worker in the form of reduced compensation. . . . Even though it is impossible to ascertain the precise amount of employer tax that falls upon the worker, it seems unreasonable to assume that no such shifting takes place. On the other hand, the assumption that the entire amount of the employer taxes is automatically borne by the worker, too, appears stringent.

Is the Payroll Tax Fair?

The payroll tax has been criticized as unfair by numerous people. There have been three major criticisms: (1) that the tax is regressive and a heavy burden on the poor; (2) that the tax is unfair to certain groups of beneficiaries, given the benefits they are likely to receive; and (3) that younger workers who are now paying taxes (and those who will pay in the future) are likely to get an unfair deal. We will examine each of these criticisms in turn.

First is the issue of a regressive tax structure and its impact on the poor. In general, a regressive tax is one in which the amount of tax paid is a *declining* proportion of income as incomes *increase*. Because the OASDI payroll tax is levied only on earnings up to the "earnings base" and not on earnings above the maximum earnings ceiling, the tax is partly regressive. That is, the proportion that contributions represent of total earnings falls for *earnings levels above the ceiling*. Moreover, if one looks at the payroll tax in relation to *total* income (not just earnings), it is clearly a regressive tax.

During the 1950s and 1960s the maximum ceiling was low relative to average earnings. The proportion of total earnings in covered employment subject to the payroll tax fell from slightly more than 90 percent during the early years of the program to a low of 71 percent in 1965. Thus, for example, in 1972, when the earnings base was $9,000, about one-quarter of the workers paying social security taxes had earnings that *exceeded* the maximum. With the significant increase and indexing of the earnings ceiling that began in 1973, the proportion of total earnings in covered employment had risen to over 90 percent. Thus, today the tax is proportional (not regressive) over a wide range of earnings levels but regressive with regard to total income.

Thus, what concerns many critics is not so much the burden on worker earnings near or above the maximum but, rather, the tax burdens on low wage earners. The payroll tax contrasts sharply with the personal income tax, falling more heavily on persons with relatively low incomes. There are several reasons for this:

1. As discussed above, the maximum taxable earnings ceiling places a limit ($72,600 in 1999) on earnings subject to the payroll tax.
2. Unlike the federal income tax, the payroll tax rate is a constant percentage at all earnings levels below the maximum.
3. Unlike the income tax, the payroll tax has no exemption or deduction provisions.
4. Income from interest, rents, and profits—the bulk of which is received by people in the higher income brackets—is not subject to the payroll tax.

Why should people with poverty-level incomes have to pay any taxes—including social security? The principal answer given over the years by supporters of the payroll tax is that the *benefit* structure of the program is heavily weighted in favor of low earners and that tampering with the tax structure threatens to turn the program into a welfare program—thereby undermining its general political acceptability. J. Douglas Brown (1973) in a memorandum sent to the U.S. Senate Special Committee on Aging argues:

Overall, the advantages of uniform proportionate contributions toward one's social insurance protection are of great psychological, social and political importance. They clearly differentiate benefits as a matter of right from those available only on individual proof of need. They reflect a natural desire for self-reliance. They refute a criticism of dependency. They also are a factor in avoiding a class-conscious society in which some classes give and some classes get. Proportionate contributions are a force for political restraint in the evolution of a total system, both in respect to excessive demands for liberality in the benefit structure and the condoning of abuses in unwarranted payments.

As payroll tax rates have risen over the years, however, concerns have increased. About one-third of workers now pay more payroll taxes than income taxes. However, despite growing criticism, little change has occurred over the years in the basic payroll financing mechanism. Concerned about the growing payroll tax burden on low earners, Congress has approached the problem in a different way. Instead of modifying the payroll tax structure, it has instituted a policy of income tax offsets.

The 1975 Tax Act contained a one-year provision known as the "earned income tax credit" (EITC) for low-income workers *with at least one "qualified child."* Under this act, an eligible individual was allowed a tax credit equal to 10 percent of earned income up to $4,000 a year. Under provisions of the law, the tax credit declined (until it reached zero at income levels of $8,000) by 10 percent of "adjusted gross income" (or, if greater, the earned income) that exceeded $4,000 per year.

The major justification given for the amendment was to remove the work-disincentive effect of social security taxes on low-income workers. In 1975 this credit offset most of the payroll taxes paid on earnings of $4,000 or less.

Most of the early opposition to this "work bonus amendment" was based on its welfare character. Senator Sam J. Ervin, for example, charged in one floor debate over the credit that "it is robbery to take social security money and use it for welfare purposes." In addition, the Nixon administration came out against an early version of the work bonus, arguing that the provision would create serious administrative problems and that it would complicate the development of sound income-maintenance policy by "adding yet another program to the many present assistance programs." The Ford administration, using similar arguments, also argued against the provision.

Despite this initial opposition, the EITC has been continuously renewed in all subsequent tax legislation. For example, the 1978 tax law extended its application to the first $10,000 of earnings. Subsequent liberalizations occurred in 1986, 1993, and 1996. The effect of these changes was to eliminate almost the entire social security tax (including the employer's share) for eligible families whose income is under the phase-out lower limit.

But the credit has become much more than a device to deal with the payroll tax. It is now seen as a major part of attempts to improve welfare policies for the poor (Howard, 1994). It appeals, for example, to those policymakers who want to give greater work incentives to low-income households, and it is seen by some as a good way to help deal with the plight of children in poor families. Thus, currently it is the largest social assistance program for the poor.

Starting in 1991, (1) the credit amounts were expanded; (2) higher credits were given to families with more than one child and/or an infant less than a year old; (3) a special credit was given to families who buy health insurance; and (4) the requirement that more than half of one's support be from nonpublic assistance sources in determining eligibility was eliminated. In 1997, almost 19 million workers received credits totalling $27 billion.

The earned income tax credit varies with earned income level and the number of children. If the credit amount exceeds what the taxpayer would otherwise owe in taxes, a payment from the U.S. Treasury is mailed for the difference. In 1997, the credit equaled, for example, 34 percent of earned income for a taxpayer with one child, up to a maximum of $2,210. John Scholz (1993–1994) estimates that 81 percent to 86 percent of persons *eligible* for the credit were *recipients* of it in 1990; and another study (Center on Budget and Policy Alternatives, 1998) estimates that in 1996, the EITC lifted 4.6 million people above the poverty level.

Is Social Security a "Good Buy"?

Just as in the case of asking who pays the payroll tax, determining the relative cost-benefit equity of social security is extremely difficult (see Leimer, 1994 and U.S. General Accounting Office, 1999). The wide range of rates of return estimated by various researchers demonstrates the difficulty of giving an unequivocal answer to the question of whether social security is a "good buy." Results are highly sensitive to the assumptions and methodology used for the analysis. *In general, however, the studies indicate that social security benefits will continue to remain a "good buy" for almost anyone—and remain so for many years to come.*

Brittain (1972) raised a basic question, however:

Why should one ask whether a person ultimately recoups in benefits the equivalent of his taxes when the same question is rarely asked about other taxes? . . . Since the taxes and later benefits assigned to a person are not at all closely related, as they are under private insurance, a strong case can be made for a completely separate analysis and evaluation of the tax and benefit structures on their own merits.

While many would agree with this point of view, others see social security taxes differently—as special earmarked taxes associated with a *compulsory* pension program, which necessitates analysis of who pays and who should pay.

Henry Aaron has correctly pointed out that most, if not all, of the controversy in this area arises from the fact that analysts have approached the various issues with different frameworks. Some view social security as an annual tax-transfer program that redistributes income from wage earners to retirees. Others see it basically as a lifetime compulsory retirement saving program within a "life-cycle model" of individual decision-making about saving and labor force participation.

Moreover, Aaron points out that much of the controversy over whether social security is "a good deal" for different types of workers arises from our not knowing what is the "correct," or "right," minimum **discount rate** to use. Aaron (1982) argues:

[C]alculations of the internal rate of return or of the present discounted value, though not without interest for certain purposes, miss most of the interesting and important questions about whether different cohorts of workers get their money's worth from social security and whether reserves should be accumulated. They place no value on the full protection against inflation that only social security now provides. In addition, the calculations do not address the fundamental question of the political, economic, and social value at the margin of social security benefits.

There is general agreement, however, that calculations of returns from social security are useful to help focus attention on possible differences in treatment of various groups within the population. Both Boskin and Brittain emphasize, for example, that the wide spread in social security rates of return indicates substantial income redistribution among categories of participants. Brittain points out, for example, that the college graduate who starts work at age 22 may fare much better than the high school graduate who starts work at 18, if both earn the same average earnings over their respective work lives. Their social security benefits will be very similar, but the college graduate, entering the workforce later, will pay fewer total payroll taxes over his career. Leimer (1979), however, cautions against giving too much weight to such hypothetical findings when evidence indicates that there are more offsetting factors in real-life experiences (discussed further later).

Money's Worth and the Debate over Rates of Return

The most common way of evaluating whether benefit recipients get their "money's worth" from social security is "the internal rate of return approach." This approach is based on the fact that the benefits workers eventually receive reflect an implicit rate of return on their contributions (i.e., payroll tax payments). The implicit rate of return equals the average interest rate workers would hypothetically have to earn on their contributions in order to pay for all the benefits they and their families will receive from social security. To be accurate and consistent, rate of return estimates must reflect all contributions and other revenues associated with the benefits that will eventually be received—including employer payroll taxes, any increased taxes needed to balance future revenues and benefits, and contributions/benefits for survivors, dependents and the disabled.

There are a very large number of studies calculating social security rates of return (e.g., Brittain, 1972; Boskin et al., 1986; Duggan et al., 1993;

Table 5–2
Internal Rates of Return under OASI for Selected Birth Cohorts

Birth Cohort	Rate of Return[a] (percent)
1876	36.5
1900	11.9
1925	4.8
1950	2.2
1975	1.9
2000	1.7

Source: Dean R. Leimer, "Lifetime Redistribution and the Social Security Program: A Literature Synopsis," *ORES Working Paper Series*, No. 81 (Washington, D.C.: SSA Office of Research, Evaluation, and Statistics, 1999), Table 1.

Steurle and Bakija, 1994). These rates of return studies can be divided into two groups: (1) studies that focus on redistribution across groups of individuals born in different years (**between cohorts**) and (2) studies that focus on how rates of return differ among different subgroups (such as women) within one particular age group of people (**a particular cohort**).

Between Cohorts

As we just discussed above, the Social Security Administration began paying benefits in the 1940s to people who had not contributed into the program over their entire lifetime (primarily to alleviate poverty and deal with high unemployment rates). Thus, people retiring during the program's start-up years received very high rates of return. As the program matured, however, the balance between taxes and benefits naturally became less favorable for later retirees. Table 5–2 shows inflation-adjusted internal rates of return for selected birth cohorts. The rates of return decline from over 36 percent for the 1876 birth cohort to less than 2 percent for birth cohorts beginning their work lives in recent years.

Looking at a Particular Cohort

Probably the nation's leading authority on rates of return, Dean Leimer (1999), concludes the following about subgroup internal rates of return within particular birth cohorts:

• Given their greater life expectancy, women tend to fare better than men, even when other factors (such as earnings) are held constant.

- Given spouse benefits, couples tend to fare better than single persons.
- Given the progressivity of the benefit formula, whites tend to fare worse than nonwhites, despite the lower survival probabilities for nonwhites.

The conclusions above are based on studies using historical data. What about future retirees? Most studies to date focusing on the future have generally reached conclusions similar to those summarized above (e.g., Boskin and Puffert, 1987; Myers and Schobel, 1992; and Steuerle and Bakija, 1994).

Private-Public Comparisons

Another comparative approach is to focus on the rates of return that might be realized if some or all money for retirement were shifted from social security to private plans investing in stocks (i.e., equities). Viewed this way, conservatives argue that social security is not a good deal. For example, economist Martin Feldstein (1998) asserts:

In contrast to the 2.6 percent "equilibrium" return on social security contributions, the real pretax return on nonfinancial corporate capital averaged 9.3 percent over the thirty-five-year period since 1960. That is the return that each individual's retirement saving could have earned in a fully funded government system or in a privatized system if the government credited the corporate tax receipts back to each account.

Similarly, Stephen Moore (1997) of the Cato Institute has asserted: "If Congress were to allow a 25 year old working woman today to invest her payroll tax contributions in private capital markets, her retirement benefit would be two to five times higher than what Social Security is offering."

A number of other studies, however, challenge such conclusions (e.g., Geanakoplos et al., 1998; Baker and Weisbrot 1999; and U.S. General Accounting Office, 1999). Baker and Weisbrot argue that claims for high rates of return from privatizing social security are vastly overstated for four reasons:

- Past stock market performance is not likely to be repeated, given lower economic growth projections.
- The higher administrative costs of private accounts will reduce actual returns by at least 1–2 percent.
- Most people are not likely to invest 100 percent in stocks but, to reduce risk, are likely to choose a mixture of stocks and lower-yielding bonds.
- Converting to privatized accounts would require large transition taxes (amounting to about 1.6 percent) to pay the existing obligations of individuals under the current social security OASI program.

When all these factors are taken into account, Baker estimates that the rates of return on privatized accounts would fall below 2 percent, and perhaps even below 1 percent.

"Money's worth" debates will continue to be one of the most controversial issues in the policy discussion regarding the future of social security. But as the U.S. General Accounting Office (1999) has observed, "Simply comparing the current Social Security program's implicit rate of return with historical returns on market investments reveals little about what workers have to gain from alternative reform proposals. Rather, if rates of return are to be compared, they should ideally be compared among complete reform proposals to capture all the costs the proposals imply and to reflect the latest projections of future economic and demographic trends." We discuss some such proposals below.

Women and Social Security Financing

Certain specific groups have been singled out for attention by some critics of social security. The treatment of women, for example, has come under scrutiny. In the financing area, the most controversial issue has been the differential treatment of working and nonworking women. Currently, a spouse first claiming benefits at the normal retirement age is entitled to a benefit equal to 50 percent of the working partner's basic benefit—regardless of whether or not the spouse participates in the social security program. A spouse who works, however, may become eligible for a regular benefit on the basis of that work. The law stipulates that such a person can get only one benefit—that from the spouse's earnings record or his or her own pension, whichever is larger.

An issue arising from this treatment of working spouses is the low rate of return on the contributions of the spouse. A working wife may pay social security taxes toward retirement protection, but the resulting benefits of the family may be *no higher* if the spouse doesn't work a sufficient number of quarters to achieve eligibility or has low earnings. Moreover, because of anomalies in the benefit structure, a couple composed of two retired workers can receive lower total benefits than a couple with the same average lifetime earnings credits all earned by one spouse (see Chapter 4).

Although a working woman's retirement benefits may be little more or no more than a nonworking spouse's, she does receive certain protection under social security not available to a nonworking wife:

1. Disability protection
2. Benefits payable at or after age 62, even if her husband continues to work
3. Monthly benefits to her children if she becomes disabled or dies

As we discussed in Chapter 4, the economic role of women has been shifting over time (see also Kahne, 1975). As a result, a number of social security reform bills have been introduced in Congress over the years to deal with the working woman issue. Thus far, no legislative action has been taken.

Differential Life Expectancies

Another issue that has been raised in relation to women, and also by various ethnic minority groups, is the extent to which differences in average life expectancy should be taken into account. Women, *on average*, tend to live longer than men; nonwhites, *on average*, have shorter life expectancies than whites. For benefit purposes, current social security policy ignores these or any other differences in life expectancies. Some private pensions, however, have in the past paid differential pension benefits based on sex, causing certain women's organizations to successfully challenge in the courts such differentials in benefits.

Some nonwhites argue that they should receive preferential social security benefits because of adverse life expectancy rates. For example, the 1971 White House Conference on Aging "special concerns session" on aged blacks recommended: "The minimum age-eligibility requirement for primary beneficiaries of Old Age, Survivors, Disability, and Health Insurance (OASDHI) under social security should be reduced by eight years for black males so as to erase existing racial inequities."

The average life expectancy *at birth* is different for whites and nonwhites, in large part because of higher infant mortality rates for nonwhites. Differences in life expectancies at other ages are not nearly as great. *At age 65, for example, there are almost no differences between white and nonwhite men.*

Ubadigbo Okonkwo investigated intragenerational equity under social security for subgroups of the United States population differentiated by race, marital status, education, and region of residence. Calculating "internal rates of return" by race, Okonkwo (1975) found that returns are higher for all groups of nonwhite workers except nonwhite couples with sixteen or more years of schooling. The highly favorable mortality experience of white female college graduates results in a more favorable internal rate of return for these couples. Okonkwo concludes:

In general, the progressivity of the social security benefit structure tended to redistribute lifetime earnings in favor of subgroups with low earnings, exemplified by nonwhites and workers with relatively few years of schooling. However this redistributive effect was weakened, but not reversed, by the relatively smaller probabilities of survival experienced by these subgroups. (Okonkwo, 1975)

Similar conclusions are reached by Leimer (1979), Wolff (1987), and Duggan et al. (1993). Specifically, they examine the validity of the arguments made by some critics of social security that the disadvantaged (nonwhites, low earners, and women) get a poorer deal from social security (see, for example, Aaron, 1977; and Duggan et al., 1993). Contrary to some critics, the consensus of investigations suggests that future nonwhite, low-earner, and/or women retirees will generally fare well and often better than their counterparts (Steuerle and Bakija, 1994).

Prior hypothetical worker studies in this area have all found that entrants to the labor force at early ages have lower rates of return from social security because they contribute payroll taxes over a longer work life. Because going to college may delay entry into the labor force and result in higher lifetime earnings, most researchers have concluded that the actual impact of delayed entry into the labor force is very important. Leimer (1979), however, analyzes data showing that workers with high ultimate education attainment have substantial earnings *during* the education period. This offsetting factor tends to reduce the importance of the delayed entry factor in actual case histories.

Viscusi (1979) argues more generally against public pension differentials based on life expectancy. He cites the widespread resentment that would probably be generated by an explicit set of different eligibility criteria or benefit levels, and he points out the administrative and practical difficulties in taking account of all differentials—smokers versus nonsmokers, drivers of safer cars, persons in occupations or industries with environmental settings that may affect health. Finally, he argues that these differentials are not as important as equalizing benefits per unit of need: "Once we accept the notion that the principal focus of Social Security should be on equalizing income for the periods one is alive, the need to adjust for differing lengths of lifetimes is not only unnecessary, but is also detrimental to this more fundamental objective."

SOCIAL SECURITY FINANCIAL REFORM PROPOSALS

The real bottom line [in reforming social security] is adjusting to lower mortality and fertility rates. In a world in which people live longer and have fewer children, we have to stop imagining that those children will be able to support their parents during ever-longer retirements. Thinking that this is just a Social Security issue is like believing that Cinderella's only issue was her shoe size. (Steuerle and Spiro, 1999)

Numerous proposals for changing the financing of social security have been put forth. This section looks at five such approaches: (1) incremental change of the present program, (2) privatization of some benefits, (3) substantial general revenue financing, (4) changing the payroll tax structure; and (5) changes in tax policy with regard to social security.

Incremental Change of the Present Programs

The 1996 Social Security Advisory Council focused on OASDI's future financing situation. The Council could not reach a consensus but instead divided into three groups with three different financing recommendations. One group, led by former Commissioner of Social Security Robert M. Ball, argued that no major changes were needed in the present system but that a number of incremental changes were needed to meet future financing needs. In addition, to deal with current perceptions of the general public that social security benefit promises were unreliable, they recommended some of social security's reserves be put into a fund of passively managed private equities—indexed to a broad spectrum of stocks.

The incremental changes the Ball group suggested were (1) a small increase in payroll taxes; (2) mandating social security participation for all new hires in state and local governments; (3) correcting inflation measurement procedures (downward); and (4) raising the earnings computation period from 35 to 38 years. Other options suggested were: raising the maximum earnings ceiling or raising the normal retirement age.

Ball (1997) argues that there is no financial need to make radical changes in social security. "The situation with Social Security is similar to that of homeowners living in a sound house. They like it very much; they only need to have its mortgage refinanced. There is no need to tear the house down, remodel it, or trade it for a different house. The need is only to improve its long-range refinancing."

Critics respond that the financial situation is far worse than the Ball group will admit and that small changes will not suffice. Moreover, they argue that an unfunded, or partially funded, pension system causes major distortions in the supply of labor and in worker compensation (Feldstein, 1998); and most important of all, they argue that workers' retirement income could be much higher if funds were mandated to go into individual private pension accounts and private savings rates were raised.

Pension Privatization

Two privatization approaches were recommended by some members of the 1996 Social Security Advisory Council. The "individual accounts" approach reduces social security benefits to a level that can be financed with the current 12.4 percent payroll tax; this would reduce benefits by about 30 percent. But it then adds a new employee contribution of 1.6 percent of earnings, which would go into individual pension accounts.

These accounts would be administered by the government, but workers would be permitted to choose from a variety of broad-based stock index funds, bond funds, and money market funds in which to invest their money. The approach is designed to give workers some choice in retirement income planning and, at the same time, to keep administrative costs down for the individual accounts—while preserving a major role for social security in minimizing investment risks.

The other approach, the "personal savings account," would replace the current old-age benefit with a flat benefit. This benefit would be at a level close to what is provided currently by the SSI (Supplemental Security Income) program for aged, blind, and disabled people with poverty-level incomes. Five percentage points of the current payroll tax would be diverted into individual accounts managed by private investment firms chosen by workers. The social security revenues lost would be replaced by a massive new government borrowing operation, with this new debt to be retired over a 72-year period using the proceeds of an additional 1.5 percent payroll tax.

The supporters of this approach argue that it makes each generation responsible for its own retirement, that it is simpler to understand, creates a direct link between worker contributions and the benefits received, promotes saving, does not encourage retirement, and is immune to demographic shifts (Combs, 1997).

Critics of these two approaches raise concerns about the high transitional costs of operating two programs simultaneously; the risks and complexity of individuals making investment decisions; the likely disadvantaged position of low earners, women, and racial minorities; huge marketing and administrative costs; and a weakening of disability protection.

General Revenue Financing

Many see the blanketing-in of large groups of persons during the initial years of social security as a burden that need not be financed by the payroll tax. These people call for general revenue financing without abandoning the basic structure of the current system.

General revenue financing was first suggested by the Committee on Economic Security, a presidential committee whose recommendations formed the basis of the original Social Security Act. The idea was also supported by the first Advisory Council on Social Security in 1937–1938 and one in 1947. Later Advisory Councils, however, did not see an immediate need for this additional source of financing or opposed general revenue financing as destructive of the insurance principles embodied in the program.

In 1944, Congress (over presidential veto) prevented a scheduled increase in the payroll tax rate and authorized an appropriation from general revenue to the trust fund for "such additional sums as may be required to finance the benefits and payment under this title." Rather than representing an enthusiastic endorsement by Congress of the concept of general revenue financing, this action, at the time, was really a by-product of a disagreement in Congress over when and how large social security reserves should grow. Ignoring the 1947 Advisory Council on Social Security's recommendation for a "government contribution," both the House Committee on Ways and Means and the Senate Finance Committee in 1949–1950 stated that the system "should be on a completely self-supporting basis," and Congress in 1950 repealed the general revenue provision.

Many who agree with the idea of general revenue financing favor restricting these payments to help meet the costs of "windfall benefits" (i.e., those given without contributions equal to the actuarial value of these benefits). In a working paper prepared for the U.S. Senate Special Committee on Aging, Nelson H. Cruikshank, then president of the National Council of Senior Citizens, presented such a proposal:

Workers already close to retirement age when the [social security] system was first started, or when coverage was extended to their employment, received full benefits even though the contributions they and their employers paid would finance only a small part of the benefit. While this was sound public policy and kept many old people off relief, it did mean that these benefits had to be financed from future contributions. There is no justification for expecting presently covered workers to pay for this "accrued liability"—estimated in the long run to amount to one-third of the total cost of the program—through a regressive payroll tax. A far fairer method would be to finance this share from general revenue sources to which all taxpayers contribute and through a more progressive tax structure. (U.S. Senate Special Committee on Aging, 1970)

During the debates leading up to the 1977 social security amendments, President Carter proposed a general revenue financing mechanism: to limit general revenue contributions to the amount of social security revenues lost as a result of an unemployment rate in excess of 6 percent. When workers lose their jobs, they (and their employers) do not pay payroll taxes on their behalf, causing a shortfall in projected revenues. Through this proposed mechanism, general revenue financing would not be open-ended but would be used only when economic activity falls significantly short of full employment levels. The proposal was not accepted by the Congress, however, when it considered the 1977 amendments.

As the costs of social security increased and the burden on low earners rose, the pressures for general revenue financing also rose. The 1979 Advisory Council on Social Security, for example, unanimously recommended "that the time has come to finance some part of social security with nonpayroll tax revenues." Its suggestion: finance the hospital insurance program entirely through earmarked portions of the personal and corporation income taxes. Reporting soon after the Advisory Council, the National Commission on Social Security also recommended (by a close vote) general revenue financing for half of the hospital insurance program costs. In addition, it recommended a cap on future payroll tax rates of 18 percent (9 percent each for employees and employers), with general revenue making up the difference.

When the Congress developed its financing legislation in 1983, it did not adopt any provision to move the Medicare program toward what some viewed as general revenue financing. It did adopt, however, a more restrictive general revenue provision. To help meet short-term funding shortfalls, it authorized an immediate and one-time transfer of about $20 billion from general revenue to cover benefits that will be paid to veterans of World War II and the Korean War. Military personnel during this period were credited with tax contributions to social security that they did not actually make. This general transfer in effect accelerates payments from general revenue to cover these costs. Also, the taxation of benefits legislated in 1983 may also be viewed as a kind of general revenue transfer.

A variety of arguments have been raised against general revenue financing. The major ones are:

1. That it would encourage excessive increases in benefits
2. That it tends to integrate social security into the annual budget review process and makes it more "political"
3. That it is contrary to the insurance and contributory principles of the program, which promote the political acceptability of social security
4. That social security would increasingly be viewed as a welfare program, with an associated decline in congressional and public support.

Opposition to any major expansion of general revenue financing still seems to be strong in Congress, especially given the budget debates of recent years.

Changing the Payroll Tax Structure

Over the years, a variety of proposals have been made to change the payroll tax. Some people would like to make the payroll tax rate progressive. One method would be to provide lump-sum earnings exemptions to the tax in the same way as exists in the current income tax law—perhaps similar to what is currently done in Canada. (The late union leader Walter Reuther, for example, proposed in 1967 a $600 exemption per earner.) Other proposals would allow exemptions for dependents, and some propose a "standard deduction" amount equal to that in the federal income tax law.

Alternatively, it has been proposed that the payroll tax be integrated with the income tax. The present tax withholdings for both social security and income taxes would continue, but at the end of the year the total amounts collected would be added together and applied to satisfy the individual's or couple's income tax liability. The earned income tax credit (discussed earlier) is a currently operational variant of this approach but not available to everyone paying into social security.

Arguments against the above two proposals are similar to those against general revenue financing.

Taxing Social Security Benefits

The 1979 Advisory Council on Social Security made a major recommendation designed to make social security financing more equitable. A majority of the council recommended that half of social security benefits be taxable income under the federal income tax:

The . . . tax treatment of social security was established at a time when both social security benefits and income tax rates were low. In 1941 the Bureau of Internal Revenue ruled that social security benefits were not taxable, most probably because they were viewed as a form of income similar to a gift or gratuity.

The Council believes that this ruling was wrong when made and is wrong today. The right to social security benefits is derived from earnings covered employment just as is the case with private pensions. (Advisory Council on Social Security, 1979)

When the Advisory Council's recommendation was announced, there was an immediate outpouring of criticism from Congress. In less than two months, nine bills (one with 241 co-sponsors) were introduced in the House to reaffirm the tax exemption of social security benefits, and within seven months, resolutions opposing taxation were passed in both Houses.

With this history in mind, it is somewhat hard to believe that three years later Congress actually passed legislation to tax social security benefits. But confronted with a short-term financing crisis, Congress moved quickly on a group of recommendations proposed by the National Commission on Social Security Reform, a commission that included key leaders of Congress in the social security area. Their recommendation included changes designed to deal with both short- and long-term financial problems.

The strategy developed by congressional leaders was to get Congress to vote on the changes as a whole package, allowing no amendments. As expressed by House Ways and Means Committee Chairman Dan Rostenkowski, "Voted on separately, very few of the controversial elements of our bill can survive. But taken together, the sacrifice they demand is fairly spread." Timothy Clark (1983) interprets what happened: "With a single-minded concentration rarely found on Capitol Hill, leaders of Congress pushed the legislation first through the House and then through the Senate. . . . Faced with the choice between legislation that appeared to distribute its painful burden evenly and the alternative of possible failure to agree on a substitute set of reforms, Congress was quick to grasp the former."

The question that remains is how much of social security should be taxed. As discussed previously, beginning in 1984 a portion of social security and railroad retirement benefits has been included in taxable income for certain high-income beneficiaries, and the percent taxed was again raised for the years after 1993.

CHAPTER 5 HIGHLIGHTS

Financing issues associated with social security are many and complex. Some of the major points we emphasized in this chapter were:

1. As social security expenditures grow, there is increased controversy over how to finance current and future benefits and the equity of various financing provisions.

2. It is important to distinguish between long-term financing problems arising from demographic factors and short-term problems resulting from an essentially pay-as-you-go financing system confronted by cyclical instability of an unexpected magnitude.

3. Experts do not agree on the existence or extent of financing inequities related to younger workers, women, and minorities covered by social security. But for most Americans social security remains a "good buy."

4. General revenue financing of a portion of social security continues to be looked upon unfavorably by Congress, but the historic opposition to income taxing of benefits collapsed in 1983 when Congress was confronted by an OASI financing "crisis."

5. Social security does not increase the federal budget deficit; in fact, its current surpluses reduce the deficit—by sizable amounts. Some argue that it would be better to cut payroll taxes, reduce these surpluses, and raise the necessary taxes closer to the time the baby boom cohort retires; others see these surpluses as a way of facilitating increased national saving and (it is hoped) economic growth.

SUGGESTED READINGS

Aaron, Henry J. *Economic Effects of Social Security*. Washington, D.C.: Brookings Institution, 1982. Chapter 6 of this excellent book contains a perceptive discussion of pension equity considerations and an assessment of prior studies.

Aaron, Henry J., B. P. Bosworth, and G. Burtless. *Can America Afford to Grow Old?* Washington, D.C.: Brookings Institution, 1989. Here is a good place to start if you want to learn more about the social security surplus question and the economic issues involved.

Annual Report of the Board of Trustees of the Federal Old-Age and Survivors Insurance and Disability Insurance Trust Funds. Washington, D.C.: U.S. Government Printing Office (annually). Assessment of the financial status of the programs is made by sophisticated actuarial projections of future expenditures and revenues.

Baker, Dean, and Mark Weisbrot. *Social Security: The Phony Crisis*. Chicago: University of Chicago Press, 1999. A passionate and informed view of why social security should not be privatized.

Ball, Robert M. *Straight Talk about Social Security*. New York: Century Foundation Press, 1998. A clear exposition of the incremental reform approach to social security, written by one of the foremost experts in the field.

Feldstein, Martin S., ed. *Privatizing Social Security*. Chicago: University of Chicago Press, 1998. A collection of papers that looks at the theoretical and practical issues related to privatizing social security, including country studies of privatized pension programs in Chile, the United Kingdom, Mexico, Australia, and Argentina.

Kingson, Eric R., and James H. Schulz, eds. *Social Security in the 21st Century*. New York: Oxford University Press, 1997. This book contains excellent chapters on the "money's worth" issue, the economic role for the trust funds, and other financing issues. In addition, it ends with two excellent survey chapters on social security reform, presenting two very different perspectives.

Salisbury, Dallas L., ed. *Assessing Social Security Reform Alternatives*. Washington, D.C.: Employee Benefit Research Institute (EBRI), 1997. Conference papers reporting on the findings of an EBRI simulation model investigating social security reform and presenting a wide range of other views on various reform proposals, including those of the 1996 Social Security Advisory Council.

Thompson, Lawrence H. *Older and Wiser: The Economics of Public Pensions*. Washington, D.C.: The Urban Institute Press, 1998. A basic primer for understanding the rationale for public pensions and related economic issues—effects on saving, labor supply, and international competitiveness.

U.S. Joint Economic Committee, Subcommittee on Fiscal Policy. "Issues in Financing Retirement Income." Paper No. 10. *Studies in Public Welfare*. Washington, D.C.: U.S. Government Printing Office, 1974. An excellent summary of the early financial history of social security and issues that have been discussed over the years.

Chapter 6

Health, Disability, and SSI Benefits

United States policies with regard to health care access and finance are very unusual when compared with most other countries in the industrialized world. Twenty-four countries out of 29 provide government-assured health insurance to at least 99 percent of their citizens. The United States covers only 33 percent—with heavy reliance on employer coverage for the rest but with many people having no insurance coverage of any kind (Anderson and Poullier, 1999).

As with pensions, the future of health care policy is debated amid growing concern. The concern focuses, as with *private* pensions, on the widespread lack of insurance coverage and on the financial burden of national health care—currently costing over one trillion dollars (yes, trillion) for one year (Smith, Heffler, and Freeland, 1999). That amount is 14 percent of the nation's **Gross National Product**. Medicare and Medicaid expenditures alone reached $232 billion in 1999; and, thus, as yearly costs climb rapidly toward two trillion dollars, many analysts think that the costs of health care in the United States are out of control.

On the other side are the elderly themselves who are confronted with the prospects of paying large and growing amounts of money out-of-pocket, despite existing government programs to assist them. Many health expenses (especially long-term care) still fall substantially on individuals or their families. The situation has not improved much since 1972, when J. Douglas Brown (1972) wrote in his *An American Philosophy of Social Security*: "Fear of a long and costly final illness haunts many old people. To end one's life as a ward of the state, or to drain the resources of one's children, is an all-too-frequent prospect for old persons in America."

Health care costs are not the only concern, however. Access to health care and the quality of care ultimately received are as important as affordability. When one looks at the health care provisions in any country, the issues of costs, access, and quality of care are inexorably intertwined. In large part that reality accounts for the difficulties policymakers are currently having in their attempts to reform the existing situation.

In this chapter, we look at the health care system for the elderly, how it is financed, and the problems remaining to be resolved (emphasizing economic issues). The second part of the chapter discusses two other important areas—disability programs and the financial help we provide for the destitute elderly.

HEALTH INSURANCE FOR THE ELDERLY

The most important legislation to help the elderly meet health care costs was passed in 1965: hospital insurance and supplementary medical insurance (collectively known as Medicare) and a means-tested medical assistance program (Medicaid). We look first at Medicaid.

Medicaid

Medicaid is a means-tested program for persons in financial need. Amendment of the Social Security Act in 1950 provided for federal financial participation in providing medical care to public assistance recipients. Then in 1960 another amendment authorized additional federal matching for medical care payments resulting from the health care needs of Old Age Assistance recipients. The Medicaid program enacted in 1965 as Title XIX of the Social Security Act, however, went far beyond these prior actions. It provided expanded eligibility, additional benefits, and major financial support, to achieve much better access to a range of basic health services for low-income people.

Medicaid is not limited to aged persons. About 32 million people of all different ages received Medicaid financial services in 1995; a little less than three million were age 65 or older. All states cover recipients of Aid to Families with Dependent Children (AFDC), most aged, blind, and disabled recipients of Supplemental Security Income (SSI), and low-income pregnant women and children. In addition, more than two-thirds of the states cover "medically needy" persons who are aged, blind, or disabled. Also included (at the option of states) are poor children and members of families ineligible for cash assistance but not able to afford medical services and institutionalized individuals with inadequate economic resources. Needy individuals *excluded* are single people who are neither aged nor disabled, couples without children, and in many states, two-parent families with children.

General guidelines for eligibility are established by the federal government, but specific eligibility requirements are determined separately by each state. As a result, a wide measure of discretion is allowed states under the Medicaid legislation with regard to what income and asset tests will be applied to various individuals. Not surprisingly, actual practice among the states varies greatly. In addition, within broad federal guidelines, states determine the duration and amount of services offered and have broad discretion in determining reimbursement procedures and rates.

Participating states are required to provide a wide range of services, including both inpatient and outpatient hospital services, skilled nursing home or home health care services, family planning services, and physicians' services. Other services—such as nursing facility services for the aged and disabled, drug therapy, eye and dental care, and physical therapy—are provided at the option of each state.

Medicaid provides federal funds appropriated from general revenue to states with qualified medical assistance programs. This federal cost-sharing ranges from 50 percent to 83 percent, based on a formula that increases the percentage to states with lower per-capita income. As a result, the federal government pays about 57 percent of total Medicaid costs (U.S. House Committee on Ways and Means, 1998).

A substantial proportion of the Medicare population over 65 (about 15 percent) is also covered by Medicaid. For these dual enrollees, Medicare is the first payer for Medicare services, and Medicaid is responsible for the Medicare cost-sharing provisions (deductibles and coinsurance). For services not covered by Medicare, Medicaid has primary responsibility.

The financing of long-term care services through Medicaid is very important. Given the high costs of nursing homes, 70 percent to 80 percent of the elderly today cannot afford out of current income a stay of even one year (Tell et al., 1987). In fact, 70 percent of the elderly living alone cannot finance nursing home care on their own beyond 13 weeks (U.S. House Select Committee on Aging, 1987). Medicaid, however, pays for such care when private assets are exhausted, but participating individuals are required to pay to the nursing home all income in excess of a "personal needs allowance" established by the state. Because of this situation, a major issue over the years has been how to protect the spouses of nursing home residents from becoming impoverished under various state Medicaid rules. Legislation passed by Congress in 1989 introduced more liberal changes in three areas: (1) spouses remaining at home can now receive a greater proportion of the nursing home resident's income; (2) national rules were established for allocating a couple's assets between nursing home expenses and the spouse's needs; and (3) national rules for the treatment of assets *transferred* from the nursing home resident to the at-home spouse (or to someone other than a spouse) were also established.

Four years later, however, Congress passed new cost-recovery legislation in the Omnibus Budget Reconciliation Act of 1993. This law requires states to recover the costs of long-term care services from the estates of Medicaid beneficiaries.

Medicare

The Medicare program is very different from Medicaid; it is a universal program that covers almost all aged persons and is funded entirely through federal mechanisms. According to the National Commission on Social Security (1981), Medicare arose historically from three principal premises:

1. That the cost of medical care was not something that could be budgeted in preparing for retirement, because it varied from time to time and from person to person. Therefore, insurance against this cost was necessary to retirement security.
2. That for most retired people, the premium cost of adequate health insurance was too high to pay out of retirement income or savings. Therefore, a new prepayment approach and government aid were required to make health insurance in retirement feasible.
3. That adequate and affordable private-sector health insurance was generally available only through group coverage. But retired people usually could not easily be brought together into groups suitable for such coverage.

The "hospital insurance" program (often called Part A) provides benefits financed by *compulsory* payroll taxes (currently 1.45 percent paid by both employee and employer) and covers (1) all persons age 65 or over entitled under either OASDI or the railroad retirement system; (2) most social security disability beneficiaries under age 65; and (3) certain workers and their family members with kidney disease. Hospital insurance benefits are also available to *noninsured* persons who were over age 65 in July 1966 and to other persons age 65 and over who voluntarily enroll and pay a premium rate that meets the entire cost of their protection.

"Supplementary medical insurance" (often called Part B) is a *voluntary* program for nonhospital health care financed by participant premiums ($45.50 per month in 1999) and a matching but much higher contribution for aged participants by the federal government out of general revenue. With certain minor exceptions, any person age 65 or over in the United States can participate.

Part A Benefits

The hospital insurance program provides a variety of hospital and post-hospital benefits (with the patient subject to certain deductible and cost-sharing charges). Reimbursement for services provided are made directly to hospitals, skilled nursing facilities, and home health service agencies. With regard to hospitalization, an individual was subject to an initial deductible of $768 in 1999 (but no more than the actual hospital charge). After the first 60 days, the individual must pay a co-payment of $192 per day; and after 90 days, he or she can choose to pay $384 per day up to 60 "lifetime reserve" days, instead of paying the actual hospital charges.[1] In addition, 20 days of skilled nursing care are provided without cost to eligible persons for each spell of illness, and 80 days following are provided on a cost-sharing basis ($96 per day in 1994).

Certain posthospital extended care services are provided if skilled nursing care is provided in an institution or section of a hospital that qualifies as a skilled nursing facility. Payment for up to 150 days is provided, but the patient is charged a coinsurance payment equal to 20 percent of the national average daily cost of such facilities.

Also, certain home health services can be provided under a care plan established by a doctor (while he is providing care to the individual). These services may include part-time or intermittent care by a visiting nurse or by a physical, speech, or occupational therapist. Full-time nursing is not included; neither are various nonmedical care needs such as housekeeping, meal preparation, or shopping.

Finally, **hospice** services for the terminally ill are available. Patients are responsible for $5 of the daily costs of both the respite care and each prescription for drugs.[2] Hospice benefits are limited to 210 days unless the person is recertified as terminally ill.

Part B Benefits

The supplementary medical insurance program covers certain nonhospital medical costs, primarily the cost of physician services. In general the program reimburses 80 percent of "reasonable charges" after an initial deductible of $100 per calendar year (with certain carry-over provisions). There are, however, two very different payment procedures available for reimbursing covered services. The doctor who accepts "assignment" and thereby agrees to accept the government reimbursement amount as payment in full is paid directly by the government (after taking into account any deductible and coinsurance). If the doctor does not accept assignment, the patient is responsible for the doctor's actual charges and must pay charges above the Medicare reimbursement rate out-of-pocket. However, federal legislation passed in 1989 limits the amount physicians *not* accepting assignment are allowed to bill their Medicare patients for actual charges in excess of the Medicare payment. Physicians can charge (to Medicare patients) no more than 115 percent of the Medicare allowable fee.

Over the years, a great many doctors have not accepted assignment—many because they would receive lower fees, some because of strong personal views against dealing with government agencies and having fees "dictated" by them, others because it has been the American Medical Association's recommended action, and still others because of alleged delays in receiving payments. In 1984 incentives were introduced to encourage physicians to accept assignment, but the percent of acceptances continued to decrease. The proportion of physicians accepting assignment has fallen from an initial level of about 85 percent to below 50 percent (U.S. Congressional Budget Office, 1990).

Beginning in 1999, persons eligible for Medicare may select from several new coverage options. The "Medicare+Choice" plans include several types of managed care plans, medical savings accounts, and private fee-for-service plans. Managed care plans are plans with a Medicare-approved network of doctors, hospitals, and other providers who agree to give care in return for a set monthly payment from Medicare. The most common type of managed care plan is the now-familiar health maintenance organization (HMO).

What Is Not Covered

One of the common misperceptions is that Medicare covers most medical expenses. But a look at the coverage exceptions makes it clear that in addition to the considerable deductions and co-payments mentioned above, there are many important and potentially expensive needs not covered. Below is a list of some key expenses not covered:

• Most prescription drugs and "over-the counter" medicines
• Routine physicals, eye exams, most immunizations, and routine foot care
• Vision glasses and orthopedic shoes
• Dental care and false teeth
• Private nurses and most chiropractic services

Given these gaps in coverage, elderly persons are exposed to substantial out-of-pocket health care costs. For example, the elderly, on average, paid out in 1995 about one-fifth of their income to meet uncovered costs (Crystal et al., 2000). This cost burden varied widely, however. Those in the lowest fifth of the income distribution paid out an average of 32 percent, while those in the top fifth paid out only 9 percent. Those with Medicaid coverage spent the lowest percentage of income out-of-pocket.

Medigap Insurance

Even before the elderly were confronted by Medicare cutbacks, many sought additional insurance protection from private plans. These "medigap" policies are designed to cover various medical expenses not covered by the government program and are currently purchased by nearly 70 percent of the elderly population. In 1987, Robert Ball, former commissioner of Social Security, offered the following evaluation of these programs:

The so-called Medigap policies of private insurance are very expensive for the protection furnished. A considerable portion of premium income goes for administration—15 to 35 percent—partly because the individual claims, on average, are small in amount. . . . They seldom fill [all] the gaps in coverage (such as prescription drugs) and do not deal at all with the cost of long-term care where the need is primarily for personal services, such as feeding, dressing, toileting, or helping the patient move about. (Ball, 1987)

Hearings in Congress over the years have highlighted "abuses in the marketing of such policies, perceptions that enforcement of medigap standards has been inadequate, confusion of seniors in purchasing such policies, and concerns about the value and cost of such policies" (U.S. Senate Special Committee on Aging, 1991). Federal legislation in 1990 authorized grants to states to support or establish health insurance counseling programs. Also, a core group of benefits was defined by the legislation and is common to all packages offered by insurers; uniform language and format is required to facilitate comparisons, and provisions were enacted to prevent duplicate coverage and policy cancellation solely on the basis of health status. Beginning in 1992, private medigap programs are limited to 10 standardized plans.

Company Retiree Health Plans

Another type of private insurance available is from plans sponsored by employers for their *retired* employees. In 1983 there were 4.3 million (one out of six) aged persons covered by employer-sponsored health insurance plans. By 1988 the number had increased to 7 million retired workers and 3.5 million spouses (U.S. General Accounting Office, 1989a); 43 percent of public- and private-sector workers over age 39 were covered—either on their own or through a spouse (EBRI, 1993). The plans fall into two main categories: (1) "Medicare supplement plans" that pay claims according to a schedule of payments for specified services; and (2) "carve-out plans" that pay the amount that is paid by the company's insurance for active workers, reduced by Medicare payments.

A Brandeis University study (Leavitt et al., 1987) looked at retirees in three large companies providing supplemental insurance protection. It found, as would be expected, much lower personal health insurance purchases by those retirees electing the company coverage; however, retirees were required to contribute financially to the costs of such insurance, discouraging election. Yet no matter how comprehensive their coverage, almost all covered retirees (even those who personally bought additional private insurance) had *noninsured* medical expenses for a wide variety of uncovered services. For many of the retirees surveyed in the study, these expenses were substantial. In addition, the study found that retirees with company-sponsored plans were confronted with difficult decisions with regard to buying additional gap insurance on their own. The gap plans did not "mesh" well with the company plans, *forcing retirees to buy outside coverage they did not need in order to get the protection they wanted.*

The costs of these corporate-sponsored plans have become a major concern to employers. For example, General Motors estimated in 1994 that every vehicle it produced cost the company (and, hence, the car buyer) an additional $1,500 just to cover the health expenditures for its workers and retirees (Employee Benefit Plan Review, 1994). Employer apprehension about the future arises from a number of factors. Retiree populations in many companies, particularly in the slow growth or declining sectors of the economy, are growing dramatically relative to employees still working. Discussions surrounding the Medicare cutbacks of recent years have also alerted employers to the possibility that their future liabilities will rise, even if health care costs in general are kept under control—given the coordination through integrated payment rules that exists between public and private programs. Finally, unlike pension plans, virtually no prefunding by employers of retiree health benefits has occurred, and consequently projected employer expenditures in the future (if nothing changes) will be extraordinarily large—according to one estimate, $402 billion in future liabilities as of 1988 (U.S. General Accounting Office, 1989a).

Until recently, these large future costs were not very visible. However, a Financial Accounting Standards Board ruling requires companies to report these accrued liabilities on their balance sheets, making present and potential shareholders more aware of the drain on future profits of these costs.

In response to rising costs and increased uncertainties about the future, some companies have been cutting back on their health programs for retirees by deliberalizing or even eliminating these benefits. More frequently employers are shifting part or all of the costs to participants. For example, General Motors, for the first time in 1994, required retirees and many salaried workers to make contributions to health care costs.

Retirees and unions have vigorously opposed cutbacks, often in the courts. Decisions in a number of court cases to date seem to severely limit the ability of employers to change or eliminate promised benefits made in the past, so employers now make sure there is a clause in the plan that clearly reserves the right to change or terminate benefits at its option. A study of 2,395 employers by A. Foster Higgins & Co. (Swoboda, 1994) indicates that a significant number of companies, in fact, have already terminated benefits.

What is the company health benefit promise worth? Increasingly, workers feel that this is not a retirement benefit that they can count on in future years (see, for example, Warshawsky, 1992).

LONG-TERM CARE

The tragedy of old age is not the fact that each of us must grow old and die but that the process of doing so has been made unnecessarily and at times excruciatingly painful, humiliating, debilitating and isolating through insensitivity, ignorance and poverty. (Butler, 1975)

At no time are older persons more sensitive to the issue Robert Butler raises in the above extract than when they confront the issue of long-term care. In 1996, there were 16,840 nursing homes with 1.76 million beds (Rhoades and Krauss, 1999). At age 65 individuals face about a 40 percent risk of entering a nursing home during their remaining lifetime. Of those who enter a nursing home, about one-third will spend less than three months (Kemper and Murtaugh, 1991), but 20 percent will spend five or more years (Rich, 1991).

Probably one of the greatest fears of old age is what will happen at the onset of severe and chronic illness or loss of capacity. The independence of living arrangements and lifestyles so cherished by most Americans is threatened (and often lost) when physical and/or mental capacities diminish. In addition, as we explain below, the financial burden of dealing with this issue falls heavily upon the individual and his or her family. For all but the rich, the costs of long-term care can quickly wipe out most financial reserves. And finally, but certainly not least in importance, there is the emotional strain placed upon individuals and their families in making decisions on how to meet the new medical, service, and financial demands.

There is one fact that seems relatively clear. The majority of (but not all) older persons with severe health and physical limitations prefer to remain out of an institutional care facility if at all possible. Hence, the major effort over the past decade or so has been to develop alternatives to institutionalization.

Yet the fact is that at present our programs and policies are still, despite improvements, heavily biased toward institutional care. Most public money for long-term care currently goes for institutional care, and the inadequate availability of community care services (and restrictions under public programs in the use of those available) encourage overutilization of institutional options.

In addition to the problem of institutional bias, it is generally recognized that the following major long-term care problems continue to exist (Callahan and Wallack, 1981):

1. The general quality of care is often poor.
2. Services and financing are fragmented.
3. There remain large amounts of unmet needs and a geographic maldistribution of available benefits.
4. Costs are rising rapidly, and public expenditures are not under acceptable control.
5. There is an absence of adequate case management (i.e., no centralized mechanisms for information, referral, prescription, allocating resources, and so forth).
6. The current situation places heavy burdens on individuals and families.

As yet no consensus has emerged in the United States as to what action is appropriate to deal with these issues.

Long-Term Care Providers

Hospitals still provide a significant amount of long-term care to the aged. While most hospitals are designed for short-term stays, many (especially city and county hospitals) treat patients requiring more than 60 days of care. Also, while the numbers have declined significantly, many elderly still receive care in psychiatric hospitals and residential treatment centers.

The trend has been to move the elderly from hospitals and mental institutions into other care facilities. The most common option is use of nursing homes. Over the past few decades there has been phenomenal growth in the number of such facilities, most being occupied predominantly by older people. In 1995, about 4 percent of the aged were residents in nursing homes.

The growth of nursing homes is not the result of satisfaction with the services provided. The quality of care provided in many of these homes has been notoriously poor. During the 1970s and 1980s, investigations found that many nursing homes fail to meet basic standards of safety and service (see, for example, U.S. HEW, 1978 and U.S. General Accounting Office, 1987). Problems cited included physical and safety hazards, the

Figure 6–1
Sources of Payments for Nursing Home Costs, 1997

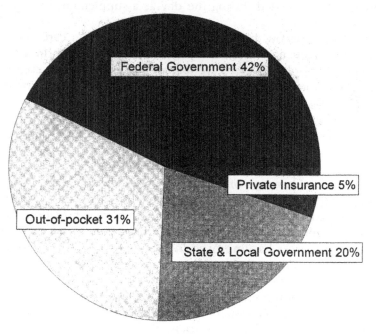

Source: U.S. House Committee on Ways and Means, *1998 Green Book* (Washington, D.C.:
U.S. Government Printing Office, 1998).

overuse of medications, the administration of drugs by untrained staff,
the rarity of physician visits, and poor quality staffing with high turnover
(to name only a few).

The growth of nursing homes arises from a number of factors. A growing elderly population, and an even faster growing *very old* population,
increases demand. It is estimated, for example, that by the years 2016–
2020, 51 percent of nursing home residents will be age 85 or older,
compared with 42 percent in 1986–1990 (Rivlin and Wiener, 1988). Another reason is that federal payment procedures to hospitals still encourage these institutions to discharge patients as soon as their health
condition permits—often to a nursing home.

The average stay in a nursing facility is between two and three years
and is often preceded by a lengthy period of care at home. The average
cost of that care is $51,100 per year (Palma, 1999).

The United States currently spends about $83 billion a year on nursing
home costs. Figure 6–1 shows the distribution of those costs among those
who pay for them. Currently, government is the primary payee.

Two alternatives to nursing homes for some people are *day-care* pro-

grams and *home care*. Day care is designed for people who do not require 24-hour institutional care and provides a protective environment
and treatment as needed during the day as a supplement to spouse or
family care at night.

To the older person, however, in many ways home care is a more
attractive option than institutionalization. For every person in a nursing
home (age 65 or older), there are almost two living in the community
requiring some form of long-term care (U.S. Senate Special Committee
on Aging, 1991). Almost all those not in institutions rely heavily on unpaid sources of care, mostly family help. In 1989, 27 percent received
some paid care; only 3 percent used paid care only (Pepper Commission,
1990).

Ideally, support for the elderly is provided in these programs by making available a wide range of community services that make it possible
for elderly persons to remain in their homes. Unfortunately, the various
publicly funded programs that cover community care provide only frag-
ments of the full range of services needed. However, Medicaid coverage
of home care services has improved in recent years. Under Section 2176
of the Omnibus Budget Reconciliation Act of 1981, state governments
may institute a variety of home- and community-based services for individuals who, but for the services, would be in long-term care institutions.
However, as mentioned above, both home care and nursing home benefit
regulations require individuals to "spend down" almost all of their wealth
in order to achieve eligibility for the services. (Increasingly, private profit
and nonprofit organizations are offering these services to people who
can pay for them.)

Finally, it is important to emphasize that over the years—and still today—it is the families of the chronically ill elderly who provide the largest
amount of care. Currently, over 3 million families provide major assistance to the impaired elderly living outside institutions; this includes
physical, personal, and financial help. For most families, caregiving is a
mixture of satisfactions and frustrations. Experiences are as varied as the
individuals who live them. Typically, families invest a great deal of time
and energy in caregiving in order to avoid sending a relative to a nursing
home. As Elaine Brody (1985) observes, *"Nowadays adult children provide more care and more difficult care to more parents over much
longer periods of time than they did in the good old days. . . .* Prior to
institutionalization, most families have endured severe personal, social,
and economic stress." They endure this stress, in most cases, willingly—
in an effort to return some of the care and love they received when they
were very young; and, as pointed out by Wiener and Illston (1995), "the
strong role of the family in long-term care runs counter to the myth that
American families, who supposedly took care of their aging relatives at

home 'in the good old days,' are now 'dumping' them in nursing homes" [emphasis added].

Covering the Costs of Long-Term Care

Not all individuals will confront the need to meet lengthy, costly long-term care expenses, but for those that do, it will be very expensive. As indicated above, the probability at age 65 of needing nursing home care before one dies is about 40 percent, and about 20 percent of those elderly using these services remain institutionalized over five years. As a result, roughly 13 percent of all elderly use 90 percent of all nursing home resources (Tell et al., 1987).

Lack of information and misinformation about long-term care is common. In 1993 a poll was taken by the Gallup organization, asking people about the financing of long-term care costs. Nearly half believed, erroneously, that Medicare pays for these costs when you get old (*Productive Aging News*, 1993a). Moreover, survey data indicate that most Americans (75 percent) do not think they will ever need long-term care (EBRI, 1992).

The only government program that pays a significant amount for long-term care is Medicaid. But Medicaid is means-tested, which means that one must deplete most financial assets before becoming eligible. (Most states allow one to keep only $2,000—some a little more or less.)

Thus, considerable anxiety exists as health declines. A survey found that 43 percent of individuals had experienced a need in their immediate family for long-term care, and 54 percent of the respondents reported worrying about future needs for themselves or their family (*Employee Benefit Plan Review*, 1993). When asked about special long-term care insurance, 68 percent of those surveyed indicated a strong interest in purchasing private insurance, and 74 percent said they would support government action, even if it meant increased income taxes (EBRI, 1992).

Many people would like to avoid the Medicaid option of long-term care financing. People who have saved for a lifetime do not want to see their financial assets wiped out. Others want to avoid reliance on government payments from a means-tested, "welfare" program. Some fear that Medicaid eligibility will make it difficult to enter a nursing home of their preference, since home operators claim they lose money on Medicaid patients.

But long-term care insurance is expensive. An individual age 65 who is in good health can expect to pay $2,000 to $4,000 per year for one of the better policies. Numerous studies conclude, however, that only 10 to 20 percent of the current elderly can afford those prices.

Currently, at least 130 private insurance companies offer policies to cover the costs of certain long-term care expenses—up from only 16 companies in 1984 and 70 in 1987 (*Consumer Reports*, 1991).

A report by Consumers Union raised serious questions about the extent to which many of these plans will help to meet the costs of long-term care and about the marketing techniques used by various companies (*Consumer Reports*, 1991). Major findings with regard to the long-term care policies surveyed were that:

1. Policy holders must obtain long-term care services from providers that meet qualifications set by the insurance companies, requirements that are often highly restrictive.
2. The process of determining that a policy holder is eligible for benefits varies greatly among plans, and information on exactly what determines eligibility is often difficult to obtain.
3. Only a small minority of plans offer benefits inflation protection that continues as long as the policy stays in force.
4. Forfeiture of benefits provisions are very strict, resulting in loss of the policy holder's entire equity if she or he can no longer afford to continue coverage or wishes to switch to another company.

With regard to getting good information so that one is well-informed before buying a policy, the experience of the Consumers Union investigation was very discouraging. A reporter (a trained expert) posed as a relative of an older person seeking protection and listened to fourteen sales representatives of nine of the largest sellers of coverage. Consumers Union reports that:

She [the investigator reporter] heard lies. She witnessed ignorance or deceit. She saw ethical standards violated and state law ignored.

Every sales agent misrepresented some aspect of the policy, the financial condition of the insurer, or the quality of a competitor's product. Not one sales agent properly explained the benefits, restrictions, and policy limitations. . . . Not only did agents fail to explain their policies properly, they didn't bother to leave written information that would. (*Consumer Reports*, 1991)

In 1997, Consumers Union did a follow-up investigation of the way long-term care policies were sold. This time their reporter sat through thirteen sales pitches in California, Colorado, and Texas. Again, the findings were troubling. While there were fewer high-pressure tactics, "many agents appeared clueless about the policies they were selling. They imparted misinformation, misleading information, or no information" (*Consumer Reports*, 1997).

German Action?

In 1995, Germany began a new compulsory state insurance scheme for persons of all ages needing long-term care. The scheme is financed largely by a 1 percent increase in payroll taxes, to be split equally between employers and employees. Thus, the country that initiated social security has expanded it to deal with this growing health care issue. Many people in the United States have proposed that we do something similar. (See Moon, 1996.)

One major question dominates the long-term care discussions: How can we adequately meet the needs of care recipients without generating politically unacceptable program costs and without undermining the historically important role of the family in this area? We still are far from agreement on the answer.

FINANCING HEALTH CARE

Health costs and, consequently, health program costs have risen rapidly over the years. Health care expenditures (for people of all ages) are about $3.4 billion each day of the year.

The percentage of the U.S. gross national product (GNP) devoted to health care services has risen to above 14 percent. In 1950 the typical stay in a hospital was eight days, at an average cost to the hospital for the entire period of $127. Contrast this with the costs in recent years. While the average stay has declined, the average cost of a hospital admission (utilizing updated knowledge and technology) soared to around $10,000.

The United States spends more per capita on health than other industrialized nations. Despite high spending, public dissatisfaction is high. A 1990 international survey of consumer satisfaction with health care found that people generally think major changes are needed to make the existing health system work better (*Ageing International*, 1990). People were asked whether they agreed with the statement: "On the whole, the [health] system works pretty well and only minor changes are needed to make it work better." The proportion of people who agreed with this statement were over 40 percent in Canada, the Netherlands, Germany, and France; around 30 percent in Australia, Sweden, Japan, and the United Kingdom; but only 12 percent in Italy and a low of 10 percent in the United States.

Comparison of health systems among various countries is difficult and needs to be treated with caution. Supporters of current American practice often assert that the United States provides the highest quality of care, that the country leads the world in medical research, and that Americans have more freedom to choose among various providers, service delivery systems, treatment methods, and insurance coverage levels. But the rapidly escalating levels of medical costs raise fears that expenditures on other important and necessary public and private goods and services will be "squeezed out." For example, focusing solely on health care, there is growing concern that escalating costs will make it difficult (if not impossible) to solve the long-term care needs (discussed earlier) and the problem of the millions without any health insurance protection at all.

Prospective Payment

In an attempt to deal with rising costs, Congress passed important legislation in 1983. Social security amendments in that year specified a major change in the way the government pays claims for inpatient hospital services. Medicare now pays a fixed amount (determined in advance) for various expense categories. Hospitals must consider these reimbursements as payments in full and are prohibited from charging beneficiaries any additional amount, apart from the statutory deductible and coinsurance amounts.

Under this new "prospective payment system (PPS)," payment amounts are determined by *the average cost of providing the treatment for a particular diagnosis*, adjusted to reflect the wage level in the local community, the higher costs of teaching hospitals, whether the hospital has an exceptionally large number of low-income, Medicaid patients, and whether the hospital is in an urban or rural area. Under this system, each hospital admission is assigned to one of 477 diagnosis-related groups (DRGs), and this determines the payment amount.

This payment system provides an incentive to hospitals to minimize tests, treatment procedures, and overall hospital stays. If these three aspects of care can be provided by the hospital at lower cost than the DRG payment, it is permitted to keep the difference. If the hospital's costs are more, the hospital cannot make up the difference (as in prior years) by charging the government for the costs of the care they provided. Thus, the DRG payment system is designed to discourage overtreatment and reduce administrative costs by eliminating the processing and review of numerous treatment/test charges involved in any hospital admission. While a relatively simple concept, the DRG payment system in practice is very complicated.

Designed to encourage improvement in hospital management, the system may cause hospitals to give too much weight to financial matters in the provision of health care. For example, because length of stay is a critical factor in determining payments, providers seek to keep their costs down by making discharge decisions that are in accord with the average length of stays assumed in the DRG payment schedule. Concern has been voiced that as a result of this process, some patients are being discharged prematurely from hospitals. Alternatively, the DRG payment system may affect patient care before they even enter the hospital—influencing hospital admissions policies. Some private hospitals have been charged with "creaming" the ill population—sending the more difficult (more expensive) cases to public hospitals.

As physicians and hospitals have adjusted to the new rules, more services have been moved out of the hospital and into ambulatory settings, leading to an increase in spending for physician and other outpatient services (Holahan et al., 1990). The annual increase in Medicare hospital costs dropped from 12 percent to 1 percent four years after introducing DRGs; however, as a result of cost shifting to ambulatory facilities, overall hospital expenditures had returned to pre-DRG levels by 1992 (Propac, 1993).

There have been many ad hoc adjustments by Congress in the PPS system since 1984. According to Moon (1996), "a consistent theme of federal budget reduction efforts has been to fund lower increases in payment rates to hospitals than that established in the original legislation." Hospitals complain that as a consequence, they are being penalized for finding ways to cut costs.

The result of these changes by the government has been a steady decline in the ability of hospitals to recover all their costs of treating Medicare patients. In some cases, particularly in high-cost teaching hospitals, all costs have not been recovered. Hospitals have responded by cutting admissions, reducing the average length of patient stays, and reducing the number of staff per patient. Of course, "from the federal government's perspective, PPS has been very successful. It has achieved substantial reductions in benefit payments over time, not in absolute dollars, but in terms of what Medicare would otherwise have had to pay for care" (Moon, 1996).

In 1989, Congress radically changed the way physicians are reimbursed under Medicare. The legislation mandated that physicians be paid in accordance with a "resource based relative value scale" (RBRVS). Scheduled to start in 1992, the new payment system came under attack from various medical organizations and doctors. Criticism and political pressure were particularly strong when the Health Care Financing Administration (HCFA) issued a draft of the implementing regulations in June of 1991. After much debate and threats from Congress, HCFA changed the final regulations to respond to many of the objections.

The RBRVS for any medical service has three components: (1) a measure of the work provided by physicians in providing the service, (2) a measure of their office expenses, and (3) a measure of malpractice insurance costs. Work is measured by the *time* and *intensity* of effort required. A "geographic practice cost index" is used to adjust for differences among localities. Physician reimbursement amounts under the new procedure are determined by multiplying the RBRVS by a dollar "conversion factor," adjusted geographically. The new payment system results in different fees for different services or specialties. For example, primary care physicians receive higher Medicare payments, while surgeons and radiologists receive relatively lower fees for their particular services.

The two major goals of the reform were to reduce the rate of growth in physicians' costs under Medicare and to create a much simpler fee schedule to replace the highly complex one that had been used for the first twenty-four years of the program. However, since this new type of payment system is still essentially a fee-for-service approach, incentives for increasing physician incomes through increasing the volume of services still exist. In recognition of this problem, the legislation established a "volume performance standard rate of growth" (i.e., a target growth rate) for physicians as a group—with physicians receiving increases in Medicare payment rates that are less than their growing costs, if the "target" is not achieved.

In the initial years of the new fee schedule, Medicare payments for surgical and testing services have grown (as expected) much less than payments for primary care service. Moreover, there is no indication that patient access to care has been impacted negatively (Moon, 1996).

Rising Costs

Not surprisingly, a disproportionate share of health care services goes to the elderly; about 12 percent of the population accounts for about one-third of total health care expenditures. The personal health care costs of older persons are between two and three times higher than what one would expect from aggregate statistics for people of all ages (Zook and Moore, 1980). Here again, however, differences among the elderly are important. Many of the aged are healthy and use a moderate amount of health care services, while others require extensive services. In fact, in 1982 only 9 percent of the elderly accounted for 70 percent of all Medicare payments (for the aged), and 40 percent of the aged receive no Medicare reimbursed services in any particular year (Davis, 1982).

As discussed above, Medicare is financed by a payroll tax (currently 1.45 percent) for Part A expenses. Payments by the federal government from general revenues finance most of Part B (and some transitional expenses connected with Part A). Coinsurance payments by eligible individuals are used to help finance both Part A and Part B services.

The rising costs of general health care (and the Medicare program more specifically) are a result of many factors (in ranked order of importance):

1. Expanding (and expensive) medical technology developments and increased utilization of expanding services.
2. The fact that the United States, unlike other countries, has not imposed severe spending limits on physicians and hospitals.
3. General inflation but inflation in health care costs especially, with health costs rising much faster than the more general Consumer Price Index.
4. An increased number of persons receiving services, especially the aged.
5. The high administrative costs of a very decentralized array of insurance programs.

In recent years there has been concern that Medicare financing was inadequate. Projections indicated a shortfall of funds in the near future. As is appropriate, Congress acted to improve the financing situation. The 1999 report of the Trustees of the Medicare Trust Fund stated that the Part A trust fund for hospital services will be able to meet all costs at least up to the year 2015. This is an increase of seven years over the estimate in their 1998 report. The improvement is the result of "robust economic growth," cost savings resulting from the Balanced Budget Act of 1997, and generally lower increases in health care costs. Large expenditures loom in the future, however, as the retirement of the Baby Boomers approaches.

To keep up with inflation, the deductible for Part A has risen from the original $40 to $764 (in 1998). Hospital coinsurance has been increased from $10 to $191 per day for days 61 through 90 in the hospital and from $20 to $382 per day for the 60 hospital "reserve days." Also, with regard to Part B, the government has shifted more of the total cost to the aged. The Part B premium has been increased substantially, with the annual Part B deductible ($75 in 1982) increased to $100.

As we indicated above, people covered by Medicare still pay out large amounts for health care. Table 6–1 shows the proportion of income these expenditures represent. While overall 14 percent of after-tax income is paid out, there are large differences by income level—with those people just above the poverty line median spending over half their income.

Repeal of Catastrophic Illness Insurance

When it was enacted, Medicare was visualized as a fairly comprehensive program, comparable to the better private health insurance plans then available for people at younger ages. But as we discussed above, rising health costs and increases in deductible and coinsurance payments have created a large gap between the total costs of health care (for a typical elderly person) and the protection provided by Medicare. This problem is especially serious for the persons experiencing exceptional or "catastrophic" medical costs. It is estimated, for example, that in 1987 there

Table 6–1
Median Out-of-Pocket Health Care Spending as a Percent of After-Tax Income, 1995

Income Level of Individuals	Percent of Income	Percent of Aged in Group
Below the Poverty Line	21	9
Poverty Line to 1.25% of Line	61	5
1.25% to 200%	45	21
200% to 400%	16	38
Over 400%	7	27
All Incomes	14	100

Source: U.S. House Committee on Ways and Means, *1998 Green Book* (Washington, D.C.: U.S. Government Printing Office, 1998), Table 3.40.

were over two million elderly who experienced catastrophic health care expenses (U.S. Congressional Research Service, 1987).

In 1986, Secretary of Health and Human Services Otis R. Bowen proposed new government action to help Americans meet the costs of catastrophic illnesses requiring long hospital or nursing home stays. The Bowen plan called for expanding Medicare Part B to better cover the elderly and a combination of state and private initiatives to cover the rest of the population. A major debate followed around a number of alternative approaches to the catastrophic illness problem.

Congress passed new legislation in 1988 putting a cost cap on out-of-pocket costs for Medicare-covered services (for 1988, the cap was about $1,800) and requiring only one deductible ($544 in 1988). The new provisions also expanded *short-term* nursing home and home health care benefits, and for the first time, coverage for prescription drugs was to be made available, with Medicare paying 80 percent of the costs after an initial deductible was met. To finance the new provisions, the monthly premium for Part B of Medicare was to be raised $4 in 1988 and an additional premium charge for the drug benefit was to be phased in. This basic premium increase was to be supplemented by an additional premium (also called a surtax) charged only to those beneficiaries who paid federal income taxes (estimated to be about 40 percent of beneficiaries in 1988).

Enacted quickly by Congress with relatively little debate, the passed legislation stirred a massive outcry of negative reaction, *especially among the elderly*. For the first time in history, Congress was asking the elderly to pay the entire cost of a Medicare benefit, and a great many older people did not like it. Critics of the financing scheme claimed the legislation was a fundamental redistribution of the income of America's senior citizens. Some critics labeled this premium an "indirect means test" and pointed out that a group of the aged were being asked "to do what was expected of no one else: to pay a special tax for benefits for their age group" (Holstein and Minkler, 1991).

Another major reason that many opposed the new law was that large numbers of the elderly already had private supplemental health insurance paid for by former employers, and many thought they would never use the program's main benefits. And "the fact [that] the new projections would annually benefit only those few (22 percent) unfortunate enough to incur significant out-of-pocket health costs was not appealing enough to many Americans" (U.S. Senate Special Committee on Aging, 1991).

Given the intense opposition to the approach adopted by Congress (as well as new evidence that the cost of the drug benefits had been seriously underestimated), legislators spent much of the year after enactment of the legislation trying to find a way to make the law more acceptable. However, a suitable compromise could not be reached. And early in October of 1989, the House of Representatives voted 360 to 66 for repeal of the catastrophic provisions—retaining only a few provisions relating to Medicaid. The Senate tried harder to keep some of the law's major provisions, but the House would not agree in the legislative conference trying to resolve the differences. Therefore, in November 1989, the Congress repealed what many had earlier hailed as the most significant expansion of Medicare since its inception in 1965.

OTHER SOCIAL SECURITY PROGRAMS: DISABILITY AND SSI

In previous chapters we have referred to a number of programs other than health and retirement pensions that have an important impact on the economic welfare of the aged. It is appropriate at this point to discuss two of them, because they are important complements to health and pension programs.[3]

Disability Programs

At an intuitive level the desire to help those with functional limitations springs from a deep-seated moral sense that they are among the least advantaged in modern societies. Simple altruism calls upon us to help our neighbors who are in need because of disabling physical or mental conditions.

Jerry Mashaw (1997)

Unfortunately, responding to this desire to help the disabled has turned out to be very difficult—but not for a lack of trying. The social security disability programs discussed below are only two of many disability programs; more than 85 types of public and private programs in the United States deal with disability—including workers' compensation, the black lung program, veterans' programs, vocational rehabilitation, railroad disability, sick leave, short- and long-term private programs, and so on. Coordination problems among these various programs create a number of difficult adequacy and equity issues related to attempts to help physically impaired individuals.

Social security's Disability Insurance program (DI) and the Supplemental Security Income program (SSI) provide benefits to people who have severe long-term disabilities. Disability protection under the DI program is currently provided to: (1) disabled insured workers and their dependents; (2) disabled widows and widowers of insured workers; and (3) adult (age 18 or older) sons and daughters who become disabled before age 22 of insured disabled, retired, or deceased workers. The DI program is financed by a 0.9 percent payroll tax paid by both workers and employers.

Disability protection as part of social security was not legislated until 1956. Early social security advisory groups disagreed about the predictability of disability program costs and about whether one could administratively determine eligibility for this type of benefit (i.e., distinguish legitimate disability from malingering). Although it was proposed repeatedly in the early years of social security, major groups effectively fought against its introduction.

When the first major legislation for disability protection was debated in 1949 and 1950, strong criticism and opposition were voiced by the American Medical Association, the United States Chamber of Commerce, the National Manufacturers Association, and representatives of private insurance organizations. After the defeat of the 1949/1950 bill, strong opposition continued in succeeding years to the various new proposals that were introduced—including the disability freeze amendment of 1954. This was a provision that prevented periods of disability from reducing or eliminating retirement and survivors' benefits by "freezing" the individual's rights at the time of disablement.

All the disability proposals were attacked as potentially costly, difficult to administer, and the beginning of "socialized medicine." Given this strong opposition over the years, the ultimate passage of disability legislation in 1956 is viewed by many as a major development in the legislative history of social security in the United States (Cohen, 1957).

Restrictive Program

Many people today wonder why it is so difficult to become eligible for the DI program. Some historical perspective is important in understanding the problems and criticisms of inadequacy surrounding the current DI program. The strong opposition of major groups to the program and fears about administering the program (discussed earlier) influenced Congress to severely restrict the scope of the program passed in 1956. Key features of the *original* program that reflected these concerns were:

1. The establishment of not one but three different tests of insured status
2. A very narrow and "severe" definition of disability
3. The denial of benefits to anyone under age 50 or to any dependent
4. Creation of a separate trust fund to help monitor program costs
5. Vocational rehabilitation programs to help move people off the disability rolls

A major barrier to getting disability benefits under the OASDI program is the multiple tests of eligibility status built into the disability laws. To be eligible for social security disability payments, a worker must be screened successfully on three levels: (1) determination of insured status; (2) assessment of physical condition and level of functional impairment; and (3) determination of ability to work. To achieve insured status, the worker must have one quarter of work coverage credit for each year since 1950 (or since age 21, if later) and 20 quarters of coverage during the 40-quarter period prior to disability.[4] Disability, for purposes of benefit entitlement, is defined as "an inability to engage in any substantial gainful activity by reason of any medically determinable physical or mental impairment which can be expected to result in death or which has lasted or can be expected to last for a continuous period of not less than 12 months." The impairment must be a degree of severity that renders the person unable to engage in *any kind of substantial gainful work* that exists in the economy, regardless of whether such work exists in the person's immediate geographic area. However, consideration may be given to a person's age, education, and work experience, if a disability determination cannot be made on the basis of medical evidence alone.

This strict disability definition excludes many people with relatively severe incapacities. *Surveys have found that two-thirds of the self-described severely disabled do not receive social security disability payments* (e.g., Van de Water, 1979).

The DI program is administered under a federal–state partnership; program administration is carried out by each state and is paid for by the federal government under negotiated agreements. The determination of an applicant's disability is by a state agency whose primary function is to gather together the medical, vocational, and other necessary evidence. Evaluation teams, consisting of a physician and a disability evaluation specialist, are responsible for making the initial disability determination. They evaluate the information available and make a determination based upon it.

Applicants who are rejected may appeal this decision. This appeals process is very elaborate. If an application is rejected by the initial local/ state review, the person can, successively, (1) request reconsideration; (2) ask for a hearing before an administrative law judge; (3) request a review by the Social Security Appeals Council; and (4) undertake a civil action in a U.S. district court.

Fear that disability applicants would attempt to manipulate and inappropriately influence the eligibility determination was a prime motivation for the restrictive policies described above. They did not solve this problem, however. As Deborah Stone points out:

Despite the intentions of the framers of disability benefit programs to make them highly restrictive through the vehicle of clinical criteria, the boundaries between ability to work and disability remain extremely flexible. Disability determinations depend on diagnostic judgments which are themselves not overly reliable and are subject to manipulation by patients and physicians. The criteria for disability must still be formulated by a process of group consensus. And the essential problem of the relationship between subjective experience and inability to work remains unsolved. This indeterminacy and resultant flexibility . . . means that it [disability determination] is particularly subject to external pressures. (Stone, 1984)

DI Benefit Levels

Like retirement benefits, disability pensions are based on average indexed earnings (excluding the disablement period) and are calculated using the same formula and the same minimum benefit provisions as the retirement program. Initially, the social security disability benefit was reduced dollar-for-dollar by any workmen's compensation benefits received by the worker. Then in 1958 this deduction was removed, creating considerable controversy. Turnbull, Williams, and Cheit (1967) report that with the deduction removed, "it became possible in some states for a seriously injured worker to receive combined benefits that would exceed his wages prior to his disability." Faced with the criticisms of those who feared the encroachment and possible supplantation of federal disability insurance for state and private programs, Congress reintroduced an offset provision in 1965. However, controversy continued over program coordination and how to "cap" the benefit level.

In 1981 Congress passed a disability "Megacap." The new provision specified that a person's disability benefits (including any benefits for the spouse or children) were to be reduced (if necessary) so that the sum of all benefits payable under certain federal, state, and local public programs did not exceed 80 percent of the person's "average current earnings" (a concept defined in the law). The intent of Congress in passing this new provision was to reduce the overlapping and duplication of public disability programs and to avoid work disincentives arising out of the old law.

In 1998, $77 billion in disability benefits were paid out to 11 million people under the OASDI and/or the SSI program. The average DI benefit paid was $733 per month ($8,796 yearly); the average SSI benefit was $380 ($4,560). It has been estimated that, for example, a relatively young, average earner (with a family) who becomes disabled would receive about $285,000 over his or her lifetime (Social Security Advisory Board, 1998). Moreover, the Social Security Administration's actuaries have estimated that nearly one out of three young men, and nearly one out of four young women, who are now age 20 will become disabled before reaching age 65.

Do disability benefits at current levels discourage many people from working? One early study (Haveman et al., 1984) indicates that they do not. The research found that rising disability benefit levels in the past have had a relatively small effect on the work effort choices of older workers.

However, entitlement to benefits will always produce some encouragement not to work. But many factors are influencing the work decision, not just this one. For example, a major reason American disability beneficiaries may not return to work is their health benefits. After a typically very long wait to achieve eligibility for disability benefits and the accompanying Medicare coverage, beneficiaries may see the continuation of these health benefits as the major reason for not returning to work. But as Mashaw (1997) points out, "any critique of disability policies based on the simple claim that they create perverse incentives should . . . be viewed as seriously unhelpful. The important policy issue is whether we can somehow do better in balancing our desire to preserve work incentives against other purposes such as adequacy, security, and administrative simplicity."

Who Is Covered?

About one out of every six social security beneficiaries receives a disability benefit or is a dependent of a beneficiary with a disability. In 1998 there were 4.7 million disabled workers, 190,000 disabled widows, and 658,000 adults who have been disabled since childhood (see Table 6–2). Average benefits ranged from $182 per month for spouses of disabled workers to $733 per month for the disabled workers themselves. In ad-

Table 6–2
Federal Disability Beneficiaries, 1998[a]

Program and Beneficiary Category	Number (in thousands)	Average Monthly Benefit (in dollars)
Disability Insurance[b]		
Disabled workers	4,698	$733
Children of disabled workers	1,446	208
Spouse of disabled workers	190	182
Disabled adult children	54	300
Old Age and Survivors Insurance[b]		
Disabled adult children	658	494
Others	234	NA
Supplemental Security Income		
Disabled adults	4,178	344
Disabled children	885	430

[a]OASDI and SSI disability benefits as of December 1998.
[b]Among the 7.2 million OASDI beneficiaries were roughly 1 million who were also receiving a federal SSI payment.
Source: U.S. Social Security Administration (SSA), *Social Security and Supplemental Security Income Disability Programs: Managing for Today, Planning for Tomorrow* (Washington, D.C.: SSA, 1999).

dition, slightly over 5.1 million individuals received a federal SSI payment based on a disability.

Although 58 percent of disabled workers are men, the proportion of women has been rising over time. Over the last decade there has also been a sharp increase in the number of beneficiaries who come on at younger ages with mental impairments.

Controversy over Administration

The costs of the initial disability program in the early 1960s proved to be much lower than had been anticipated, encouraging a liberalization of the program by Congress. Almost immediately, however, expenditures began to grow faster than revenues. In response, Congress tightened the definition of disability. Even under the revised definition, however, claims mushroomed, with the number of disability beneficiaries tripling between 1965 and 1978 to a total of about 5 million disabled workers and their eligible dependents.

During the same period, the costs of the program grew from $1.5 billion in 1965 to $11 billion in 1977. If not for a 1977 legislative reallocation of OASDHI payroll tax revenues—less to the retirement (OASI) and health (HI) programs and more to disability (DI)—the disability program would have exhausted its reserves and been faced with a financial crisis. While some part of the increased costs resulted from program maturation (i.e., more workers meeting the years-of-coverage requirements), much of the increase came from an unanticipated increase in claims (Cardwell, 1976).

DI's financial problems in the 1970s caused policymakers to take a long, hard look at the program. The result was "belt-tightening" legislation passed in three years (1977, 1980, and 1981). These amendments were designed to address the financial problems of the program and, at the same time, to improve its operation.

Increased scrutiny of the disability program's operations resulted in a major disability controversy in the 1980s. The federal disability program and its administrative procedures came under additional criticism when a 1980 General Accounting Office report estimated that over a half-million people on the disability roles were capable of working. Congress responded by directing the Social Security Administration to review the eligibility status of benefit recipients every three years.

Reagan administration officials, newly in office, responded enthusiastically to the directive, hastily setting into place a review process. They saw the review mandate as consistent with their cost-cutting and antifederal views and pushed the review program forward with a vengeance. Over 30,000 cases a month were sent out to state officials who (we now know) were unprepared to review them. Between 1981 and 1984, about 1.2 million cases were reviewed; 491,000 benefits were terminated as a consequence of these reviews before any appeal by the recipient could take place. About 200,000 of these terminations were eventually reversed upon appeal. In one reversal, federal District Court Judge Joseph S. Lord III wrote, "If the purpose of the U.S. Department of Health and Human Services is to crush defenseless human beings, as it seems to be, it would succeed unless . . . courts interposed a protective arm" (*Newsweek,* 1984). A U.S. General Accounting Office report stated that at least eight people committed suicide because of benefit terminations.

Faced with an almost unprecedented refusal by Reagan administration officials to institute more humane policies, the courts, state governors, and members of Congress joined in a fight to stop the worst review practices. Some governors directed their disability agencies not to cooperate with federal officials. Court actions were frequently initiated.

The disability review process lasted until the spring of 1984. "By then opposition was so powerful and the chaos was so complete that the administration was compelled to suspend the review and wait for Congress to try to restore order with new legislation" (Derthick, 1990). The response of the Congress to the mess was to pass the 1984 Social Security Disability Benefits Reform Act. The law required the Social Security Administration, among other things, to terminate benefits only if *new* medical or assessment evidence was presented of an improved medical condition or if the earlier determination was shown to be in error. With the passage of this legislation, a review process was again started in 1986, but the number of reviews has been much lower.

Current Problems

In 1998 the Advisory Board to the Social Security Administration issued a report on ways to improve the disability programs under SSA management. The Board began its report with the following observation:

Today's problems have a long history. They stem, at least in part, from the complex administrative structure under which the programs operate, as well as from the fact that determining whether an individual is disabled is fundamentally a judgmental process in which different decision makers will frequently have different views. Today, as in the past, there are serious concerns about the lack of consistency in decision making; unexplained changes in application and allowance rates; the complexity, slowness and cost of the application and appeals process; the lack of confidence in the system; and the fact that few beneficiaries are successfully rehabilitated so that they can become part of the economic mainstream. (Social Security Advisory Board, 1998)

For individuals the biggest problem is what Mashaw (1997) has called "entitlement security." Mashaw points out that few people comprehend the requirement that *to be eligible for a disability benefit, a person must be unable to do any job that is available in the economy, whether or not the person would be hired for such a job*. As a result, most people do not understand benefit rejection decisions.

Once on the rolls, there is the fear of termination in eligibility. In part this arises from the fact that a beneficiary's health status often fluctuates, sometimes improving temporarily and calling eligibility into question.

Another major problem is the time it takes for a decision. In 1997, the average length of time for an initial disability decision was 70 days for DI and 80 for SSI. But if an individual's application is rejected and he or she appeals the case to an Administrative Law Judge (65 percent of cases), the wait is over a year—given a huge backlog in cases (Social Security Advisory Board, 1998).

THE SUPPLEMENTAL SECURITY INCOME PROGRAM

A new cash-assistance program for needy persons who were aged (age 65 or older), blind, or disabled went into operation at the beginning of

Figure 6–2
SSI Recipients, by Category and Age, December 1998

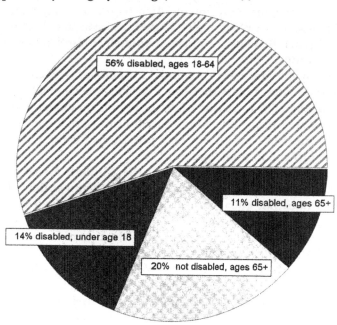

56% disabled, ages 18-64

11% disabled, ages 65+

14% disabled, under age 18

20% not disabled, ages 65+

Source: Web site of the U.S. Social Security Administration (www.socsec.gov).

1974. This Supplemental Security Income program (SSI) replaced federal grants to three programs: the state-administered programs of (1) old-age assistance; (2) aid to the blind; and (3) aid to the permanently and totally disabled (see Figure 6–2). The SSI program is administered by the federal government and financed from general revenues. It establishes uniform eligibility requirements and benefits levels for the whole nation. In addition, states are encouraged (and some are required) to supplement the federal benefits with their own payments. In cases where they do, the states have the option of administering the supplementary payments themselves or contracting with the federal government.

Eligibility for SSI requires that the individual satisfy both an income and an asset test. Nonexcluded assets were set by the most recent legislation not to exceed $2,000 for an individual and $3,000 for a couple. The major assets excluded from the test are (1) the value of one's home; (2) the value of household goods and personal effects up to $2,000; (3) an automobile (up to $4,500); and (4) life insurance (face value up to $1,500).

SSI benefits are reduced dollar for dollar (100 percent) by all *unearned* income and by 50 percent of any *earned* income above a $65-per-month "disregard." Unearned income up to $20 per month is also disregarded.

In 1996, SSI guaranteed recipients (before any state supplementation) a monthly income of $490 if single ($5,800 per year) and $725 if a couple ($8,700 per year). Benefits are adjusted annually for inflation by the Consumer Price Index.

In 1996, SSI assistance was prohibited for persons who are not citizens of the United States, unless they meet certain special eligibility requirements. Also, eligibility by reason of disability was no longer permitted for individuals where drug addiction or alcoholism were a contributing factor. Finally, the 1996 law set out new provisions for the review of eligibility related to children under age 18.

States have the option to supplement the SSI floor for all or selected categories of persons. States *are required to supplement* the federal level if that level does not equal or exceed the benefits provided under the state old-age assistance programs in December 1973 (just before SSI started), plus, in general the amount of federal benefits increases after 1979. About 6.6 million people were receiving federally administered SSI payments in 1999. Most of these recipients are disabled persons—not aged. The number of aged in the program was 2.4 million in 1999. Total program expenditures totaled about $31 billion in 1999.

The Historical Origins of SSI

To better understand the issues related to SSI today, it is important to look back in history at our earlier collective actions taken in response to the poverty of various groups in the American population.

Initial efforts to deal with the needs of the poor in early America were influenced a great deal by the poor laws in England. Three principles of welfare became established early in America's history and continued to dominate policies down through the years (Schottland, 1970):

1. That principal responsibility for providing and administering welfare programs was to reside with state governments and local communities.
2. That aid was to be available primarily to persons who were established residents of a community.
3. That relatives were to be held responsible for support of their needy kinsmen.

However, over the years one other major principle has dominated the development of welfare policies in the United States: that those in need who were unable to work were to be viewed much more favorably than those able to work—whether the latter had a job and irrespective of whether they could earn a living wage. Children, the disabled, and the aged in America have always received more favorable welfare treatment than the working poor. Just before the passage of the Social Security Act in 1935, for example, over half the states had an old-age assistance law, and all but two had programs for needy widowed mothers. While the benefits available under these programs were small, their very existence contrasted sharply with the lack of assistance provided by governments in the United States to the unemployed and their families.

The Great Depression changed the way the nation viewed many issues. Francis E. Townsend, a 60-year-old physician who had lost his job during this depression as assistant medical officer in Long Beach, California, was one of those galvanized into action by frustration and anger. His reform idea was presented initially in a letter to the *Long Beach Press-Telegram* on September 20, 1933. When Townsend proposed a universal pension plan for the aged, the idea spread rapidly and grew dramatically into a nationwide movement of 2 million people organized in 7,000 clubs. Although the Townsend movement never achieved its objective of a flat pension for all Americans age 60 or over, the movement itself had a major political impact, paving the way for the more moderate proposals encompassed in the Social Security Act.

In addition to old-age insurance, the new social security law provided grants to the states for assistance to the *needy* aged, blind, and dependent children. But the act did not mandate participation by the states. Rather it established minimal federal standards for receipt of the funds, keeping the responsibility for "welfare assistance" within the states and allowing them wide discretion in dealing with these issues. By 1938 all but one state (Virginia) had a qualified plan, and over 22 percent of Americans age 65 and over (2 million) were receiving "old age assistance."

The Social Security Act required that an individual's income and assets be considered in determining need (except for certain special exceptions) but did not specify a standard of living to be used by the states in establishing benefit levels. Consequently, each state developed its own definition of both the amount of resources to be used in determining eligibility and the levels of assistance to be provided to those meeting the eligibility requirements.

States generally defined assistance levels in terms of the number, kinds, and cost of certain specified consumption items included in various "assistance budgets." All states took food, clothing, shelter, fuel, and utility needs into account. Most states included items for personal care, nonprescription medicines, and household supplies; and many, but not all, states recognized "special needs," such as special dietary requirements or requirements for special transportation. One of the largest variations among (and within) states was the availability and cost of rental living units for assistance recipients.

Once a state established its full standards of need, financing considerations often played an important role. In some states, actual money payments to recipients were below the amount of determined need. This was a result of limits placed on state funds made available to meet these needs. In 1972, the largest payments were more than twice the levels in the poorest-paying states.

But differences in payment levels were only the beginning. Big differences in eligibility requirements, estate recovery, and relatives' financial responsibility also existed. Seventeen states required grown children, if they had the means, to help support needy parents. Some of these states held an applicant ineligible when a child was able to contribute to his support even though the child did not and would not do so (Schorr, 1960). More than one-half of the states permitted the state or local public assistance agency to obtain unsecured or secured claims against the real or personal property of recipients. In extreme cases, claims on real estate might be exercised, even though a surviving spouse or dependent was still occupying the premises.

Perhaps the most complex and widespread differences in state practices related to eligibility requirements:

Under the old system [of assistance to the aged, blind, and disabled], however, one State required an aged person to use up his last dollar before receiving relief; another allowed a cash reserve equal to 1 month's cost of living; six limited cash reserves to $300 or $350. Even "liberal" New York denied relief to an old person with liquid resources greater than $500 and specified that this counted the face value of life insurance "for burial." One State barred relief to anyone whose house had a value more than $750 above that of "modest homes in the community," and the rules of some states required applicants to sell their car before obtaining help. (Burke and Burke, 1974)

In addition to the above, there were also differences in residence and citizenship requirements and differences in the treatment of residents in institutions.

Dissatisfaction with the state programs grew over time. It would be wrong, however, to think that the new SSI program originated primarily as a federal response to the inadequacies of these state programs and dissatisfaction with the variation among them. The establishment of a federal program guaranteeing a minimum income to the aged, blind, and disabled came about in a much more indirect way. As we indicated above, Congress and presidents over the years had been sensitive to the problems of the "deserving poor," and they were concerned about the elderly, especially given the perception that old-age politics had been a significant factor in past elections and could be important in future elections.

The federal response, however, was not to focus on public assistance programs to help the needy; quite the opposite. Congress and various presidents turned to the social security programs that were not means-tested. By liberalizing these programs and thereby raising the living standards of all the elderly, they sought to reduce the role of the less popular "welfare" programs in the various states but help the poorest aged at the same time.

OASI became the cornerstone of those efforts. But over the years, as OASI was liberalized, a serious dilemma became apparent to increasing numbers of people. The problem with a strategy of combining in OASI the objectives of both social adequacy and individual equity was that neither could be satisfactorily carried out because of the inherent contradiction between the goals. As understanding and sensitivity to this dilemma grew, authoritative calls for dealing with welfare problems outside of OASI were voiced.

According to Vincent and Vee Burke (1974), in their book on welfare reform, SSI

solved a problem for key politicians—the defense of the social security wage-related "insurance" system against encroachments by welfare. . . . Social Security Commissioner Ball told the congressional tax writers [U.S. House Committee on Ways and Means] that there were limits as to how far "they could go in making the social security system itself a complete replacement for an income-determined or means-tested welfare benefit" without imperiling the wage-related and contributory nature of the system.

When President Nixon initially proposed his welfare reform legislation in 1969, SSI as we know it today was not part of the package. Instead, Nixon recommended a new "national minimum standard" to determine the amount of aid for the aged, blind, and disabled needy. But the standard was to operate under the existing state programs and under the hodgepodge of state rules on eligibility and administration.

It was not until 1971, when the House Ways and Means Committee redrafted the Nixon proposal that SSI was created. Although hailed by a few as a revolutionary development in income maintenance policy, SSI won congressional acceptance in 1972 with hardly any discussion and no floor debate. At the time, most of the attention of Congress was on welfare reform proposals for the nonaged—proposals that were hotly debated but never passed. Also, at the time, congressional attention was given to major changes in OASDI—that is, benefit liberalization and indexation (discussed in Chapter 4).

SSI in Practice

Figure 6–3 shows the ages of SSI beneficiaries. The big increases have been among the nonaged population, especially poor people with disabilities and young children.

Figure 6–3
Number of SSI Recipients, by Age, 1974–1998

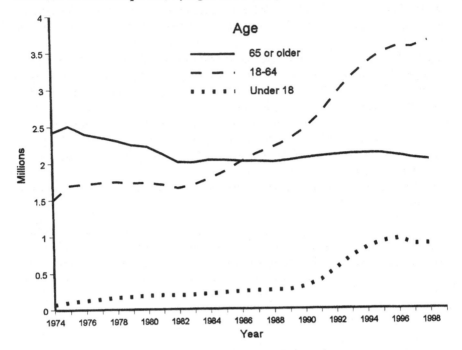

Source: Web site of the U.S. Social Security Administration (www.socsec.gov).

When SSI was legislated, its supporters argued that it would reduce many of the traditional problems associated with other programs to help the poor—that it would produce more efficient program administration, less stigma to recipients, and more adequate benefits using a national standard. During the first years of the program, the Social Security Administration had difficulty coping with the responsibilities and the additional workload suddenly thrust upon it as the chief administrator of the new federal program. In 1977, three years after its operations began, the SSI program was described by the U.S. Senate Committee on Finance staff as follows: "The early months of the program were characterized by near total administrative breakdown, primarily as a result of insufficient and inaccurate planning and inadequate resources. The crisis stage has passed, and steady improvements in administrative capabilities are taking place."

A major concern arose early in the program with regard to the low participation level of persons eligible for the SSI program. Studies indicated that about 40 percent of the aged eligible for SSI do not participate in the program (for example, Leavitt and Schulz, 1988).

Research investigating nonparticipation indicates that the two key reasons that many aged do not participate are lack of knowledge about it and stigma (for example, Drazaga et al., 1982). The Drazaga study found that 45 percent of nonparticipants had not even heard of the SSI program. But large numbers of those who knew of SSI still did not participate, indicating a reluctance to become involved in a means-tested program.

That some people are reluctant to participate in a means-tested program is illustrated by a surprising occurrence arising out of one Social Security (SSA) study of nonparticipation. After the study was completed, SSA sent a letter to about 300 of the nonparticipants in the study who were probably eligible. The letter stated that the individuals might be eligible for SSI payments and encouraged them to contact their local SSA office. But even personal letters from SSA did not substantially increase participation. Only about 10 out of the 300 individuals contacted by SSA subsequently applied for and received payments! Thus, while an early study by Tissue (1978) indicates that most SSI *participants* do not find SSI stigmatizing, there seems to be a significant minority of nonparticipants who do and, as a result, never apply.

Another major issue associated with SSI is the asset test. Studies show that most low-income elderly have few assets. Yet the asset test for SSI is so stringent that some people with inadequate incomes are denied assistance because of small amounts of savings and other resources. A study by Leavitt and Schulz (1988) of the low-income elderly found that in 1984, about one-third of those eligible for SSI *based on income* were ineligible for benefits because they had *assets* exceeding SSI eligibility maximums. But the study then went on to show that many of these ineligible older persons and couples had minimal amounts of financial assets—leaving them economically impoverished. Over half had "money income producing assets" of less than $5,000 and nearly two-thirds had less than $10,000 worth of these assets.

A more recent study of SSI applicants in 1989 (Kochhar, 1992) also found many with minimal assets. The study reports that 43,392 aged and nonaged applicants were denied benefits because of "excess countable resources." The approximately 16,000 *aged* applicants denied had assets with a mean value of $10,500; only 17 percent of these aged had liquid assets (mostly bank accounts) of $10,000 or more.

The National Commission on Social Security recommended in its final report that the asset test be eliminated. It argued that this action would simplify program administration, while providing SSI to many more needy persons. Various other groups studying the program have made a number of other recommendations for improving SSI, but thus far Congress has not changed the program significantly from the original provisions legislated in 1972.

CHAPTER 6 HIGHLIGHTS

The programs discussed in this chapter complement the retirement pension programs providing the bulk of income for older persons no longer working. Some important points to remember:

1. The cost of health care services for the elderly is now a major item in the federal budget and is growing rapidly—most say too rapidly.

2. Medicare pays the bulk of hospitalization costs and a major portion of doctors' bills for persons age 65 and older. Supplemental private insurance sponsored by previous employers or through individual purchases is used by many to meet growing out-of-pocket health care expenditures.

3. Congress continues to search for ways to keep health care cost down—through co-payments, restrictions on physician reimbursement, and managed care (to name a few developments).

4. Families in the United States do not "dump" relatives in nursing homes; they continue to be the major providers of long-term care to chronically ill elderly persons, providing about 70 percent of personal and physical care needs.

5. Because of strong opposition (in the past and currently) to government disability programs, the disability programs under social security determine participant eligibility using a very narrow and stringent definition of disability that excludes many people with relatively severe incapacities.

6. SSI, a means-tested program designed to provide needy aged, blind, and disabled persons with minimum income, is limited in the help it gives by participation problems, low benefits, and stringent eligibility tests that have not been adjusted for inflation over the past couple of decades.

SUGGESTED READINGS

Binstock, Robert H., and Stephen G. Post. *Too Old for Health Care?* Baltimore, Md.: Johns Hopkins University Press, 1991. An excellent discussion of issues related to "health care rationing."

Butler, Robert N., L. K. Grossman, and M. R. Oberlink, eds. *Life in an Older America*. New York: Century Foundation Press, 1999. See the chapters by Moon, Stone, and Binstock.

Consumer Reports, June 1991 and October 1997. These issues contain consumer-oriented articles on buying long-term care insurance.

Mashaw, Jerry L. "Disability: Why Does the Search for Good Programs Continue?" In Eric R. Kingson and James H. Schulz, eds., *Social Security in the 21st Century*. New York: Oxford University Press, 1997, pp. 105–126. An excellent discussion of disability program problems.

Moon, Marilyn. *Medicare Now and in the Future*, 2nd ed. Washington, D.C.:

Urban Institute Press, 1996. This book focuses on the costs, financing, and coverage of Medicare.

Schechter, Malvin. *Beyond Medicare: Achieving Long-Term Care Security*. San Francisco: Jossey-Bass, 1993. A comprehensive overview of issues related to long-term care, from geriatrics to politics.

Chapter 7

What Role for Employer-Sponsored Pensions?

More retirement benefits from employer-sponsored pension plans are now paid to people than are paid from social security. In 1994, for example, $313 billion employer-sponsored retirement benefits were paid out—in contrast to $312 billion OASD benefits from social security (EBRI, 1997a). These plans now play a major role in retirement income security.

Pension plans set up by private industry or employee groups did not appear in the United States until the end of the 19th century. One of the first company pension plans was established by the American Express Company in 1875 but provided benefits only to permanently incapacitated workers over age 60 who had at least twenty years of service. Thereafter, plans were established in the railroad industry and by a few firms in other industries. However, a congressional study reports that such pension schemes "were by and large slow in developing and [that] there were probably fewer than ten plans in operation by the end of the 19th century" (U.S. House Committee on Education and Labor, 1972).

The Civil Service Retirement Act was enacted in 1920, providing pension coverage for the first time to federal civilian employees. A year later the implementation of private plans was encouraged by the Revenue Act of 1921.[1] This legislation exempted from income taxation both the income of pension and profit sharing trusts and the employer contributions to these plans.

Although between 3 million and 4 million workers were participating in private pension plans prior to the establishment of social security in the 1930s, coverage was concentrated in only a few older, big businesses.

Benefits were very limited; less than 15 percent of the workforce was covered. Payments were made only if certain very stringent age and service requirements were met.

It was not until the 1940s and 1950s that the growth of private pensions mushroomed. Private employer coverage rose from about 4 million employees in the late 1930s to roughly 20 million by 1960. In 1990, there were about 42 million workers in private-sector, employer-sponsored pension plans (U.S. Department of Labor, 1993).

Many factors have been cited as responsible for the rather dramatic increases in private pension coverage during the immediate post–World War II period:

1. Continued industrialization of the American economy, together with a movement of workers out of agriculture, which stimulated increasing interest in alternatives other than the family for providing retirement security.
2. The introduction of company pensions by some employers as a way of creating employee loyalty and discouraging job shifting, because most early plans called for the worker to lose the rights to the pension upon switching jobs.
3. Wage freezes during World War II and the Korean War that encouraged fringe benefit growth in lieu of wages.
4. A series of favorable tax inducements offered by the federal government, beginning with the Revenue Acts of 1921, 1926, 1928, and 1942.[2]
5. A favorable decision by the Supreme Court in 1949 supporting the National Labor Relations Board's decision that pensions were a proper issue for collective bargaining.
6. The report of the Steel Industry Fact-Finding Committee in 1949, which included a recommendation that the industry had a social obligation to provide workers with pensions.
7. Growing recognition, especially by unions, of the inadequacy for most workers of social security benefits and the consequent need for supplementation.
8. The development of multiemployer pension plans—particularly in the construction, transportation, trade, and service industries.

Over the years, serious problems have undermined the worker protection provided under employer-sponsored pensions. Workers have unexpectedly lost benefit rights as a result of unemployment, company mergers, plant closures, or firm bankruptcies—often after long years of service. Changing jobs, for any reason, often meant the loss of significant retirement benefits. Pension reserve funds, supposedly put aside to guarantee benefits to workers, were sometimes mismanaged or misused. Benefits, when actually paid, were often inadequate, and inflation seriously eroded their purchasing power.

These problems (and others) resulted in pension reform. This chapter focuses on the progress that has been made in creating employer-sponsored pensions that are a viable mechanism for providing income in old age. Plans have improved significantly over the years, in part as a result of new government regulations, but many problems remain.

The role that pensions will ultimately play in the economics of aging depends on the resolution of a number of issues. We begin with three of the most important and controversial issues, relating to plan coverage, benefit protection, and the impact of inflation on pensions.

WHO IS COVERED?

Some analysts use the term "pension covered" to refer to all workers in a company or government agency with a pension plan, whether or not all workers actually *participate* in the plan. In fact, some workers may not be eligible to participate (e.g., *part-time workers* are often excluded). Other workers cannot participate until they reach a certain age (typically age 21) and achieve a minimum tenure on the job (typically one year). In this book, we use the term "pension covered" to refer to workers actually participating and accruing benefit rights in a pension plan.

The total number of workers covered under private pension plans has increased from 12 percent of the *private* wage and salary labor force in 1940 to about 45 percent in 1990 (U.S. Department of Labor, 1993). The major increases in coverage occurred in the 1940s and the 1950s, averaging about 12 percent and 7 percent a year, respectively. The growth rate slowed in the 1960s and 1970s to a little over 3 percent a year. In the 1980s, the pension coverage rate actually went down, in large part as a result of poor economic conditions and general employment declines in industries with traditionally high rates of pension coverage.

According to EBRI (1997a), retirement benefits coverage for *full-time* employees in *medium* and *large* private establishments was 80 percent in 1995, but coverage in small private establishments was only 42 percent in 1994.

In contrast, a high proportion of state and local employees are covered. In 1994, 96 percent of full-time state and local workers were participating in plans (EBRI, 1997a). And most federal employees are covered by a variety of different plans.

Almost 52 million workers in 1990 did *not* participate in a pension plan on their current job. Who are the uncovered?

Table 7–1 shows for 1988 the characteristics of those working full time. A majority not covered by pensions work in two industries: trade and service. *But the two key factors in understanding coverage are union status and the size of the employing firm.* Almost all full-time workers without pension coverage are nonunion and work for firms with a rela-

Table 7–1

Which Full-Time Workers[a] Were Not Pension Covered[b] in May 1988?

Selected Worker Characteristics	Percent Not Covered
Under age 21[c]	84%
Age 25-29	57
Age 45-49	42
Age 60+	52
Race:	
White	52%
Black	57
Other	51
Size of firm:[c]	
Less than 10 workers	89%
50-99 workers	59
250 or more workers	31
Union	24%
Nonunion	56
Men	50%
Women	57
Job tenure:[c]	
Less than 1 year	81%
1-4 years	62
15-19 years	26
Industry:[c]	
Construction	68%
Manufacturing	
Durable goods	34
Nondurables	39
Trade	
Wholesale	51
Retail	68
Services	
Professional	54
Other	74

[a]Private wage and salary workers.
[b]Only actual participants in a pension plan (defined benefit or defined contribution [including profit share, thrift, stock bonus, and IRAs]) are included.
[c]Percentage of coverage for other categories not shown are available in the source article.
Source: Based on data in John R. Woods, "Pension Coverage Among Private Wage and Salary Workers: Preliminary Findings from the 1988 Survey of Employee Benefits," *Social Security Bulletin* 52 (October 1989): 2–19.

tively small number of employees. Also, most part-time workers are not covered.

More recent data for 1995 (EBRI, 1997a) show that coverage varies by occupational categories. Medium and large establishment coverage in that year was 87 percent for full-time professional and technical employees, 85 percent for full-time clerical and sales personnel, and 73 percent for full-time production and service workers.

It has been especially difficult to extend private pension coverage to employees in small firms. Coverage for example, that provides benefits for full-time production and service workers was only 35 percent in 1994. Among the factors that have been cited to explain the low coverage are:

1. The high costs per employee of establishing and maintaining a private plan.
2. The lack of pressure in these companies from employees or unions.
3. The fact that small business firms are often relatively young and, on average, short-lived.
4. The fact that small employers tend to view pensions as personal costs.
5. The personality of the small business owner who tends to emphasize individual self-reliance in financial matters.
6. The often unstable and insecure financial status of many small businesses and competitive pressures for cost-cutting.

As a result of these and other factors, a sizable proportion of the American workforce in small firms is not likely to be covered by traditional types of private pensions. There has been increasing interest, therefore, in a wider variety of employer-sponsored mechanisms to provide retirement income. Let us look more closely at the range of pension types.

Controversial Types of Coverage

Private pension plans vary greatly. In fact, there is disagreement among experts over just what type of arrangement should be called a "pension." We begin by looking in this section at three controversial arrangements. Then in the next section, we discuss the more typical plans.

Profit-Sharing Plans

Most estimates of pension coverage include workers who are covered only by a **deferred profit-sharing plan**. Yet profit-sharing plans are very different from the traditional private plans. Contributions into profit-sharing plans usually vary with the amount of a particular company's profits and consequently are more directly tied to the vicissitudes of the economy. Hence, profit-sharing plans—less certain with regard to ultimate payout—are a more debatable way of insuring adequate retirement benefits for the millions of workers with *only* this type of coverage. In contrast, the pension plans described later make a benefit promise that is generally independent of fluctuations in the economy or the prosperity of a particular business enterprise (as long as it stays in business).

The pension history at the Sears and Roebuck Company is a good example of the problems that can arise. Initially, the company provided retiring workers with only profit-sharing benefits, invested in Sears stock. In the 1970s over 20 percent of Sears common stock was owned by Sears employees through the company's profit-sharing plan. In the company's high profit years of the 1960s and early 1970s, employees experienced huge investment gains through the plan, as the price of Sears stock rose. But later, business conditions became poor; the price of Sears stock fell dramatically. The potential gains from the plan declined dramatically, and as a result many workers became angry. Sears responded by creating a "regular" pension plan to complement the profit-sharing plan, thereby giving more security to workers approaching retirement.

Today, millions of workers covered only by profit-sharing plans still face the question raised by the Sears example: How adequate and how secure is the retirement income promise? The U.S. Department of Labor (1993) reports that in 1990 there were 418,587 profit-sharing or thrift-savings (discussed later) plans; about three-quarters of these plans provided the primary or only benefit to workers covered by them. In 1994, 13 percent of full-time employees in small, medium, and large establishments had a deferred profit-sharing plan as either a primary or secondary plan (EBRI, 1997a).

A representative survey of private companies with 100 or more employees (Coates, 1991) found that 40 percent of participants in profit-sharing plans are in plans with no predetermined formula for employer contributions. In most cases, the determinations are made by the company's board of directors. Moreover, in 60 percent of the plans, participants do not have a choice of how the profit-sharing distributions are invested.

Thrift and 401(K) Plans

Another mechanism that helps workers prepare for retirement is the company thrift (or savings) or a 401(K) plan. Most companies with thrift or 401(K) plans also provide a "regular" pension plan for employees. Some companies, however, just have thrift plans.[3]

The most common and most important of these plans is designed to take advantage of the special tax advantages available under various sections of the Internal Revenue Code. Although there have been a number of changes over recent years in the tax laws affecting retirement, perhaps the most important was the Revenue Act of 1978, which added section 401(K) to the tax codes.[4] Section 401(K) permits employees to make *tax-*

deferred contributions to an employer-sponsored plan. Prior to this pro-vision, such contributions could only be made by workers using money upon which federal income taxes had been paid. Section 401(K) stimu-lated a major expansion of these types of plans.

While many plans under section 401(K) are profit-sharing or are vol-untary employee contribution plans with no employer contribution, the majority are thrift plans. In thrift plans the company *matches* some pro-portion of the employee's contribution. The amount of annual dollar contribution by employees to 401(K) plans is limited by law. Originally $30,000, the Tax Reform Act of 1986 reduced the limit to $7,000 per year. This ceiling, however, is indexed annually for inflation and is now over $30,000.

Election by employees to have a portion of their compensation con-tributed to a pension plan under the 401(K) provision has been growing rapidly. More than 39 million workers were covered in 1993, up from 7 million in 1983 (EBRI, 1997b).

The average account balance in a sample of 401(K) plans in 1996 was slightly over $37,000 (EBRI, 1999a). Poterba et al. (1992) argue that 401(K) plans represent "a significant and increasingly important com-ponent of retirement saving" and that 401(K) saving largely represents net new saving. But others worry about the retirement income adequacy implications of greater reliance on such savings plans. Steven Sass (1993), of the Boston Federal Reserve Bank, comments, for example: "Unless participants [in savings plans] jump in more quickly and take on better yielding though riskier investments, the future is not promising for sav-ings vehicles. . . . Fidelity, Boston's mutual fund giant with millions of 401(K) accounts on its books, recently initiated a major program to ed-ucate participants in the trade-offs they face."

Hybrid Pension Plans

In recent years there has been a trend toward the creation of what have become known as "hybrid pension plans" (EBRI, 1996). These plans com-bine features of both defined benefit (DB) and defined contribution (DC) plans. For example, one group of hybrid plans is called "floor-offset plans." This type of plan is actually two separate but associated plans—one a defined benefit "floor" and the other a defined contribution "base." As the name implies, the DC plan is the basic plan that in most cases determines the employees ultimate pension. But if the DC plan for any particular worker provides less than the minimum benefit (the floor) specified by the DB plan, the DB plan makes up the difference. This type plan is designed to offset one major concern with regard to DC plans; its retirement income adequacy is vulnerable to the adverse and often unexpected investment experience of funds in an individual's DC account. Thus, the employer in this type of hybrid plan retains some of the investment risk, which in ordinary DC plans is shifted entirely to the worker.

Another type of hybrid plan is "cash balance plans." These are DB plans but with one significant difference. Employees receive information about their benefits not in terms of a promised benefit formula calculation but, similar to a DC plan, in terms of an individual retirement account. The accounts, however, are hypothetical but serve to more effectively communicate the current value of an employee's accrued benefit at any point in her or his work career.

Serious concerns have been raised about many cash balance plans. Most employers argue that the new approach is a response to the pension needs of young and mobile employees; others argue that it is also a way for employers to save on pension expenses. It is argued that workers with long years of service are losing benefits when companies change to the hybrid plan. With most cash balance plans the percent of pay set aside for workers' pensions basically stays the same each year. Traditional DB plans, in contrast, increase a worker's pension accrual toward the last years on the job. Because of this difference, some companies are giving workers a choice between the old and new plans, but not all give this option. Among several lawsuits challenging cash balance conversions is a class action suit alleging age discrimination. The plaintiffs argue that the drastic pension cuts that occur when companies switch to the cash balance approach violate the Age Discrimination in Employment Act.

Individual Retirement Accounts

Individual retirement accounts (IRAs) are considered by some people to be one of the most important mechanisms created to deal with the need to extend private pension coverage. In a message to Congress on December 8, 1971, President Nixon proposed that pension legislation be enacted that would contain saving incentives. The legislation was ultimately enacted as part of the private pension reform legislation (ERISA) that became law in September 1974.

President Nixon's proposal, and the subsequent law, permitted wage and salary earners to set up their own individual retirement plans (IRAs) *if they were not covered by any qualified pension plan*. In addition, the 1974 pension reform legislation liberalized existing limitations on contributions to retirement plans by the self-employed (called Keogh plans).

Currently, individuals under age 70 1/2 can contribute $2,000 yearly into an IRA account (subject to certain conditions). Full eligibility is restricted to workers in families without pension coverage, pension-covered workers with "adjusted gross income" below $25,000 (for individuals) and $40,000 (for families), or nonworking spouses with a working husband or wife.

It is estimated that about 55 percent of all workers ages 21 to 64 are eligible to participate (EBRI, 1991). Many do not (discussed later). However, all IRA accounts, even those set up by individuals not eligible for IRA tax deductibility at time of pay-in, will continue to accumulate investment earnings on these accounts.

The amount of money accumulated in these accounts is now quite large. In 1997, there were almost $2 trillion worth of financial assets held in IRA accounts (EBRI, 1999c).

When President Nixon proposed the original IRA legislation, he argued that it would encourage people to save and that public policy should reward and reinforce this type of activity. In transmitting the legislation, he said:

Self-reliance, prudence, and independence are qualities which our government should work to encourage among our people. These are also the qualities which are involved when a person chooses to invest in a retirement savings plan, setting aside money today so that he will have greater security tomorrow. In this respect pension plans are a direct expression of some of the best elements in the American character. Public policy should be designed to reward and reinforce these qualities.

Whether the IRA mechanism has in fact increased total savings over the years is still being debated (see the summaries of the research in Gravelle, 1991; and Skinner, 1992).

The president also argued that this legislation would be responsive to the inequity that existed between those people who were covered by private pensions and those who were not. People covered by private pensions receive favorable tax treatment because contributions made by the employer on their behalf are not taxable. These private pension contributions are only taxable at the time they are paid out, often at a lower tax rate because retirement income is typically lower than income when working.

These were the president's two principal arguments in favor of such legislation. Other people have argued that by encouraging people to save for retirement individually, one allows them greater control over their investments. They can decide what they want to invest in and the amount of risk they want to take. In contrast, members of a collective plan usually have nothing to say about the investment policy of the plan.[5] Often the gains of good investment accrue only to the employer. But those who are sophisticated about financial matters and economics might be able to do better on their own, especially if they are willing to take more risks. Current evidence indicates, however, that many individuals often invest too conservatively, when given responsibility for managing retirement funds (see, e.g., Mikkelsen, 1993).

Finally, it has been argued that this approach is an alternative to social security and other social welfare programs that currently exist to help older people. Such tax incentives, it is argued, give people the option to build upon their social security base and give them the freedom to choose how to do it. Attorney Peter J. Ferrara (1986), a harsh critic of the current OASDI program, has proposed a "super IRA" scheme. He would allow individuals to redirect a major part of the payments going into social security into private retirement accounts.[6]

Only a small minority (10%) of private wage and salary workers not covered by an employer-sponsored pension plan contributed to an IRA in 1987 (Woods, 1989). Other research shows that the proportion of *lower-paid* workers who take advantage of this opportunity for tax-sheltered saving is much smaller than that of more highly paid persons. The fear that such tax-exemption proposals would turn into tax loopholes for higher-income people was the principal argument voiced in Congress against the legislation when it was proposed and continues to be an argument made today, based on actual experience.

Roth IRAs

A new IRA option ($2,000 maximum) was initiated in 1998—the Roth IRA. It is available to virtually everyone, but "adjusted gross income" must be below specified levels ($160,000 for couples).

The most important difference between a regular IRA and a Roth is that regular IRA contributions are deducted from the year's taxable income. The Roth IRA contributions are not tax deductible. Despite this, Roth IRAs are generally more advantageous, since no taxes are levied on both the resulting investment income (similar to regular IRAs) and also any income paid out after five years or more (*unlike* regular IRAs). Since the investment income growth component of an IRA (not the contribution component) is typically the largest part of the final payout, many people, especially those investing at younger ages, will come out ahead. However, which IRA is best also depends to a degree on an individual's or couple's tax bracket at pay-in and pay-out, on the number of years of contributions, and the rate of return on IRA investments.

Future Coverage

The availability of private pension benefits is affected by the Employee Retirement Income Security Act of 1974 (ERISA). ERISA extensively regulated the provision of many types of private pension benefits in an attempt to make sure promised benefits were actually paid (described further later). ERISA *did not obligate*, however, any employer without a pension plan to establish one. Thus, ERISA contained no provision beyond the tax incentives provided in the federal tax laws to encourage the expansion of existing private plan coverage. Rather, *the principal focus of ERISA was on expanding the supervision and regulation of private plans* by the federal government and creating tax-exempt IRAs. Many people argue that this regulation discourages the expansion of coverage.

Regulation costs money. In addition to the costs to taxpayers for the federal supervisory agencies and their staffs, considerable regulatory costs are imposed on the businesses with pension funds. These costs arise from the necessity of providing information to the government in order for the regulators to carry out their various supervisory roles. Because of the complexity of the laws and regulations, businesses must often either develop staff and/or hire outside lawyers and consultants to provide them with the expertise necessary to ensure compliance with ERISA and other pension-related laws. Pension management has become big business in the United States.

Employers have reacted negatively to the growing regulatory prohibitions and costs. Pension consultant Rebecca Miller, testifying during Internal Revenue Service pension hearings, commented, "Every time the rules are changed, clients say, 'I'm going to junk this thing' " (*Tax Notes*, 1990). Over the years there has been an outpouring of complaints from pension consultants and employers before congressional committees about the high costs of reporting required information to the government and the costs of simply understanding the law. Some companies have terminated their plans because of the increased administrative burdens and costs. Many pension experts say that employers without plans are increasingly reluctant to start new ones.

When we look at the coverage trend over the last couple of decades, we see a slowing down in coverage beginning prior to ERISA. This slowdown results primarily from the fact that job growth has shifted to smaller, nonunionized firms, while large corporations have been reducing employment. A profile of small employers without pension plans would include the business proprietors found on any typical small-town Main Street or any large city neighborhood shopping center: the small retailer, the local restaurant, the service station, repair service stores, the barber and beauty shop, the doctor and dentist, the auto dealer, and many, many more small employers of wage and salary workers. The profile would also include partnership operations such as law firms, consulting engineers, accounting firms, real estate firms, and small manufacturing plants operated as corporations or by self-employed owners.

An EBRI (1999b) survey of small employers (100 or fewer employees) found that the two most important reasons these employers do not offer pension coverage is uncertainty and the nature of their workforce. They say their sales and revenue are too uncertain to insure the long-term financial viability of a pension plan. Others say that pensions are not appropriate, since a large proportion of their workers are seasonal or part-time, and many quit after a short period of time.

Coverage Equals What Benefit?

As our discussion below on **vesting** emphasizes, workers covered by a plan do not always receive a benefit. Some employees do not work long enough to achieve vesting. Others receive only a lump-sum payout when they leave their job, and still others who are eligible for very small benefits may also receive a cashed-out lump sum. ERISA permits employers to do this for benefits less than $3,500 in order to eliminate the administrative costs arising from keeping track of these small benefits and their recipients. In 1992, about 40 percent of the elderly age 65 or older received some income from pensions (using the broadest definition of this income source); among recent retirees, however, the proportion is much higher—over half (EBRI, 1994). Often the amount received, however, is relatively small; sometimes it is very large.

Recent Legislation

Legislation passed by Congress in recent years to broaden private pension coverage includes "simplified employee pensions" (SEPs), employee stock option plans (ESOPs),[7] and IRAs (discussed above). SEPs significantly reduce the amount of paper work, record keeping, and reporting requirements involved in managing a plan. Also, larger annual contributions can be made under an SEP than with an IRA. In 1986, Congress changed some details of the law relating to SEPs, trying to make them more attractive. However, utilization of SEPs by employers has been low, with only 1 percent to 4 percent of small-business employees participating in an SEP (U.S. General Accounting Office, 1992b). One explanation is offered by the Employee Benefit Research Institute:

Among employers that have heard of SEPs, interest in flexibility of contributions and simplicity of administration may be tempered by concern about the [government's] nondiscrimination requirements. The employer must make contributions on behalf of employees who may not remain long with the employer, thus diverting funds the employer might wish to use to reward longer-service employees. Because employees vest immediately in employer contributions, employers may feel that such a retirement arrangement does little to encourage employees to remain with the employer. (EBRI, 1990)

PRIVATE PLAN CHARACTERISTICS

It is difficult to generalize about the provisions of private pension plans because of the large number of different plans with widely varying characteristics. In 1995, there were 693,404 private-sector pension plans in the United States (U.S. Department of Labor, 1999). Most are *single employer* plans; a few are *multiemployer* plans—about 3,000 plans covering approximately 6 million workers (U.S. Department of Labor, 1993). Multiemployer plans are usually the result of bargaining between unions and management. They tend to be concentrated in particular industries (mining, construction, trade, transportation, and service) and, in these industries, affect more than 50 percent of all pension-covered workers. Multiemployer plans usually require employers to make contributions into a central fund (typically a specified percentage of payroll or cents-per-hours-worked), and employees can qualify for benefits from the fund by meeting eligibility requirements through employment in the various firms participating in the program. Reciprocity agreements among some of these multiemployer plans (and a few single-employer plans) allow workers to move between plans. Another important difference between the two types of plans is in their administration. Single-employer plans are generally managed by the employer alone; multiemployer plans are almost invariably administered by a group of trustees, with equal representation from labor and management (in accordance with terms of the federal Taft-Hartley Act).

Another common way of classifying private plans is to distinguish between *contributory* and *noncontributory* plans. Contributory plans require that the employee pay part of the cost, whereas noncontributory plans are financed solely by the employer. In the United States, most covered workers in *private* employment (about 95 percent) participate in noncontributory plans (Mitchell, 1999), in part because employers' contributions are tax-free under current laws, while employee contributions (unless sheltered by special arrangements) are not. Also, noncontributory plans do not require the employer to put aside money for each worker at the time benefit rights accrue. This means that employers have more flexibility in funding and administration. For example, they can use actuarial assumptions that take into account employee turnover (reducing current pension expenses) and provide for funding of the plan over an extended period of years.

In surveying the specific provisions of various pension plans, there are four key characteristics that are generally considered most important: the benefit formulas, vesting and portability requirements, the availability of survivors' benefits, and early retirement options.

Benefit Determination

While there is a great deal of variation among private plans in the way benefits are calculated, three major types can be identified:

Defined Benefit Plans:

1. *Dollar amount times service*—benefits are determined by multiplying a specified dollar amount by the number of years of employed service credited under
   the plan.
2. *Combined service/earnings formulas*—benefits are calculated based upon (1)
   the employee's earnings over a specified period of employment (e.g., career,
   high five of the last 10, or last 10 years of earnings); and (2) years of service.

Defined Contribution Plans:[8]

3. Money-purchase arrangements—periodic **contributions** are set aside according to a predetermined, or agreed, formula (usually a percentage of earnings).
   Pensions are paid out based on the accumulated funds (contributions plus
   investment income) in individual employee accounts.

The overwhelming proportion of workers covered by *single employer
plans* belong to plans that use *defined benefit* formulas that base benefits
on earnings. In contrast, only a small proportion of workers under multiemployer plans participate in plans using earnings-based formulas. Instead, most multiemployer plans use the "dollar amount times service"
formula. Defined *contribution* plans are most common in small businesses and nonprofit organizations.

*Half of workers in the United States are covered by defined benefit
plans.* This type of plan has been popular among both workers and employers for a number of reasons:

1. The benefit determination process is usually easy for workers to understand
   (although the actual details and regulations can be very complex).
2. Unlike defined contribution plans, workers assume little, if any, risk related to
   preretirement inflation and fluctuating financial returns on different investments.
3. The plans reward workers who stay a long time with a particular employer.
4. Even workers who join a company later in life can still accrue significant benefits.

In recent years, however, an increasing number of *new* pension plans
have used the defined contribution approach, and the overall proportion
of workers covered by these plans has increased significantly (Figure 7–
1). Some positive features of defined contribution plans include:

1. Administration and compliance with government regulation is much easier and
   less costly, especially for small companies.
2. Mobile workers are less likely to lose benefits.
3. Future costs for employers are more predictable.

Figure 7–1
A Growing Number of Workers Are in Defined Contribution Plans

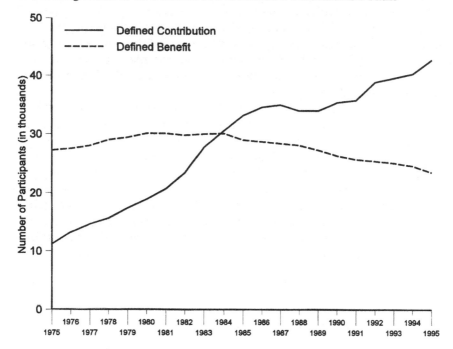

Source: U.S. Department of Labor, *Private Pension Plan Bulletin*, Abstract of 1995, Form 5500 Reports, No. 8 (Washington, D.C.: Pension and Welfare Benefits Administration, Office of Policy and Research, Spring 2000), Tables E8 and E23.

Because defined contribution plans have been more popular with small employers and most new plans are small, the popularity of defined contribution among *new* plans is not surprising. Some benefit experts have speculated, however, that regulatory and financing issues associated with defined benefit plans are causing some employers with *older* plans to rethink pension design and encouraging them to view defined contribution plans more favorably (see, for example, Clark and McDermed, 1989). Commenting on the growing popularity of defined contribution plans (even among some larger companies), Sass (1993) observes:

This set up suits the emerging model of corporate employment—one of abbreviated careers and tenures. Firms recruiting workers with professional training or specific experience are hiring workers at older ages. They are retiring their employees earlier—corporate careers now commonly end between 58 and 62 years of age. And the new volatility of corporate employment makes survival to retirement less likely.

Reacting to the high inflation rates of the 1980s, another important trend has been a shift to basing benefits (in defined benefit plans) on earnings just prior to retirement. The major advantage of this type of formula is a built-in adjustment for inflation prior to retirement (because earnings over time are usually adjusted upward for cost-of-living increases). In 1997, 95 percent of defined benefit plans using formulas based on earnings used the last three or five, or used the high three or five years (Mitchell, 1999).

In March 1999, David M. Strauss, Executive Director of the Pension Benefit Guaranty Corporation (discussed below), testified before Congress about pension trends (Strauss, 1999). He voiced concern about the drop in defined benefit coverage. The Clinton administration, he said, thought that these plans needed to be made more attractive to employers—given their favorable characteristics in promoting workers' retirement security. To this end, President Clinton proposed a simplified defined benefit plan for small business. This plan was designed to keep administrative and pension insurance costs low, while making contributions into the plan 100 percent vested at all times. No action, however, was taken on this proposal.

Receipt and Level of Benefits

In 1994, among all *retirees* ages 40 and older, 49 percent were receiving, had received, or expected to receive some kind of employer-provided pension benefit (U.S. Department of Labor, 1995). This benefit was either in the form of a lifetime **annuity** or a lump-sum monetary distribution. Overall, 70 percent of *government* retirees "received" pensions, in contrast to 42 percent of retirees employed in the *private* sector. Another contrast is the 58 percent "receipt" of private and public retired *men*, as contrasted with only 41 percent for retired *women*.

The proportion of retirees who are receiving annuity-type pensions has been decreasing over recent years. However, the number is still significant, and the value of benefits received has been steadily increasing. For annuity recipients who first began receiving pensions in 1993 or 1994, the median annual benefit was $8,400—increasing from $7,770 in 1988–1989 (U.S. Department of Labor, 1995).

When private pensions are combined with social security, how adequate is the result? For persons receiving their initial benefits in 1993 or 1994, the median replacement rate for "final years earnings" was 58 percent (U.S. Department of Labor, 1995). This is much higher than the replacement rate for those persons receiving only social security retirement benefits—a median replacement rate of only 40 percent.

Figure 7–2 shows that there is considerable variation in replacement

Figure 7-2
Pension Replacement Rates* by Earnings Quintiles, 1993–1994

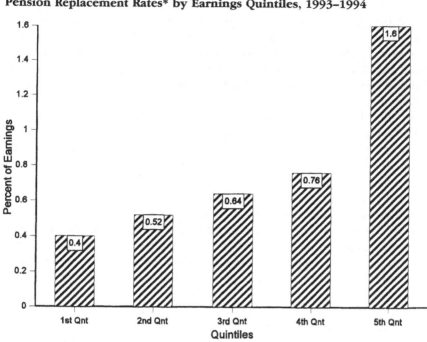

*Combined social security and employer-sponsored pension as a percent of final-year earnings.
Source: U.S. Department of Labor, *Retirement Benefits of American Workers* (Washington, D.C.: Pension and Welfare Administration, 1995).

rates. However, a little over 60 percent of pension recipients received combined replacement rates that were two-thirds or better.

Vesting and Portability Requirements

Vesting and portability are related pension concepts but are not identical. Vesting refers to the provision in pension plans that guarantees that those covered by the plan will receive all or part of the benefit that they have earned (i.e., accrued), whether or not they are working under the plan at the time of their "retirement." Through vesting, the pension rights of otherwise qualified workers are protected—whether they are discharged, furloughed, or quit voluntarily. Prior to ERISA, vesting was sometimes nonexistent. Where vesting was available, eligibility conditions varied greatly, and many workers lost their pension rights—sometimes after long years of service and sometimes just prior to retirement. For example, in the early years of pension development it was common for plans to require twenty to thirty years of continuous service to achieve any vesting.

ERISA originally required all plans covered by the law to provide minimum vested benefits meeting one of three alternative standards. In fact, most companies adopted the same option: vesting of 100 percent of accrued benefits after ten years of service. Hence, those workers who changed jobs before accumulating ten years of service received no pension credits.

The Tax Reform Act of 1986 mandated more rapid vesting beginning in 1989. Full vesting now begins at the end of five years of employment for most workers. Companies, however, have the option of using an alternative vesting schedule vesting: 20 percent of the benefit after three years and increasing the vested amount to reach 100 percent at the end of seven years. Thus the new law goes a long way toward eliminating the loss of pension credits as a result of job change and has resulted in 64 percent of workers covered by plans being vested in 1988 (Reno, 1993).

Another problem arises, however, in connection with vesting. Vested benefits left in a pension plan after a worker voluntarily or involuntarily leaves the firm are not adjusted upward if the pension plan's formula for continuing workers is changed either to compensate for inflation or to provide a higher level of real benefits. Also, vested benefits left in plans with earnings-related formulas do not reflect the rise in earnings that would occur if the worker remained employed by the firm. The result is that an employee who changes jobs and achieves vesting in more than one "similar" plan is likely to receive lower benefits than a worker with equal years of vesting who works for only one employer.

"Portability" of pension rights permits employees to transfer the money value of these rights into another plan, and it is hoped, by this process to reduce the inflationary losses that arise when benefits are left behind. Unfortunately, although portability has received a lot of public attention (and is often confused with vesting), the administrative, financial, and actuarial complexities of setting up such arrangements have discouraged any significant action in this area. The multiemployer plan, however, reduces the problems associated with job change by introducing limited portability (i.e., within the boundaries of the plan) through a centralized pension fund.

The 1974 pension reform law (ERISA) permits a separated employee to transfer tax-free the value of a vested benefit into an IRA permitted by the plan, or to another plan, if permitted by both plans. In fact, an employer with a noncontributory plan has a positive financial incentive not to agree to this transfer, because he can earn interest or dividends on any "funded" money he keeps and need not pass on any of these earnings to the former employee.

Survivor Benefits

In 1989, about 3 million widowed elderly (age 65 and over) received an employer-sponsored survivor's benefit; 95 percent were women (U.S. General Accounting Office, 1992a). The median benefit was $4,296.

The survivor benefits of private plans are of three main types:

1. *Joint and survivor annuity.* Regular payments are made during the combined retirement lifetimes of retiree and spouse. Joint and survivor annuities are typically calculated by reducing the worker's benefit to pay for the additional costs of survivor protection. Survivor benefits are usually 50 percent (most common), 67 percent, or 100 percent of the worker's benefit amount.

2. *Accrued pension survivor's benefit.* Some employers with defined benefit plans pay to survivors a portion of the accrued annuity that would have been paid to the employee had she or he retired the day before death; no reduction in the benefit is imposed. When an employee covered by a defined contribution plan dies, his or her survivor receives all of the contributions that were made to the plan, and any vested employer contributions. The entire amount is usually paid in a lump sum, although payments for life or a fixed period may be offered as an option.

3. *Qualified preretirement survivor annuity.* This is a regular payment (typically 50 percent) for survivors of workers who die before retirement. The protection is usually provided automatically by the employer, with no elective reduction in the worker's accrued retirement benefits. When an extra cost is imposed, it is assessed as a reduction in the amount the employee would have received had he or she retired the day before death.

There is great variation in the provisions various private companies have made for dealing with problems arising from the death of an employee; private pensions are just one of a number of mechanisms.

The existing data indicate that the most important means of providing survivor protection through private pensions continues to be the joint and survivor option, typically at the cost of a lower benefit paid to the retiring worker (which discourages its election). Survivor benefits provided over and above the joint and survivor option are not widespread, are of generally limited duration, and are often of small magnitude. Some firms do provide life insurance and/or supplemental plans that add to the level of benefits provided. Nevertheless, current benefits often do not reflect the needs of employees and their survivors.

Death protection through private pensions was not a high priority item in the early years of pension planning. Consequently, until recently some pension plans made little or no provision for the survivors of workers. In 1974, before ERISA became effective, for example, about 20 percent of the workers covered by defined benefit plans were in plans with *no survivor provisions of any kind*. The most common type of survivor benefit in those private plans that did have provisions was the joint and survivor equity.

Federal pension law now mandates that all pension plans subject to ERISA provide (at a minimum) any worker with vested benefits an opportunity to elect a joint and survivor option. Originally under ERISA, only participants eligible for early retirement or age 55 (whichever was later) could elect such coverage. Now this option must be offered at *all* ages.

Even though ERISA requires employers to *offer* survivor benefits, the decision to provide these benefits legally rests with the worker. In prior years some workers, without the knowledge of their spouse, did not elect the extra protection; in other cases, the worker and spouse together decided to opt for the bigger retirement benefit, gambling (for that is what it is) that the survivor benefit wouldn't be needed.

The Retirement Equity Act of 1984 sought to deal more effectively with this issue. Under the provisions of this law, it is mandated that employers obtain the *spouse's consent in writing*—notarized or witnessed by a representative of the plan—if the worker wishes to reject the survivor option. Before mandating, only 17 percent of large plans had any sort of written consent requirement. But a study by the U.S. General Accounting Office has found that the percentage of retired married men retaining the joint and survivor annuity rose from 65 percent in 1983 to 80 percent in 1988–1989, indicating that the 1984 legislation probably made a significant difference (U.S. General Accounting Office, 1992a).

Even with mandating, however, potential problems remain. A study by the U.S. General Accounting Office (1989b) reported that 42 percent of companies surveyed did not provide workers with any formal retirement counseling and even fewer counseled spouses. Moreover, the study found that many of the consent forms developed by companies omitted key information necessary to make informed decisions and that there were many language and design problems that made the forms difficult to read and confusing.

Early Retirement Option

During the past two decades we have witnessed a tremendous push toward early retirement. We learned earlier that increasing numbers of workers are retiring early under social security. Federal employees can retire on full benefits at age 55 with thirty years of service. Most state and local government employee plans also have very liberal retirement provisions; early retirement is usually possible after twenty to thirty years of service—often as early as age 50 or 55.

Less well-known are the retirement options provided under private pension plans. The generous provisions of the big plans—for example, in the auto industry—are well-known. In the rubber and metal industries, special "early retirement benefits" supplement regular pension benefits until the plan's normal retirement age or until age 65, when the retiree becomes eligible for unreduced social security benefits.

Few data are published on the hundreds of thousands of plans in other industries. A study of pension plans by the U.S. Bureau of Labor Statistics (1980), however, found that more than half of covered workers were eligible to receive *normal* retirement benefits before age 65 (i.e., benefits not reduced because of age), and almost a third were eligible for normal benefits at age 60 or earlier.

But these numbers do not tell the whole story. "Virtually all defined benefit plans incorporate stiff financial penalties for working past the age of 65, and a very sizeable fraction have similarly stiff penalties for working past the plan's early retirement age, often as young as 55" (Lumsdaine and Wise, 1990). More than 90 percent of all workers covered by private pensions are in plans having early retirement options. When a worker retires early, that is, before the "normal" retirement age, the benefit may be reduced. A large number of employers, however, encourage their employees to retire early by absorbing some of the costs of paying pensions over a longer period of time. Thus, while some plans reduce benefits by the full actuarial discount, the majority of plans, in effect, give actuarial bonuses to workers who retire early (Hatch, 1981).

Kotlikoff and Wise (1989) have found that many pension plans contain substantial incentives designed to encourage retirement at certain early ages. If a worker delayed retirement beyond these earlier ages, it was "not unusual for the reduction in pension benefit accrual after these retirement ages to equal the equivalent of a 30 percent reduction in wage earnings."

Thus, we see that social security is not the sole force pushing workers into retirement. Certainly, social security income, when it becomes available, encourages workers to retire. But for many workers it is federal, state/local, private or military plans that make it truly attractive to retire at increasingly early ages.

Inflation Protection

What happens to the value of a private pension when **inflation** occurs? It is appropriate to divide the answer to that question into two parts: the postretirement versus the preretirement period. Almost no employer-sponsored plan in the private sector *automatically* adjusts the pensions being paid in retirement for increases in the cost of living. In contrast, social security pensions and also federal military and civilian pension are automatically adjusted; and most state/local government employee plans adjust automatically but with stringent "caps" on the adjustment process.

Many private companies adjust benefits going to retirees on an ad hoc basis. Allen et al. (1993) have used the information provided by Employee Benefit Surveys carried out by the federal government to study these ad hoc changes in defined benefit plans. They report that during the high inflation period of 1977–1982, surveyed pension plans increased retiree benefits, on average, by only 19 percent of the total inflation increase. During the 1983–1988 period, benefits were increased by only 10 percent of inflation.[9]

If we look at the preretirement years, the situation is very different. Most defined benefit plans deliberately base benefits on some measure of average earnings in *the final years of employment*. These earnings are generally higher, not only because of seniority but because earnings tend to change over time in response to inflation. Thus, plans with "final earnings" measures have a built-in, automatic mechanism to adjust for inflation—to the extent that a worker's wage adjustments keep up with inflation.

Less protection is afforded employees covered by defined contribution plans. Benefits from these plans are based on contributions, not earnings. Employee protection from inflation depends on the investment performance of the funds in the individual's account and are thus, in part, dependent on the investment options provided by the plan and the financial knowledge of the person selecting the type of investment fund into which the money will go. Historically, few types of financial securities have closely tracked the pattern of inflation. The result is significant inflation risk for those covered by defined contribution plans.

Another major problem that we discussed above is the fact that the vested benefits of employees who change jobs are not protected from inflation. The result is that many workers find vested pensions from an early job worth very little (in real dollar terms) when they reach retirement.

PRIVATE PENSION REGULATION

Benefit formulas, vesting, survivors' provisions, and early retirement options are four of the most important aspects of private pensions. Another area of major concern is the danger of lost pension rights as a result of inadequate pension funding, misuse of pension funds, or the termination of plans because of plant closures, bankruptcy, or other reasons.

In August 1978 the Professional Drivers Council, a dissident Teamsters union group, charged that millions of dollars were being drained from the union's pension funds because of mismanagement and corrupt practices. The dissident group claimed that, among other abuses, multimillion-dollar loans had been made to individuals and groups with questionable backgrounds or to entities running deficits when the loans were made (BNA, 1978). That same month a U.S. district court ruled that a $20 million loan by pension trustees of Teamsters' Local 281 violated ERISA regulations; the money was loaned to finance a thousand-plus room hotel and gambling casino in Las Vegas. Earlier, a reform group called Miners for Democracy acted to displace the United Mine Workers' leadership, charged with illegal financial transactions and the use of union pension funds for personal gain. In 1985 a jury awarded $1.2 million to the Iron Workers Local 272 in Florida. The award was based on charges of fraud and negligence brought against the former trustees of the pension fund and the insurance consultant they used. In the trial it was brought out that the former trustees had purchased whole life insurance policies recommended by a consultant who had been convicted of grand larceny and stock manipulation and whose insurance license had been suspended (BNA, 1986).

A great deal of attention has been given to problems related to managing pension funds safely and wisely. Over the years there has been a number of investigating groups and legislative committees concerned about the adequacy of our laws in this area. Congressional concern for the protection of employee benefit funds resulted in the enactment of the Welfare and Pension Plan Disclosure Act in 1959 but placed primary responsibility for policing the plans on the participants themselves. As the problems grew, Congress saw that much more comprehensive and stronger regulatory supervision was needed. The Employee Retirement Income Security Act (ERISA), passed in 1974, set up a much more comprehensive set of safeguards, establishing participation, vesting, funding standards, plan termination insurance, and extensive reporting and disclosure requirements.

The following are the major provisions of ERISA:

1. Minimum vesting standards are established.

2. A plan termination insurance mechanism is established.

3. Funding standards are established, and fiduciary standards are strengthened.

4. Certain employees are permitted to establish individual retirement accounts (exempt from federal income taxation).

5. Disclosure regulations are established, permitting participants to request once each year a statement from the plan administrator of total accrued benefits, both vested and nonvested, and the earliest date on which invested benefits will become nonforfeitable.

6. The Social Security Administration is directed to receive reports from employers (through the Treasury Department) of vested benefits due separated workers; Social Security notifies employees of all vested pension rights at the time they apply for social security.

7. Conditional on the consent and cooperation of their employers, employees

are permitted to transfer, upon job separation, their vested pension rights on a tax-free basis from one employer to another; or the employee may transfer the funds to an individual retirement account.

Passed by both houses of Congress by wide vote margins, ERISA is an attempt to provide greater certainty that private pension promises will be fulfilled. But the legislation does not deal with all private pension problems.

Critics were quick to cite the limitations of the original legislation (as they saw them):

1. Universal coverage was not mandated.
2. State and local government pension plans were excluded from the law.
3. There were no strong "portability" provisions and inadequate vesting standards.
4. Survivors' provisions were seen as weak.
5. No provision was made for **indexing** pensions to deal with inflation.

While the drafters of the 1974 private pension legislation admitted in debate that the legislation did not deal with all problems, they argued that it was a major step forward. The legislation itself called for further study of many of the unresolved issues, and in the years that followed, the law has been modified in a number of important ways. Four major changes are discussed elsewhere in the chapter. They include: (1) liberalization of vesting; (2) changes in survivor provisions and coverage requirements; (3) revised procedures for plan termination insurance; and (4) IRA liberalization and then cutbacks in these liberalization provisions.

ERISA HELPS BUT . . .

A recent court case illustrates how ERISA can help workers in a significant way. At the same time, the case dramatically shows that workers covered by private pensions must be ever vigilant against employer attempts to give—in this case "the pension promise"—with one hand and take it away with another.

In 1991 the Continental Can Company agreed to pay $415 million to settle a class action suit (*Employee Benefit Plan Review*, 1991). The lawsuit had charged that the company deliberately fired employees before they became eligible for benefits. As a result of the settlement, more than 3,000 former employees were awarded an average of $90,000 each.

In 1977, Continental Can agreed to a labor contract that provided substantial pension, health, and life insurance benefits and also a $400 monthly supplement benefit to eligible workers placed on long-term layoff. To be eligible, a worker was required to have a combined age and years of service totaling between 65 and 75. Internal corporate memos submitted at the trial revealed that the company adopted a secret computer program designed to identify workers approaching eligibility for the costly benefit package. Numerous workers found themselves laid off just before reaching that point. Moreover, the computer program included red warning flags that flashed when employees identified for termination were inadvertently summoned back to work. According to U.S. District Judge H. Lee Sarokin, "The plan was shrouded in secrecy and executed companywide at the specific direction of the higher levels of corporate management. It was intended to save hundreds of millions of dollars in unfunded pension liabilities" (*Employee Benefit Plan Review*, 1991).

The Continental Can settlement is one of the largest payments made in an ERISA case. Over the years there have been thousands of other court cases over pension rights, most related to the ERISA laws. This litigation serves as a stark reminder of the risks attached to private pensions and a warning to anyone with a pension not to become complacent about a "personal asset" potentially worth, for some, hundreds of thousands of dollars. The next section looks at the many problems surrounding pension financing and the resulting threats to worker benefits. Despite many years of government study and regulation, concerns about the financing of plans have increased, not decreased, over the years.

Another example, totally different from the Continental Can case, dramatically illustrates the dangers facing people trying to prepare financially for retirement. Kurt Eichenwald's book *Serpent on the Rock* (1995) describes the biggest and most costly financial scandal that the United States has ever seen. More than $8 billion worth of special investment opportunities, called "limited partnerships," were sold in the 1980s as conservative and safe investments to people saving for retirement, pensioners, and others. In reality, the partnerships were highly risky and financially unsound from the very beginning.

As Eichenwald observes: "[The fraud] was not engineered by the shady penny-stock promoters or crooked savings and loan operators. . . . Rather, the scheme emerged full-blown from the New York headquarters of one of the brokerage industry's brightest lights, an investment firm with a name that conveyed the essence of reliability and trust: Prudential-Bache Securities."

Regulatory authorities took years to uncover the fraud. But even when they did, most of the investors got little or nothing back—despite the fact that the parent company (Prudential) had untold billions in assets.

FINANCING PRIVATE PENSIONS

It now seems like a long time ago, but in 1963 an important event occurred in American pension history. The Studebaker Corporation, a small producer of automobiles, closed its operations in the United States. The company had established, fourteen years before, a pension plan that ultimately covered about 11,000 employees. When the company closed its South Bend, Indiana, plant, there were assets worth $24 million in the pension fund. But these assets were insufficient to meet all the pension rights that had been accumulated. The result: about 4,500 workers received an average of $600 apiece, or only 15 percent of the value of their legally promised benefits; and those workers who had accumulated years of service but had not achieved pension vesting status got nothing.

Because of the number of workers affected and the prominence of the auto industry, the Studebaker case immediately became a favorite example in the days before ERISA, cited by those persons calling for private pension reform. Studebaker and hundreds of other defaults illustrate the major goal—but also the major hazard—of private pension financing: to insure that there are adequate funds so that promised benefits are, in fact, paid.

Prior to ERISA, most private plans financed pensions on a reserve basis, with a few operating on a partial or full pay-as-you-go basis. Now all plans covered by ERISA are required to meet minimum funding standards.

In reviewing financing practices, it is useful to group plans into three categories: (1) noninsured or trusteed plans; (2) insured plans; and (3) multiemployer plans. The majority of plans are noninsured or trusteed plans whose reserves are either self-administered by the individual company or administered by a trustee, in most cases commercial banks. Significantly, the great bulk of these reserves are administered by only about 25 banks. Insured plans are administered by various insurance companies. Multiemployer funds, usually the result of union collective bargaining, are typically run jointly by the union and employer trustees.

About one-fifth of private plans require employee contributions to the plan; the rest are financed entirely by the employer. A major reason for the prevalence of noncontributory plans is that employee contributions from earnings are subject, with certain exceptions, to federal income taxes. In contrast, the money employers put into a "qualified" pension fund is not subject to any taxes. In addition, employee contributions greatly complicate the administration of a plan, requiring the establishment of a pension account for each worker and policies regulating these accounts; and, as we indicated earlier, noncontributory plans usually reduce employer pension costs during the early years.

Although most firms have established reserve funds to be built up over the years as their pension liabilities grow, some of the pension rights granted under certain plans remain in jeopardy as a result of "past service credits." When new plans are established or old plans liberalized, the usual practice is to give workers full pension credits for their years of work prior to the plan's establishment or liberalization. While the pension liabilities for these past service credits accrue immediately, employers usually adopt a payment schedule for funding these liabilities that in the past extended over a 10- to 40-year period (and sometimes longer). As long as unfunded liability remains, a plan that terminates will be unable to pay all of its promised future pension benefits. This is what happened in the Studebaker case. In fact, many plans have terminated over the years—with a resultant loss of pension rights to thousands of workers.

In the aggregate, single-employer plans are adequately funded, with $1.2 trillion in assets to deal with $1.1 trillion in liabilities. Most individual pension plans are overfunded; that is, their assets exceed their liabilities. However, a minority of plans are underfunded. In 1996, the aggregate total for these plans with underfunding was $83 billion (PBGC, 1998).

Many pension plans, especially in the 1980s, have been terminated by companies. These terminations have been motivated by two very different sets of circumstances: on the one hand, there were the *problems* of plans in economically distressed companies, and on the other hand, there were the *opportunities* arising out of overfunded plans in some companies, which sought to use this unexpected pension wealth for other corporate purposes. Falling into the first category, for example, were the January 1987 terminations of three LTV Corporation steel worker plans with unfunded liabilities exceeding $2.1 billion![10] In contrast, there were nearly 500 overfunded terminations in 1985 alone (Leavitt, 1986). Between 1980 and 1987 there were more than 1,600 defined benefit plans that terminated (or announced an intent to terminate) with more than $1 million in "excess assets" (PBGC, 1987).

What happens to workers when a plan terminates without adequate funds or excess funds?

Terminations with Inadequate Funding

In the spring of 1982, Braniff Airlines shut down. Even before Braniff filed for bankruptcy, there were dramatic reductions in the number of employees working for the company. A few years before the shut-down there were about 15,000 employees working for Braniff (in their heyday). Just before filing for bankruptcy, there were only 9,500 employees left. Thus, a significant number of people left Braniff—were forced to leave Braniff, in most cases prior to the bankruptcy. What happened to the pension rights of these particular employees? And after Braniff filed for bankruptcy and terminated its pension plans, what happened to the workers still employed, who were covered by the plan and had expected to receive benefits?

One thing is certain. Those people who had fewer than ten years of service working for Braniff Airlines—whether they had left before the bankruptcy or whether they were working at the point of bankruptcy filing—got nothing under the old ERISA standards. However, ERISA, at the time, required that employees with more than ten years of service, which was the most popular alternative of the three vesting options available at the time, receive benefits when they retire.

Those former Braniff employees retired and receiving pensions and those eligible for vested benefits were protected by the Pension Benefit Guaranty Corporation (PBGC). This government organization, part of the Labor Department, was set up under ERISA to guarantee the continued payment of benefits to retired workers and the future payment of benefits to vested workers (limited in 1991 to $2,250 monthly). When a plan terminates without sufficient funds to meet these obligations, the PBGC takes over the plan and assumes responsibility for paying the benefits. Each company or union with a plan covered by ERISA must make contributions (insurance premiums) to the PBGC to cover the costs of providing this insurance protection.

Terminations by Overfunded Plans

Rising to a peak in 1985, there was a dramatic increase in the 1980s of "overfunded" defined benefit plans terminating voluntarily. Upon termination there has been a reversion of large sums of money to the sponsoring company. Getting these funds to use for other purposes has often been the primary motivation for these plan terminations. In recent years, these companies have been able to capture, on average, nearly 50 percent of the assets in these terminated plans through this termination/asset reversion process.

A major contributing factor to this situation was the existence of high interest rates in the early 1980s, followed by a sharply rising stock market before mid-1987. Investment performance widely exceeded the conservative assumptions of pension plan actuaries, resulting in the overfunding of many plans (using standard actuarial evaluation practices).

A study at the Brandeis University Policy Center on Aging (Leavitt, 1986), found that overfunded terminations up to 1986 had not resulted in immediate harm to plan participants. However, the study argued that in the longer run, many employees were likely to be adversely affected by (1) some terminated plans not being replaced by another plan; (2) replacement of some plans by less generous or more risky plans (e.g., profit sharing); and (3) the weakened funding situation of some new plans.

Critics have also argued that any excess assets belong to plan participants and beneficiaries, based on the idea that pension contributions by employers are deferred compensation. Employers usually respond that because they are meeting their legal obligations in providing promised benefits, there is no reason for sponsors not to recover these assets.

What is clear in this debate is that current law does not prohibit employer terminations for any purpose; however, in an attempt to reduce this practice, the Tax Reform Act of 1986 instituted a 10 percent excise tax on these reversions. This tax has since been increased, rising to as high as 50 percent under certain circumstances.

The Pension Benefit Guaranty Corporation[11]

As we discussed above, Congress created the Pension Benefit Guaranty Corporation (PBGC) to protect workers if certain inadequately funded defined benefit plans terminate.[12] For example, PBGC was there to step in when the poor economic conditions of the 1970s and 1980s caused plan terminations to rapidly increase. Most terminating plans can meet their obligations; however, some cannot. Between 1975 and 1992, about 135,000 single-employer plans terminated; of these, the PBGC needed to provide financial support to meet the pension claims in 1,785 plans (U.S. House Committee on Ways and Means, 1993).

Currently, the PBGC is responsible for the pensions of nearly a half million workers and retirees covered by 2,700 terminated plans that were inadequately funded. Table 7–2 shows the industries of these terminations, the amount of claims involved, and the number of people dependent on PBGC for protection of their pension "rights." The biggest problems have been in the steel and air transportation industries.

The Costs of Pension Insurance

In 1983, the head of the PBGC went before Congress and testified that the agency would run out of funds unless Congress increased the premium on single-employer plans from its then-current level of $2.60 per employee covered. He stated that due to underfunded terminating plans, PBGC liabilities were far higher than had been anticipated. This statement shocked both the Congress and the business community paying the premiums, because this was the first time the agency had publicly revealed its severe financial problems. "A major cause of the PBGC's problems was the ease with which economically viable companies could terminate underfunded plans and dump their pension liabilities on the termination insurance program" (U.S. Senate Special Committee on Aging, 1987).

Table 7–2
PBGC Protection of Pension Rights, by Industry, Claims, and Number of People, 1998

Industry	Number of Plans	Claims (millions of dollars)	People Eligible for Current or Future Benefits
Steel and other metals	423	$2,247	83,138
Air transportation	16	1,447	77,035
Industrial machinery	166	572	29,171
Motor vehicle equipment	66	200	10,814
Rubber and plastics	53	219	10,080
All other industries	1,931	1,342	268,645
Total	2,655	$6,027	478,883

Source: Pension Benefits Guaranty Corporation (PBGC), "Pension Insurance and the American Workforce," *Facts* (Washington, D.C.: PBGC, 1999).

The possibility of rapidly escalating premiums caused many employers to call for changes in the reinsurance program. They argued that companies with fully funded plans were, in effect, subsidizing unfunded plans, as a result of legal loopholes that allow companies to dump their unfunded pension liabilities on the PBGC.

A major debate over these issues took place for several years, primarily in various committees of the Congress. In April 1986, legislation was finally passed that made it more difficult for employers to pass on unfunded plan liabilities to PBGC.[13] The key feature of the 1986 law was to distinguish between *standard* and *distress* terminations. When a standard termination occurs—where the employer is *not* in financial distress—employers must pay all benefit commitments under the plan. Only when a company has filed for bankruptcy, would clearly go out of business unless the plan were terminated, or where the cost has become unreasonably burdensome does the financial support of the PBGC come into play. However, in such cases, the new law gave higher priority than before to PBGC claims in bankruptcy proceedings, thereby substantially increasing its claims on the distressed company's assets and reducing the practice of "dumping" unfunded liabilities onto the PBGC. The 1986 law also addressed the financial problems of the PBGC by increasing the premium for single-employer termination insurance.

No sooner was the new legislation passed in 1986 than the PBGC was confronted with distressed terminations of unprecedented proportions. PBGC's deficit nearly tripled, and its liabilities more than doubled to $5.6 billion. Reacting to a deteriorating situation, Congress acted in late 1987, again in 1990, and still again in 1994. A "variable rate premium" was established. As of January 1, 1991, a base rate of $19 per employee participant was levied on all plans. An additional charge of $9 per $1,000 of unfunded vested benefits was levied on underfunded plans. This additional premium, however, was not to exceed $53 per plan participant.

In yet another effort to deal with the financial insecurity created by pension underfunding, Congress passed the Retirement Protection Act of 1994. This law:

1. Removed the premium cap for underfunded plans, raising PBGC premiums dramatically for these companies.
2. Requires companies with underfunded plans to better inform their employees about the situation and the limits of the PBGC guarantee.
3. Calls for companies to provide more financial and pension funding information to the PBGC.
4. Mandates more uniform life-expectancy and interest rate assumptions in the actuarial determinations of funding status and required employer contributions into pension funds.
5. Gives the PBGC greater leverage to encourage and monitor the progress of underfunded plans and to collect money from companies if plans are terminated.

The PBGC currently protects about 42 million workers covered by 44,000 private, defined benefit plans (PBGC, 1999). Nine million of these workers are in multiemployer plans, with the rest in single-employer plans. In 1999, the PBGC guaranteed pension benefits up to $16.25 per month for each year a person worked under a particular plan (up to a maximum of $38,659 per year). To provide this insurance, PBGC collected total premiums from employers of $990 million in 1998.

Unlike its earlier years, the financial situation of the PBGC is currently quite good. Its multiemployer plan fund is currently in surplus by $241 million, and the fund for single-employer plans has moved from a deficit of $2.7 billion in 1992 to, for the first time in its history, a surplus beginning in 1996. In 1998 it had jumped to over $6 billion (PBGC, 1998).

WOMEN AND PRIVATE PENSIONS

Women are not as likely to be covered by an employer-sponsored pension. In 1995, 48 percent of working women were covered, versus 57 percent of men (Sunden and Surette, 1998).

Women are also not as likely as men to receive private pension benefits. A 1982 survey of "new social security beneficiaries" found low levels of pension receipt among retired *working* women, both in absolute terms and relative to men. "Only 27 percent of the women were receiving a pension—24 percent from their own employment and 3 percent with survivor benefits only. Among men, the incidence of pension receipt was 53 percent, twice the rate for women" (Woods, 1988).

A federal Task Force on Sex Discrimination (U.S. Department of Justice, n.d.) pointed out that women, because of their home and family responsibilities, are likely to accumulate far fewer total years of service with any one employer. With regard to spouses, the Task Force observed: "The retirement income protection provided for most women as wives of workers covered under private pension plans is generally both insecure and inadequate. . . . [ERISA] has done little to change the fact that most women, as housewives, are only one man away from poverty" (U.S. Department of Justice, n.d.).

Legislation to address these issues was passed by the Congress in 1984 and 1986. The Retirement Equity Act of 1984 and the 1986 Tax Reform Act:

1. Changed the age before which years of service can be excluded for vesting purposes from age 22 to 18.
2. Set the minimum age for plan participation for most workers at age 21 (with one year of service), instead of age 25.
3. Liberalized break-in-service rules.
4. Specified 100 percent vesting after five years' service (and three other vesting alternatives).
5. Required that pension plans provide automatic joint and survivor protection to participants with vested benefits (including terminated employees).
6. Specified that pension beneficiary decisions and changes to them must be carried out with the direct consent of spouses.

Despite these changes, the pension coverage of women is still lower than men. This difference arises from the fact that more women are employed in low-wage jobs, small firms, and low-coverage occupations. Table 7–3, for example, shows that differences in coverage rates virtually disappear if one groups men and women by level of earnings.

Thus, in her review of recent trends, Sophie Korczyk (1993) reports: "There is both good news and bad news about pension coverage among women. The good news is that women's pension coverage has increased despite both their market disadvantages and the declines among men. . . . The bad news is that women's coverage rates remain below those of men."

GOVERNMENT EMPLOYEE PENSION PLANS

Our discussion of employer-sponsored pension plans would not be complete without mentioning one other important category: federal,

Table 7–3
Total Participation Rates by Earnings and Gender

Earnings	All Workers		Pension Participants	
	Men	Women	Men	Women
Less than $10,000	10%	23%	13%	13%
$10,000-19,999	31	46	36	46
$20,000-29,999	27	21	63	64
$30,000-49,999	23	9	74	75
$50,000 or more	8	1	79	77
Total	100%	100%	50%	43%

Source: Sophie M. Korczyk, "Gender and Pension Coverage," in John A. Turner and D. J. Beller, eds., *Trends in Pensions, 1992* (Washington, D.C.: U.S. Government Printing Office, 1992).

state, and local plans for government employees. These plans have many characteristics similar to the private plans discussed above but are unique in some respects.

Federal Civil Service Plans

Most civilians working for the federal government (90 percent of full-time workers) are covered by the civil service retirement pension system (CSRS). In 1992 about $33 billion in benefits was paid out to 2.2 million beneficiaries under this program. In 1986, however, an alternative system was also established (described later).

Benefits under the original CSRS program are quite generous. A worker employed for 35 years with a final salary over $30,000 will generally receive enough *from his federal pension alone* to maintain his or her standard of living in retirement (Hartman, 1983). In fact, Robert Hartman argued, in his 1983 book *Pay and Pensions for Federal Workers*, that federal pensions were much better than those in the private sector and, as a result, too costly to taxpayers. Moreover, he argued that many aspects of the system were inequitable, favoring highly paid and long-term workers and those people who return to government service late in their career. Over the years Hartman and many others (e.g., the Universal Social Security Coverage Study Group, 1980) have called for major changes in this pension program.

One of the activities that received the most criticism was the "double-dipping" of civil servants who receive both a good federal pension and, in addition, social security. Until 1984 federal civilian employees were *not* covered by social security. However, the relatively low number of quarters needed to qualify for social security in the past often permitted (and encouraged) them to obtain coverage through employment in non-government jobs. Many federal employees worked part time while employed by the government. Others, after retirement (often early retirement) from government employment, took a new job to obtain social security eligibility and eventually obtained a minimum (or better) social security benefit. In fact, among those age 62 or older, the proportion of civil service annuitants eligible to receive social security retirement benefits was 63 percent in 1979 (U.S. Social Security Administration, 1982). Over the years, the cost and inequity of providing social security benefits to federal pensioners (who already had good federal pensions) was condemned by many, and recommendations were frequently made to cover all government employees. It was not until 1984, however, that all *new* federal employees were mandatorily covered by social security.

Pension eligibility requirements, financing, and benefits were significantly revised under provisions of the Federal Employees' Retirement System Act of 1986. The new system (FERS), effective January 1987, covers all federal civilian employees hired on or after that date and virtually all earlier hires with fewer than five years of nonmilitary service on December 31, 1986.

Older employees covered by the original federal pension plan (CSRS) will remain under that system (unless they opt to shift to the FERS). To be eligible for unreduced benefits under CSRS, an employee must be age 62 with at least five years of service; age 60 with twenty years; or age 55 with thirty years. Retirement benefits under CSRS continue to be based on the employee's average annual earnings during the three highest consecutive years of employment. The formula used is: 1.5 percent of average annual earnings during the first five years of service, plus 1.75 percent for each of the next five years of service, plus 2 percent for each year of service in excess of ten. For thirty years of service, the result is a benefit equal to 56.25 percent of average annual earnings. As of 1987, a "thrift savings plan" option was available that allows employees to invest up to 5 percent of pay in a tax-deferred plan, but there is no matching contribution by the government.

The *new* civil service retirement program (FERS) consists of three benefits: social security, a defined benefit plan, and a thrift savings plan. Under social security, employees pay an OASDI tax up to the taxable wage ceiling in addition to the Medicare tax that all federal employees pay. They receive regular benefits under the program and are subject to all the provisions.

The second benefit is the new CSRS, to which employees contribute 0.8 percent of salary. Age and length of service requirements to obtain benefits are as described above for employees under the old CSRS, but the benefit formula is different. The annual benefit is calculated at 1.0

percent of a retiring employee's average annual earnings for the three highest consecutive years, multiplied by the number of years of service. If the employee is age 62 or older at retirement, the calculation factor is 1.1 percent. If younger, the employee receives a supplement equal to the estimated social security benefit that would be payable based on current federal service under social security, calculated as if the employee were age 62. The supplement, which is subject to reduction if outside earnings exceed certain limits, ceases at age 62, when the retiree begins drawing actual social security benefits.

The third benefit is from a thrift savings plan. It offers three types of tax-deferred investment options: special government securities, fixed income securities, or a stock index fund. The government contributes an amount equal to 1 percent of each employee's pay to the plan, even if the employee does not participate. In addition, the government contributes a dollar for each employee dollar contributed up to 3 percent of pay, and 50 cents for each employee dollar up to the next 2 percent of pay. The employee can contribute beyond 5 percent (without a government match) up to a maximum of 10 percent of pay.

The Federal Employees' Retirement System Act (FERS) limits automatic cost-of-living adjustments payable from the CSRS fund. Annual adjustments will be: (1) the actual twelve-month rise in the Consumer Price Index, if it is less than 2 percent; (2) 2 percent, if the rise is 2 percent to 3 percent; and (3) the rise minus 1 percentage point, if the rise is 3 percent or more. These adjustments apply to all retirees (both old and new programs), beginning at age 62. Previously, the formula provided for unreduced adjustments for all retirees, regardless of age.

The new retirement system (FERS) was designed to save the government money—$42 million in 1987 and rising to $2.67 billion in 1991. Even with the less liberal cost-of-living and lower CSRS formula, many government and union official contend that FERS, with social security, is a better system for many workers (for example, workers who eventually leave the government and take a job in the private sector). However, few workers covered by the old system have exercised their option to switch to FERS. The law creating FERS contained a provision allowing those retiring under either CSRS or FERS to withdraw their contributions in a lump sum when they retired. A 1990 law suspended (with exceptions) this option for five years, beginning on December 1, 1990.

Military Pensions

In 1995, 1.8 million retirees and survivors received military retirement benefits costing nearly $28 billion. "Of all pension plans, probably none is better than the military's," observed Congressman Les Aspin (1976). The liberal attributes of this plan come at a high price. The current average lifetime cost of a pension for a high-ranking military officer retiring after thirty years of service is well over a million dollars.

Since 1935, over twelve advisory panels or commissions have recommended *major* changes in the military pension program, with little resulting action. Former Director of the Office of Budget and Management David Stockman in a highly publicized moment of candor, described the program as a "scandal" (Bickerman, 1985).

The military retirement program:

1. Provides full benefits that begin immediately upon retirement, typically before age 50.
2. Vests and pays benefits after (but not before) twenty years of service.
3. Requires no financial contribution from military personnel.
4. Pays at least 50 percent of basic pay to those with twenty years of service and 75 percent after thirty years.[14]
5. Is indexed for inflation over the lifetime of the pensioner.
6. Does not subject benefits to an earnings test, allowing military personnel to retire and take other jobs while receiving a military pension.

The current median age of "retirement" is 42 for enlisted personnel and 46 for officers, with less than 10 percent of all nondisabled persons leaving military service after age 50; almost 90 percent of military retirees are under age 65, and 50 percent are under age 50.

This "early out" option has been justified over the years as necessary to maintain the youth and fighting vigor of the military forces. Critics point out, however, that the overwhelming majority of current military personnel are noncombatants and that the current pension program strips the service of the experienced, highly trained personnel increasingly needed to run our modern, technologically sophisticated military program.

Reacting more to budget issues than military manpower considerations, Congress in the 1980s made two major changes in the military pension law. In 1985 it created the Military Retirement Trust Fund, establishing mechanisms to move the program toward a funded system. Then in 1986 Congress deliberalized the pension program for *new* personnel covered by the plan. In addition to lowering pensions paid to people leaving with less than thirty years of service, cost-of-living adjustments (COLA) were changed. Pensions under the new law are indexed by the Consumer Price Index (CPI) *less 1 percent* each year. At age 62 the pension benefit level is adjusted upward to restore the "lost" COLA adjustments over the prior period. But once again in subsequent years, the new higher benefit level is adjusted for inflation by the "CPI minus one" rule. The result is significant cost savings to the government.

Military pensions still remain the best pension in the United States and the most expensive. Many feel they are too generous and should not be available at very early ages. Debate over these issues continues, but no change is expected in the near future.

State and Local Pension Plans

In 1992, there were nearly 2,307 "state and local retirement systems" covering 13.6 million state and local government active employees and paying $44.2 billion in benefits to 4.7 million retirees (EBRI, 1997b). These plans are similar in many ways to private employer plans. Writing in 1975, James A. Maxwell summarized some of the differences: "Overall, the state and local government pension systems provide more generous benefits than do private systems. The normal retirement age and service requirements are more generous. . . . And they are more likely to have generous disability and survivor coverage. . . . [Most] require employee contributions, whereas most private plans do not." The differences remain today, as verified by Mitchell and Carr (1995).

With regard to inflation protection, a study (Crown et al., 1990) of the 76 major teacher and state-employee retirement plans found that 41 plans in 1982 had automatic adjustment mechanisms, with annual ceilings on these adjustments of 2 percent to 5 percent. Only two of these plans did not have ceilings: Maryland, for employees hired before 1980; and New Jersey, which adjusts pensions for 60 percent of the change in the Consumer Price Index.

When social security was passed, state and local governments were free to choose whether to cover their employees under social security; however, the option to *withdraw* from social security (once having joined the system) was eliminated in 1983. About 75 percent of state and local government employees are currently covered by both social security and a state or local pension plan (Mitchell and Carr, 1995). Again, for workers not covered by social security, dual coverage is often achieved by early retirement from state or local service followed by work for a nongovernment employer.

Regarding benefits, a study by Lovejoy (1988) found that "at 40 years of service, replacement rates for each of the public sector groups exceeded 75 percent." In 1989, the median benefit paid out was $7,200, replacing 42 percent of preretirement earnings. For those not receiving social security benefits, the median replacement rate was much higher—50 percent (Phillips, 1992).

Congressional interest in federal regulation of state and local plans was a major issue when ERISA was passed in 1974. These plans were formally exempted from the ERISA legislation, however, because it was not clear that Congress had the constitutional authority to regulate the states in this area. However, over the years legislation has been introduced in Congress to establish minimum reporting, disclosure, and financial responsibility standards for state and local plans. Supporters of the legislation believe it is constitutional and will improve the security of pensions for employees in the states. Strong opposition to the legislation has come from state and local government organizations. They maintain that regulation is unnecessary and argue that such action would be an undesirable invasion of states' rights.

Over the years there has been concern about the financial condition of state and local plans. Studies have indicated serious problems for plans in certain states and cities (Maxwell, 1975; U.S. House Committee on Education and Labor, 1978). A 1993 survey of plans by the Public Pension Coordinating Council indicated that *in the aggregate*, underfunding is not a major problem, with the value of assets as a percent of benefit liabilities averaging 93 percent. Some plans, however, remain severely underfunded.

CHAPTER 7 HIGHLIGHTS

Private and government employee pensions play important roles in the United States. Some key points to remember are:

1. While many government employee pensions were in place relatively early in this century, the rapid development of private pensions did not begin until the 1950s.

2. Still not covered by private plans are many people who work for small businesses; the uncovered are also more likely to be nonunion, female, part time, lower paid, and in the trade or service industries.

3. Many pension-covered workers are in noncontributory defined benefit plans with five-year vesting, optional survivors' benefits, and nonindexed benefits based on years of service and final years of earnings. Coverage in defined contribution plans, however, has grown dramatically in recent years.

4. The 1974 Employee Retirement Income Security Act (ERISA) set up a comprehensive set of minimum standards, financial safeguards, and disclosure requirements, seeking to ensure that benefits promised to workers would be realized.

5. The ERISA provisions have been strengthened by major new legislation (since ERISA) in the areas of vesting, plan termination and reinsurance, survivors' protection, and pension integration provisions.

6. The major private pension issues currently being debated are: (1) the adequacy of coverage; (2) how to reduce the risk of pension loss; and (3) the extent to which benefits should be protected from inflation.

SUGGESTED READINGS

Atkinson, A. B., and Martin Rein. *Age, Work and Social Security*. New York: St. Martin's Press, 1993. An informative collection of papers on economic well-being in old age, changing work policies, and issues regarding early retirement.

Burkhauser, Richard V., and Dallas L. Salisbury. *Pensions in a Changing Economy*. Washington, D.C.: Employee Benefit Research Institute, 1993. An excellent summary of contemporary private pension issues.

Employee Benefit Research Institute (EBRI). *Fundamentals of Employee Benefit Programs*, 5th ed. Washington, D.C.: EBRI, 1997. An up-to-date and authoritative compendium on pensions and other employee benefits.

Employee Benefit Research Institute (EBRI). *Pension Tax Expenditures: Are They Worth the Cost?* Washington, D.C.: EBRI, 1993. Some people argue that the federal government should reduce its tax subsidies to encourage private pensions. This monograph explores the issue.

Hannah, Leslie. *Inventing Retirement—The Development of Occupational Pensions in Britain*. Cambridge: Cambridge University Press, 1986. An excellent history of the evolution of private plans in Great Britain, which is quite relevant to the American situation.

Hushback, Clare. "Public Employee Pension Funds: Retirement Security for Plan Participants or Cash Cow for State Governments?" Washington, D.C.: AARP Public Policy Institute, 1993. An overview of state pension plan funding issues.

Kotlikoff, Laurence J., and David A. Wise. *The Wage Carrot and the Pension Stick*. Kalamazoo, Mich.: W. E. Upjohn Institute, 1989. A theoretical and empirical examination of the interaction between private pensions and labor force participation, providing excellent insights into the "early retirement" phenomenon.

Mitchell, Olivia S. *New Trends in Pension Benefit and Retirement Provisions*. NBER Working Paper No. 7381. Cambridge, Mass.: National Bureau of Econom Research (NBER), 1999. This study illustrates and interprets plan benefit provisions over the last two decades.

Schulz, James H., and K. Burnes. *Older Women and Pension Privatization in the United States*. Waltham, Mass.: National Center on Women and Aging, Brandeis University, 1999. This monograph focuses on the impact of defined contribution plans on retirement income adequacy, especially the economic situation of women.

U.S. Congressional Budget Office. *Federal Insurance of Private Pension Benefits*. Washington, D.C.: U.S. Government Printing Office, 1987. A review of the structure of employer-sponsored pensions in the United States, the role of the Pension Benefit Guaranty Corporation, and the controversy over reinsurance of plan benefits.

U.S. Department of Labor. *Trends in Pensions*. Washington, D.C.: Pension and Welfare Benefits Administration, 1989 and 1992. A major source of data on pensions, with in-depth studies on pension characteristics, financing, and foreign systems.

Chapter 8

Population Aging:
Generational Conflict?

The significant, semi-hidden story in the . . . federal budget is that America's public resources are increasingly being mortgaged for the use of a single group within our country: the elderly.

The above quotation is similar to many statements made in recent years. But it was voiced close to three decades ago by columnist David Broder (1973), writing in the *Washington Post*. Broder's article was one of the first assessments to raise serious questions about growing federal expenditures for the elderly.

Two more recent articles in *Forbes* magazine typified media attention. A feature article in 1980 titled "The Old Folks" was headlined: "The myth is that they're sunk in poverty. The reality is that they're living well. The trouble is there are too many of them—God bless 'em" (Flint, 1980). Eight years later, *Forbes*, in an article titled "Consuming Our Children," again raised the alarm: "Many young people complain that they can't live as well as their parents did. They may well be right. We are witnessing nothing less than a massive transfer of income and wealth from the younger generations to the older" (Chakravarty and Weisman, 1988).

Before the end of the Cold War, economist Barbara Boyle Torrey (1982) summarized the issue in this way: "The traditional tradeoff between guns and butter may in the future be better characterized as a tradeoff between guns and canes." This was followed by demographer Samuel H. Preston's assertion that the real trade-off was between canes and baby bottles:

Since the early 1960s the well-being of the elderly has improved greatly, whereas that of the young has deteriorated. Demographic trends underlie these changes: in the family, in politics, and in industry the growing number of older people and the declining number of children have worked to the advantage of the group that is increasing in size. (Preston, 1984)

GENERATIONAL CONFLICT?

In 1994, columnist Robert J. Samuelson directly raised the specter of generational conflict, a concern that has been voiced again and again by many in the United States: "Everything about an aging America tells us it contains the seeds of huge social and political problems. Is it fair to impose such large tax burdens on workers to pay for retirees, many [of] whom are now (and will be in the future) relatively healthy and well off?" (Samuelson, 1994).

Thus, "a new policy question has arisen: how should we adjust economic and social arrangements to allow for a rising and permanently higher proportion of old people? This question has never been posed or answered before, and its very novelty may provoke alarm" (Jackson, 1998).

If you want to understand the generational conflict issue, the place to start is with demographics. The so-called rising "burden" of the elderly in terms of pension and medical costs, for example, has its origins in the nation's changing population structure. "The real bottom line is adjusting to lower mortality and fertility rates. In a world in which people live longer and have fewer children, we have to stop imagining that those children will be able to support their parents during ever-longer retirements. Thinking that this is just a Social Security issue is like believing that Cinderella's only issue was her shoe size" (Steuerle and Spiro, 1999).

A recent report published by the National Academy on an Aging Society cautions, however, that "demography is not destiny" (Friedland and Summer, 1999). We agree. In this chapter we suggest that the fears of Samuelson and others are overstated, that the nature of the "demographic aging problem" is frequently misstated, and that many of the complexities of analysis related to this issue are often ignored in discussions of it. More important, we conclude with the view that the future well-being of the whole population (of all ages) has very little to do with "population aging" and much to do with technological change, investments in human and business capital, management skills, and all the other nonaging factors that have a major impact on economic growth.

AGING POPULATIONS

Population aging was unknown before the 20th century. Now there are aging populations around the world. Demographers classify countries

Table 8–1
The World's "Oldest" Countries, 1999

Country	Percent of Population Age 65 and Over
Italy	17.9
Sweden	17.3
Belgium	16.9
Greece	16.8
Spain	16.6
Japan	16.5
Bulgaria	16.3
Germany	16.1
France	16.0
United Kingdom	15.7

Source: Kevin Kinsella, "The Demographics of Aging," *Coalition '99*, No. 12 (July/August 1999).

into "young," "mature," and "aged" populations according to the proportion of population age 65 and over. Cowgill and Holmes (1970) have suggested that countries with 4 percent to 6 percent aged should be classified as young, 7 percent to 9 percent as mature, and 10 percent or more as aged.

Table 8–1 shows the percentage of aged persons for the world's ten oldest countries. In 1999, persons age 65 or older were 12.7 percent of the U.S. population. This age group has increased more rapidly than the whole population. Yet, as Siegel (1976) points out, the growth of this age group during the 1960s and early 1970s was below its growth during the 1950s and the preceding decades. Given relatively stable mortality and net immigration rates, fluctuations in population growth since World War II have largely been due to fluctuations in the **fertility rate**. Figure 8–1 shows the changing fertility rate over the 1970–1989 period. In the early 1970s, the rate declined dramatically, then leveled off, and has been increasing in recent years. Currently, the fertility rate is close to the population "replacement level" (2,100 births per 1,000 females).

Given past and current rates, there is a "graying" of the U.S. population, with the demographic structure exhibiting the following major characteristics (U.S. Bureau of the Census, 1996):

1. The 65-and-over population will rise to about 75 million in 2040 and represent 20 percent of the total population.

Figure 8–1
Fertility Rates, 1925–1997

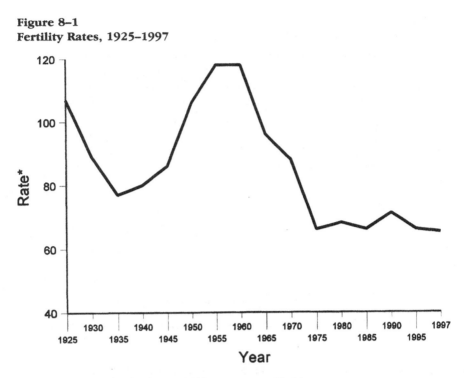

*Fertility rates are live births per 1,000 women ages 15–44 years.
Source: National Center for Health Statistics.

2. The "very old" (ages 85 and older) will become an increasingly larger fraction of the elderly population, rising to 18 percent of the 65 and over population.

3. Because women's life expectancy exceeds that of men by a growing number of years, the proportion of widows will rise, and they will face an ever longer widowhood.

4. Given the baby boom of the 1940s and 1950s, the aged population will begin to increase exceptionally rapidly around the year 2010.

The progressive aging of the population and the longer life expectancy of women creates a new situation. Older men are usually married and relatively few live alone. In contrast, almost two-thirds of older women are widowed, divorced, or single, and almost half of them live alone or with nonrelatives.

DEPENDENCY RATIOS

The increase in the number of the aged has caused concern. Many people worry about an increase in the number of nonworkers who must be economically supported by the working population.

Some people are concerned about the increased competition that may arise among age cohorts as each strives for a larger share of the nation's output. For example, improving retirement income by increasing social security often heads the list of demands by the aged segment of the population; in contrast, this is a relatively unimportant priority for younger workers.

As we discussed in Chapter 3, individuals "store up" claims (while working) to later output (produced after they stop working) by acquiring financial assets (wealth) and by the accrual of pension credits (a special kind of wealth). Retirement income is provided to the individual through social security, public assistance, employer-sponsored pensions, private charity, and/or personal savings. At the same time, the fundamental economic fact remains that the part of national output consumed in any particular year by the *retired* spending this income is produced by the then-working population—regardless of the mix of mechanisms employed. Some of society's total output is produced by elderly persons still in the labor force. However, most of the aged do not participate in the production process; they must consume output produced by others.

To assess the changing relationship among consumption by the elderly, government expenditures for the elderly, and total economic output, it has been common to calculate what are called **dependency ratios**. These dependency ratios seek to measure the number of persons in the society not engaged in producing output relative to those in the labor force who are.

It is important to realize, however, that the recent interest in dependency ratios has arisen primarily as a result of concern about the so-called increasing burden of the aged that might arise with changes in the demographic structure and economic support patterns. Hence, the prejudicial term chosen for these discussions has been "dependency ratios"—emphasizing the economically nonproductive potential of certain groups, such as children and retired persons.

The President's Commission on Pension Policy, a blue-ribbon panel appointed by President Jimmy Carter, was one of the first groups to sound the alarm:

After the turn of the century, an unprecedented shifting of older workers into retirement will begin to take place as the so-called "baby boom" generation grows older. Quite literally, this country's population will be coming of age.

As the population of the country matures severe strains will be placed on our already overburdened retirement income system. The inequities and inadequacies of the present retirement income system will become critical as more people retire and the active work force to support their retirement shrinks. (President's Commission on Pension Policy, 1981)

The commission's focus on the retired population relative to the work-ing population has also been the focus of policymakers, researchers, and the media who have raised fears about the growing aged population. The concern is not limited to the United States. An article in the *Economist* (1984), for example, commented: "Today's finance ministers [around the world] may think they have a tough job trying to restrain public spending, but their successors in the twenty-first century will envy them. Thirty years from now, the industrial countries will be bulging with pensioners. The costs will turn their children gray."

But, as pointed out by Cowgill (1981), "from a demographic standpoint such fears are not warranted. The analysis on which they are based is one-sided and misleading." Cowgill points out that *most modernized countries of the world, all with relatively aged populations, have quite low dependency loads, much lower than developing nations*. As we show below, historically *total labor force* dependency ratios in the United States have been declining, and projections indicate that they are likely to continue to decline until around the year 2010 and will not rise dra-matically in the years following.

The definition of dependency ratio used by the President's Commission focuses only on dependents arising as old people retire from the work force. As many demographers have pointed out, this is a very biased meas-ure of the nonworking segment of the population. There are many other individuals who are not working: children, "nonworking" spouses, un-employed workers, and the severely disabled. Children have always con-stituted the major proportion of dependents in societies. While that burden has been sharply reduced in industrialized countries, children still represent a major dependency burden in developing countries. Thus, between 1975 and 2025, the *aged* dependency ratio is expected to almost double for Latin America and to rise even more sharply for East Asia; *total* dependency, however, is projected to fall in both regions as a result of declining fertility rates (Schulz, 1991 and 1997).

Labor Force Dependency Ratios

As a recent report (Friedland and Summer, 1999) points out, "although the ratio of total 'dependents' to people of working age is projected to increase between now and 2040, it is not expected to grow as large as it was in the 1950s, 1960s, and 1970s." Figure 8–2 shows that there were *90 people* under age 20 or over age 65 for every 100 ages 20–65 in 1960. But it is projected that there will be *only 80 "dependents"* in 2040.

In a detailed analysis of dependency ratios, Schulz, Borowski, and Crown (1991) calculated labor force dependency ratios for the years 1950–2020. The labor force dependency ratios were calculated by first multiplying labor force participation rates at various ages by population

Figure 8–2
Number of Children and Elderly per 100 People of Working Age, 1960–2040*

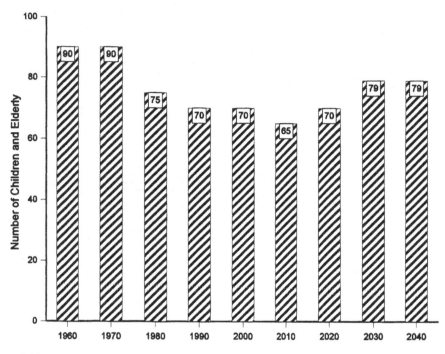

*Children are defined as under age 20, and the elderly are age 65 or older.
Source: *Annual Report of the Board of Trustees OASDI Trust Funds, 1997* (Washington,
D.C.: U.S. Government Printing Office, 1997), Table II.H1.

projections for each corresponding age group to find the "total working population." The ratio was then calculated by dividing the difference between "the total number in the population and the working population" (that is, the dependent population) by the "working population" and multiplying the result by 100.

Trends in these ratios are shown in Figure 8–3. The total labor force dependency ratio *declines* from about 15 in 1960 to about 11 in 2020. Figure 8–3 also decomposes the ratio into three age groups—children, younger adults, and older persons. The shape of the total labor force dependency ratio over the years 1960–2000 is dominated by declines in child and younger adult dependency, the latter being the result of increased labor force participation among women. From 2000–2020, the total ratio is influenced mainly by the rising aged dependency ratio.

Overall, projections indicate that aged dependency will never approach the levels of youth dependency in the 1960s and 1970s and that total dependency will be lower.

Figure 8–3
Historical and Projected Labor Force Dependency Ratios: United States,
1950–2020

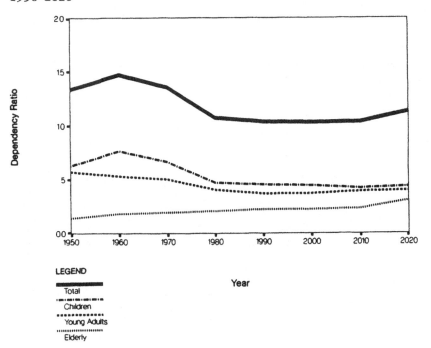

Sources: James H. Schulz, Allan Borowski, and William H. Crown, *Economics of Population Aging: The "Graying" of Australia, Japan, and the United States* (Westport, Conn.: Auburn House, 1991), p. 78; and James H. Schulz, *The Economics of Aging*, 6th ed. (Westport, Conn.: Auburn House, 1995), p. 271. Reprinted by permission of Auburn House, an imprint of Greenwood Publishing Group, Inc., Westport, Conn.

Economic Implications of Demographic Change

There are now many treatises on the aging of populations. To cite only one, the editors of *Our Aging Society: Paradox and Promise* (Pifer and Bronte, 1986) alert us to a "demographic revolution" taking place and ask the question, given the resulting population structure: "Would such [an aged] society, or anything approaching it, be viable?"

The alarming tenor of this question is typical of most writing on this topic today. Yet when one looks closely at recent books and articles, one finds that the writing is highly speculative and supported by very little sophisticated research. There have been frequent examinations of *demographic* statistics but almost no *economic* analysis of the evolving situation. A kind of "voodoo demographics" has developed that raises the specter of lost opportunities and an intolerable economic burden arising from growing numbers of older people and a resultant rise in intergenerational conflict (see, for example, Wattenberg, 1987 or Peterson, 1999).

Most of the discussions rely heavily (often exclusively) on dependency ratio statistics. Dependency ratios are useful in understanding changes in the composition of dependency relationships over time. But as we have emphasized, they must be used with great caution. Such ratios enable policymakers to make crude estimates of the speed at which dependency relationships have changed in the past and are expected to change in the future. It is important to remember, however, that the validity of dependency ratio analysis rests on the calculation procedures and a number of assumptions. In addition to the issues discussed, one of the most important considerations is the assumption that the per person costs associated with different types of "dependent persons" are the same. But the per capita private and public costs associated with supporting children are not the same as those related to the consumption expenditures of the elderly. In addition, most reported dependency ratios do not take account of economic growth—growth that will lower the support "burden" associated with rising aged dependency.

Schulz, Borowski, and Crown (1991) weight the demographic data (shown in Figure 8-3) to reflect the "private support costs" associated with different age groups of nonworking persons and also look at the potential effect of economic growth. Based on this extension of the demographic statistics to include economic differences, they conclude, first, "that the economic impact of demographic aging is not as bad as those doomsayers who use simplistic dependency ratios would have us believe. Second, as in other areas of social policy, relatively small increases in economic growth rates have the potential to substantially moderate the ill effects of other factors that have a negative impact." In fact, they conclude from their research that the future overall "support burden" will be less in the years 2030–2050 than it was during 1950–1970 (see, also, Adamchak, 1993).

But even if the economic requirements are manageable, the changing composition of the support burden raises a major political question. Parents directly pay for most of the expenditures on children (education in the early years is usually the big exception).[1] In contrast, the elderly receive much of their economic support through (1) employer-sponsored programs; and (2) government programs supported by various taxes (taxes that will almost certainly need to rise in order to pay future benefits to older people). Much of the concern about the future burden of the elderly should be interpreted as concern about governments' ability to tax (that is, voters' willingness to pay taxes) and employers' willingness to sponsor group plans to meet the needs of groups like the aged who in today's world rely heavily on payments outside the family—both government- and employer-sponsored health and pension benefits.

FINANCING AN AGING POPULATION

Providing adequately for the retirement period is an expensive proposition. As the retirement age continues to decline, we face the prospect of providing individuals with income and services for a twenty- to thirty-year period outside the labor force. Increasingly, people are developing expectations that retirement can and should be an enjoyable period of life and that economic resources should be sufficient to avoid the limitations imposed on retirement living by financial stringency. Unfortunately, if individuals begin to worry and seriously plan for their own retirement only shortly before the event, the magnitude of the financing problem becomes insuperable for most. The best and easiest way of accumulating the resources necessary for retirement is to begin very early. But historically most people have shown a reluctance to think about retirement until it is *almost* a reality or until it is a reality. The result in years past was a great deal of poverty among the aged.

Collective Approaches

Public and private pension programs and, before them, families have stepped in to provide needed economic support for many of these people—often preventing destitution. The level of public pension support has often been very low and inadequate for preventing a sharp drop in the living standard during retirement. Yet, as we discussed previously, the rising financial burden imposed on the working population, even at these low levels of support, has created political concern, and now there is growing concern regarding the *future* burden.

There is considerable debate over what the future costs of social security will be. Despite the lack of agreement, it is clear that sizable amounts of resource transfers will be required. How willing are people to finance the required levels of support?

One of the best answers is provided by the individuals *now covered* both by good private pensions and by social security. The combined reduction in their take-home pay to provide social security and a good private pension is quite large (about 16 percent to 20 percent). Yet there is little complaining from this group (probably in large part because these costs are taken out of their salaries before they ever get their earnings check). Many European countries have payroll taxes for OASDI that are over 17 percent. Despite these high rates, there has been relatively little political opposition in these countries to this level of taxation *for retirement purposes*. Rather, as in the United States, there has been a lot more concern in past years about government deficits caused by slow growth and record high levels of unemployment. Survey data from a variety of opinion polls indicate, in fact, a willingness of American workers to pay for even better benefits (Sherman, 1989 or Reno and Friedland, 1997).

Some people—such as Peterson and Howe (1988)—have argued that social security expenditures are out of control and too costly to maintain in what they foresee as a no-growth economic environment. They predict that if nothing is done, payroll taxes will reach unbelievably high levels and workers will rebel at such high taxes. Their conclusions, however, are disputed by most social security experts (Kingson and Schulz, 1997).

There is, however, almost unanimous agreement (as we discussed in Chapter 6) that medical care expenditures, if left unchecked, could "break the bank." In contrast, most experts see the finances of the pension programs (OASDI) as under control and think that the funding increases that will be required in the future are economically and politically feasible if moderate economic growth continues. Thus, the 1999 Report of the Social Security Trustees states that the long-term [social security] financial problem is significant "but can be solved by small gradual changes."

This difference between health care and pension costs is one reason so much recent attention has been focused on medical care reform and on health care cost containment. But even with regard to health care costs, there is a tendency to focus disproportionately on the old. In Chapter 6, we listed the major factors increasing health care costs. Studies show that "aging" as a factor in these costs is dwarfed by other factors, such as the intensity and utilization rates of health services across the age spectrum and expanding medical technology (Binstock, 1993). A study by Mendelson and Schwartz (1993), for example, found that population aging was a relatively negligible factor when compared with the more general rise in spending on hospitals, physicians, and other health components.

"The Days of Cheap Gas and Social Security Are Gone"

Older Americans can remember when fuel for automobiles was 26 cents a gallon. Those prices are gone forever.

Certainly, we must be sensitive to both the economic and political realities associated with retirement costs. The recent years of economic chaos are a vivid reminder of the uncertainties that lie ahead. We must constantly monitor developments and seek to anticipate problems. Some of the problems that must be dealt with—such as escalating health costs and the baby boom phenomenon—can be seen clearly. Most future developments, both negative and positive, are hidden from our view. The debate, consequently, often centers around two points of view: the pessimist sees the glass half empty but the optimist sees it half full.

Despite this dilemma, it is foolish to think we can escape the cost of providing an individual with an adequate retirement income by keeping the cost of social security down. *If we do not provide for older Americans through taxation, then we will do so by other but perhaps less visible means—for example, by reducing a workers' take-home pay to finance private pensions or by transferring income within families from the young to the old.* Times have changed. When we reach old age, we are no longer willing to live as paupers in retirement. We expect that there will be programs and policies that make it possible to live comfortably in old age.

Certainly, the days of cheap social security, like the days of cheap gasoline, are gone forever. We will have to do some very hard thinking and some belt-tightening. But there is no rational justification for the hysteria that is being promoted today by some people who are attacking social security and raising the specter of the aged burden in an aging society. As we point out elsewhere (Schulz et al., 1991), even moderate rates of real economic growth will enable us to substantially increase real per capita support of nonworkers without increasing substantially (if at all) the burden on the workers of the future.

In 1961, then Secretary of Health, Education, and Welfare Abraham Ribicoff stated that he thought the limit to public acceptance of the social security payroll tax was 10 percent. But we passed through that hypothetical ceiling in 1980 without difficulty. Now people worry about the high rates of payroll taxes that will be needed in the years after 2010. But as economist Martin Feldstein (1975) has pointed out:

An increase in the social security tax rate to 16 or 20 percent would be a substantial increase. . . . There are some who believe that such high rates would create an intolerable burden on low-income and middle-income families. This is a false argument that ignores the substantial increase in real earnings that these families will enjoy at the same time that tax rates rise. Even a tax rate increase of 10 percentage points over the next 50 years is only an increase of 0.2 percent per year. The higher tax would absorb only one tenth of the annual real wage growth of 2 percent. Stated somewhat differently, with a 2 percent annual rate of growth, real wages would rise by 200 percent between now and 2030, and the higher social security tax would absorb no more than 10 percentage points of this 200 percentage point increase in real wages.

Thus, it is important to keep in mind the greater political acceptability of *gradual* increases in tax rates. This suggests that rising pension costs should be phased in over a period of years—similar to the way many other countries have introduced the major improvements in their pension programs; and it is probably wise to anticipate the demographic bulge and consequent sharp rise in costs beginning around the year 2010 as a result of the World War II baby boom.

Also, there is a need for a greater awareness of the changing demographics and the intra- and intergenerational equity issues. As the costs of aged retirement living increase, more attention will need to be given to these issues in order to maintain public confidence in and support for the programs and to use with maximum effectiveness the money allocated.

THE GENERATIONAL EQUITY DEBATE

Probably three basic changes, above all others, have been the fuel for the intergenerational concerns that have been raised: (1) the improved economic status of the elderly; (2) the declining economic status of children; and (3) large government deficits. Many commentators have linked the first two and have asserted that the economic problems of children are the result of government expenditures on the elderly and that future children are likely to be worse off when the baby boom cohort retires.

It is true that elderly poverty has declined, and poverty among children has risen.[2] *But the trends in child and elderly poverty are due to totally different factors.* As we discussed in Chapter 1, the elderly improvement is the result of major improvements in public and private pensions and a new public assistance program (SSI). In contrast, poverty among children in the United States is largely a result of family breakdown. According to policy analyst Isabel Sawhill, "as a first approximation, the rapid growth in the number of children living in single-parent families can explain virtually all the growth [in their poverty] since 1960" (Gill and Gill, 1994). For example, one recent study found "that after divorce the percentage of children in poverty doubles from 19 percent to 38 percent" (Gill and Gill, 1994).

When single-parent families with children need economic help, where does it come from? Public assistance is provided by state-controlled programs that in large part have been cutting eligibility and have allowed *real* benefit levels to decline with inflation over many years. Contrast this to SSI, where federal law prohibits states from cutting benefits and where these benefits are indexed to keep pace with inflation. Quadagno (1988) shows that the history of state old-age assistance programs before SSI was very much like public assistance today for the nonaged; benefits and eligibility requirements varied greatly from state to state, and matters of race often influenced the political decision-making, especially in the South.

More recently, cutbacks during the Reagan administration illustrate the perverse distributional impacts that have occurred. When the Reagan administration took office in 1981, the aged felt the effects of the first broad action taken to cut back expenditures for the elderly. President Reagan's budget request for 1983 called for $6.5 billion less expenditure for aged programs than occurred under pre-Reagan policies. Ultimately, $5.2 billion in cuts, over half related to Medicare, were legislated.

These cuts, however, affected various subgroups of the elderly differently. In a review of both these spending decreases and the tax reductions occurring during this period, Storey (1983) concludes that the impacts varied greatly by level of income. The well-to-do aged received substantial tax cuts and escaped major benefit cuts; the middle-income aged were helped a little by tax cuts but were more affected by benefit cuts; and the low-income aged received no tax-cut benefits and bore the brunt of many of the largest spending cuts. "The net result of the policy changes . . . [1981–1983] has been to squeeze the resources available to the neediest among our Nation's elderly populations" (Storey, 1983).

Thus, the results we see today are the result of politics driven much more by attitudes toward "the deserving poor" and the "undeserving poor" than they are a matter of scarce government revenues going from one age group to another. Even if social security benefits were cut in half, it is unlikely that many (if any) of the "freed" dollars would go to poor children, especially given all the other needs of other competing interests—national defense, environmental protection, the "information superhighway," and so on.

However, instead of focusing on the historic evidence regarding the politics and economics of what President Lyndon Johnson called "the war on poverty," people continue to argue generational conflict on the basis of a crude demographic determinism. Thus, Senator David Durenberger, in an address to the Americans for Generational Equity, asserted: "We have entered an era in which the date of one's birth has become the prime determinant of one's prospects for realizing the American dream" (quoted in Quadagno, 1991).

Not so!

The "Entitlement Controversy"

Federal budget deficits have been a big concern until recent years—the result primarily of President Reagan's huge tax cut in 1986 and massive increases in defense expenditures during the same period. Successive administrations have searched unsuccessfully for ways to reduce the resulting gap between federal revenues and expenditures. Even with the end of the Cold War and cuts in military expenditures, tax revenues in the period of sluggish growth were far below expenditures. Thus, in an environment of "no new taxes," no easy answer was found.

Two retired but highly respected U.S. senators, Republican Warren Rudman and Democrat Paul Tsongas, formed an organization called the Concord Coalition. The organization's primary concern is large federal budget deficits and the effect of these deficits on economic growth. In a 1993 report (Concord Coalition, 1993), they wrote that:

Entitlement spending is the major contributor to the growing federal budget deficit . . . [and] Social Security is the largest entitlement program. . . .

The centerpiece of The Zero Deficit Plan [that the Concord Coalition proposes] and its single largest component of deficit reduction is a proposal to means-test entitlement programs. . . . Entitlement payments to individuals, including the two "megaprograms," Medicare and Social Security, would be subject to a sliding-scale, across-the-board means test starting at a family income level of $40,000.

As the extract indicates, two major aspects of the **entitlement** controversy are: (1) the extent to which federal expenditures for the elderly contribute to the federal deficit; and (2) the merits of means-tested versus universal income support programs.

The term "entitlement" is used currently by people who want cutbacks; it refers to any program that provides legally enforceable statutory rights to payments from the federal government. In 1993, the ten largest programs (in order of outlays, bigger to smaller) were social security, Medicare, Medicaid, civil service retirement, unemployment, military retirement, food stamps, SSI, farm subsidies, and veterans' benefits (Cahill, 1993). Social security, Medicare, and Medicaid account for about two-thirds of all entitlement spending, but that does not necessarily mean that they are the source of the past federal deficit problems.

As we discussed in Chapter 5, the federal government is currently running (and will run for many years) large surpluses in the social security accounts. Despite the "self-financing" aspects of social security and its current surpluses (not deficits), critics continue to argue that cuts in entitlements are the solution to federal deficit problems. Moreover, social protection programs must compete with our need to pay for defense, environmental cleanup, the savings and loan debacle, and other federal programs. It is not surprising that "entitlement cuts" receive such serious attention when politicians are confronted with the obvious but painful alternative of tax increases.

With regard to means testing, we have given this topic extensive attention in Chapters 4, 5, and 6. Major problems associated with means testing are: the creation of "poverty traps," high administrative costs, imprecise targeting (i.e., including or excluding the wrong people), the stigma related to "poor people" receiving benefits, the abuse of power by those determining eligibility, and adverse work and saving incentives. The result has been widespread hostility to means testing over the years by the majority of both citizens and policymakers alike (see Skocpol, 1990, for an elaboration of this point).

In 1994, a group of social security experts headed by former Social Security Commissioner Robert Ball issued a joint statement on the Concord Coalition proposal. It argued, in part:

We oppose means testing for various reasons. Many of us believe that means testing would not actually lower the deficit because it would lead to reductions in Social Security taxes as benefit outgo declined. Many believe that the denial of benefits to higher income households would lead to demands that they be permitted to opt out of the system. Such withdrawals by high-earning households would deprive Social Security of the taxes these workers and their employers pay and place an unsustainable burden on average earners.

One concern often raised is that entitlements are poorly targeted and that they subsidize the wealthy (e.g., Howe and Longman, 1992). However, Gist and Aleksa (1994) report that the percent of OASDHI benefits going to those with pre-tax income below $20,000 is almost as great (70–75%) as for means-tested Medicaid (83%). Moreover, only about 2 percent of OASDHI goes to households with incomes in excess of $100,000. Gist and Aleksa contrast this with the government benefits resulting, for example, from the deductibility of homeowner mortgage interest in paying the federal income tax. Twenty-five percent of this government benefit goes to people in the $100,000+ group.

One thing has become clear in the debate about the federal budget. Because federal expenditures are so large, almost everyone is sure that there is great potential to cut the budget in many areas. But in almost every *specific* area of government activity, supporters have been generally able to make good arguments against cuts. The "cut programs but not my programs" debate has often resulted in political stalemate. The current focus on "entitlements" should be viewed as part of the more general attempts of interest groups to shift the cuts to somebody else. Recent efforts to characterize the elderly as better off than the rest of the population (which we argued in Chapter 1 is a gross distortion of the truth) is, in part, an effort to shift attention from growing inequality and high-income people of *all ages*—especially from those who have received and will receive millions of dollars in government subsidies from nonaging programs and policies.

The American Dream at Risk?

The American dream is that for native sons and immigrants alike, ever-rising prosperity will guarantee each generation of people that works hard a high standard of living, with each generation living better than its predecessor. But has the end of the dream arrived?

Central to this discussion is the debate that has arisen in the United States over the causes of lagging economic growth and what has come to be known as the "**productivity** slowdown." There is still no consensus among economists on the extent and reasons for the slowdown in the 1970s and early 1980s. More important, no one knows for sure whether what happened then is just another "statistical blip" or instead reflects a long-term decline in American competitiveness and economic leadership. The higher rates of growth in the 1990s seem to support those who argue that growth has its ups and downs. One highly regarded study (Baumol et al., 1989) concludes that "there is absolutely no evidence of a long-term slowdown in the sectors of the economy that are most progressive in terms of productivity growth."

In 1999, the federal government announced the findings of a comprehensive review and revision of the nation's statistical accounts-measuring output. The government reported that the productivity slowdown was less severe in the 1970s than originally thought. And the productivity rate increases in the years that followed have also been larger than initially reported. Although the puzzle (and arguments) over productivity changes continue, the revised statistics support a more optimistic view of future growth. The numbers suggest that recent productivity gains are not just short-term gains but are based on positive structural shifts that will endure for many years to come.

While such findings offer encouraging prospects for the future, the economic difficulties of the recent past have had a negative impact on many people. Easterlin et al. (1990) point out that the baby boom generation has reacted to these adverse economic conditions and has sought to moderate the problems in three major ways: (1) increasing numbers have avoided parenthood and opted for childless living arrangements; (2) families with children have had a smaller number of children; and (3) more married women have been entering the paid labor force. Easterlin et al. predict, as a result, "that contrary to popular impression, the baby boom cohorts, on average, are likely to enter old age in an even better economic position than pre-boom cohorts." (A recent set of simulation projections by Lewin-VHI, Inc. [1994] agrees.)

Once again, it is important to point out that future productivity and economic growth have little to do with demographic aging: (1) There is no consensus (only major controversy) among economists that providing for a growing elderly population depresses investment through lower savings (see Chapters 3, 4, and 5); (2) most older workers are workers with productivity equal to or better than other workers (see Chapter 2 and below); (3) as just discussed, social security is not the cause of (or solution to) reducing a federal deficit; (4) and, while equity issues abound, the social security mechanism remains an economically efficient and politically effective way of providing a major part of the economic support all people require in old age.

If you ask economists what are the major factors determining our future economic growth, you will get a long list of items but little agreement on which are most important: saving, investment, research and development, "deficit reduction," political stability, managerial skills, incentive approaches, education and improvement of human capital, effective worker-retraining programs, minimizing "business cycles," and so on. "Population aging" might appear on a few lists but would be absent from most.

The demographic aging phenomenon may affect economic growth in ways we do not yet fully comprehend. Based on our past economic history and analysis to date, however, it seems clear that, while certainly worthy of study, the phenomenon should not be very high on the list of issues worrying policymakers concerned with economic growth in the future.

"PUT THE OLD FOLKS BACK TO WORK!"

A new buzzword is currently popular in discussions of social policy— "the Third Way" (for example, Giddens, 1999). The Third Way contrasts itself, on the one hand, with sole reliance on markets for economic and social welfare and, on the other hand, with almost exclusive reliance on social security to moderate the economic and social problems that arise from markets. The Third Way emphasizes programs (1) that help people to succeed in markets through the creation of jobs and employment opportunities, (2) that encourage those workers in the labor force to continue working, (3) that make people "marketable" through education and training programs, and (4) that provide incentives through wage subsidies, child and elder care, and transportation to where the jobs are (Myles and Quadagno, 2000).

With regard to old age, the Third Way focuses primarily on pension policy and the retrenchment of public plans. Despite the problems facing older workers (discussed in Chapter 2), there is a rising expectation that people should work longer, take more responsibility for their retirement planning, and expect less from government. This attitude is particularly strong among those who worry about the "rising tide" of the elderly in future years. Their solution: put the elderly back to work!

The composition of the labor force in the United States is undergoing a fundamental change as our population ages. Fewer younger people are entering the workforce each year. Beginning in 1981, there has been a sharp annual decline in the number of new entrants (see Figure 8–4). The result is a changing pattern of workers by age available for the workforce. Table 8–2 shows the decline in the younger worker categories and the very large growth rates for age 45 and above.

There are some in the United States who have very clear notions as to what our reaction to this change should be: if the number of younger workers is declining, then there will be more need (and better job opportunities) for older workers, *who are healthy, living longer, and should work more.*

Figure 8–4
Number of U.S. Workers Added to the Labor Force Each Decade (millions)

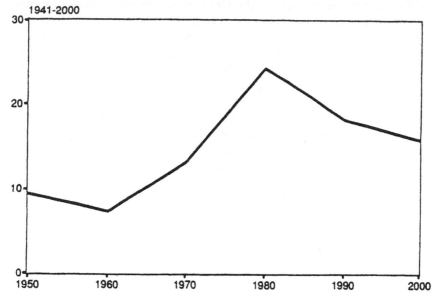

Source: Based on data in *America in the 21st Century: A Demographic Overview* (Washington, D.C.: Population Reference Bureau, 1989).

Table 8–2
Changes in the Number of American Workers by Age, 1986–2006

	Percent Change	
Age Group	1986–1996	1996–2006 (projected)
16-19	-02%	+14%
20–24	-13	+16
25–34	-02	-09
35–44	+34	-03
45–54	+49	+33
55–64	+02	+54
65+	+27	+10

Source: H. N. Fullerton, "Labor Force 2006: Slowing Down and Changing Composition," *Monthly Labor Review* (November 1997): Table 7.

However, that conclusion does not necessarily follow from what we know about past practice and current attitudes. The fact is that employers may not need, or be inclined to hire, older workers. Moreover, older people may not want the new jobs, even if they are offered.

Without dramatic changes in the ability of countries to moderate business cycles and keep unemployment low over the long run, there may be little change in current provisions that encourage retirement and early retirement. As in the past, we can expect employers, unions, politicians, and workers themselves to support mechanisms that encourage older workers to retire at increasingly early ages when unemployment is high (see Chapter 2).

The issue is further complicated by current attitudes of older workers toward work and training. As we grow older, most of us become very choosy about the work we do—especially if retirement becomes financially feasible through pension benefits. Also, with increasing age comes an understandable reluctance to uproot oneself and make the geographic move often associated with attractive employment opportunities.

Good Jobs, Bad Jobs

A stereotypical scenario of America's job situation in the future runs something like this: Under the pressure of foreign competition, the changing U.S. economy is producing overwhelming numbers of unappealing, low-paying jobs for people of all ages. With the declines in traditional manufacturing industries, more and more American workers (both young and old) will be forced in the future to sell chicken nuggets and hamburgers at Kentucky Fried Chicken and McDonald's.

Growth in jobs, according to this stereotype, lies in two typical areas: the expansion of eating and drinking establishments and the mushrooming computer industry. Both areas are seen as unattractive sources of jobs for many older workers. Work at McDonald's is tedious and pays poorly, whereas computer jobs are too demanding in their education and skill requirements. Hence, the argument goes, it will be hard to match the work desires of older workers with the jobs becoming available, unless older workers are ready to settle for "lousy jobs."

This view is incorrect. A closer look at the shifts taking place in our economy indicates that older workers can indeed be matched with appropriate jobs. *The problem lies not so much in the nature of the jobs and their skill requirements but in the attitudes of both older workers and their potential employers, in the rigid structure of the workplace, in current hiring practices, in the prevailing wage structure and compensation policies, and in attitudes toward training older workers.*

Look first at the nature of new jobs in the future. Working in fast food service jobs is not bad for all older workers. For some of them (especially those in semiretirement), a job at McDonald's is a good match: part-time, flexible schedules, pleasant surroundings with lots of people, low skill requirements, and a convenient distance to travel from home.

However, the overwhelming proportion of new jobs in the future will not be related to selling hamburgers. If one looks at Bureau of Labor Statistics predictions of the top dozen occupations with the largest future job growth potential, three points immediately stand out (Schulz, 1990). First, the range of jobs in the top growth categories is very diverse. Second, there is no concentration of future job openings in just a few occupational areas. Third, the list of most rapidly expanding jobs is not dominated by occupations (such as computer programmers, engineers, lawyers, physicians, and so on) that require long training or unique skills. Neither is it dominated by dead-end jobs.

Most of the new jobs in the future will be in a broad span of industries—including business services, medical services, construction, financial services, and information processing of many types. A large number of the new jobs in these industries are unexotic but often challenging, and can be done by a wide range of workers of any age. Examples are jobs as health care specialists, clerks, drivers, salespeople, maintenance personnel, and receptionists.

The Need for Retraining

The picture is not all rosy, however. In the major production efforts of the future, microchips, computers, and telecommunication equipment will probably play the same key roles as oil, steel, and automobiles did during the postwar era. But unlike steel and autos, production processes will be much less labor-intensive. Peter Drucker (1986) has pointed out, for example, that the manufacturing costs of a semiconductor microchip are about 70 percent knowledge (research, development, and testing); less than 12 percent of the costs are for labor going into production.

This shift in the nature of productive capacity, and the skill requirements associated with it, does indeed represent a significant threat to older workers—both in raising the probability of job obsolescence and in increasing the difficulty of making new job matches. Clearly, the transmission of new knowledge to older workers will take on new importance in the future.

Without a doubt, the most serious barrier to the reemployment of older workers today is the attitudes of the workers themselves and their potential employers, especially with regard to the issue of productivity and our ability to train older workers. Conventional notions about workers' abilities die hard. Many older workers and most employers truly believe that productivity almost always declines with age and, as the old saying goes, "old dogs cannot learn new tricks." Moreover, American work environments remain very rigid with regard to making adjustments to job requirements and remuneration patterns, making it nearly impossible to easily match older workers with existing employment opportunities.

How Will Business Respond?

Clearly, there is a need for major changes in our attitudes and practices regarding the training and employment of individuals over the life cycle. As the rate at which young people are entering the labor force slows, businesses will be forced to rethink how they will get the labor necessary for producing their products and services.

It is important to realize that firms can respond to this issue in a number of ways; recruiting and hiring different types of workers (such as older workers) is *only one of many ways*. They can invest in more physical capital that reduces labor needs; encourage liberalization of immigration policies favoring applicants with needed skills; encourage more women with children to stay in the labor force by, for example, offering day care facilities; or shift production processes to developing countries with labor surpluses and cheap wages.

Thus, the new demographic profile evolving in the United States (and other industrialized countries) does not necessarily mean there will be serious labor shortages in the future. Neither does it mean that all older workers will find that it is much easier to obtain suitable reemployment after losing or shifting jobs. However, the new demographics do provide an opportunity to devise and promote better policies and programs for a more efficient use of potential labor force participants. Raising the size and productivity of the labor force through manpower policies is a major alternative to current calls by some for cutbacks in retirement benefits for the old.

The biggest retirement issue of the next century is likely to be whether both workers and employers see the need and are willing to modify the retirement "right" to include what each group sees as viable work options in later life to complement the retirement life everyone now expects and almost all enjoy.

AGE IS NOT THE KEY VARIABLE

As this and prior chapters have shown, the question of a nation's ability to support various age groups at "appropriate levels" is very complex. Much of what is written today on the issue is too simplistic; it encourages us to look for solutions in the wrong places. Today, as in the past, the most important determinants of the future economic welfare of people (of all ages) are the factors we discussed above: savings and **investment** in human and business capital, technological change, entrepreneurial and managerial skills, government provision of infrastructure, and so on. Thus, we cannot overemphasize our belief that the debate over how best to run an economic system is not primarily an aging discussion. In fact, the aging of populations may have little to do with the outcome.

However, economic trade-offs must always be made. As a result, one thing is clear about the future costs of an aging population and our ability to meet those costs. The major economic issue we need to confront is not whether—in the face of other public expenditure problems such as urban blight, national defense, and pollution—we can have better pensions and services for the aged. *The key issue is how to promote general economic growth and whether we want that growth to provide a higher standard of living in our retirement years at the expense of a lower standard in our younger years.* While trade-offs must be continually made in the short run, rising incomes in retirement are closely related over the long run to sacrifices in consumption made in the earlier years. Whether we like it or not, the "economics of aging" begins for most of us quite early in life.

CHAPTER 8 HIGHLIGHTS

What are the economic implications of the "graying of America"? Some of the important points made in this chapter are:

1. The American population is aging, primarily as a result of declining fertility. Some people, often reacting to crude demographic ratios, fear a large economic burden arising from a growing elderly population.

2. Historically, *total labor force* dependency ratios have been slowly declining and, contrary to often-voiced concerns, are likely to decline even further in future years.

3. The public costs of pensions will increase in future years, but there are many years and many ways to respond to this issue.

4. The current generational equity debate is dominated by a crude demographic determinism that provides little insight into the issue and fails to take into account past and current realities about the politics of income transfers among subgroups of the population.

5. The "entitlement" debate is a debate over whose income should be cut to reduce federal government expenditures, and should be viewed as a part of the more general, long-running debate about income distribution in the United States, especially between the rich and poor.

6. As was observed in Chapter 2, "everyone is in favor of keeping older people in the labor force except the unions, government, business, and older people." Current demographic and labor force trends are not likely to change that. But if we want to give more older people the chance to work, we will have to change older workers', governments', and employers' attitudes.

7. The contemporary economic growth debate is not primarily a debate about population aging.

SUGGESTED READINGS

American Association of Retired Persons (AARP). "Entitlements and the Federal Budget Deficit: Setting the Record Straight." Washington, D.C.: AARP, n.d. The report provides wide-ranging statistics and graphs that address this issue.

Coale, Ansley. "How a Population Ages or Grows Younger." In Ronald Freedman, ed., *Population: The Vital Revolution*. New York: Anchor Books, Doubleday and Co., 1964, pp. 4–57. A good place to begin for nondemographers who want to understand the fundamental aspects of any demographic aging process.

Disney, Richard. *Can We Afford to Grow Older?* London: The MIT Press, 1996. An excellent, but sometimes technical, discussion of population aging, pensions, and a variety of other relevant topics.

Easterlin, Richard A. "Economic and Social Implications of Demographic Patterns in the United States." In Robert H. Binstock and Linda George, eds., *Handbook of Aging and the Social Sciences*, 4th ed. New York: Academic Press, 1995. An excellent discussion of the relationship between demographic aging and economic growth, concluding that demographic change has not been a major determinant of growth.

Friedland, Robert B., and Laura Summer. *Demography Is Not Destiny*. Washington, D.C.: National Academy on an Aging Society, 1999. An excellent, up-to-date discussion of population aging, entitlements, and the role of economic growth.

"International Challenges of an Aging World." *Generations* 17 (Winter 1993). A collection of many short articles on the economic and political impact of demographic aging around the world.

Jackson, William A. *The Political Economy of Population Aging*. Cheltenham, U.K.: Edward Elgar, 1998. A comprehensive and highly analytical discussion of population aging issues with major attention to worker productivity, employment, retirement, and pension issues.

Kingson, Eric R., B. A. Hirshorn, and J. M. Corman. *Ties That Bind—The Interdependence of Generations*. Cabin John, Md.: Seven Locks Press, 1986. The interrelationships among demography, economics, and families with young and older persons are explored in this response to those preaching the message of intergenerational conflict.

Kingson, Eric R., and John B. Williamson. "The Generational Equity Debate: A Progressive Framing of a Conservative Issue." *Journal of Aging and Social Policy* 5(3)(1993): 31–53. An excellent survey of the controversy.

Schulz, James H. "Saving, Growth, and Social Security." In R. N. Butler, L. K. Grossman, and M. R. Oberlink, eds., *Life in an Older America*. New York: Century Foundation Press, 1999, pp. 121–150. Much of the generational conflict debate centers on an aging population decreasing savings and hence growth. This article argues that this view is bad economics.

U.S. Congressional Budget Office (CBO). *Baby Boomers in Retirement: An Early Perspective*. Washington, D.C.: CBO, 1993. This study focuses on how the incomes and wealth of Baby Boomers compare with those of their parents as young adults, assesses the financial health of current retirees as a basis for comparison, and discusses factors that will influence the well-being of retirees in the next century.

Williamson, Jeffrey G. "Productivity and American Leadership: A Review Article." *Journal of Economic Literature* 29 (March 1991): 51–68. A good introduction and comprehensive summary of the literature and debate over the "productivity slowdown."

Notes

CHAPTER 1

1. Terms in boldface type throughout the book are defined in the Glossary at the end of the book.

2. The official poverty rate for aged persons was 35.2 percent in 1959. Unofficial rates for earlier periods may have exceeded 50 percent, but such estimates are controversial due to changes over time in living standards.

3. Radner (1991) finds that the share of earnings increased slightly between 1984 and 1989 for aged "units"—families of two or more and single persons living with no relative.

4. Only income, payroll, and property taxes are included in this estimate.

5. "This credit is intended to remove inequities between individuals who receive retirement or disability income which is not tax-exempt and individuals who receive Social Security, which is mostly tax-exempt. Almost all people who are able to take advantage of the credit have annual income below $30,000" (U.S. House Committee on Ways and Means, 1993).

6. While many of the special provisions have been eliminated or modified (as discussed in the text), a new one has been added and an important one remains unchanged: the Tax Reform Act of 1986 provides an advantage to older persons. Persons receiving a large lump-sum income distribution (typically from a pension plan) can use "five-year income averaging" if they reached age 50 before January 1, 1986. Averaging reduces income taxes under the current moderately **progressive tax schedule**. There are also many special tax provisions related to the costs of physical or mental disability at all ages (see Talley, 1992).

7. The costs of renting are typically more than for owning living quarters, in large part because landlords charge for their efforts.

8. An interesting alternative approach to measuring poverty (defined as people with "equivalent disposable income" below half the median) is found in a recent seven-country comparative study (Smeeding et al., 1990).

9. An excellent detailed history of the index is provided in Fisher (1992).

10. Originally, the index distinguished between farm and nonfarm families and between male- and female-headed families. These distinctions were eliminated in 1981. At the same time the maximum family size was expanded from "7 or more" to "9 or more."

11. See Fisher (1992) for details on a number of minor changes made over the years.

12. A comparison of various scales can be found in Buhmann et al. (1988).

13. See, for example, Danziger et al. (1984), Smeeding (1989), Crystal and Shea (1990), Radner (1990), and U.S. Bureau of the Census (1991). A discussion of these and other studies can be found in Radner (1993b).

14. During periods of high inflation (e.g., the early 1980s), nominal interest rates, which include an inflation premium, often rise and can be significantly higher. Some of that additional income can be saved to offset the decline in the real value of the asset.

15. Hollister and Palmer (1972), Torda (1972), Mirer (1974), King (1976), Borzilleri (1978), Michael (1979), DRI (1980), Minarik (1981), Barnes and Zedlewski (1981), Bridges and Packard (1981), and U.S. Bureau of Labor Statistics (1988).

CHAPTER 2

1. Terms in boldface type throughout the text are defined in the Glossary at the end of the book.

2. Public pensions in Japan will in *future* years, for *future* workers, provide benefits that are as high as in other countries. The inadequate benefits received by many today are in large part a result of the pre-pension and transition years.

3. The Bureau of Labor Statistics defines a dislocated worker as someone who is age 20 or older with three or more years of job tenure and who has lost or left a job as a result of a plant closing or relocation, slack work, or the elimination of a position or shift.

4. Reporting rates are also dependent on both the extent to which recourse procedures are advertised and generally known and on potential claimants' perceptions as to how they will be treated.

5. The Medoff study finds that the relative vulnerability of those 55 and over (versus those 16 to 34) declined but cannot explain the result. As the discussion in this chapter indicates, an "age 55 and over" category is probably too large to distinguish among the wide variability in labor force behavior and employment *options* existing among workers in this age range.

6. There has been disagreement among pension analysts as to how to measure such costs. Two alternative basic methods are to evaluate "termination benefits" versus "projected benefits" (Ippolito, 1985).

7. Shanas et al. (1968), Cottrell and Atchley (1969), Atchley (1971), Streib and Schneider (1971), Atchley (1976), Atchley and Robinson (1982), Foner and Schwab (1983), and Palmore et al. (1984).

8. A prior exemption for tenured faculty, firefighters, police, and corrections officials expired at the end of 1993.

9. Work ethic was measured (1) by answers to the question: "If by some chance, you were to get enough money to live comfortably without working, do you think you would work anyway?" and (2) by the individual's score on a four-point scale based on reactions to five statements about work and retirement asked in the 1978 survey.

CHAPTER 3

1. A full description of how this estimate was made can be found in Schulz and Carrin (1972). Alternative estimates are found in Morgan (1977) and Diamond (1977).

2. See Chapters 4 and 5 for discussions of these and other social security issues.

3. Of course, those who died before, or very shortly after, retirement did not experience this positive transfer. However, in most cases their spouses did, given the widow benefit.

4. We ignore here the tax-preferred status of pensions in the United States. Also, see Lazear (1986) for the view of some labor economists that pension plans are part of an efficient contract to enhance labor productivity.

CHAPTER 4

1. The railroad retirement program was integrated with the social security system in 1974. We do not discuss the railroad retirement system in this book. Those interested in developments should see Skolnik (1975) or U.S. Senate Special Committee on Aging (1991).

2. Unless a federal employee has voluntarily transferred to the new retirement system for civil servants.

3. The 20 percent noncoverage estimate is reported in Detlefs et al. (1993).

4. Railroad workers are also technically not covered, but their pension program is closely coordinated by law with social security.

5. As we discussed previously, the goal of (nearly) universal coverage was achieved by gradually extending coverage in different years to groups not covered originally.

6. We discuss in Chapter 5 the question of who pays the employer contribution—the employee through reduced wages, consumers through higher prices, or the firm itself.

7. If the individual does not have a sufficient number of years of eligible work with some amount of earnings, zeros are entered into the averaging calculation for the "nonwork years" (to complete the 35-year requirement).

8. The law now requires that SSA, beginning in fiscal year 2000, send an annual unsolicited statement to persons age 25 and over.

9. "New" federal employees are now covered by social security (see Chapter 7).

10. For a more detailed listing and discussion or arguments for and against the test, see Schulz (1977) or Colberg (1978).

11. This figure has appeared in many reports and publications discussing social security benefit levels and is based on a methodology and estimates developed by the Office of the Actuary of the Social Security Administration.

12. The study is a sample of *workers* who were *new* recipients of benefits. Replacement rates were calculated separately for male and female retiring workers. The replacement rate for couples shown in the text is the rate for couples where the *male* worker is the "new beneficiary." Replacement rates for couples of retiring female workers were significantly higher (62 percent).

13. See Boskin et al. (1986) for alternative and much higher replacement rates based on "real career average earnings" (as opposed to the high three of the last ten). We do not think, however, that average lifetime earnings are a good basis for retirement planning or pension adequacy assessment. Most pension planners currently use some type of *final* earnings measure. See Fox (1982) for an earlier study similar to the one by Grad, discussed in the text.

CHAPTER 5

1. Copyright 1973 by the New York Times Company. Reprinted by permission.

2. A year later, the earnings base for 1974 was raised to $13,200.

3. In 1993, the earnings ceiling for the Medicare payroll tax was eliminated, effective 1994.

4. This point is discussed again in Chapter 7, when employer-sponsored plans are discussed.

5. We do not present the relatively technical explanation for this result. Interested readers should see Thompson (1974).

6. In addition, a six-month delay in granting cost-of-living increases and shifting the inflation adjustment from July of each year to the following January, not only resulted in expenditure reductions in the short run but will also have a significant impact on outlays over the long run.

7. Such amount cannot exceed the smaller of: (1) 85 percent of the social security benefits; or (2) 50 percent of such benefits, plus 85 percent of such excess over $25,00 as exceeds $9,000 (i.e., 85 percent of the excess of the "income" over $34,000).

8. Congress removed the social security trust funds from the deficit reduction guidelines (the Gramm-Rudman-Hollings deficit-reduction, budget-cutting process) in 1990.

9. See Dye (1985) for a summary of a number of empirical studies of payroll tax incidence.

CHAPTER 6

1. If another hospital admission occurs 60 days after the individual is discharged from the hospital or skilled nursing facility, he or she is subject to another deductible and any co-payments.

2. Hospice patients need not pay more than $5 for each prescription related to symptom management and pain relief.

3. Two other significant programs, unemployment insurance and the food stamp program, are not discussed.

4. A worker disabled before age 31 needs one-half the quarters after age 21, with a minimum of six such quarters.

CHAPTER 7

1. Actually, pensions were not mentioned in the Internal Revenue Codes until 1926, but plans were treated like profit-sharing and stock bonus plans.

2. Coming at a time of sharp personal and corporate federal income tax increases, the Revenue Act of 1942: (1) treated employer contributions to qualified pension plans as tax deductible; (2) excluded plan investment income from taxation; and (3) deferred taxes on participant beneficiaries until actually received in retirement. The net effect was to discourage plan formation but to encourage worker participation in existing plans.

3. Not discussed are: Employee Stock Ownership Plans (ESOP), in which companies make employee retirement contributions that are primarily in the form of the company's stock and Section 403(b) plans for certain nonprofit organizations and public schools.

4. Plans under Section 401(K) originated many years before 1978, were "frozen" in 1974, and "unfrozen" in 1978.

5. Some defined contribution plans provide options; the Teachers Insurance and Annuity Association pension plan (TIAA/CREF) is, for example, such an exception.

6. For a critique of the "super IRA" approach, see Meyer (1987).

7. We do not discuss this option in the book. For a good overview of ESOPs see EBRI (1990), Chapter 10.

8. Deferred profit-sharing plans are often listed as defined contribution plans. For the reason given previously, we exclude them.

9. Allen et al. (1993) provide data for four other time periods, showing that their estimates are sensitive to the time period chosen. They find the highest average of ad hoc adjustment by firms relative to inflation was 30 percent, measured over the 1980–1985 period. See also Schmitt (1984) on this issue.

10. The LTV Corporation and the Pension Benefit Guaranty Corporation were locked for many years in a legal battle over who should assume responsibility for the plans' liabilities. In 1990, the Supreme Court ruled that the PBGC had to assume the liabilities resulting from the terminations.

11. Because of space limitations and the complexity of the issues, we do not discuss in this section a number of major problems that have also arisen in connection with insuring multiemployer plans. Also, we do not discuss the very recent concerns about insured pension annuities and whether these benefits are (should be) protected by ERISA.

12. The PBGC covers only plans meeting section 401 requirements of the Internal Revenue Code.

13. The Single-Employer Pension Plan Amendment Act of 1986.

14. These percentages are for new personnel covered by the 1986 amendments to the military pension law. Personnel covered by the old program receive 50

percent after twenty years. Benefits for new personnel are reduced (over previous levels) by one percentage point for each year of service less than thirty.

CHAPTER 8

1. They also pay indirectly as a result of the lost wages and time given up while providing services, care, and supervision at home.

2. The proportion of children age 18 or younger residing in households with incomes below the federal poverty index rose from about 15 percent in 1974 to 22 percent in 1991 (U.S. House Committee on Ways and Means, 1993).

Glossary

Accrued benefits. Pension benefits are typically based on the number of years a person works with an employer or works under a particular plan sponsored by that employer. In addition, the worker's level of earnings in specified years is also used frequently to determine benefits. Thus, each year worked results in accumulated pension rights to future payments, if all other required conditions are met. Based on the plan rules, government regulations, the benefit formula, and actuarial assumptions, the amount accumulated can be calculated. This amount is generally called the accrued benefit.

Actuarial. Cost projections that take into account (for pensions) the number of employees retiring and dying each year, labor force turnover, the benefit formula, plan expenses, and investment income.

Advisory Council on Social Security. In accordance with federal law, an advisory group is appointed every four years to report to the Social Security Administration, Congress, and the president on social security affairs. The function of the council has usually been to review all aspects of the social security program and to recommend improvements. However, some councils have been asked to focus exclusively on certain issues or problems. The council issues a formal report, which is available to all interested persons.

Age Discrimination in Employment Act. Originally enacted by the federal government in 1967 "to promote employment of older persons based on their ability rather than age; to prohibit arbitrary age discrimination in employment; and to help employers and workers find ways of meeting problems arising from the impact of age on employment." The original act prohibited discrimination based on age against persons ages 40 to 65. Amendments in 1978 raised the upper age limit to 70 but eliminated all age limits for most federal employees. In October 1986, amendments prohibited job termination *at any age* on the basis of age—temporarily excluding for seven years police officers, firefighters, prison guards, and tenured academic faculty. Fully excluded are employees in small businesses (fewer than twelve employees).

Annuities. These financial instruments are agreements that specify that a company or government will make regular payments of income for a specified amount of time—say, twenty years or (more often) until the recipient dies. In the private sector, annuities are typically issued by insurance companies, with the amount of payment dependent on the lump-sum amount paid in at start-up and on the individual's age (which is a key determinent of probable life expectancy). Annuities often specify that upon the death of the holder, some percentage of the payment will continue to be paid to a surviving beneficiary (such as a spouse) until his or her death. The basic idea of the annuity is to provide a mechanism that allows individuals to avoid the possibility of running out of income if they live an unusually long number of years. Using the insurance principle discussed in Chapter 3, the costs of payments for persons who have exceptionally long lives is paid for by those who, unfortunately, die young.

Breaks in service. Pension plans often have requirements regarding the number of years of employment required to participate in, be vested, or accumulate a certain amount of benefits. One important aspect of this counting process is determining when a "break" in employment occurs, terminating the continued accumulation or counting of the service years necessary to comply with various plan provisions. ERISA (described below) contains very specific rules with regard to how years of service should be counted.

British "Poor Laws." Passed originally to suppress vagrancy and begging, these laws (passed in a series of legislative acts) were in effect throughout the 16th to early 20th centuries. For example, the Elizabethan Poor Law Act of 1601 provided relief at the parish level to those unable to work, but it also established unpleasant workhouses for those unemployed but able to work. The main idea of the laws was to help the poor but to make sure laziness was not rewarded by demeaning those individuals receiving the relief and punishing those unable or unwilling to work in normal jobs. After World War II, the poor laws were largely replaced by reform legislation anchored in public pensions.

Capital. In economics, the word "capital" is used in two ways. As a real investment concept it refers to actual buildings and equipment used to produce goods and services; as a financial concept it refers to the monetary funds used to finance business enterprises, including the acquisition of economic capital.

CDs. "Certificates of deposit" are financial assets issued by banks for a specified term at a specified rate of interest.

Cohort. The word cohort refers to a group. It is commonly used in demographic and economic discussions to refer to a group of people born over a specified time period ("birth cohorts"). For example, one might refer to the cohort of people born in the Great Depression years of the 1930s or to the cohort we refer to as "Baby Boomers" (born in the later 1940s and early 1950s).

Coinsurance. Coinsurance payments are often required by health insurance programs to keep costs down. Under such arrangements, individuals are required to pay (out-of-pocket or through other insurance) some percentage of the covered costs, with the primary insurer usually paying the rest. For example, under Part B of Medicare, the program pays only 80 percent of covered charges—after the deductible provision is met. (See also **deductible**.)

Comparative advantage. In an extension of the theoretical advantages of the free trade to international trade, economists assert that nations should specialize in producing and exporting goods that they are most efficient at manufacturing, and that they should import goods from other countries that they are less efficient in producing. It is argued that all nations will benefit by this economic "law of comparative advantage." The biggest issue that arises in practice is that international competition, and the resulting imports from abroad, typically result in the loss of domestic jobs related to the production of similar goods. The result is political pressure from the businesses and workers affected, who ask the governments to either protect the domestic industries or compensate the businesses and workers for some of the hardship created.

Consumer Price Index. An **index** (see definition in this glossary) developed by the federal government to measure broad changes in prices affecting individuals and households. While the index is an indicator of general changes, it does not necessarily accurately measure the impact of price changes on consumers of different characteristics and various income levels.

Deductible. A common technique for reducing the costs of insurance companies is to set an initial amount that must be paid by the person being insured, before benefits begin under the insurance policy. For example, under Part B of Medicare, an individual must pay the first $100 of covered expenses *each year* before Medicare begins paying for additional expenses. (See also **coinsurance**.)

Deferred profit-sharing plan. A plan in which the company's contributions are based primarily or exclusively on business profits. Profits are credited to employee accounts to be paid (along with interest accrued) at retirement or other stated dates or circumstances (for example, at separation or upon either disability or death). Two other types are "cash plans" that pay out when profits are determined and "combination plans" that give employees the option of deferring all or part of the profit-sharing allocation.

Defined benefit plans. Pension plans that state before retirement how much they will pay in benefits at retirement, benefits usually varying by years of service and/or earnings. These plans contrast with defined contribution plans that specify certain contributions to be made on an employee's behalf; the benefit is then determined at retirement on the basis of the total contribution accumulated.

Defined contribution plan. See **defined benefit plans**.

Deflationary economic policy. Economists have shown that government tax and expenditure policies can have a major impact on the level of total demand for a nation's goods and services. Many economists believe that government tax and expenditure policies, as a consequence, have an important effect on the levels of unemployment and inflation. Policies that result in increased government spending or reduced levels of taxation (putting more money into the hands of the private sector) are viewed as "expansionary" in terms of the general level of economic activity and, in periods of low unemployment, inflationary. Decreased spending or increased taxes are viewed as having the opposite effect—tending to reduce overall economic activity and increasing unemployment in periods of economic slack. The latter policies are referred to as "deflationary."

Dependency ratios. A numerical measure that compares (divides) the number of older and/or younger persons, typically over age 65 and under age 18, with (by) persons in the middle ages (e.g., ages 18 to 64). For example, the "aged dependency ratio" is projected to increase from its current level of 19 elderly persons (per 100 persons ages 18 to 64) to 37 per 100 in the year 2030. But simultaneously, the proportion of the population under 18 will decline over the next several decades. The net result is that the **overall** dependency ratio will be lower than it was in the 1960s.

Depreciation allowance. A charge against the current income of a business to reflect the using up or "wear and tear" on a certain amount of its assets, primarily buildings and equipment. This charge is not paid out to other businesses but is retained within the firm and entered as a bookkeeping entry.

Depression. The recurrent ups and downs in the level of economic activity that extend over a period of years are referred to as the "business cycle." Depression usually refers to extreme low levels of economic activity extending over a long period (not seasonally). The Great Depression of the 1930s extended over almost a decade and resulted, at one point, in about one-quarter of the workforce being unemployed.

Discount rate. The "present price" of something whose receipt is deferred for some period is sometimes known as a discounted value. The term "discounting" is suggested by the fact that, at positive rates of interest, $1 due in a year (i.e., deferred for a year) has a "present value" of less than $1. The lower present price of a future amount due is the "discounted" value of the future amount due. The interest rate used for discounting is known as the discount rate.

Disregard. A term used to refer to provisions in means-tested financial support programs that exempt certain amounts of financial resources in determining benefit eligibility. For example, in the SSI program, $20 per month of unearned income is disregarded in determining whether an applicant's total income falls below the level specified for payment of benefits.

Entitlement. This term is generally used to refer to government expenditures where the traditional annual budgetary review is not required. Legislation enacted in a prior year specifies that the government pay specified benefits based on a set of eligibility rules. Unless the entitlement is terminated or changed, the government is required to make the necessary funds available. Major entitlement programs are farm price supports, Medicare, old-age pensions under social security, and Food Stamps.

Equity (home equity). The accumulated value (less any liabilities) of a property or business. In the typical home mortgage situation, the homeowner gradually repays the loan used to purchase the house, while paying interest on the outstanding loan amount. Thus the portion of the home value "owned" by the person gradually increases over time and is known as his or her equity in the property.

Equivalency scale. An index (defined below) that takes account of differences in family size, composition, health status, age, sex, and other relevant characteristics when determining the level of income necessary to achieve a given level of economic well-being.

ERISA (Employee Retirement Income Security Act of 1974). Federal legislation establishing participation, vesting, funding standards, plan termination insurance, disclosure requirements, and individual retirement accounts (IRAs).

Federal Reserve. A central banking system for the United States established in 1913. There are twelve district banks and a coordinating seven-member Federal

Reserve Board of Governors in Washington, D.C. Appointed by the president to the Board of Governors for fourteen-year terms, members constitute a body that has been purposely established as an independent monetary authority.

Fertility rate. The total fertility rate is the number of births that 1,000 women would have in their lifetime if, at each year of age, they experienced the birth rates occurring in the specified calendar year. The fertility rate is an annual (or percentage) measure, even though it is expressed as a hypothetical lifetime (or cohort) measure.

FICA. The Federal Insurance Contribution Act. The legislation specifying the amount of payroll taxes that must be paid on earnings by employers, employees, and the self-employed.

Fiduciary standards. The expected or legally specified behavior of individuals or institutions entrusted with authority to make financial decisions on behalf of or affecting other persons or institutions. ERISA sets out a detailed body of law governing the behavior and decisions of people and institutions managing pension funds on behalf of future beneficiaries.

Fiscal policy. Action by the government to influence the economy (especially to promote employment and decrease inflation) through changing tax rates and expenditure levels.

Gross domestic product (GDP). A national accounting concept that measures the market value of all final goods and services *produced within* a country (i.e., excluding net production abroad), over a given period of time. (See also **gross national product**.)

Gross national product (GNP). A national accounting concept that measures the market value of all final goods and services produced by *the permanent residents* of a nation (at home and abroad), within a given period of time (typically a year). (See also **gross domestic product**.)

Health maintenance organizations (HMOs). A special kind of group medical practice operating under a prepayment plan. HMOs provide a wide range of medical services in and outside a hospital for a specified premium. Operating in a more competitive environment, providers of medical services under these plans are encouraged to keep costs down and to emphasize preventive health care, because their monetary gains depend on keeping costs under the prepaid fees received from the covered group (or their employers).

Hospice. Programs specializing in social and health care services to the terminally ill, usually emphasizing care provided in the home. To be eligible for hospice benefits under Medicare, a person's physician must judge that the person has less than six months to live.

Householder. A technical term used by U.S. statistical agencies. The term refers to the person (or one of the persons) in whose name the home is owned or rented. If the house is owned jointly by a married couple, either the husband or the wife may be listed first, thereby becoming the reference person, or householder, to whom the relationship of the other household member is recorded. One person in each household is designated as the "householder."

Income. For every dollar of goods or services produced and sold there is a dollar of income created. Thus, we speak about both the national product and the national income of a country. People, as workers or owners of capital or natural resources, receive income in return for the services provided by factors of production (land, labor, and capital) in the production process.

Index(ing). The use of mathematical ratios to make comparisons between two different periods of time (or comparisons between different locations, industries, nationalities, etc.). The consumer price index is probably the most well-known index, comparing "average" prices in a given year with those in a predetermined base year.

Individual Retirement Account (IRA). Workers in families not covered by a retirement plan who have incomes below specified ceilings (see text) can make tax-deductible contributions of 15 percent of earned income up to $2,000 per year to an individual account or annuity. Funds in IRAs may be placed in a life insurance company, a bank, a mutual fund, or in certain special government bonds. There are penalties and immediate tax liability if funds are withdrawn prematurely.

Inflation. A general and widely diffused increase in the level of prices for various goods and services. The result is a loss in the purchasing power of money, customarily measured by various price indexes (e.g., the consumer price index). Inflation hurts those whose incomes do not rise as fast as prices increase: people with fixed or slowly rising income and savers who lend money. A rise in the index of prices means that it will take more money to buy the same amount of goods and services.

Investment. Economic investment is an activity (usually by business) that uses the resources of a nation to maintain or add to its stock of physical capital (i.e., buildings and equipment). The main source of investment expenditure is the retained earnings (defined below) and depreciation allowances of business. Expenditures, however, are also made possible by savings from households (1) by direct borrowing or by sale of new stock issues or (2) indirectly via financial institutions.

Life cycle hypothesis. Economists have speculated over the years on the savings behavior of individuals. One popular hypothesis (initially proposed by Franco Modigliani) is that individuals build up savings for retirement, which are then spent down before death. Thus, the hypothesis predicts major dissavings in the later years of life (apart from assets people wish to pass on to heirs).

Life expectancy. A statistical measure of the average number of years persons born in a given year can be expected to live under the conditions prevailing in that year. Life expectancy is measured both at birth and at other years (or stages) of life.

Lifetime rate of return. The interest rate that equalizes the compounded value of total taxes paid over a lifetime and the "present value" of the expected stream of benefits. A less technical definition is the rate at which the total value of accumulated payroll taxes (increased for interest) is equated to the value of benefits (decreased for interest). The present value of a sum of money due at a future date is the amount which, put at compound interest at a given rate, will accumulate to the sum specified at the stated date. The present value of, say, $1,000 six years hence at 5 percent is $746.30, since that sum compounded at 5 percent equals $1,000.

Managed care. This term encompasses a variety of interventions in health care delivery and financing designed to reduce costs by eliminating unnecessary and inappropriate care. The major elements of managed care are: (1) reviewing and intervening in decisions about health services; (2) limiting or influencing patient choice of providers; and (3) negotiating payment terms or levels with providers. One major way to manage care is through health maintenance organizations (defined above). Another is through preferred provider organizations (PPOs) that attempt to influence patient choice of provider through offering differential cost-sharing that rewards patients who select providers from the PPO network.

Marginal tax rate. The proportion of "last income" (i.e., the most recent part of total income received) paid in taxes. Because income is sometimes taxed at different rates as income increases, the marginal rate may differ significantly from the average rate. For example, the federal income tax on individuals is based on five basic rates—15 percent, 28 percent, 31 percent, 36 percent, and 39.6 percent.

Means test. A regulation stipulating that eligibility for aid and the amount of aid provided depend not, for example, on past employment or earnings but on the fact that the income and/or assets of the person (family) requesting assistance do not exceed a specified amount.

Median. A statistical measure that is often used instead of the mean (or average) to describe the center, middle, or "average" of a set of data. It is the value of the middle data term when the items are arranged in an increasing or decreasing order of magnitude. For example, the median of the data set 13 16 18 29 40 is 18.

Monetary policy. Action by the government to influence the economy by changing the demand for and supply of money.

Money income. Income before payment of federal, state, local, or social security (FICA) taxes and before any other deductions, such as union dues or Medicare premiums. Major components of money income are wages and salaries, self-employment income, social security and SSI, public assistance, interest, dividends, rents, unemployment and workers' compensation, other pension income, and alimony/child support. Excluded in almost all reported statistics are capital gains (or losses), lump-sum or one-time payments, and in-kind income.

National income accounting. A generally accepted methodology developed by economists to assist in describing and analyzing a nation's economy. Productive activity and income generated by that activity are measured and organized in a set of standardized tables called "the national accounts." Information from these accounts is used to derive specific economic measures, such as gross national product, national income, and personal income. The tables, and statistics based on them, are usually published by the governments concerned or international agencies such as the Statistics Division of the United Nations.

Negative income tax. A type of benefit proposed to deal with the problem of poverty. As the name implies, a negative income tax is an "income tax in reverse." Income tax programs collect revenues from individuals who have taxable income in excess of certain deductions, exemptions, and credits. In contrast, a negative income tax would require the government to make payments to individuals with incomes below some specified poverty level. Thus, such plans subsidize people with low incomes.

Net worth. An accounting measure of the total value of assets minus the value of any liabilities (i.e., debts).

Overfunded pension plans. Pension plans (either by law or, in a few cases, by convention) maintain assets to meet future liabilities. When plan assets exceed liabilities, this is commonly referred to as overfunding. ERISA (discussed above) requires that only liabilities accrued up to termination be covered. Since many plan benefits are based on employee earnings (which generally increase over time), termination liabilities are typically lower than liabilities calculated on an ongoing basis. Hence, the term "overfunding" is not free from ambiguity and measurement issues.

Part-time employment. The conventional measure used by American statistical agencies to define part time is less than 35 hours of work per week. A "part-time worker" is defined as a worker who works part time in a majority of the weeks worked during the year.

Past service credits (benefits). Pension plans often credit workers for years of work with the firm prior to the actual establishment of the pension plans. Because most plans pay benefits based on formulas that raise pension levels with years of service, this provision is important for older workers.

Payroll tax. Employees and employers and the self-employed each pay mandated taxes on earnings in covered social security employment and self-employment up to a legislated maximum taxable amount. The rate for employers and employees is specified under the current Federal Insurance Contribution Act (FICA). The self-employed are covered by the Self-Employment Contributions Act (SECA).

Pension. A fixed dollar amount that is paid regularly over time by a former employer or the government to a retired, disabled, or deserving person (or his or her dependents). The amount may be increased partially or fully in later years to compensate for inflation.

Pension replacement rate. The ratio of retirement income to preretirement income. The definition (or measure) of both numerator and denominator varies. One of the most important measures is the ratio of *pension* income to preretirement earnings. Pension income is typically measured at the "normal retirement age" or at the time of initial start-up of the pension. Earnings are typically an average of the years just before retirement—last three years, high five of the last ten, and so on.

Portability. A type of vesting (defined below) mechanism that allows employees to take their pension credits with them when they change jobs. For credits to be portable, they must be vested—that is, nonforfeitable. ERISA permits portability but only if both the employee and the involved employer mutually agree.

Present value. The present value of a sum of money due at a future date is the amount that, put at compound interest at a given rate, will amount to the sum specified at the stated date. The present value of, say, "$1,000 six years hence at 5 percent" is $746.30, because that sum compounded at 5 percent (for six years) equals $1,000.

Private pensions. Pensions obtained through employment in the nongovernment sector of the economy. (See also **pension**.)

Productivity. An economic concept defined as the total output of a good or service divided by the total number of work-hours expended in producing the goods. Productivity is influenced by such major factors as the level of technology, changes in capital plant and equipment, and the quality of the labor force.

Profit-sharing plan. See **deferred profit-sharing plan**.

Progressive tax. A tax that takes a larger proportion of income in taxes, the higher the income. The key to whether a tax is progressive or not lies in the increasing percentage of income paid in taxes, not in the increasing amount paid. Thus, the payroll tax is "proportional" up to the taxable earnings ceiling, but the federal income tax is progressive.

Qualified pension plan. After a pension plan is initially set up, formal legal documents are usually prepared for submission to the Internal Revenue Service, because few employers are willing to operate a plan whose costs are not deductible for tax purposes. The usual practice is for the employer to submit these documents and ask for a "determination letter" that indicates whether or not the plan qualifies under the relevant laws for special tax treatment.

Recession. A "mild" depression. (See **depression** defined above.)

Replacement rate. See **pension replacement rate**.

Retained earnings. Business income after expenses that is not paid out in dividends or government taxes.

Transfer income. Income that results from government disbursements for which no products or services are received. Most government welfare expenditures fall into this classification—social security payments, unemployment compensation, and so on. Transfer payments, in a sense, rechannel tax revenues of the public sector back into the hands of individuals and groups in the private sector.

Unemployment rate. A measure of the number unemployed as a percentage of the (usually) civilian labor force. The percentage is determined by surveying a sample of the population: those persons who did not work during the survey week, but were available for work (except for temporary illness) and had looked for jobs within the preceding four weeks.

Vesting. The pension rights of a terminating employee depend on the plan provisions. Vesting refers to the provision that gives a participant the right to receive an accrued benefit at a designated age, regardless of whether the employee is still employed at that time. Thus, vesting removes the obligation of the participant to remain in the pension plan until the date of early or normal retirement. ERISA currently requires that covered plans vest most workers fully at the end of five years. Companies, however, have the option of using an alternative vesting schedule, vesting 20 percent of the benefit after three years and increasing the amount to 100 percent at the end of seven years. Multiemployer plans are allowed to use a form of ten-year vesting.

Wage index. A measure of the change in general wage levels. Such an index is used in the social security program to adjust recorded wages of workers before calculating benefits. Thus, if a worker earned $3,000 in 1956, retired at age 65 in 1985, and wage levels were, say, two and one-half times higher than in 1956, the indexing factor of two and one-half would be applied to the $3,000 and the index earnings would be $7,500. (See also **indexing**.)

Workers' Compensation. Various state laws have created programs—some elective and some compulsory—that provide financial compensation to workers injured in work-related activities. Benefits are financed by contributions from employers, and in return these employers are relieved of liability from common-law suits. (That is, injured workers agree to accept the benefits under the law on a no-fault basis.) Benefits usually include cash payments, medical services, and rehabilitation opportunities.

References

This chapter does not include the "Suggested Readings" listed at the end of each chapter.

Aaron, Henry J. 1977. "Demographic Effects on the Equity of Social Security Benefits." In M. S. Feldstein and R. P. Inman, eds., *The Economics of Public Service*. New York: MacMillan, pp. 151–173.

———. 1981. "Salvaging Social Security." *The Brookings Bulletin* 17 (Spring): 13–16.

———. 1982. *Economic Effects of Social Security*. Washington, D.C.: Brookings Institution.

AARP (American Association of Retired Persons). 1987. "Older Workers Are Bearing Brunt of Most Downsizing Programs." *AARP News Bulletin* 28 (December): 1, 4–5.

———. 1991. *Women and Social Security: Challenges Facing the American System of Social Insurance*. Issue Brief No. 2. Washington, D.C.: Public Policy Institution.

———. 1995. *American Business and Older Workers*. Washington, D.C.: AARP.

AARP Public Policy Institute. 1991. *Home Equity Conversion in the United States*. Policy Paper No. 9102. Washington, D.C.: American Association of Retired Persons.

Acs, Gregory, and John Sabelhaus. 1995. "Trends in Out-of-Pocket Spending on Health Care." *Monthly Labor Review* 118(12): 35–45.

Adamchak, Donald J. 1993. "Demographic Aging in the Industrialized World: A Rising Burden?" *Generations* 17 (Winter): 6–9.

Ad Hoc Advisory Committee. 1975. "Social Security: A Sound and Durable Institution of Great Value." In U.S. Senate Special Committee on Aging, *Future*

Directions in Social Security—Unresolved Issues: An Interim Staff Report. Washington, D.C.: U.S. Government Printing Office.

Advisory Council on Social Security. 1939. *Final Report.* U.S. Senate Document 4, 76th Congress. Washington, D.C.: U.S. Government Printing Office.

———. 1975. *Reports.* Washington, D.C., reproduced.

———. 1979. *Social Security Financing and Benefits.* Washington, D.C., reproduced.

Aging America: Trends and Projections. 1991 edition. Washington, D.C.: U.S. Department of Health and Human Services.

Alcon, Arnaa. 1999. *An Introduction to the Financial Planning Industry.* Waltham, Mass.: Brandeis University, National Center on Women & Aging.

Allen, Steven G., Robert L. Clark, and Ann A. McDermed. 1993. *Post-Retirement Increases in Pensions in the 1980s: Did Plan Finances Matter?* Working Paper No. 4413. Cambridge, Mass.: National Bureau of Economic Research.

Amble, Nathan, and Ken Stewart. 1994. "Experimental Price Index for Elderly Consumers." *Monthly Labor Review* 117 (May): 11–16.

America in the 21st Century: A Demographic Overview. 1989. Washington, D.C.: Population Reference Bureau.

American Council of Life Insurance. 1992. *1992 Life Insurance Fact Book.* Washington, D.C.: American Council of Life Insurance.

Americans Over 55 at Work Program: Research Reports 1 and 2. 1993. New York: The Commonwealth Fund.

Anderson, G. F., and J. P. Poullier. 1999. "Health Spending, Access, and Outcomes: Trends in Industrialized Countries." *Health Affairs* 18(3): 178–192.

Andrisani, Paul J. 1977. "Effects of Health Problems on the Work Experience of Middle-Aged Men." *Industrial Gerontology* 4 (Spring): 97–112.

Annual Report of the Board of Trustees OASDI Trust Funds, 1997. 1997. Washington, D.C.: U.S. Government Printing Office.

Arenson, Karen W. 1981. "The Low U.S. Rate of Savings." *New York Times* (December 22): D1, D7.

Aspin, Les. 1976. "The Burden of Generosity." *Harper's* 253 (December): 22–24.

Atchley, Robert. 1971. "Retirement and Leisure Participation: Continuity or Crisis?" *The Gerontologist* 11 (Spring, Part 1): 13–17.

———. 1976. *The Sociology of Retirement.* New York: Wiley/Schenkman.

Atchley, Robert C., and Judith L. Robinson. 1982. "Attitudes Toward Retirement and Distance from the Event." *Research on Aging* 4 (September): 299–313.

Baker, Dean, and Mark Weisbrot. 1999. *Social Security: The Phony Crisis.* Chicago: University of Chicago Press.

Ball, Robert M. 1978. "Income Security for the Elderly." In *The Economics of Aging: A National Journal Issue Book.* Washington, D.C.: Government Research Corp., pp. 1748–1753.

———. 1987. "Don't Drain the Social Security Fund." *Washington Post* (August 30): C7.

———. 1994. Testimony before the Bipartisan Commission on Entitlement and Tax Reform. Washington, D.C., reproduced.

———. 1997. "The Maintain Benefits Plan for Social Security." In Dallas L. Salisbury, ed., *Assessing Social Security Reform Alternatives.* Washington, D.C.: Employee Benefit Research Institute, pp. 9–96.

Barnes, Robert, and Sheila Zedlewski. 1981. *The Impact of Inflation on the Income and Expenditures of Elderly Families*. Final Report to the Administration on Aging. Washington, D.C., reproduced.

Barro, Robert J. 1978. *The Impact of Social Security on Private Saving—Evidence from the U.S. Time Series*. Washington, D.C.: American Enterprise Institute.

Bass, Scott A., and Francis G. Caro. 1992. "The New Politics of Productive Aging." *Depth* 2(3): 59–79.

Bass, Scott A., Francis G. Caro, and Yung-Ping Chen. 1993. *Achieving a Productive Aging Society*. Westport, Conn.: Auburn House.

Bassett, Preston C. 1978. "Future Pension Policy and the President's Commission." *Employee Benefit Plan Review* 33 (December): 28, 30, 91.

Baumol, William J., Sue Anne Batey Blackman, and Edward N. Wolff. 1989. *Productivity and American Leadership: The Long View*. Cambridge, Mass.: MIT Press.

Becker, Gary S. 1986. "What Really Hurts the Job Market for Older Workers." *Business Week* (October 6): 15.

Bernheim, B. Douglas. 1993. *Is the Baby Boom Generation Preparing Adequately for Retirement?* Summary Report. New York: Merrill Lynch.

Best, Fred. 1978. "Preferences on Worklife Scheduling and Work-Leisure Trade-offs." *Monthly Labor Review* 101 (June): 31–37.

Bickerman, John. 1985. "Stockman Is Right: Military Pensions Are a Scandal." *The Washington Post National Weekly* (April 1): 24–25.

Binstock, Robert H. 1993. "Healthcare Costs Around the World: Is Aging a Fiscal 'Black Hole'?" *Generations* 17 (Winter): 37–42.

BNA. 1978. *Pension Reporter* 202 (August 21): A–9.

———. 1986. *Pension Reporter* 13 (January 20): 114.

Bodie, Zvi. 1990. "Pensions as Retirement Income Insurance." *Journal of Economic Literature* 28 (March): 28–49.

Bondar, Joseph. 1993. "Beneficiaries Affected by the Annual Earnings Test, 1989." *Social Security Bulletin* 56 (Spring): 20–28.

Borzilleri, Thomas C. 1978. "The Need for a Separate Consumer Index for Older Persons." *The Gerontologist* 18 (June): 230–236.

Boskin, Michael J. 1986. *Too Many Promises: The Uncertain Future of Social Security*. Homewood, Ill.: Dow Jones–Irwin.

Boskin, Michael, J., L. J. Kotlikoff, D. J. Puffert, and J. B. Shoven. 1986. "Social Security: A Financial Appraisal across and within Generations." Working Paper No. 1891. Cambridge, Mass.: National Bureau of Economic Research.

Boskin, Michael J., and D. J. Puffert. 1987. "Social Security and the American Family." In Lawrence H. Summers, ed., *Tax Policy and the Economy*. Cambridge, Mass.: MIT Press, pp. 139–159.

Boulding, Kenneth. 1958. *Principles of Economic Policy*. Englewood Cliffs, N.J.: Prentice-Hall.

Bradford, Kenneth. 1979. "Can You Survive Your Retirement?" *Harvard Business Review* (November/December): 103–107.

Bridges, B., and M. Packard. 1981. "Prices and Income Changes for the Elderly." *Social Security Bulletin* 44 (January): 3–15.

Brittain, John A. 1972. *The Payroll Tax for Social Security*. Washington, D.C.: Brookings Institution.

Broder, David S. 1973. "Budget Funds for Elderly Grow Rapidly." *Washington Post* (January 30): A-16.

Brody, Elaine M. 1985. "Parent Care as a Normative Family Stress." *The Gerontologist* 25 (February): 19–29.

Brown, J. Douglas. 1972. *An American Philosophy of Social Security*. Princeton, N.J.: Princeton University Press.

———. 1973. Memorandum. In U.S. Senate Special Committee on Aging, *Future Directions in Social Security*, Part 3. Washington, D.C.: U.S. Government Printing Office, pp. 220–221.

Bryce, David, and Robert B. Friedland. 1997. *Economic and Health Security: An Overview of the Origins of Federal Legislation*. Washington, D.C.: National Academy on an Aging Society.

Buhmann, B., Lee Rainwater, G. Schmaus, and Timothy M. Smeeding. 1988. "Equivalence Scales, Well-being, Inequality, and Poverty: Sensitivity Estimates Across Ten Countries Using the Luxembourg Income Study (LIS) Database." *Review of Income and Wealth* 34(2): 115–142.

Burke, Vincent J., and Vee Burke. 1974. *Nixon's Good Deed. Welfare Reform*. New York: Columbia University Press.

Burkhauser, Richard V., Karen C. Holden, and Daniel Feaster. 1988. "Incidence, Timing, and Events Associated with Poverty: A Dynamic View of Poverty in Retirement." *Journal of Gerontology: Social Sciences* 43 (March): S46–S52.

Burkhauser, Richard V., and J. P. Quinn. 1985. "Planned and Actual Retirement: An Empirical Analysis." In Z. S. Blau, *Current Perspectives on Aging and the Life Cycle*, Vol. 1. Greenwich, Conn.: JAI Press.

Burkhauser, Richard V., and T. M. Smeeding. 1994. *Social Security Reform: A Budget Neutral Approach to Reducing Older Women's Disproportionate Risk of Poverty*. Policy Brief No. 2/1994. Syracuse, N.Y.: Center for Policy Research, Syracuse University.

Burtless, G., and R. A. Moffitt. 1984. "The Effects of Social Security on the Labor Supply of the Aged." In H. Aaron and G. Burtless, eds., *Retirement and Economic Behavior*. Washington, D.C.: Brookings Institution, pp. 135–174.

Burtless, Gary. 1987. "Occupational Effects on the Health and Work Capacity of Older Men." In Gary Burtless, ed., *Work, Health, and Income among the Elderly*. Washington, D.C.: Brookings Institution, pp. 103–141.

Burtless, Gary, and Alicia H. Munnell. 1990. "Does a Trend Toward Early Retirement Create Problems for the Economy?" *New England Economic Review* (November–December): 17–32.

Butler, Robert N. 1989. "Productive Aging." In V. L. Bengtson and K. W. Schaie, eds., *The Course of Later Life*. New York: Springer, pp. 55–64.

Cahill, K. 1993. *Entitlements and Other Mandatory Spending*. CRS Report for Congress. Washington, D.C.: Congressional Research Service.

Callahan, James, and Stanley S. Wallack, eds. 1981. *Reforming the Long-Term Care System*. Lexington, Mass.: Lexington Books, D. C. Heath.

"Canadians and Americans at Polar Opposites in Satisfaction with Their Health Care Systems." 1990. *Ageing International* 17 (Winter): 4–5.

Cantor, Marjorie H., and Mark Brennan. 1993. *Growing Older in New York City in the 1990s*, Vol. 2. New York: New York Community Trust.

Cardwell, James B. 1976. Testimony. In U.S. House Committee on Ways and Means, Subcommittee on Social Security, *Disability Insurance Program.* Washington, D.C.: U.S. Government Printing Office, pp. 273–281.

Centaur Associates. 1986. *Evaluation Study of the Senior Community Service Employment Program.* Washington, D.C.: Centaur.

Center on Budget and Policy Alternatives. 1998. *Strength of the Safety Net.* Washington, D.C.: The Center.

Chakravarty, Subrata N., and K. Weisman. 1988. "Consuming Our Children?" *Business Week* (November 14): 222–232.

Chen, Yung-Ping, and Stephen C. Goss. 1997. "Are Returns on Payroll Taxes Fair?" In Eric R. Kingson and James H. Schulz, eds., *Social Security in the 21st Century.* New York: Oxford University Press, pp. 76–90.

Citro, C. F., and R. T. Michael, eds. 1995. *Measuring Poverty: A New Approach.* Washington, D.C.: National Academy Press.

Clark, Robert L. 1994. "Employment Costs and the Older Worker." In Sara E. Rix, ed., *Older Workers: How Do They Measure Up?* Washington, D.C.: Public Policy Institute, American Association of Retired Persons, pp. 1–26.

Clark, Robert L., D. T. Barker, and R. S. Cantrell. 1979. *Outlawing Age Discrimination: Economic and Institutional Response to the Elimination of Mandatory Retirement.* Final Report to the Administration on Aging, reproduced.

Clark, Robert L., and A. McDermed. 1989. "Pension Regulation and Pension Structure." Washington, D.C.: American Enterprise Institute.

Clark, Timothy B. 1983. "Congress Avoiding Political Abyss by Approving Social Security Changes." *National Journal* (March 19): 611–615.

———. 1985. "Too Much, Too Soon?" *National Journal* (September 21): 2172.

Coates, Edward M. 1991. "Profit Sharing Today: Plans and Provisions." *Monthly Labor Review* 114 (April): 19–25.

Cohen, Wilbur J. 1957. *Retirement Policies Under Social Security.* Berkeley: University of California Press.

Cohen, Wilbur J., and Milton Friedman. 1972. *Social Security: Universal or Selective?* Rational Debate Seminars. Washington, D.C.: American Enterprise Institute for Public Policy Research.

Cohen, Senator William S. 1993. Prepared statement. In U.S. Senate Special Committee on Aging, *How Secure Is Your Retirement: Investments, Planning, and Fraud?* Washington, D.C.: U.S. Government Printing Office, pp. 4–5.

Colberg, Marshall R. 1978. *The Social Security Retirement Test—Right or Wrong?* Washington, D.C.: American Enterprise Institute for Public Policy Research.

Combs, Ann L. 1997. "A Retirement System for the Future: Personal Security Accounts." In Dallas L. Salisbury, ed., *Assessing Social Security Reform Alternatives.* Washington, D.C.: Employee Benefit Research Institute, pp. 107–110.

Commonwealth Fund. 1991. *Older Workers Are Good Investments.* New York: The Commonwealth Fund.

———. 1993. *The Untapped Resource.* New York: The Commonwealth Fund.

Concord Coalition. 1993. *The Zero Deficit Plan.* Washington, D.C.: Concord Coalition.

Consumer Reports. 1991. "An Empty Promise to the Elderly?" 56 (June): 425–426, 429–441.

———. 1997. "How Agents Spin the Coverage." 62 (October): 47–48.

Cook, Fay Lomax. 1989. "Social Security and 'Crisis of Support'." *Northwestern Center on Aging Newsletter* 5 (Summer): 1–3.

Cook, Fay Lomax, and R. A. Settersten, Jr. 1995. "Expenditure Patterns by Age and Income Among Mature Adults: Does Age Matter?" *The Gerontologist* 35(1): 10–23.

Cottrell, Fred, and Robert C. Atchley. 1969. *Women in Retirement. A Preliminary Report*. Oxford, Ohio: Scripps Foundation.

Cowgill, Donald O. 1981. "Can We Afford Our Aging Populations?" Paper prepared for Conference on Economics of Aging, Kansas City, Missouri, April, reproduced.

Cowgill, Donald O., and Lowell D. Holmes. 1970. "The Demography of Aging." In A. M. Hoffman, ed., *The Daily Needs and Interests of Older People*. Springfield, Ill.: C. C. Thomas, pp. 27–69.

Crown, W. H., D. Mazur, P. Mutschler, M. Stubbs, R. Loew, and J. Callahan, Jr. 1990. *Pension and Health Benefits for State, Local, and Teacher Retirees: Coping with Inflation (1982–1987)*. Report to the AARP Andrus Foundation. Waltham, Mass.: Brandeis University.

Crown, William H., Phyllis H. Mutschler, James H. Schulz, and Rebecca Loew. 1993. *The Economic Status of Divorced Older Women*. Waltham, Mass.: Policy Center on Aging, Heller School, Brandeis University.

Crystal, Stephen, R. W. Johnson, J. Harman, U. Sambamoorthi, and R. Kumar. 2000. "Out-of-Pocket Health Care Costs among Older Americans." *Journal of Gerontology* 55B(1): S51–S62.

Crystal, Stephen, and Dennis Shea. 1990. "The Economic Well-Being of the Elderly," *Review of Income and Wealth* 36(3): 227–247.

Dale, Edwin L., Jr. 1973. "The Young Pay for the Old." *New York Times Magazine* (January 14): 8ff.

Danziger, Sheldon. 1984. "Implications of the Relative Economic Status of the Elderly for Transfer Policy." In H. J. Aaron and G. Burless, eds., *Retirement and Economic Behavior*. Washington, D.C.: Brookings Institution.

Danziger, Sheldon, J. Van Der Gaag, E. Smolensky, and M. K. Taussig. 1982–1983. "The Life-Cycle Hypothesis and the Consumption Behavior of the Elderly." *Journal of Post Keynesian Economics* 5 (Winter): 208–227.

Danziger, Sheldon, J. Van der Gaag, E. Smolensky, and M. K. Taussig. 1987. "Implications of the Relative Economic Status of the Elderly for Transfer Policy." In H. J. Aaron and G. Burtless, eds., *Retirement and Economic Behavior*. Washington, D.C.: Brookings Institution.

Davis, Karen. 1982. "Medicare Reconsidered." Paper prepared for the Duke University Medical Center Seventh Private Sector Conference on Financial Support of Health Care for the Elderly and Indigent. Durham, N.C., reproduced.

Denison, Edward F. 1979. *Accounting for Slower Economic Growth: The United States in the 1970s*. Washington, D.C.: Brookings Institution.

Derthick, Martha. 1990. *Agency Under Stress: The Social Security Administration in American Government*. Washington, D.C.: Brookings Institution.

Detlefs, D. R., R. J. Myers, and J. R. Treanor. 1993. *Guide to Social Security and Medicare*, 22nd ed. Louisville, Ky.: William M. Mercer, Inc.

Diamond, P. A. 1977. "A Framework for Social Security Analysis." *Journal of Public Economics* 8 (December): 275–298.

Diamond, Stephen L. 1993. Testimony. In U.S. Senate Special Committee on Aging, *How Secure Is Your Retirement: Investments, Planning, and Fraud?* Washington, D.C.: U.S. Government Printing Office, pp. 44–45.

Doctors, S. I., Y. M. Shkop, K. C. Denning, and V. T. Doctors. 1980. "Older Worker Employment Services." *Aging and Work* 3 (Fall): 229–237.

Doeringer, Peter B., ed. 1990. *Bridges to Retirement: Older Workers in a Changing Labor Market*. Ithaca, N.Y.: IRR Press.

Donahue, Wilma, Harold L. Orbach, and Otto Pollak. 1960. "Retirement: The Emerging Social Pattern." In Clark Tibbitts, ed., *Handbook of Social Gerontology*. Chicago: University of Chicago Press, pp. 330–406.

Dowd, James J., and Vern Bengtson. 1978. "Aging in Minority Populations." *Journal of Gerontology* 33 (May): 427–436.

Downs, Alan. 1994. "Tale of a Reformed Corporate Executioner." *The Christian Science Monitor* (March 15): 8.

Drazaga, Linda, M. Upp, and V. Reno. 1982. "Low Income Aged: Eligibility and Participation in SSI." *Social Security Bulletin* 45 (May): 28–35.

DRI (Data Resources, Inc.). 1980. *Inflation and the Elderly*. Report to NRTA/AARP. Lexington, Mass., reproduced.

Drucker, Peter F. 1986. "The Changed World Economy." *Foreign Affairs* 65 (Spring): 768–791.

Duggan, James E., Robert Gillingham, and John S. Greenlees. 1993. "Returns Paid to Early Social Security Cohorts." *Contemporary Policy Issues* 6 (October): 1–13.

Dye, Richard F. 1985. "Evidence of the Effects of Payroll Tax Changes on Wage Growth and Inflation: A Review and Reconciliation." *Eastern Economic Journal* 11 (April–June): 89–100.

Easterlin, Richard A., C. MacDonald, and D. J. Macunovich. 1990. "Retirement Prospects of the Baby Boom Generation: A Different Perspective." *The Gerontologist* 30 (December): 776–783.

EBRI (Employee Benefit Research Institute). 1989. *EBRI Issue Brief*, No. 96 (November).

———. 1990. *Fundamentals of Employee Benefit Programs*. Washington, D.C.: EBRI.

———. 1991. "IRA Deduction Eligibility Falls Under TRA '86." *Employee Benefit Notes* 12 (May): 1–4.

———. 1992. "Public Opinion on Health, Retirement, and Employee Benefits." *EBRI Issue Brief*, No. 132 (December).

———. 1993. "Facts from EBRI, Retiree Health Benefits." Washington, D.C.: EBRI.

———. 1994. "Characteristics of the Part-time Work Force." *Special Report*, No. 149. Washington, D.C.: EBRI.

———. 1996. "Hybrid Retirement Plans: The Retirement Income System Continues to Evolve." *Issue Brief*, No. 171 (March).

———. 1997a. *EBRI Databook on Employee Benefits*, 4th ed. Washington, D.C.: EBRI.

————. 1997b. *Fundamentals of Employee Benefit Programs*, 5th ed. Washington, D.C.: EBRI.

————. 1999a. "401(K) Plan Asset Allocation, Account Balances, and Loan Activity." *Issue Briefs* (January).

————. 1999b. "The 1999 Small Employer Retirement Survey: Building a Better Mousetrap Is Not Enough." *Issue Briefs* (August).

————. 1999c. "Projecting IRA Balances and Withdrawals." *EBRI Notes* (May).

Economist. 1984. "A Granny Crisis Is Coming." (May 19): 55.

Eichenwald, Kurt. 1995. *Serpent on the Rock*. New York: HarperBusiness.

Eisner, Robert. 1989. *The Total Incomes System of Accounts*. Chicago: University of Chicago Press.

Ekerdt, David J. 1987. "Why the Notion Persists that Retirement Harms Health." *The Gerontologist* 27 (August): 454–457.

Employee Benefit Plan Review. 1991. "Class Action Settlement to Cost $415 Million." 46 (February): 68–69.

————. 1993. "Concern about Long-Term Care Creates Generation of Worriers." 47 (October): 42.

————. 1994. "General Motors, IBM Implement Employee Health Plan Contributions." 48 (January): 42–43.

Epstein, Lenore A., and Janet H. Murray. 1967. *The Aged Population of the United States*. Office of Research and Statistics, Social Security Administration. Report No. 19. Washington, D.C.: U.S. Government Printing Office.

Esposito, Louis, L. B. Mallan, and D. Podoff. 1980. "Distribution of Increased Benefits under Alternative Earnings Tests." *Social Security Bulletin* 43 (September): 3–9.

"Fear of Future Pervades Ranks of Pre-retirees." 1994. *Horizons* 4 (April): 2–3.

Feldstein, Martin S. 1972. "The Incidence of the Social Security Payroll Tax: Comment." *American Economic Review* 42 (September): 735–742.

————. 1974. "Social Security, Induced Retirement, and Aggregate Capital Accumulation." *Journal of Political Economy* 82 (September–October): 905–926.

————. 1975. "Toward a Reform of Social Security." *The Public Interest* 40 (Summer): 80–81.

————. 1977. "Facing the Social Security Crisis." *The Public Interest* 47 (Spring): 88–100.

————. 1994. *Fiscal Policies, Capital Formation, and Capitalism*. Working Paper No. 4885. Cambridge, Mass.: National Bureau of Economic Research.

————, ed. 1998. "Introduction." In Martin Feldstein, ed., *Privatizing Social Security*. Chicago: University of Chicago Press, pp. 1–32.

Ferber, Marianne A. 1993. "Women's Employment and the Social Security System." *Social Security Bulletin* 56 (Fall): 33–55.

Ferrara, Peter J. 1986. "Intergenerational Transfers and Super IRA's." *Cato Journal* 6 (Spring/Summer): 195–228.

Ferraro, Kenneth F. 1990. "Cohort Analysis of Retirement Preparation, 1974–1981." *Journal of Gerontology: Social Sciences* 45 (January): S21–S31.

Fields, Gary, and Olivia Mitchell. 1984. *Retirement, Pensions and Social Security*. Cambridge, Mass.: MIT Press.

Fierst, Edith U. 1990. "Social Security and Women: Why Reasonableness Doesn't

Always Work." *Of Current Interest*. Brandeis University Policy Center on Aging Newsletter 9 (February): 1–3, 8.

Fierst, Edith U., and Nancy Duff, eds. 1988. *Earnings Sharing in Social Security: A Model for Reform*. Report of the Technical Committee on Earnings Sharing. Washington, D.C.: Center for Women's Policy Studies.

Fisher, Gordon M. 1992. "The Development and History of the Poverty Thresholds." *Social Security Bulletin* 55 (Winter): 3–14.

Fitzgerald, Albert J. 1978. Testimony. In U.S. House Select Committee on Aging, Subcommittee on Retirement Income and Employment, *National Pension Policies: Private Pension Plans*. Washington, D.C.: U.S. Government Printing Office, pp. 486–494.

Flint, Jerry. 1977. "Early Retirement Is Growing in U.S." *New York Times* (July 10): 1.

———. 1980. "The Old Folks." *Forbes* (18 February): 51–56.

Flowers, Marilyn R. 1977. *Women and Social Security: An Institutional Dilemma*. Washington, D.C.: American Enterprise Institute for Public Policy Research.

Foner, Anne, and Karen Schwab. 1983. "Work and Retirement in a Changing Society." In Matilda White Riley, Beth B. Hess, and K. Bond, eds., *Aging in Society: Selected Reviews of Recent Research*. Hillsdale, N.J.: Lawrence Erlbaum Associates.

Forman, Maxine. 1987. "Consumer Perspectives on the Impact of Retirement Income Systems on Women in the United States." In M. J. Gibson, ed., *Income Security and Longterm Care for Women*. Washington, D.C.: American Association of Retired Persons.

Fox, Alan. 1982. "Earnings Replacement Rates and Total Income: Findings from the Retirement History Study." *Social Security Bulletin* 45 (October): 3–23.

Friedberg, Leora. 1999. *The Labor Supply Effects of the Social Security Earnings Test*. Working Paper 7200. Cambridge, Mass.: National Bureau of Economic Research.

Friedland, Robert B. 1994. *When Support and Confidence Are at Odds: The Public's Understanding of the Social Security Program*. Washington, D.C.: National Academy of Social Insurance.

Friedland, Robert B., and Laura Summer. 1999. *Demography Is Not Destiny*. Washington, D.C. National Academy on an Aging Society.

Friedman, B. M., and M. Warshansky. 1988. "Annuity Prices and Savings Behavior in the United States." In Z. Bodie, J. Shoven, and D. Wise, eds., *Pensions in the U.S. Economy*. Chicago: University of Chicago Press, pp. 53–84.

Friedman, Eugene A., and Harold L. Orbach. 1974. "Adjustment to Retirement." In Silvano Arieti, ed., *The Foundation of Psychiatry*. Vol. 1, *American Handbook of Psychiatry*, 2nd ed. New York: Basic Books, pp. 609–645.

Friedman, Milton. 1971. "Purchasing Power Bonds." *Newsweek* (April 12): 86.

Fullerton, H. N. 1997. "Labor Force 2006: Slowing Down and Changing Composition." *Monthly Labor Review* (November): 23–38.

Garner, T., K. Short, S. Shipp, C. Nelson, and G. Paulin. 1998. "Experimental Poverty Measurement for the 1990s." *Monthly Labor Review* (March): 39–61.

Geanakoplos, John, Olivia S. Mitchell, and Stephen P. Zeldes. 1998. "Would a

Privatized Social Security System Really Pay a Higher Rate of Return?" *NBER Working Paper Series*, No. 6713. Cambridge, Mass.: NBER.

Giddens, Anthony. 1999. *The Third Way: The Renewal of Social Democracy*. Oxford: Polity Press.

Gill, Richard T., and T. Brandon Gill. 1994. Quoted in "A Parental Bill of Rights." *Family Affairs* 6 (Winter): 1–6.

Gist, John R., and Janemarie Mulvey. 1990. "Marginal Tax Rates and Older Taxpayers." *Tax Notes* (November 5): 679–694.

Gordon, Robert J. 1981. "The Consumer Price Index: Measuring Inflation and Causing It." *The Public Interest* (Spring): 112–134.

Gore, Al. 2000. "Gore to Make Social Security More Fair for Women." Press release. Washington, D.C.: Gore for President.

Goudy, Willis J. 1981. "Changing Work Expectations: Findings from the Retirement History Study." *The Gerontologist* 21 (December): 644–649.

Grad, Susan. 1985. *Income of the Population 55 and Over, 1984*. Washington, D.C.: U.S. Social Security Administration.

———. 1990. "Earnings Replacement Rates of New Retired Workers." *Social Security Bulletin* 53 (October): 2–19.

———. 1994. *Income of the Population 55 or Older, 1992*. Washington, D.C.: U.S. Department of Health and Human Services.

Gramlich, Edward M. 1997. "How Does Social Security Affect the Economy?" In Eric R. Kingson and James H. Schulz, eds., *Social Security in the 21st Century*. New York: Oxford University Press, pp. 147–155.

Gravelle, Jane G. 1991. "Do Individual Retirement Accounts Increase Savings?" *Journal of Economic Perspectives* 5 (Spring): 133–148.

"The Graying of America." 1977. *Newsweek* (February): 10–15.

Gruber, Jonathan, and Peter Orszag. 1999. *What to Do about the Social Security Earnings Test?* Issue Brief No. 1. Newton, Mass.: Center for Retirement Research, Boston College.

Gustman, Alan L., and F. Thomas Juster. 1995. *Income and Wealth of Older American Households: Modeling Issues for Public Policy Analysis*. Working Paper 4996. Cambridge, Mass.: National Bureau of Economic Research.

Gustman, Alan L., and T. L. Steinmeier. 1986. "A Structural Retirement Model." *Econometrica* 54: 555–584.

Hartman, Robert. 1983. *Pay and Pensions for Federal Workers*. Washington, D.C.: Brookings Institution.

Hatch, Sara. 1981. *Financial Retirement Incentives in Private Pension Plans*. Report to the Department of Labor. Washington, D.C.: Urban Institute.

Haveman, Robert. 1992–1993. "Changing the Poverty Measure: Pitfalls and Potential Gain." *Focus* 14 (Winter): 24–29.

Haveman, Robert H., B. L. Wolfe, and J. L. Warlick. 1984. "Disability Transfers, Early Retirement, and Retrenchment." In H. J. Aaron and G. T. Burtless, eds., *Retirement and Economic Behavior*. Washington, D.C.: Brookings Institution, pp. 65–96.

Heidbreder, E. M., and M. D. Batten. 1974. "ESAR II—A Comparative View of Services to Age Groups." *Facts and Trends*, No. 4. Washington, D.C.: National Council on Aging.

Herzog, A. R., R. L Kahn, J. N. Morgan, J. S. Jackson, and T. C. Antonucci. 1989.

"Age Difference in Productive Activities." *Journal of Gerontology: Social Sciences* 44 (July): S129–S138.

Hewitt, Edwin S. 1970. Testimony. In U.S. Senate Special Committee on Aging, *Economics of Aging: Toward a Full Share in Abundance*, Part 10B. Washington, D.C.: U.S. Government Printing Office.

Hipple, Steven. 1999. "Worker Displacement in the Mid-1990s." *Monthly Labor Review* (July): 15–32.

Hirshorn, Barbara A., and Denise T. Hoyer. 1994. "Private Sector Hiring and Use of Retirees: The Firm Perspective." *The Gerontologist* 34(1): 50–58.

Holahan, J., A. Dor, and S. Zuckerman. 1990. "Understanding the Recent Growth in Medicare Physician Expenditures." *Journal of the American Medical Association* 263 (March): 1658–1661.

Holden, Karen C. 1982. "Supplemental OASI Benefits to Homemakers through Current Spouse Benefits, a Homemaker Credit, and Child-Care Drop-Out Years." In R. V. Burkhauser and K. C. Holden, eds., *A Challenge to Social Security*. New York: Academic Press, pp. 41–65.

Holden, Karen C., and Timothy M. Smeeding. 1990. "The Poor, the Rich, and the Insecure Elderly Caught in Between." *Milbank Quarterly* 68(2): 191–219.

Hollister, Robinson G., and John L. Palmer. 1972. "The Impact of Inflation on the Poor." In Kenneth Boulding and M. Pfaff, eds., *Redistribution to the Rich and Poor*. Belmont, Calif.: Wadsworth, pp. 240–270.

Holstein, Martha, and M. Minkler. 1991. "The Short Life and Painful Death of the Medicare Catastrophic Coverage Act." In M. Minkler and C. L. Estes, eds., *Critical Perspectives on Aging: The Political and Moral Economy of Growing Old*. Amityville, N.Y.: Baywood, pp. 189–206.

Holzmann, Robert. 1991. "The Provision of Complimentary Pensions: Objectives, Forms, and Constraints." *International Social Security Review* 44(1–2): 75–93.

Honig, Marjorie, and C. Reimers. 1989. "Is It Worth Eliminating the Retirement Test?" *AEA Papers and Proceedings* 79 (May): 103–107.

Howard, Christopher. 1994. "Happy Returns: How the Working Poor Got Tax Relief." *The American Prospect*, No. 3 (Spring): 46–53.

Howe, Neil, and Philip Longman. 1992. "The Next New Deal." *Atlantic Monthly* (April): 88–99.

Hurd, Michael D. 1990. "Research on the Elderly: Economic Status, Retirement, and Consumption and Saving." *Journal of Economic Literature* 28 (June): 565–637.

———. 1993a. *The Effect of Labor Market Rigidities on the Labor Force Behavior of Older Workers*. Working Paper No. 4462. Cambridge, Mass.: National Bureau of Economic Research.

———. 1993b. *The Effects of Demographic Trends on Consumption Saving and Government Expenditures in the U.S.* Working Paper No. 4601. Cambridge, Mass.: National Bureau of Economic Research.

Institute on Poverty, University of Wisconsin. 1983. "The Relative Economic Status of the Aged." *IRP Focus* 6 (Spring): 1–4, 11–14.

Ippolito, Richard. 1985. "The Labor Contract and True Economic Pension Liabilities." *American Economic Review* 75: 1031–1043.

Irelan, Lola M., and K. Bond. 1976. "Retirees of the 1970s." In Gary S. Kart and

Barbara B. Manard, eds., *Aging in America—Readings in Social Gerontology*. Sherman Oaks, Calif.: Alfred, pp. 231–251.

Jackson, J. J. 1970. "Aged Negroes: Their Cultural Departures from Statistical Stereotypes of Rural-Urban Differences." *The Gerontologist* 10 (Summer): 140–145.

Jackson, William A. 1998. *The Political Economy of Population Aging*. Cheltenham, U.K.: Edward Elgar.

James, Estelle, James Smalhout, and Dimitri Vittas. 1999. "Administrative Costs of Individual Account Systems: How to Keep Them Low." Paper presented at the World Bank Conference on "New Ideas about Old Age Security." Washington, D.C.: World Bank Web site.

Johnson and Higgins Inc. 1979. *1979 Study of American Attitudes toward Pensions and Retirement*. New York: Johnson and Higgins.

Juster, F. Thomas. n.d. "Current and Prospective Financial Status of the Elderly Population." In Phillip Cagan, ed., *Saving Retirement*. Washington, D.C.: American Council of Life Insurance.

Juster, F. Thomas, and Frank P. Stafford. 1991. "The Allocation of Time: Empirical Findings, Behavioral Models, and Problems of Measurement." *Journal of Economic Literature* 29 (June): 471–522.

Kahne, Hilda. 1975. "Economic Perspectives on the Roles of Women in the American Economy." *Journal of Economic Literature* 13 (December): 1249–1292.

Kanter, R. M. 1994. "U.S. Competitiveness and the Aging Workforce: Toward Organizational and Institutional Change." In J. A. Auerbach and J. C. Welsh, eds., *Aging and Competition: Rebuilding the U.S. Workforce*. Washington, D.C.: National Council on Aging.

Kemper, P., and C. M. Murtaugh. 1991. "Lifetime Use of Nursing Home Care." *New England Journal of Medicine* 324(9): 595–600.

Kenworthy, Tom. 1991. "60 to 38 Senate Vote Kills Social Security Tax Cut." *Washington Post* (April 25): 1.

King, Jill. 1976. *The Consumer Price Index*. Technical Paper V, The Measure of Poverty Reports. Washington, D.C.: U.S. Department of Health, Education, and Welfare.

Kingson, Eric R. 1979. "Men Who Leave Work Before Age 62: A Study of Advantaged and Disadvantaged Very Early Labor Force Withdrawal." Ph.D. dissertation, Florence Heller Graduate School, Brandeis University.

Kingson, Eric R., and James H. Schulz, eds. 1997. *Social Security in the 21st Century*. New York: Oxford University Press.

Kinsella, Kevin. 1999. "The Demographics of Aging." *Coalition '99* no. 12 (July/August).

Kochhar, Staya. 1992. "Denial of SSI Applications Because of Excess Resources." *Social Security Bulletin* 55 (Summer): 52–56.

Korczyk, Sophie M. 1993. "Gender Issues in Employer Pensions Policy." In R. V. Burkhauser and D. L. Salisbury, eds., *Pensions in a Changing Economy*. Washington, D.C.: Employee Benefits Research Institute, pp. 59–66.

———. 1998. *How Americans Save*. Washington, D.C.: AARP.

Kotlikoff, Laurence J. 1989. "On the Contribution of Economics to the Evaluation and Formation of Social Insurance Policy." *American Economic Review* 79 (May): 184–190.

Kotlikoff, Laurence J., Avia Spivak, and Lawrence Summers. 1982. "The Adequacy of Savings." *American Economic Review* 72 (December): 1056–1069.

Kotlikoff, Laurence J., and David A. Wise. 1989. *The Wage Carrot and the Pension Stick.* Kalmazoo, Mich.: W. E. Upjohn Institute.

Kreps, Juanita M. 1977. "Age, Work, and Income." *Southern Economic Journal* 43 (April): 1423–1437.

Kreps, Juanita M., and Joseph J. Spengler. 1966. "The Leisure Component of Economic Growth." In National Commission on Technology, Automation, and Economic Progress, *Technology and the Economy.* Appendix 2: The Employment Impact of Technological Change. Washington, D.C.: U.S. Government Printing Office.

Lapkoff, Shelly. 1981. "Working Women, Marriage, and Retirement." Chapter 42 in the Appendix of the President's Commission on Pension Policy, *Coming of Age: Toward a National Retirement Policy.* Washington, D.C.: Commission on Pension Policy.

Lawrence, Jim. 1986. "House Votes to End Mandatory Retirement." *Boston Globe* (September 24): 5.

Lazear, Edward P. 1986. "Incentive Effects of Pensions." In D. A. Wise, ed., *Pensions, Labor, and Individual Behavior.* Chicago: University of Chicago Press, pp. 253–278.

———. 1991. "Labor Economics and the Psychology of Organizations." *Journal of Economic Perspectives* 5 (Spring): 89–110.

Leavitt, Thomas D. 1983. *Early Retirement Incentive Programs.* Waltham, Mass.: Policy Center on Aging, Brandeis University.

———. 1986. *The Impact of "Overfunded" Pension Terminations on Workers.* Publication 8603. Washington, D.C.: AARP Public Policy Institute.

Leavitt, Thomas D., and James H. Schulz. 1988. *The Role of the Asset Test in Program Eligibility and Participation: The Case of SSI.* Publication No. E-2. Washington, D.C.: Public Policy Institute, American Association of Retired Persons.

Leavitt, Thomas D., James H. Schulz, S. Fournier, K. Sohn, and L. Diamond. 1987. *Corporate Health Benefits for Medicare Eligible Retirees: An Analysis of Retiree Experience and Attitudes.* Washington, D.C.: American Association of Retired Persons.

Leimer, Dean R. 1979. "Projected Rates of Return to Future Social Security Retirees Under Alternative Benefit Structures." In *Proceedings of the Workshop on Policy Analysis with Social Security Record Files.* Washington, D.C.: Social Security Administration.

———. 1994. *Cohort-Specific Measures of Lifetime Net Social Security Transfers.* ORS Working Paper Series No. 59. Washington, D.C.: Office of Research and Statistics, U.S. Social Security Administration.

———. 1999. "Lifetime Redistribution under the Social Security Program: A Literature Synopsis." *ORES Working Paper Series.* Washington, D.C.: Social Security Administration, Office of Research, Evaluation, and Statistics.

Leonard, Herman B. 1986. *Checks Unbalanced: The Quiet Side of Public Spending.* New York: Basic Books.

Leonesio, Michael V. 1993. "Social Security and Older Workers." In Olivia S. Mitchell, ed., *As the Workforce Ages*. Ithaca, N.Y.: ILR Press, pp. 183–204.

Lesnoy, Selig D., and D. R. Leimer. 1981. *Social Security and Private Saving*. Working Paper No. 22. Washington, D.C.: Office of Research and Statistics, SSA.

Leuthold, Jane H. 1975. "The Incidence of the Payroll Tax in the United States." *Public Finance Quarterly* 3 (January): 3–13.

Levene, Tony. 1998. "Prudential: New Sales Row." *The Guardian* (August 10): Home News.

Lewin-VHI, Inc. 1994. *Aging Baby Boomers: How Secure Is Their Economic Future?* Washington, D.C.: American Association of Retired Persons.

Lewis, Robert. 1994. "For Whom the Job Bell Doesn't Toll." *AARP Bulletin* 35 (February): 2, 12.

Liang, J., and T. J. Fairchild. 1979. "Relative Deprivation and Perception of Financial Adequacy among the Aged." *Journal of Gerontology* 34 (September): 747–760.

Lopez, Eduard A. 1991. "Déjà Views: The Social Security Debate of 1937." *The New Republic* (April 22): 20–21.

Lovejoy, Lora Mills. 1988. "The Comparative Value of Pensions in the Public and Private Sectors." *Monthly Labor Review* 111 (December): 18–26.

Lumsdaine, Robin L., and David A. Wise. 1990. "Aging and Labor Force Participation: A Review of Trends and Explanations." Working Paper No. 3420. Cambridge, Mass.: National Bureau of Economic Research.

Mackey, Scott, and Karnen Carter. 1994. *State Tax Policy and Senior Citizens*, 2nd ed. Denver, Colo.: National Conference of State Legislatures.

Mallan, Lucy B. 1975. "Young Widows and Their Children: A Comparative Report." *Social Security Bulletin* 38 (May): 3–21.

Markides, Kyriakos S. 1993. "Trends in the Health of the Elderly in Western Societies." In A. B. Atkinson and Martin Rein, eds., *Age, Work, and Social Security*. New York: St. Martin's Press, pp. 3–16.

Mashaw, Jerry L. 1997. "Disability: Why Does the Search for Good Programs Continue?" In Eric R. Kingson and James H. Schulz, eds, *Social Security in the 21st Century*. New York: Oxford University Press, pp. 105–126.

Maxwell, James A. 1975. "Characteristics of State and Local Trust Funds." In David J. Ott, Attiat F. Ott, James A. Maxwell, and J. Richard Aronson, eds., *State-Local Finances in the Last Half of the 1970s*. Washington, D.C.: The American Enterprise Institute, pp. 35–62.

McConnel, Charles E., and F. Deljavan. 1983. "Consumption Patterns of the Retired Household." *Journal of Gerontology* 38 (July): 480–490.

McGarry, Kathleen, and R. F. Schoeni. 1997. "Transfer Behavior within the Family: Results from the Asset and Health Dynamics Study." *Journals of Gerontology*, Series B, vol. 52B (special issue): 82–92.

McGee, J., and R. Brown. 1992. *What Makes HMOs Drop Their Medicare Risk Contracts?* Princeton, N.J.: Mathematica Policy Research, Inc.

McNaught, William, and M. C. Barth. 1991. *Older Americans: Ready and Able to Work*. Report No. 1. Washington, D.C.: The Commonwealth Fund.

Medoff, James L. 1993. "Middle-Aged and Out-of-Work." DSC Report Series. Washington, D.C.: Democratic Study Center.

Menchik, Paul L., and Martin David. 1983. "Income Distribution, Lifetime Savings, and Bequests." *American Economic Review* 73 (September): 672–690.

Mendelson, D. N., and W. B. Schwartz. 1993. "The Effects of Aging and Population Growth on Health Care Costs." *Health Affairs* 12(1): 119–125.

Meyer, Charles W., ed. 1987. *Social Security—A Critique of Radical Reform Proposals.* Lexington, Mass.: Lexington Books.

Michael, Robert T. 1979. "Variations across Households in the Rate of Inflation." *Journal of Money, Credit, and Banking* 2 (February): 32–46.

Mikkelsen, Curtis. 1993. "A Corporate Response to Pension Reform." In Richard V. Burkhauser and Dallas L. Salisbury, eds., *Pensions in a Changing Economy.* Washington, D.C. and Syracuse, N.Y.: EBRI and Syracuse University, pp. 107–108.

Minarik, Joseph J. 1981. Testimony before the U.S. Senate Special Committee on Aging. Hearings on Social Security Oversight: Cost-of-Living Adjustments, Part 3. Washington, D.C.: U.S. Government Printing Office.

Miranda, M. R. 1988. "The Older Worker." *Aging Network News* (November): 5, 12.

Mirer, Thad W. 1974. "The Distributional Impact of Inflation and Anti-inflation Policy." Discussion Paper No. 231-74. Madison, Wisc.: Institute for Research on Poverty, University of Wisconsin–Madison.

Mishel, L., and R. A. Teixeira. 1991. *The Myth of the Coming Labor Shortage: Jobs, Skills, and Incomes of America's Workforce 2000.* Washington, D.C.: Economic Policy Institute.

Mitchell, Olivia S. 1993. "As the Workforce Ages." In Olivia S. Mitchell, ed., *As the Workforce Ages.* Ithaca, N.Y.: ILR Press, pp. 3–15.

———. 1999. *New Trends in Pension Benefit and Retirement Provisions.* Working Paper 7381. Cambridge, Mass.: National Bureau of Economic Research.

Mitchell, Olivia S., and R. Carr. 1995. *State and Local Plans.* Working Paper No. 5271. Cambridge, Mass.: National Bureau of Economic Research.

Modigliani, Franco. 1987. "The Key to Saving Is Growth, Not Thrift." *Challenge* 30 (May–June): 24–29.

Moehrle, Thomas. 1990. "Expenditure Patterns of the Elderly: Workers and Nonworkers." *Monthly Labor Review* 113 (May): 34–41.

Moeller, Charles. 1972. "The Role of Private Pension Plans in the Economy." In *Financing Retirement: Public and Private.* Conference Proceedings. New York: The Tax Foundation, Inc.

Moody, Harry R. 1993. "Age, Productivity, and Transcendence." In Scott A. Bass, Francis G. Caro, and Yung-Ping Chen, eds., *Achieving a Productive Aging Society.* Westport, Conn.: Auburn House, pp. 27–40.

Moon, Marilyn. 1996. *Medicare Now and in the Future,* 2nd ed. Washington, D.C.: Urban Institute Press.

Moore, Stephen. 1997. Testimony before the U.S. House Ways and Means Committee, Social Security Subcommittee, June 24, reproduced.

Moore, Thomas S. 1996. *The Disposable Workforce.* New York: Aldine De Gruyter.

Morgan, James N. 1977. "An Economic Theory of the Social Security System and Its Relation to Fiscal Policy." In G. S. Tolley and Richard V. Burkhauser, eds., *Income Support Policies for the Aged.* Cambridge, Mass.: Ballinger, pp. 107–126.

———. 1978. "Intra-Family Transfers Revisited: The Support of Dependents Inside the Family." In G. Duncan and J. Morgan, eds., *Five Thousand American Families*, Vol. 8. Ann Arbor: Survey Research Center, IRS, University of Michigan.

———. 1980. "Retirement in Prospect and Retrospect." In G. Duncan and J. Morgan, eds., *Five Thousand American Families*, Vol. 8. Ann Arbor: Survey Research Center, IRS, University of Michigan.

———. 1983. "The Redistribution of Income by Families and Institutions and Emerging Help Patterns." In G. J. Duncan and J. N. Morgan, eds., *Five Thousand American Families*, Vol. 10. Anne Arbor: Institute for Social Research, University of Michigan, pp. 1–59.

Morrison, Peter A. 1982. "Demographic Links to Social Security." *Challenge* 24 (January/February): 44–48.

Mothner, Ira. 1985. *Children and Elders: Intergenerational Relations in an Aging Society*. New York: Carnegie Foundation.

Munnell, Alicia H. 1977. *The Future of Social Security*. Washington, D.C.: Brookings Institution.

———. 1979. "Are Private Pensions Doomed?" *New England Economic Review* (March/April): 5–20.

———. 1982. *The Economics of Private Pensions*. Washington, D.C.: Brookings Institution.

Munnell, Alicia H., and L. E. Blais. 1984. "Do We Want Large Social Security Surpluses?" *New England Economic Review* (September/October): 5–21.

Myers, Robert J. 1987. "Social Security Roller Coaster." *Washington Post* (August 20): A23.

———. 1990. "Real Wages Went Up in the 1980s." *Wall Street Journal* (August 21).

———. 1991. *Social Security*, 4th ed. Philadelphia: University of Pennsylvania Press.

Myers, Robert J., and Bruce D. Schobel. 1992. "An Updated Money's-Worth Analysis of Social Security Retirement Benefits." *Transactions* 44: 47–70.

Myles, John, and Jill Quadagno. 2000. "Envisioning a Third Way: The Welfare State in the Twenty-First Century." *Contemporary Sociology* 29(1): 156–167.

Myrdal, Gunnar. 1963. *Challenge to Affluence*. New York: Pantheon Books.

National Academy of Social Insurance. 1988. *The Social Security Benefit Notch: A Study*. Washington, D.C.: The Academy.

National Center of Women & Aging. 1988. *Financial Challenges for Mature Women*. Waltham, Mass.: Heller Graduate School, Brandeis University.

National Commission on Social Security. 1981. *The Social Security in America's Future*. Report of the Commission to the President. Washington, D.C.: National Commission on Social Security.

NCOA (National Council on the Aging). 1975. *The Myth and Reality of Aging in America*. Washington, D.C.: NCOA.

———. 1981. *Aging in the Eighties*. Washington, D.C.: NCOA.

Nelson, Richard. 1997. "How New Is New Growth Theory?" *Challenge* 40(5) (September–October): 29–58.

Newsweek. 1984. "The Social Security Scandals" (September 24): 32–33.

Nordhaus, W., and J. Tobin. 1973. "Is Growth Obsolete?" In National Bureau of

Economic Research, *The Measurement of Economic and Social Performance*. New York: National Bureau of Economic Research, pp. 509–532.

NOW (National Organization of Women). 1987. *Social Security: The Economic Marginalization of Workers*. Washington, D.C.: NOW.

O'Grady-LeShane, Regina. 1993. "Changes in the Lives of Women and Their Families: Have Old Age Pensions Kept Pace?" *Generations* 17 (Winter): 27–31.

Okonkwo, Ubadigbo. 1975. "Intragenerational Equity under Social Security." Washington, D.C., reproduced.

Okun, Arthur. 1975. *Equality and Efficiency—The Big Trade-Off*. Washington, D.C.: Brookings Institution.

Orshansky, Mollie. 1978. Testimony. In U.S. House Select Committee on Aging, *Poverty Among America's Aged*. Washington, D.C.: U.S. Government Printing Office.

———. 1988. "Commentary: The Poverty Measure." *Social Security Bulletin* 51 (October): 22–24.

O'Shaughnessy, Carol. 1985. *Title V of the Older Americans Act—Community Services Employment Programs for Older Americans: Program Description, Evaluation, and Legislative History*. Report No. 85-155-GOV. Washington, D.C.: Congressional Research Service.

Packard, Michael D. 1990. "The Earnings Test and the Short-Run Work Response to Its Elimination." *Social Security Bulletin* 53 (September): 2–16.

Packard, Michael D., and Virginia P. Reno. 1988. "A Look at Very Early Retirees." In Rita Ricardo-Campbell and Edward P. Lazear, eds., *Issues in Contemporary Retirement*. Stanford, Calif.: Hoover Institute Press, pp. 243–265.

Palma, James. 1999. "Long-Term Care Insurance Revisited." *Women & Aging Letter* 3 (April): 1–8.

Palmer, Bruce A. 1989. "Tax Reform and Retirement Income Replacement Ratios." *Journal of Risk and Insurance* 56 (December): 702–725.

Palmore, Erdman, G. G. Fillenbaum, and L. K. George. 1984. "Consequences of Retirement." *Journal of Gerontology* 39 (January): 109–116.

Parnes, Herbert S. 1981. "From the Middle to the Later Years." *Research on Aging* 3 (December): 387–402.

Parnes, Herbert S., and Gilbert Nestel. 1979. "The Retirement Experience." In H. S. Parnes, G. Nestel, T. H. Chirikos, T. N. Daymont, F. L. Mott, and D. O. Parsons, eds., *From the Middle to Later Years*. Columbus: Center for Human Resources, Ohio State University.

Parnes, Herbert S., and David G. Sommers. 1994. "Shunning Retirement: Work Experience of Men in Their Seventies and Early Eighties." *Journal of Gerontology* 49(3): S117–S124.

Pattison, David, and David E. Harrington. 1993. "Proposals to Modify the Taxation of Social Security Benefits: Options and Distributional Effects." *Social Security Bulletin* 56 (Summer): 3–21.

PBGC (Pension Benefit Guaranty Corporation). 1987. *Annual Report to Congress, Fiscal Year 1987*. Washington, D.C.: PBGC.

———. 1998. *Pension Insurance Data Book*. Washington, D.C.: PBGC.

———. 1999. "Defined Benefit Pension Plans." *Facts*. Washington, D.C.: PBGC.

Pechman, Joseph A., Henry J. Aaron, and Michael K. Taussig. 1968. *Social Security: Perspectives for Reform*. Washington, D.C.: Brookings Institution.

Pepper Commission (U.S. Bipartisan Commission on Comprehensive Health Care). 1990. *A Call for Action*. Washington, D.C.: U.S. Government Printing Office.

Peter D. Hart Research Associates, Inc. 1979. *A National Survey of Attitudes Toward Social Security*. A report prepared for the National Commission on Social Security. Washington, D.C., reproduced.

Peterson, Peter G. 1999. *Gray Dawn: How the Coming Age Wave Will Transform America—And the World*. New York: Time Books.

Peterson, Peter G., and Neil Howe. 1988. *On Borrowed Time: How the Growth of Entitlement Spending Threatens America's Future*. San Francisco: Institute for Contemporary Studies.

Phillips, Kristen. 1992. "State and Local Government Pension Benefits." In John A. Turner and Daniel J. Beller, eds., *Trends in Pensions, 1992*. Washington, D.C.: U.S. Government Printing Office.

Pifer, Alan, and Lydia Bronte, eds. 1986. *Our Aging Society: Paradox and Promise*. New York: W. W. Norton.

Poterba, James M., Steven F. Venti, and David A. Wise. 1992. *401(K) Plans and Tax-Deferred Saving*. Working Paper No. 4181. Cambridge, Mass.: National Bureau of Economic Research.

Poverty Studies Task Force. 1976. *The Measure of Poverty*. A Report to Congress as Mandated by the Education Amendments of 1974. Washington, D.C.: U.S. Department of Health, Education, and Welfare.

President's Commission on Pension Policy. 1981. *Coming of Age: Toward a National Retirement Income Policy*. Report of the Commission. Washington, D.C.: Commission on Pension Policy.

Preston, Samuel H. 1984. "Children and the Elderly in the U.S." *Scientific American* 251 (December): 44–49.

Productive Aging News. 1993a. "Does Medicare Cover Long-Term Care?" No. 74 (September): 5–6.

———. 1993b. "NIA Expert Sees a Revolution in Living for 21st Century Americans." (July/August): 6–9.

Propac (Prospective Payment Assessment Commission). 1993. *Medicare and the American Health Care System: Report to Congress*. Washington, D.C.: Propac.

Pursell, Donald E., and William D. Torrence. 1979. "Age and the Jobhunting Methods of the Unemployed." *Monthly Labor Review* 102 (January): 68–69.

Quadagno, Jill. 1988. *The Transformation of Old Age Security, Class and Politics in the American Welfare State*. Chicago: University of Chicago Press.

———. 1991. "Interest-Group Politics and the Future of U.S. Social Security." In John Myles and Jill Quadagno, eds., *States, Labor Markets, and the Future of Old-Age Policy*. Philadelphia, Pa.: Temple University Press, pp. 84–104.

Quadagno, Jill, and Melissa Hardy. 1995. "Work and Retirement." In R. H. Binstock and L. K. George, eds., *Handbook of Aging and the Social Sciences*, 4th ed. San Diego, Calif.: Academic Press, pp. 326–345.

Quinn, Joseph F. 1993. "Is Early Retirement an Economic Threat?" *Generations* 17 (Winter): 10–14.

———. 1999. *Retirement Patterns and Bridge Jobs in the 1990s*. EBRI Issue Brief (February). Washington, D.C.: Employee Benefit Research Institute.

Quinn, Joseph F., Richard V. Burkhauser, and Daniel A. Myers. 1990. *Passing the Torch: The Influence of Economic Incentives on Work and Retirement.* Kalamazoo, Mich.: W. E. Upjohn Institute for Employment Research.

Radner, Daniel B. 1982. "Distribution of Family Income: Improved Estimates." *Social Security Bulletin* 45 (July): 13–21.

———. 1989. "Net Worth and Financial Assets of Age Groups in 1984." *Social Security Bulletin* 52 (March): 2–15.

———. 1990. "Assessing the Economic Status of the Aged and Nonaged Using Alternative Income-Wealth Measures." *Social Security Bulletin* 53 (March): 2–14.

———. 1991. "Changes in the Incomes of Age Groups, 1984–89." *Social Security Bulletin* 54 (December): 2–18.

———. 1993a. "Economic Well-Being of the Old Old: Family Unit Income and Household Wealth." *Social Security Bulletin* 56 (Spring): 3–18.

———. 1993b. *An Assessment of the Economic Status of the Aged.* Studies in Income Distribution, No. 16. Washington, D.C.: Office of Research and Statistics, U.S. Social Security Administration.

Rauch, Jonathan. 1987a. "Uncle Sam Inc." *National Journal* (September 5): 2242.

———. 1987b. "False Security." *National Journal* 19 (February 14): 362–365.

Rebick, Marcus. 1993. "The Japanese Approach to Finding Jobs for Older Workers." In Olivia S. Mitchell, ed., *As the Workforce Ages.* Ithaca, N.Y.: ILR Press.

Reich, Murray H. 1977. "Group Preretirement Education Programs: Whither the Proliferation?" *Industrial Gerontology* 4 (Winter): 29–43.

Reich, Robert B. 1994. "A Global, Technological Economy." In J. A. Auerbach and J. C. Welsh, eds., *Aging and Competition: Rebuilding the U.S. Workforce.* Washington, D.C.: National Council on the Aging, pp. 41–48.

Reno, Virginia. 1971. "Why Men Stop Working at or Before Age 65: Findings from the Survey of New Beneficiaries." *Social Security Bulletin* (June): 3–11.

———. 1993. "The Role of Pensions in Retirement Income." In R. V. Burkhauser and D. L. Salisbury, eds., *Pensions in a Changing Economy.* Washington, D.C.: Employee Benefit Research Institute, pp. 19–32.

Reno, Virginia P., and Robert B. Friedland. 1997. "Strong Support but Low Confidence: What Explains the Contradiction?" In Eric R. Kingson and James H. Schulz, eds., *Social Security in the 21st Century.* New York: Oxford University Press, pp. 178–194.

Reno, Virginia P., and Susan Grad. 1985. "Economic Security, 1935–85." *Social Security Bulletin* 48 (December): 5–9.

Reschovsky, Andrew. 1994. *Do the Elderly Face High Property Tax Burdens?* Washington, D.C.: Public Policy Institute, American Association of Retired Persons.

Rhoades, Jeffrey A., and N. A. Krauss. 1999. *Nursing Home Trends, 1987 and 1996.* MEPS Chartbook No. 3. Rockville, Md.: Agency for Health Care Policy and Research.

Rich, Spencer. 1990. "Warning Signs at Social Security." *Washington Post* (April 20): 1.

———. 1991. "900,000 Could Need Long-Term Care." *Washington Post* (March 8): 2.

Riley, Matilda White. 1993. "First Annual Pepper Lecture on Aging and Public Policy." Florida State University, reproduced.

Rivlin, Alice M., and Joshua M. Wiener. 1988. *Caring for the Disabled Elderly: Who Will Pay?* Washington, D.C.: Brookings Institution.

Rix, Sara E. 1999a. "The Older Worker in a Graying America." In R. N. Butler, L. K. Grossman, and M. R. Oberlink, eds., *Life in an Older America*. New York: Century Foundation Press, pp. 187–216.

———. 1999b. "Maintenance of the Skills and Employability of Older Workers: Skills Training and Retraining." Paper presented at a conference on "Active Strategies for an Ageing Workforce," Turku, Finland, reproduced.

Robinson, Pauline, Sally Coberly, and C. E. Paul. 1984. "Work and Retirement." In Robert H. Binstock and Ethel Shanas, eds., *Handbook of Aging and the Social Sciences*, 2nd ed. New York: Van Nostrand Reinhold, pp. 503–527.

Rones, Philip L. 1983. "The Labor Market Problems of Older Workers." *Monthly Labor Review* 106 (May): 3–12.

Rosenblum, M., and H. Sheppard. 1977. *Jobs for Older Workers in U.S. Industry: Possibilities and Prospects*. Report to the U.S. Department of Commerce, Economic Development Administration. Washington, D.C., reproduced.

Ross, C. M., S. Danziger, and E. Smolensky. 1987. "Interpreting Changes in the Economic Status of the Elderly, 1949–1979." *Contemporary Policy Issues* 5: 98–112.

Ross, Jane L., and Melinda M. Upp. 1993. "Treatment of Women in the U.S. Social Security System, 1970–88." *Social Security Bulletin* 56 (Fall): 56–67.

Rowen, Hobart. 1978. "Rethinking That Bite in Social Security." *Washington Post* (February 16): A-10.

Rubin, Rose M., and M. L. Nieswiadomy. 1997. *Expenditures of Older Americans*. Westport, Conn.: Praeger.

Ruggles, Patricia. 1990. *Drawing the Line: Alternative Poverty Measures and Their Implications for Public Policy*. Washington, D.C.: Urban Institute Press.

Ruhm, Christopher J. 1990. "Determinants of the Timing of Retirement." In Peter B. Doeringer, ed., *Bridges to Retirement: Older Workers in a Changing Labor Market*. Ithaca, N.Y.: ILR Press, pp. 23–32.

Rupp, Kalman. 1983. *Eligibility and Participation Rates of Older Americans in Employment and Training Programs*. Research Report Series, RR-83-11. Washington, D.C.: National Commission for Employment Policy.

Samuelson, Robert J. 1994. "Generational Economics." *Boston Globe* (April 19): 46.

Sandell, Steven H. 1987. "Prospects for Older Workers: The Demographic and Economic Context." In Steven H. Sandell, ed., *The Problem Isn't Age: Work and Older Americans*. New York: Praeger, pp. 3–14.

Sass, Steven. 1993. "Crisis in Pensions." *Regional Review* (Spring): 13–18.

Schieber, Sylvester J. 1978. "First Year Impact of SSI on Economic Status of 1973 Adult Assistance Populations." *Social Security Bulletin* 41 (February): 18–51.

Schmitt, Donald G. 1984. "Postretirement Increases under Private Pension Plans." *Monthly Labor Review* 107 (September): 3–8.

Schmundt, M., E. Smolensky, and L. Stiefel. 1975. "The Evaluation of Recipients of In-Kind Transfers." In I. Laurie, ed., *Integrating Income Maintenance Programs*. New York: Academic Press, pp. 189–207.

Scholen, Ken, and Yung-Ping Chen. 1980. *Unlocking Home Equity for the Elderly*. Cambridge, Mass.: Ballinger.

Scholz, John Karl. 1993–1994. "Tax Policy and the Working Poor: The Earned Income Tax Credit." *Focus* 15 (Winter): 1–13.

Schorr, Alvin L. 1960. *Filial Responsibility in the Modern American Family*. Washington, D.C.: U.S. Government Printing Office.

Schottland, Charles I. 1970. *The Social Security Program in the United States*, 2nd ed. New York: Appleton-Century-Crofts.

Schram, S. F., and D. F. Osten. 1978. "CETA and the Aging." *Aging and Work* 1 (Summer): 163–174.

Schulz, James H. 1974. "The Economics of Mandatory Retirement." *Industrial Gerontology* 1(1), New Series (Winter): 1–10.

———. 1977. "The Social Security Retirement Test: Time for a Change?" *The Urban and Social Change Review* 10 (Summer): 14–18.

———. 1991. *The World Aging Situation, 1991*. Vienna: United Nations Centre for Social Development and Humanitarian Affairs.

———. 1997. *Ageing in Asia: The Growing Need for Social Protection*. Bangkok: International Labor Office.

———. 1999. "Saving, Growth, and Social Security." In R. N. Butler, L. K. Grossman, and M. R. Oberlink, eds., *Life in an Older America*. New York: Century Foundation Press, pp. 121–150.

———. 2000. "Global Lessons from Pension Privatization." *Challenge* (January–February): 93–104.

Schulz, James H., Allan Borowski, and William H. Crown. 1991. *Economics of Population Aging: The "Graying" of Australia, Japan, and the United States*. New York: Auburn House.

Schulz, James H., and Guy Carrin. 1972. "The Role of Savings and Pension Systems in Maintaining Living Standards in Retirement." *Journal of Human Resources* 7 (Summer): 343–365.

Schulz, James H., and T. D. Leavitt. 1983. *Pension Integration: Concepts, Issues, and Proposals*. Washington, D.C.: Employee Benefit Research Institute.

Schulz, James H., and John Myles. 1990. "Old Age Pensions: A Comparative Perspective." In Robert H. Binstock and Linda George, eds., *Handbook of Aging and the Social Sciences*, 3rd ed. New York: Academic Press, pp. 398–414.

Schulz, James H., Kazuo Takada, and Shinya Hoshino. 1989. *When "Lifetime Employment" Ends*. Waltham, Mass.: Policy Center on Aging, Brandeis University.

Scott, Hilda, and Juliet F. Brudney. 1987. *Forced Out*. New York: Simon and Schuster.

Secretary of State for Social Security. 1998. *A New Contract for Welfare: Partnership in Pensions*. London: HMSO.

Shanas, Ethel, Peter Townsend, Dorothy Wedderburn, Henning Friis, Poul Milhog, and Jan Stehouwer. 1968. *Old People in Three Industrial Societies*. New York: Atherton.

Sheppard, Harold L. 1977. "Factors Associated with Early Withdrawal from the

Labor Force." In S. L. Wolfbein, ed., *Men in the Pre-Retirement Years*. Philadelphia, Pa.: Temple University Press.

Sheppard, Harold L., and A. Harvey Belitsky. 1966. *The Job Hunt*. Baltimore, Md.: Johns Hopkins University Press.

Sherman, Sally R. 1989. "Public Attitudes toward Social Security." *Social Security Bulletin* 52 (December): 2–16.

Siegel, Jacob S. 1976. *Demographic Aspects of Aging and the Older Population in the United States*. Current Population Reports, Special Studies. Series P-23, No. 59. Washington, D.C.: U.S. Government Printing Office.

Siegfried, Charles A. 1970. "The Role of Private Pensions." In American Enterprise Institute, *Private Pensions and the Public Interest*. Washington, D.C.: The American Enterprise Institute.

Skinner, Jonathan. 1992. "Individual Retirement Accounts: A Review of the Evidence." *Tax Notes* (January 13): 201–212.

Skocpol, Theta. 1990. "Sustainable Social Policy: Fighting Poverty without Poverty Programs." *The American Prospect* 1 (Spring): 58–70.

Skolnik, Alfred M. 1975. "Restructuring the Railroad Retirement System." *Social Security Bulletin* 38 (April): 23–29.

Smeeding, Timothy M. 1989. "Full Income Estimates of the Relative Well-Being of the Elderly and the Nonelderly." *Research on Economic Inequality* 1: 83–122.

———. 1990. "Economic Status of the Elderly." In Robert H. Binstock and L. George, eds., *Handbook of Aging and the Social Sciences*, 3rd ed. New York: Academic Press, pp. 362–381.

Smeeding, Timothy M., Michael O'Higgins, and Lee Rainwater. 1990. *Poverty, Inequality, and Income Distribution in Comparative Perspective*. Washington, D.C.: Urban Institute Press.

Smith, Sheila, Stephen Heffler, and Mark Freeland. 1999. "U.S. Health Care Spending Growth." *Health Affairs* 18 (July/August): 86–95.

Sobel, Irvin, and Richard C. Wilcock. 1963. "Job Placement Services for Older Workers in the United States." *International Labor Review* 88: 129–156.

Social Security Advisory Board. 1998. *How SSA's Disability Programs Can Be Improved*. Washington, D.C.: Social Security Advisory Board.

Soldo, Beth J. 1981. "The Living Arrangements of the Elderly in the Near Future." In S. B. Kiesler, J. N. Morgan, and V. K. Oppenheimer, eds., *Aging: Social Change*. New York: Academic Press.

Solow, Robert M. 1975. "The Intelligent Citizen's Guide to Inflation." *The Public Interest* 38 (Winter): 30–66.

Sparrow, Paul R. 1986. "Job Performance among Older Workers." *Ageing International* 13 (Autumn/Winter): 5–6, 22.

Stapleton, David, David Kennell, and Richard Iovanna. 1993. *Health Care Costs and Older Workers*. Washington, D.C.: Lewin-VHI, Inc.

Sterns, Harvey L., and Michael A. McDaniel. 1994. *Job Performance and the Older Worker*. Washington, D.C.: American Association of Retired Persons (AARP).

Steuerle, C. Eugene, and J. M. Bakija. 1994. *Retooling Social Security for the 21st Century*. Washington, D.C.: Urban Institute Press.

Steuerle, C. Eugene, and C. Spiro. 1999. "What Does Fixing Social Security Actually Fix?" *Straight Talk*. Briefs from the Retirement Project, No. 1. Washington, D.C.: Urban Institute Press.

Stevenson, Richard W. 2000. "House Backs End to Earnings Limit on Social Security." *New York Times* (March 2): A1, A18.

Stone, Deborah A. 1984. *The Disabled State*. Philadelphia, Pa.: Temple University Press.

Storey, James R. 1983. Testimony before the House Select Committee on Aging, Health and Long-Term Care Subcommittee (May 5), reproduced.

Strauss, David M. 1999. Statement before the U.S. House Committee on Ways and Means, Subcommittee on Oversight. Washington, D.C., reproduced.

Streib, Gordon F., and Clement J. Schneider. 1971. *Retirement in American Society*. Ithaca, N.Y.: Cornell University Press.

Sunden, Annika E., and Brian J. Surette. 1998. "Gender Differences in the Allocation of Assets in Retirement Savings Plans." *AEA Papers and Proceedings* 88(2): 207–216.

Suzman, Richard M., David P. Willis, and Kenneth G. Manton, eds. 1992. *The Oldest Old*. Oxford: Oxford University Press.

Swoboda, Frank. 1994. "Fewer Retirees Get Health Coverage." *Boston Globe* (May 31): 35.

Talley, Louis Alan. 1992. *Federal Income Tax Treatment of the Elderly*. CRS Report for Congress. Washington, D.C.: Congressional Research Service, Library of Congress.

Taplin, Polly T. 1989. "Spencer Survey of Preretirement Counseling: Ongoing, Early Retirement Programs Described." *Employee Benefit Plan Review* 44 (August): 14–18.

Tax Notes. 1990. "IRS Hears Pension Witnesses Sing the 'Plan Dropout Blues'." (October 1): 9.

Tell, Eileen J., M. A. Cohen, and S. S. Wallack. 1987. "Life Care at Home: A New Model for Financing and Delivering Long-Term Care." *Inquiry* 24 (Fall): 245–252.

Thompson, Lawrence H. 1974. *An Analysis of the Factors Currently Determining Benefit Level Adjustments in the Social Security Program*. Technical Analysis Paper No. 1. Office of Income Security Policy, Office of the Assistant Secretary of Planning and Evaluation. Washington, D.C.: Department of Health, Education, and Welfare.

———. 1990. "The Financing Debate: A Scorecard." *Social Insurance Update*, No. 12. National Academy of Social Insurance (March): P1–P8.

———. 1998. *Older and Wiser: The Economics of Public Pensions*. Washington, D.C.: Urban Institute Press.

Thompson, Lawrence H., and Paul N. Van de Water. 1975. "The Short-Run Behavior of the Social Security Trust Funds." *Technical Analysis Paper*, No. 8. Washington, D.C.: Office of Income Security Policy, Department of Health, Education, and Welfare.

Thurow, Lester. 1976. "Tax Wealth, Not Income." *New York Times Magazine* (April 11): 32.

Tibbitts, Clark. 1977. "Older Americans in the Family Context." *Aging* (April–May): 6–11.

Tissue, Thomas. 1978. "Response to Recipiency under Public Assistance and SSI." *Social Security Bulletin* 41 (November): 3–15.

Torda, Theodore S. 1972. "The Impact of Inflation on the Elderly." *Federal Reserve Bank of Cleveland Monthly Review* (October–November): 3–19.

Torrey, Barbara Boyle. 1982. "Guns vs. Canes. The Fiscal Implications of an Aging Population." *American Economic Review*. Papers and Proceedings (May): 309–313.

Torrey, Barbara Boyle, and C. M. Taeuber. 1986. "The Importance of Asset Income among the Elderly." *The Review of Income and Wealth*, Series 32 (December): 443–449.

Turnbull, John G., C. Arthur Williams, Jr., and Earl F. Cheit. 1967. *Economic and Social Security*, 3rd ed. New York: Ronald Press.

U.S. Bureau of the Census. 1983. *Estimating After-tax Money Income Distributions Using Data from the March Current Population Survey*. Current Population Reports, Series P-23, No. 126. Washington, D.C.: U.S. Government Printing Office.

———. 1988. *Who's Helping Out? Support Networks among American Families*. Current Population Reports, Series P-70, No. 13. Washington, D.C.: U.S. Government Printing Office.

———. 1991. *Measuring the Effect of Benefits and Taxes on Income and Poverty: 1990*. Current Population Reports, Series P-60, No. 176-RD. Washington, D.C.: U.S. Government Printing Office.

———. 1992. *Home Ownership: 1981 to 1991*. Statistical Brief No. SB/92-7. Washington, D.C.: U.S. Department of Commerce.

———. 1993. *Measuring the Effects of Benefits and Taxes on Income and Poverty: 1992*. Current Population Reports, P-60-186RD. Washington, D.C.: U.S. Government Printing Office.

———. 1996. *Resident Population of the United States: Middle Series Projections, 2035–2050, by Age and Sex*. Washington, D.C.: Census Web site: www.census.gov.

———. 1998. *Measuring 50 Years of Economic Change Using the March Current Population Survey*. Current Population Reports, P60-203. Washington, D.C.: U.S. Government Printing Office.

U.S. Bureau of Labor Statistics. 1980. *Employee Benefits in Industry: A Pilot Survey*, Report 615. Washington, D.C.: U.S. Government Printing Office.

———. 1989. "An Analysis of the Rates of Inflation Affecting Older Americans Based on an Experimental Reweighted Consumer Price Index." In U.S. Senate Special Committee on Aging, *Cost-of-Living Adjustments and the CPI: A Question of Fairness*. Hearing, October 5, 1988. Washington, D.C.: U.S. Government Printing Office, pp. 50–81.

———. 1991. *Employee Benefits in Medium and Large Firms, 1989*. Bulletin 2363. Washington, D.C.: U.S. Government Printing Office.

———. 1994. *Employment and Earnings*, No. 1. Washington, D.C.: U.S. Government Printing Office.

U.S. Congressional Budget Office (CBO). 1986. *Earnings Sharing Options for the Social Security System*. Washington, D.C.: CBO.

———. 1990. "The Federal Deficit: Does It Measure the Government's Effect on National Saving?" Washington, D.C.: CBO.

————. 1993. *Assessing the Decline in the National Saving Rate.* Washington, D.C.: U.S. Government Printing Office.

————. 1999. *Raising the Earliest Eligibility Age for Social Security Benefits.* Washington, D.C.: CBO.

U.S. Congressional Research Service (CRS), Library of Congress. 1987. *Catastrophic Health Insurance: Medicare.* Issue Brief No. IB 87106. Washington, D.C.: CRS.

U.S. Department of Justice. n.d. *The Pension Game: American System from the Viewpoint of the Average Woman.* Task Force on Sex Discrimination, Civil Rights Division. Washington, D.C.: U.S. Government Printing Office.

U.S. Department of Labor. 1965. *The Older American Worker.* Washington, D.C.: U.S. Department of Labor.

————. 1988. *BLS Reports on Worker Displacement.* Washington, D.C.: U.S. Government Printing Office.

————. 1991. "Report on Programs and Activities Related to Aging." In U.S. Senate Special Committee on Aging, *Developments in Aging: 1990*, Vol. 2. Washington, D.C.: U.S. Government Printing Office, pp. 512–514.

————. 1993. *Private Pension Plan Bulletin* (Summer).

————. 1994. Communication and Report of the Secretary of Labor to Senator David Pryor, Chairman, U.S. Senate Special Committee on Aging, reproduced.

————. 1995. *Retirement Benefits of American Workers.* Washington, D.C.: Office of Research and Economic Analysis, Pension and Welfare Benefits Administration.

————. 1999. *Private Pension Plan Bulletin*, No. 8. Abstract of 1995 From 5500 Annual Reports. Washington, D.C.: U.S. Government Printing Office.

U.S. General Accounting Office (GAO). 1987. *Medicare and Medicaid: Stronger Enforcement of Nursing Home Requirements Needed.* Washington, D.C.: GAO.

————. 1988. *Social Security: The Notch Issue.* Washington, D.C.: GAO.

————. 1989a. *Employer Benefits: Companies' Retiree Health Liabilities Large, Advance Funding Costly.* Washington, D.C.: GAO.

————. 1989b. *Private Pensions: Spousal Consent Forms Hard to Read and Lack Important Information.* Washington, D.C.: GAO.

————. 1992a. *Pension Plans: Survivor Benefit Coverage for Wives Increased after 1984 Pension Law.* Washington, D.C.: GAO.

————. 1992b. *Report on SEP Participation.* Washington, D.C.: GAO.

————. 1999. *Social Security: Issues in Comparing Rates of Return with Market Investments.* Washington, D.C.: GAO.

U.S. HEW (Department of Health, Education, and Welfare). 1978. "Major Initiative: Long-Term Care/Community Services." Memorandum, Office of the Secretary. Washington, D.C., July 14, reproduced.

U.S. HEW Task Force (on the Treatment of Women Under Social Security). 1978. *Report.* Washington, D.C.: U.S. Department of Health, Education, and Welfare.

U.S. HHS (Department of Health and Human Services). 1986. "Increasing the Social Security Retirement Age: Older Workers in Physically Demanding Occupations or Ill Health." *Social Security Bulletin* 49 (October): 5–23.

U.S. House Committee on Education and Labor. 1972. *Interim Staff Report of Activities of the Pension Study Task Force*. Washington, D.C.: U.S. Government Printing Office.

———. 1978. *Pension Task Force Report on Public Employee Retirement Systems*. Washington, D.C.: U.S. Government Printing Office.

U.S. House Committee on Ways and Means. 1967. *President's Proposals for Revision in the Social Security System*. Hearings, Part 1. Washington, D.C.: U.S. Government Printing Office.

———. 1985. *Reports on Earnings Sharing Implementation Study*. Washington, D.C.: U.S. Government Printing Office.

———. 1991. *1991 Green Book*. Washington, D.C.: U.S. Government Printing Office.

———. 1993. *1993 Green Book: Overview of Entitlement Programs*. Washington, D.C.: U.S. Government Printing Office.

——— 1998. *1998 Green Book*. Washington, D.C.: U.S. Government Printing Office.

U.S. House Select Committee on Aging. 1978. *Poverty Among America's Aged*. Hearings. Washington, D.C.: U.S. Government Printing Office.

———. 1987. *Longterm Care and Personal Impoverishment*. Washington, D.C.: U.S. Government Printing Office.

U.S. Joint Economic Committee, Subcommittee on Fiscal Policy. 1974. "Issues in Financing Retirement Income," Paper No. 10. *Studies in Public Welfare*. Washington, D.C.: U.S. Government Printing Office.

U.S. Office of Technology and Assessment (OTA). 1985. *Technology and the Aging in America*. Washington, D.C.: OTA.

U.S. Senate Committee on Finance. 1975. *Report of the Panel on Social Security Financing*. Washington, D.C.: U.S. Government Printing Office.

U.S. Senate Special Committee on Aging. 1984. *The Costs of Employing Older Workers*. Washington, D.C.: U.S. Government Printing Office.

———. 1987. *Developments in Aging: 1986*, Vol. 1. Washington, D.C.: U.S. Government Printing Office.

———. 1991. *Developments in Aging: 1990*, Vol. 1. Washington, D.C.: U.S. Government Printing Office.

———. 1993. *Developments in Aging: 1993*, Vol. 1. Washington, D.C.: U.S. Government Printing Office.

U.S. Social Security Administration (SSA). 1981. "Erroneous Public Perception of SSA Administrative Expenses." *Social Security Bulletin* 49 (August): 5–19.

———. 1982. "Federal Civil Service Annuitants and Social Security." *Research and Statistics Note*, Report No. 6. Washington, D.C.: Office of Research and Statistics, Social Security Administration.

———. 1998. *Income of the Population 55 or Older, 1996*. Washington, D.C.: SSA Office of Policy.

Universal Social Security Coverage Study Group. 1980. *The Desirability and Feasibility of Social Security Coverage for Employees of Federal, State, and Local Governments and Private Non-Profit Organizations*. Report of the Study Group. Washington, D.C.: U.S. Department of Health, Education, and Welfare.

Van de Water, Paul N. 1979. "Disability Insurance." *American Economic Review* 69 (May): 275–278.

Venti, Steven F., and David A. Wise. 1990. "Aging and the Income Value of Housing Wealth." Working Paper No. 3547. Cambridge, Mass.: National Bureau of Economic Research.

Viscusi, W. Kip. 1979. *Welfare of the Elderly*. New York: Wiley-Interscience.

Wall Street Journal. 1990. "Old Time Religion" (January 31): 40.

Wallich, Henry. 1969. "Adjustable Bonds: Purchasing Power Bonds." *Newsweek* (November 24).

Warshawsky, Mark J. 1992. *The Uncertain Promise of Retiree Health Benefits*. Washington, D.C.: The American Enterprise Press.

Wattenberg, Ben J. 1987. *The Birth Dearth*. New York: Pharos Books.

Weitzman, L. J. 1985. *The Divorce Revolution*. New York: The Free Press.

Wiener, J. M., and L. H. Illston. 1995. "Health Care for the Aged." In Robert A. Binstock and Linda George, eds., *Handbook of Aging and the Social Sciences*, 4th ed. New York: Academic Press.

Wolff, Nancy. 1987. *Income Redistribution and the Social Security Program*. Ann Arbor, Mich.: UMI Research Press.

Woods, John R. 1988. "Retirement-Age Women and Pensions: Findings from the New Beneficiary Survey." *Social Security Bulletin* 51 (December): 5–16.

———. 1989. "Pension Coverage among Private Wage and Salary Workers: Preliminary Findings from the 1988 Survey of Employee Benefits." *Social Security Bulletin* 52 (October): 2–19.

YSW (Yankelovich, Skelly, and White Inc.). 1985. *A Fifty Year Report Card on the Social Security System—The Attitudes of the American Public*. An opinion poll conducted for AARP. Washington, D.C.: YSW.

Zook, C., and F. Moore. 1980. "High-Cost Users of Medical Care." *New England Journal of Medicine* 302 (May): 96–102.

Index

Aaron, Henry, 108, 123, 152, 159, 183, 191–92
AARP Public Policy Institute, 26. *See also* American Association of Retired Persons
Acs, Gregory, 14
actuarial soundness, 174
Adamchak, Donald, 291
adverse selection, 116, 117–18
Advisory Council on Social Security. *See* social security advisory councils
age discrimination, 73
Age Discrimination in Employment Act, 75, 90–91, 250
Aid to Families with Dependent Children (AFDC), 206
Alcon, Arnaa, 126
Allen, Steven, 264
Allied Chemical and Alkali Workers v. Pittsburgh Plate Glass, 55
Alzheimer's disease, 3
Amble, Nathan, 51
American Association of Retired Persons (AARP), 75, 79, 88, 161
American Council of Life Insurance, 118

American Express pension plan, 243
American Medical Association (AMA), 226
Americans for Generational Equity, 296
Andrisani, Paul, 86
annuities, 116, 117, 258
Archer, Congressman Bill, 155
Arenson, Karin, 123
Aspin, Congressman Les, 277
assets: amount held by elderly, 26–28, 49; and economic status, 3; housing, 23–24; income from assets as a share of total income, 7; and inflation, 49, 53–54; liquid vs. nonliquid, 23; "locked in" assets, 24, 25; measurement difficulties, 28; and medical expenditures, 23–24; motives for accumulating, 23; net worth, 26–28; net worth differences by marital status, 26; in private pension plans, 269; role of home equity, 28; saving rates in old age, 24; test in SSI, 223; and the "tweeners," 46
"assignment," in Medicare, 209–10

Atchley, Robert, 89
average indexed monthly earnings, 138

B&Q plc, 84
baby boom: aging of population, 284–86; budget surplus, 186; cost implications, 290–91; fears of, 178, 169; financing issues, 292–95; generational equity, 295–96; impact on children, 284; social security, 179–81, 182; "voodoo demographics," 292
Baker, Dean, 194–95
Bakija, J. M., 197
Ball, Robert, 143, 149, 161, 167, 172, 187, 198, 211, 297
Bass, Scott, 62, 63
Batten, M. D., 79
Baumol, William, 181
Becker, Gary, 90
Belitsky, Harvey, 79
Bernheim, Douglas, 109
Bickerman, John, 278
Binstock, Robert, 293
black elderly, 17–19
Blais, L. E., 176
Board of Trustees of the Social Security Trust Funds, 171
Bodie, Zvi, 106
Bond, Kathleen, 4
Borowski, Allan, 288, 291
Boskin, Michael, 105, 192, 194
Boulding, Kenneth, 107, 108, 113–14
Bowen, Otis, 224
Bowen plan, 211
Bradford, Kenneth, 68
Brandeis University Policy Center on Aging, 270
Braniff Airlines, 269–70
"bridge jobs," 88–89
British poor laws, 64, 153, 234
Brittain, Joseph, 188, 191, 192
Broder, David, 283
Brody, Elaine, 216
Bronte, Lydia, 290
Brown, J. Douglas, 109, 135, 174, 189, 205–6

Brudney, Juliet, 85
Bryce, David, 154
budget cuts and surpluses. *See* federal budget
Burke, Vee, 236, 237
Burke, Vincent, 236, 237
Burkhauser, Richard, 17, 96, 161
Burtless, Gary, 69, 86
Butler, Robert, 62, 213

Callahan, James, 214
Cardwell, James, 231
career centers, 82–83
Caro, Frank, 62, 63
Carr, J., 279
Carter, President Jimmy, 171, 200
Carter, Karnin, 21
catastrophic illness insurance, 223–25
Centaur Associates, 83
Chakravarty, S. N., 283
Challenge to Affluence, 1
Chamber of Commerce, 226
Charles D. Spencer and Associates, 128
Cheit, Earl, 228
Chen, Yung Ping, 25
Chile's pension system, 154
Church, Frank, 148
"circuit breaker," 21
Citro, C. F., 37
civil service pensions. *See* government employee pensions
Civil Service Retirement Act (1920), 243
Clark, Robert, 78, 91, 257
Clark, Timothy, 203
Clinton, President Bill, 168, 258, 287
Coates, Edward, 248
Coberly, Sally, 93
Cohen, Wilbur, 31–32, 115, 141, 153, 226
Cohen, William, 125
Combs, Ann, 199
Commonwealth Fund, 84, 96
comparative advantage, 80
Comprehensive Employment and Training Act (CETA), 81
compulsory pensions, 108–10

Concord Coalition, 296–97
Congressional Budget Office, 45, 123, 163, 210
Congressional Research Service, 224
Consumer Expenditure Survey, 35
Consumer Price Index (CPI): to adjust federal pensions, 277; defined, 47; and health costs, 223; military pensions, 278; OASI special minimum benefits, 140; private pensions, 263–64; social security benefits, 148; tax "standard deduction," 21
Consumers Union, 218
consumption: age differences, 14; health expenditures, 14; patterns, 12–14; and the price index, 51; role in constructing poverty index, 44–45
Continental Can Company, 266–67
Cook, Fay, 14, 147
Council of Economic Advisors, 34
Cowgill, Donald, 285, 288
CPI. *See* Consumer Price Index
Crown, William, 40, 279, 288, 291
Cruikshank, Nelson, 200
Crystal, Stephen, 210
Current Population Survey, 5, 8, 36

Dale, Edwin, 171
Danziger, Sheldon, 24, 43, 45
David, Martin, 24
Days Inn of America, 84
deferred profit-sharing plans, 247–48
defined benefit pensions, 78, 116, 117, 256. *See also* pensions
defined contribution pensions, 120, 256
delayed retirement credit, 141–42
Deljavan, F., 12
Denison, Edward, 181
dependency ratios, 286–89
Derthick, Martha, 166, 167, 232
"the deserving poor," 62
Diamond, Peter, 109
Diamond, Stephen, 125
disability benefits, 166, 225–32
divorce, 39, 137
Doctors, S. I., 84

Doeringer, Peter, 89
Doggette, Herbert, 167
Donahue, Wilma, 59
"double decker," 153–54
"double jeopardy," 18
Downs, Alan, 77
Drazaga, Linda, 239
DRGs, 220–21
Drucker, Peter, 303
"dual pensioners," 19
Duff, Nancy, 163–64
Duggan, James, 197
Durenberger, Senator David, 296

early retirement: early retirement benefits, 16; economic impact, 66; impact of illness, 86; impact of social security, 87; incentive programs, 72; private plans, 88; trends, 69, 91
early retirement incentive programs, 72
earned income credit, 190–91
earnings: base in social security, 173; of elderly, 7, 12; index for inflation, 48; just before retirement, 150; pension replacement rates, 103–4, 149–52; and retirement planning, 103–4; and the social security maximum, 173; trends, 7
earnings sharing, 162–64
earnings test (social security), 87, 137
Easterlin, Richard, 299
economic status of the elderly, 1, 2, 17, 44–47
economy food plan, 35
Eichenwald, Kurt, 267
Eisner, Robert, 62
Ekerdt, D. S., 68
"elder engagement," 63
Employee Benefit Research Institute, 71, 243, 245, 249, 251, 253–54, 279
Employee Retirement Income Security Act (ERISA), 252–53
employee stock option pension plans (ESOPs), 254
employer-sponsored pensions. *See* pensions; private pensions
employment. *See* work

"entitlements," 296–98
Equal Employment Opportunity Commission (EEOC), 75
equivalency scale, 42–43
ERISA. *See* Employee Retirement Income Security Act
Ervin, Senator Sam, 190
ethnic differences in economic status, 17–18
expenditures. *See* consumption

Fairchild, T. J., 96
Fair Employment Council of Greater Washington, 75
Family Assistance Act, 148
Feaster, Daniel, 17
federal budget: Gramm-Rudman-Hollings, 184; impact of an aging population, 297–98; impact of social security expenditures, 183–87; surpluses, 184–87
federal civil service pension plans, 275–77
Federal Employees Retirement System Act, 276–77
Federal Home Loan Bank Board, 25
Federal Housing Administration, 25
Feldstein, Martin, 123, 149, 151, 188, 194, 198, 294
Ferrara, Peter, 252
Ferraro, Kenneth, 128
fertility rate, 285
Fidelity (Investments), 249
Fierst, Edith, 163–64
Financial Accounting Standards Board, 212
Fisher, Gordon, 36
Fitzgerald, A. J., 55
Flint, Jerry, 89
Food Consumption Survey, 35
food plans and food budgets (in poverty measurement), 32
food stamps, 2, 45, 50
Ford administration, 190
Forest Service, 83
Forman, Maxine, 163
401(K) plans, 248–49

Freeland, Mark, 205
Friedland, Robert, 154, 182, 284, 288, 293
Friedman, B. M., 117
Friedman, Eugene, 60
Friedman, Milton, 54, 115
Fuller, Ida, 131
The Full Monty, 80

Gardner, T. K., 37
Geanakoplos, John, 194
gender differences, 17–19
General Accounting Office, 166–67, 178, 191, 194, 195, 211, 212, 214, 231, 254, 261, 262
General Motors Corp., 212
general revenue financing of pensions, 199–200
generational equity and conflict, 284, 295–96
Giddens, Anthony, 300
Gill, Richard T., 295
Gill, T. Brandon, 295
Gist, John, 21, 298
Gordon, Robert, 51
Gore, Albert, 161
Goss, Stephen, 188
Goudy, Willis, 96
government employee pensions, 50, 258, 274–80
Grad, Susan, 36, 41, 151
Gramlich, Edward, 115
Gramm-Rudman-Hollings, 184
Great Depression, 105–6, 177, 235
"greedy geezers," 62

Hardy, Melissa, 87
Harrington, David, 180
Hartman, Robert, 275
Hatch, Sara, 263
Haveman, Robert, 35, 229
Health and Retirement Study, 86, 88
health care: catastrophic illness, 223–25; employer-sponsored health plans, 211–12; financing, 219–23; views of the public on costs, 219. *See also* HMOs; Medicaid; Medicare

Health Care Financing Administration (HCFA), 221
health maintenance organizations. *See* HMOs
Heffler, Stephen, 205
Heidbreder, Elizabeth, 79
Herzog, A. R., 60
Hewitt, Edwin, 121
HEW Task Force, 158
Hipple, Steven, 74–75
Hirshorn, Barbara, 84
HMOs, 210
Holahan, J., 221
Holden, Karen, 17, 46–47, 162
Holmes, Lowell, 285
Holstein, Martha, 225
home care, 216
homemaker credits, 161–62
home ownership of elderly, 24
homestead exemption, 21
hospice care, 209
House Committee on Education and Labor, 243, 280
House Committee on Ways and Means, 200, 237, 271
"householder," 5
House Select Committee on Aging, 35, 207
housing: as an asset, 24–25; expenditures on, 13; and inflation, 49; property taxes, 21–22; special government programs, 24–25; and the "tweeners," 46
Howard, Christopher, 190
Howe, Neil, 293, 298
Hoyer, Denise, 84
Hurd, Michael, 4, 71, 94
Hybrid pension plans, 249–50

Illston, L. H., 216
income distribution of the elderly, 4–7
income replacement standard. *See* replacement rates
income sources (elderly), 7–8
indexed bonds, 53–55
indexing, 21, 178, 181
"index of impairment," 86
Individual Retirement Accounts (IRAs):

accumulations, 251; eligibility, 250–51; history, 250–53; Roth IRAs, 252
inflation: and assets, 49; defined, 47–48; erosion of pensions, 3, 243, 247; German experience, 118, 219; impact on elderly, 1, 3, 47–53; indexation of government programs; 2; and long-term care, 218; pension indexing, 182; pension protection, 258, 279; and private pensions, 263–64; retirement planning, 100, 102; risks in defined contribution plans, 256; role of taxes, 48; and social security benefits, 1, 132, 133, 140, 151
in-kind income, 28–90, 36, 37, 45
Institute for Social Research, 60
Institute on Poverty, 45
"institutionalization of retirement," 59–60
insurance principle, 106
inter- and intrafamily transfers, 29–31
intergenerational conflict, 284
intergenerational equity, 295–96
IRAs. *See* Individual Retirement Accounts
Irelan, Lola, 4

Jackson, James, 18
Jackson, William, 284
job discrimination. *See* older workers
Job Training Partnership Act, 82
Johnson, President Lyndon, 183, 296
Johnson and Higgins Inc., 96
Juster, Thomas, 28, 60

Kemper, P., 213
Kennedy, President John F., 124
Keogh plans, 250
King, Gwendolyn, 47
Kingson, E. R., 15, 154, 286
Kochhar, Staya, 239
Korczyk, Sophie, 274
Kotlikoff, Laurence, 88, 108, 109, 263
Krauss, N. A., 213
Kreps, Juanita, 64, 66–68, 69

labor force participation: and dependency ratios, 288–90; and health, 86; in Japan, 71; male trends, 71–73; of older workers, 70–73, 96; private pension impact, 72, 262; by race, 71; source of statistics, 8; women, 70
Landon, Al, 174
Lapkoff, Shelly, 161
Lawrence, James, 90
Lazear, Edward, 90
Leavitt, Thomas, 114, 212, 238, 239, 270
Leimer, Dean, 191, 192, 193–94, 197
leisure and retirement, 40, 60–62, 63, 68–69, 71
Leonard, Herman, 133
Leonesio, Michael, 87
Lesnoy, Selig, 123
Leuthold, Jane, 188
Lewin-VHI, Inc, 299
Lewis, Robert, 75
Liang, Jersey, 96
"life cycle hypothesis," 115, 123
life expectancy: aging populations, 286; and annuities, 117–18, 196–97; Ida Fuller, 131; and retirement needs, 106–7; retirement planning, 100
life-long learning, 79–81
living arrangements, 6–7, 30
Longman, Philip, 298
long-term care: costs and financing, 217–19; fear of, 214–17; financing, 207–8; German reforms, 219; home care, 216; institutional bias in service provision, 214; institutions, 213; private insurance, 218; providers of, 214–17; quality of care, 214–15
Lord, Judge Joseph S., 231
Louis Harris Associates, 94–97, 165, 181–82
Lovejoy, Lora, 279
lump-sum pension distribution, 258
Lumsdaine, Robert, 263

Mackey, Scott, 21
McConnel, Charles, 12

McDaniel, Michael, 94
McDermed, Ann, 59
McGarry, Kathleen, 30
McGill, Daniel, 93
mandatory retirement, 2, 64, 72, 85, 89–94
Mashaw, Jerry, 225, 229, 332
Maxwell, James, 279, 280
means-test, 110, 144–47
Medicaid: eligibility, 50, 206–7; financing, 207; history and provisions, 206–8; as in-kind income, 29; legislation, 2, 206. *See also* long-term care
medical care. *See* health care
Medicare: all aspects of cost, 208–13; assignment, 209–10; benefits, 209; coverage, 210; description and history, 2, 208–10; growth of, 222–23; as in-kind income, 28–29, 36; payment system, 220–22
medigap insurance, 211
Medoff, Jeff, 76
Megacap, 216
Menchik, Paul, 24
Mendelson, D. N., 293
Mexican-American aged, 18
Michael, R. T., 37
Michigan Panel Study of Income Dynamics, 30
military pensions, 50, 277–79
Miller, Rebecca, 253
Mills, Wilbur, 148
Minarik, Joseph, 51
minimum benefit, 136, 139–40
Minkler, M., 225
minorities, 17–19, 38
Miranda, M. R., 84
Mishel, L., 69
Mitchell, Olivia, 73, 255, 258, 279
Modigliani, Franco, 123
Moehrie, Thomas, 13
Moeller, Charles, 122
Moody, Rick, 63
Moon, Marilyn, 219, 221, 222
Moore, F., 222
Moore, Stephen, 194
Morgan, James, 15, 222

Morrison, Peter, 181
Moynihan, Senator Daniel, 172, 186–87
multiemployer pension plans, 255, 256, 268
"multiple hazard," 118
Mulvey, Janemarie, 21
Munnell, Alicia, 69, 123, 160, 176, 186
Murtaugh, Carrin, 213
Myers, Robert, 172, 181, 194
Myles, John, 300
Myrdal, Gunnar, 1

National Academy of Sciences, 37
National Academy of Social Insurance, 178
National Center on Women and Aging, 126
National Commission on Social Security, 162–63, 164, 184, 201, 208, 239
National Commission on Social Security Reform, 164, 202
National Council on the Aging (NCOA), 83, 95, 96
National Institute of Industrial Gerontology, 79
National Longitudinal Survey, 86
National Manufacturers Association, 226
National Research Council, 33
negative income tax, 152
Nelson, Richard, 185–86
Nestel, Gilbert, 91
net worth. *See* assets
Nieswiadomy, M. L., 14
Nixon, President Richard, 148, 237, 250–51
Nixon administration, 2, 190
Nordhaus, William, 61
NOW (National Organization of Women), 88
nuclear families, 107
nursing homes, 214–16

Office of Technology and Assessment, 79

O'Grady-LeShane, Regina, 159
Okonkwo, Ubadigbo, 196
Okun, Arthur, 122
old age assistance, 2
older workers: attitudes toward work, 300–304; and the changing economy, 71–73; economic problems, 73–79; employment assistance, 83–84; encouraging to retire, 229; job discrimination, 73; job-seeking behavior, 88–89, 94–96; job services, 84; job termination, 73–75; retirement decision, 85–89; retraining, 81–82; training of, 79–84; unemployment, 73–75
"oldest old," 17
Omnibus Budget Reconciliation Act, of 1990, 184, 216
Orbach, Harold, 59, 60
Orshansky, Molly, 4, 35
Osten, D. F., 82

Packard, Michael, 15
Palma, James, 215
Panel Study of Income Dynamics, 30
Panel Study on Social Security Financing, 176
Parnes, Herbert, 86, 91, 96
part-time work, 71
Pattison, David, 180
Paul, C. E., 93
payroll tax: changes in rates, 171–73; disability pension financing, 226; equity, 189–91; to finance long-term care in Germany, 219; incidence, 187–88; for Medicare, 208; proposals for change, 201–2; relative to benefits, 208
Pechman, Joseph, 108, 152, 159
Pension Benefit Guaranty Corporation (PBGC), 269, 270, 271–73
pensions: **benefits**: adequacy, 111–12; benefits (private), 255–59; certainty, 112; levels, 2, 138–39, 147–52, 258, 278; survivor benefits, 261; **characteristics**: compulsory, 108–10; equity, 113, 187–97; flexibility, 112; general characteristics, 111–15; in-

flation issues, 118–19, 263–64; integration, 114; plan problems, 244; private plan characteristics, 254–64; treatment of women, 273; vesting and portability, 259–60; **coverage**, 19, 119–20, 243–54, 257; **financing**: administrative costs, 113, 119; aggregate amounts paid (private), 243; costs and financing, 78, 268–71; funding issues (private), 263–73; rates of return, 192–95; and saving (national), 122–23; **history**: and the "institutionalization of retirement," 60; origins of private plans, 243–44; plan terminations, 269–73; privatization of pensions, 154–57; rationale for, 106–8; regulation of private plans, 264–66; **impact on labor force**: designed to promote retirement, 88; early retirement provisions, 262–63; **preretirement planning**, 105; **types**: 401(K), 248–49; government employee plans, 243; "hybrid plans," 249–50; military, 277–79; mix of public/private, 115, 124; profit sharing plans, 247–48; thrift plans, 248–49. *See also* Employee Retirement Income Security Act; employee stock option plans; Individual Retirement Accounts; mandatory retirement; Simplified Employee Pensions

Pepper, Claude, 90
Pepper Commission, 216
Personal Pensions (United Kingdom), 156–57
personal savings accounts, 199
Peter D. Hart Research Associates, 50, 147
Peterson, Peter, 291, 293
Philips, Kirsten, 279
Pifer, Alan, 290
Pollak, Otto, 59
poor laws, 64
population aging, 179–81, 197
portability of pensions, 259–60
Poterba, James, 249
poverty: in America, 1, 117; concep-

tual and measurement issues, 31–33; current measures, 32–41; extent among elderly, 38–40; "hidden," 5; index, 4, 32–37; male-female differences, 39; new measures proposed, 37–38; "traps," 297; trends, 6–7, 38–40; and the "tweeners," 46; young vs. old, 44–46
Poverty Studies Task Force, 32, 35
President's Commission on Pension Policy, 164, 287, 288
Preston, Samuel, 283–84
private pensions, 121–23, 243–74. *See also* pensions
privatization of pensions, 154–57
"productive aging," 62–64
productivity: and mandatory retirement, 93–94; older workers, 94–95; "slowdown," 181, 298; social security costs, 181
Professional Drivers Council, 264
profit-sharing plans, 247–48
PROPAC, 221
property taxes, 2, 20–21, 23
prospective payment system, 220–22
Public Pension Coordinating Council, 280
purchasing power bonds, 53–55
Puffert, D. J., 194
Prudential-Bache Securities, 267
Pursell, Donald, 79

Quadagno, Jill, 87
Quinn, Joseph, 69, 72, 86, 88, 295, 300

Radner, Daniel, 9, 17, 28, 86
Rauch, Johnathan, 186
Reagan administration, 295
Rebick, Marcus, 71
Reich, Robert, 80
Reno, Virginia, 15, 87, 182, 260, 293
replacement rates, 41, 103–5, 150–51, 258–59
Reschovsky, Andrew, 23
reserves (pensions), 174–76, 268–71
"resource based relative value scale" (RBRVS), 221

retirement: age of, 15; age of military, 278; attitudes toward work, 90–91, 94–97; "bridge jobs," 88; the decision, 72–73, 85–88; encouragement of, 59–60, 69; and health, 59; early retirement incentive programs, 72; impact on income, 11, 16; impact of social security, 132; "institutionalization" of, 59–60; patterns of, 15–17; and pensions, 87–88; planning, 40, 99–105, 125; problems of defining, 11; reasons for institutionalization, 60; savings needs, 102–3. *See also* labor force participation rates

Retirement Equity Act (1984), 274

retirement planners, 125

retirement planning, 99–128. *See also* retirement

Retirement Protection Act (1994), 273

retirement test, 144–47. *See also* social security

retraining (for jobs), 81–84

Reuther, Walter, 202

revenue acts, 244

reverse annuity mortgages, 25–26

Rhoades, Jeffery, 213

Rich, Spencer, 213

Riley, Matilda, 62, 68

Rix, Sara, 72, 74, 79

Robinson, Pauline, 62, 93

roles in later life, 62–64, 68

Rones, Philip, 74, 79

Roosevelt, President Franklin D., 117, 133, 174

Rosenblum, M., 84

Ross, C. H., 17

Ross, Jane, 162, 164

Rostenkowski, Congressman Daniel, 203

Roth IRA, 252

Rubin, Rose, 14

Rudman, Warren, 296

Ruggles, Patricia, 35, 36, 44–45

Ruhm, Christopher, 87

Rupp, Kalman, 82

Sabelhaus, John, 14

sales tax, 21

Samuelson, Robert, 284

Sandell, Stephen, 81

Sarokin, Judge H. Lee, 267

Sass, Steven, 249, 257

saving: adequacy of, 102–5; and economic growth, 122; frauds, 125; government surpluses, 185; inadequate amounts of, 109; over the life cycle, 115; and private pensions, 122–23; requirements of individuals, 104–5; Sweden, 123

Sawhill, Isabel, 295

Schneider, Clement, 91

Schobel, Bruce, 194

Schoeni, R. F., 30

Scholen, Kenneth, 25

Scholz, John, 191

Schottland, Charles, 234

Schram, S. F., 82

Schulz, James, 69, 71, 114, 115, 122, 185, 238, 239, 288, 291, 293, 294

Schwartz, W. B., 293

Scott, Hilda, 85

Sears, 248

Senate Committee on Finance, 200, 238

Senate Special Committee on Aging, 78, 125, 167, 184, 186, 211, 216, 225

Senior Community Service Employment Program (SCSEP), 83–88

Settersten, R., 14

Shaw, Congressman Clay, 155

Sheppard, Harold, 79, 84, 87

Sherman, Sally, 293

Siegel, Jacob, 285

Siegfried, Charles, 121

simplified employee pensions (SEPs), 254

Smeeding, Timothy, 45, 46–47, 161

Smith, Sheila, 205

Smolensky, Eugene, 17, 24

Sobel, Irvin, 79

social security: **benefits**: benefit levels and adequacy, 1, 137–40, 147–52; early retirement benefits, 136, 140; indexing, 137, 176, 177; and inflation, 2, 49, 118; minimum benefits,

136, 139–40; redistribution of income, 116, 117; replacement rates,
138, 178; the retirement test, 135,
144–47; share of income, 7; spouse
benefits, 137, 158–60; survivor benefits, 137, 142–43, 160, 161, 179–80;
tax treatment, 172, 202–3; treatment of women, 157–64; types of
benefits, 136–37; **changes**: amendments of 1939, 132; amendments of
1983, 173; changes over time, 132–
33; **characteristics**: age of retirement, 164; constitutionality, 109;
coverage, 133; delayed retirement,
140; 109; eligibility requirements,
136, 176–77; **financing**: administration and costs, 118, 165–68; annual
reports, 133, 139, 293; expenditures, 172; financing equity, 187–97;
financing history, 133–34, 171–203;
inter-/intragenerational equity, 187–
97; projections, 134; reserves, 175–
76; **foreign provisions**, 105, 110–
11, 118, 119, 120, 153, 154–57,
201, 292; **principles/rationale**: arguments for, 116; compulsory coverage debate, 109–10; criticisms of,
116; economies of scale advantage,
113; principles, 134–35; rationale
for, 106–10; **reform**: privatization
of benefits, 154–57, 198–99; reform
proposals, 197–203. *See also* earnings sharing; federal budget; homemaker credits; pensions; trust funds
Social Security Advisory Board, 229,
232
social security advisory councils, 148,
153, 155, 174, 182, 198, 199, 202
Social Security Appeals Council, 228
Soldo, Beth, 30
Solow, Robert M., 47, 123
Sommers, David, 96
Sparrow, Paul, 93
Special Committee on Aging. *See* Senate Special Committee on Aging
special minimum benefit (social security), 136, 140
Spengler, Joseph, 64, 66–68

Spiro, C., 197, 284
Stafford, Frank, 60
Stapleton, David, 78
state and local pension plans, 279–80
statistics, economics of aging: eco-
nomic status, 1–55; income, 4–7;
national output and growth, 299;
poverty among the elderly, 38–40;
reliability of, 9–10; sources, 4, 7–10
Sterns, Harvey, 94
Steuerle, Eugene, 197, 284
Stewart, Kenneth, 51
Stockman, David, 178
Stone, Deborah, 228
Storey, James, 296
Strauss, David, 258
Streib, Gordon, 91
Studebaker Corporation, 268
Summer, Laura, 284, 288
Sunden, Annika, 273
Supplemental Security Income (SSI),
2, 50, 165–66, 232–39
Surette, Brian, 273
Survey of Income and Program Partici-
pation (SIPP), 30, 37
Survey of New Entitled Beneficiaries,
87
Suzman, Richard, 17

Taeuber, Cynthia, 24
Taft-Hartley Act and private pensions,
255
Taplin, Polly, 128
target replacement rates, 103–4
Task Force on Sex Discrimination, 274
Taussig, Michael, 24, 108, 152, 159
Tax Act of 1975, 190
taxation of the elderly, 20–23
Tax Reform Act (1986), 274
Teamsters, 264–65
Technical Committee on Earnings
Sharing, 163
Teixeira, R. A., 69
Tell, Eileen, 207, 217
tenure and reverse annuity mortgages,
25
Thatcher, Margaret, 156

Thompson, Lawrence, 120–21, 182, 186
thrift savings plans, 248–49
thrifty food plan, 35
Thurow, Lester, 122
Tibbitts, Clark, 107
Tissue, Thomas, 239
Tobin, James, 53, 61
Torrence, David, 79
Torrey, Barbara, 24, 283
Townsend, Francis, 135, 235
transfers, 29–31
Travelers Corporation, 84
Treasury Inflation Indexed Securities, 54
trust funds (OASDHI), 171–72, 174–75, 223
Tsongas, Paul, 296
Turnbull, John, 228
"tweeners," 46

unemployment, 74, 75–76, 79, 145
"unified budget," 184. *See also* federal budget
United Kingdom pension experience, 156–57
Universal Social Security Coverage Study Group, 275
Upp, Melinda, 162, 164
U.S. government agencies. *See respective agency names*

Van Der Gaag, E., 24
Van de Water, Paul, 182, 227
Venti, Steven, 25
vesting, 259–60
veterans' benefits, 201
viager, 24
"voodoo demographics," 290

Wallack, Stanley, 214
Wallich, Henry, 32
"War on Poverty," 277
Warshansky, M., 117

Warshawsky, Mark, 213
Wattenberg, Benjamin, 291
Wealth. *See* assets
Weisbrot, Mark, 194–95
Weisman, K., 283
Weitzman, L. J., 158
Welfare and Pension Plan Disclosure Act, 265
White House Conference on Aging (1971), 196
widows, 3, 17, 143
Wiener, Joshua, 216
Wilcock, Richard, 79
Williams Arthur, 228
Willis, David, 17
Wise, David, 25, 88, 263
Wolff, Nancy, 197
women: early retirement, 15; earnings sharing, 162–64; financial planning, 126; homemaker credits, 161–62; income trends, 7; male-female income differences, 18; pension financing, 195–96; and poverty, 9; private pension plans, 273–74; separated women, 19, 40; social security treatment, 137; spouse benefit, 137; survivor pensions, 137, 261. *See also* divorce
Woods, John, 252, 274
Work: attitudes toward, 94–97; and "baby boom" pension costs, 300–304; defining, 62; future jobs of older workers, 302–3; government policies relating to, 64; and health, 85–86; hours worked, in United States, 60; "nonwork," 62; part-time, 71; patterns, 66; payroll tax influence on, 144; retraining, 303–4; work-leisure tradeoff, 60–62
Workforce Investment Act (1998), 82–83

Zero Deficit Plan, 296
Zink, Victor, 89
Zook, C., 222

About the Author

JAMES H. SCHULZ is Emeritus Professor of Economics, Brandeis University. A former president of the Gerontological Society of America, he has written extensively on aging, pension, retirement, and social policy.

CPSIA information can be obtained at www.ICGtesting.com
Printed in the USA
BVOW06s1917130116

432801BV00014B/181/P